SYMBOL, DREAM, and PSYCHOSIS

ROBERT FLIESS, M.D.

SYMBOL, DREAM, and PSYCHOSIS

VOLUME III
PSYCHOANALYTIC SERIES

ROBERT FLIESS, M.D.

INTERNATIONAL UNIVERSITIES PRESS, INC.

New York   New York

Library of Congress Catalog Card Number: 72–184212
ISBN: 0–8236–6287–X

Manufactured in the United States of America

CONTENTS

FOREWORD   vii

Chapter One   On the Symbol   3
     THE GENERAL THEORY OF THE SYMBOL   3
     DISCUSSION OF SOME PARTICULAR SYMBOLS   67
     POSTSCRIPT—SOME RESULTS OF SYMBOL TRANSLATION   116

Chapter Two   On the Dream   122
     TOWARD A THEORY OF DREAM HALLUCINATION   122
     ON THE SPOKEN WORD IN THE DREAM   135
     ON TYPICAL DREAMS   154
     ON THE TOPOGRAPHICAL ANALYSIS OF THE DREAM   187
     DELUSION IN DREAMS   201

Chapter Three   The Ambulatory Psychosis: A Particular Type   204
     PERTINENT LITERATURE   206
     REFINEMENTS IN TECHNIQUE OF AMNESIA REMOVAL   219
     SYMPTOMATOLOGY   220
     THE AGGRESSIVE ABUSE OF THE CHILD   243

Chapter Four   On Exceptional States   262
     BASICALLY IDENTICAL (HYPNOTIC) STATES   263
     STATES DIFFERING FROM EACH OTHER AS WELL AS
        FROM THOSE OF GROUP I.   311

NOTES ON TECHNIQUE

NOTES ON TECHNIQUE   349

Chapter Five   On the Analytic Relation   350
     ON THE ROLE OF TRANSFERENCE IN PSYCHOANALYTIC
        TREATMENT   352

RESISTANCES OF THE ANALYST   358
TWO "INFANTILE TRAITS" OF THE PATIENT, ESSENTIAL
    TO ANALYTIC TREATMENT   361

Chapter Six   Toward the Technique of Amnesia Removal   366
FREE-FLOATING ATTENTION   367
THE DISTINCTION OF MEMORY FROM FANTASY   368
THE IMPORTANCE OF MEMORY QUALITY   380
THE OCCASIONAL SEPARATION OF TWO SENSORY
    SPHERES FROM EACH OTHER IN THE PROCESS OF
    AMNESIA REMOVAL   388
AN ADDENDUM TO THE TECHNIQUE OF AMNESIA REMOVAL   389
MISCELLANEOUS NOTES   390
IDENTITY OF THE RESULTS OF AMNESIA REMOVAL IN
    THE NEUROTIC AND THE PSYCHOTIC ANALYSAND   391

Chapter Seven   Notes on the Diagnosis and Treatment of
    the Ambulatory Psychotic   393
DIAGNOSTIC CONSIDERATIONS   393
PROGNOSIS   401
TREATMENT   402
PSYCHOTHERAPEUTIC PREPARATION FOR ANALYSIS   403
POSTSCRIPT   411
APPENDIX: OBSERVATIONS ON AMBULATORY PSYCHOTICS   412
GLOSSARY   418
REFERENCES   421
INDEX   427

Ce qui donne du courage, ce sont les ideés.

—Clemenceau

FOREWORD

With this volume the *Psychoanalytic Series* is concluded. The first, *Erogeneity and Libido,* and the second, *Ego and Body Ego,* are interrelated with this, the final monograph, to the degree that as in any science findings are based one upon another. But the various subjects can be read, as they are dealt with, separately. For the reader not having the earlier volumes at hand, a Glossary briefly defining certain neologisms and/or concepts developed in the earlier volumes will be found at the end of this one. There are, of course, careful cross references in each volume.

As to the subjects treated here, they will be found to vary not only in content but also in the mode of their treatment. The first part of the chapter, On the Symbol, is not truly original, for it is a lengthy comment on Freud's important discovery of symbolism in the psychoanalytic sense of the word. But it had to be written. Because the literature on the subject did not satisfy me, and because the theory of symbolism is of such primary importance, I wanted to give it a comprehensive and systematic treatment. The second part of the first chapter is for the better part original inasmuch as it adds a number of hitherto unknown symbols I have been able to observe.

To write the chapter On the Dream it was necessary first to set down a theory of dream hallucination, for Freud's relatively early explanation of hallucination in dreams as a historic regression to a supposed nurseling hallucination (which he himself called a "fiction") satisfies no one. The Spoken Word in the Dream replaces an earlier article of mine on the subject—a totally inadequate discussion to which I would not today wish to sign my name. On Typical Dreams attempts to bring order into Freud's original but somewhat arbitrary treatment of this subject and to add to the number of these dreams. The fourth section, On the Topographical Analysis of the Dream, is merely a beginning, intended to further stimulate workers who have a theoretical bent. Delusions in Dreams is didactic: the explanation its *raison d'être.*

In the Foreword to Volume I of the Series, I tendered a thesis based on the discovery of the unbelievable frequency of (undiagnosed) ambulatory psychosis. My observations were continued (as clinical illustrations in both this and the previous volume attest) and corroborated verbally by others in the field, but publication had to be postponed until now. The thesis—the relation between this frequency and the etiology of the severe neurosis—is developed in the beginning of Chapter Three.

Both my observations and my thesis are at the present time bound to be rejected by many. Analysts, by and large, are not prepared to learn of this subject so close to their patients' childhood, if not their own. The reasons for my own freedom to accept what my patients proffer me were documented as early as Volume I (Foreword, xviii, fn.).

Chapter Four contains a number of findings with regard to "Exceptional States" it was my good fortune to make in the course of many years of analytic work.

Younger colleagues have sometimes asked me to write on technique. I never did. The final section however contains three chapters: On the Analytic Relation, Toward the Technique of Amnesia Removal, and Notes on the Diagnosis and (Psychoanalytic) Treatment of the Ambulatory Psychotic. Together with some further Observations on Ambulatory Psychotics, they offer my credentials for my findings.

I continue to live in indebtedness to my wife. It is with this as it was with the other volumes: without her affectionate and intelligent cooperation it could not have been brought to light.

Deep in the Country.
Fall 1969.

ON THE SYMBOL

". . . an original knowledge which adults afterwards forget . . ."
—Freud: MOSES AND MONOTHEISM

CHAPTER ONE

ON THE SYMBOL

I. THE GENERAL THEORY OF THE SYMBOL

A. A PARADIGMATIC STORY

In his *Decameron* Boccaccio tells how the young wife of a dullard, surprised with her lover by the husband, found a way to take up again in the slow-witted man's very presence what had been interrupted by his unexpected return.

The story is the most perfect introduction to the subject of symbolism that I know because almost everything in it is told in two ways, once directly and once symbolically; and the further the tale proceeds the more closely it juxtaposes the two modes of expression, with the result that one interprets the other. To read it, enjoying the literary liberty of the Renaissance—Boccaccio after all was a contemporary of Chaucer—is to be both amused and instructed, because the tale answers many questions about the symbol.

It is therefore worth summarizing Boccaccio's story by paraphrase and by direct quotation: Peronella, "fair and lovesome," is pursued by Gianello, "young gallant" of the neighborhood, until she agrees that he watch the house for the departure of her husband, a poor mason, so that they can be together. Or, as the poet says, when the husband had left *the street where she abode, which . . . being very solitary, he should come to her house. . . .*" (italics throughout are mine). He did so many times; but once the mason returned unexpectedly and found the door locked. He praised the Lord for having given him such a faithful wife: "See *how she locked the door within* as soon as I was gone out, so none might enter to do her any annoy." Peronella, "*knowing her husband by his way of knocking,*" wonders

3

whether he saw the lover enter the house. Yet she rallies quickly, hides her Gianello in a great wine vat, opens the door, and gives the mason a scolding. She ". . . said to him with an angry air, 'What is to do now, that thou returnest home so soon this morning? Meseemeth thou hast a mind to do naught today . . . On what are we to live? . . . I, who do nothing but spin day and night. . . . *and thou, thou returnest home to me with thy hands a-dangle, whenas thou shouldst be at work* (p. 327).'" She goes on volubly praising her virtue and bewailing her marital fate until the husband eventually explains that it is, unknown to both of them, a feastday and therefore he could obtain no work. He has provided for them, nevertheless, by selling a vat, which only encumbers the house, for five florins. Ah, replies Peronella, poor me, ignorant as I am of the ways of the world, I have already made a better bargain: there is a gentleman inspecting it presently who has promised me seven florins for it. At this point Gianello emerges and asks the husband: "Who are thou? *I want the woman with whom I made the bargain for this vat.*" When the mason identifies himself, the lover declares the vat sound enough but crusted over with dregs or the like and demands that the husband scrape it. While the latter goes about this, "Peronella, as if she had a mind to see that he did, *thrust her head and one of her arms, shoulder and all, in at the mouth of the vat, which was not overbig, and fell to saying 'Scrape here' and 'There' and 'There also' and 'See, here is a little left.'*" At the same time—I now let the poet speak entirely for himself—

> *Gianello, who had scarce yet that morning done his full desire, when they were interrupted. . . . seeing that he could not as he would, bethought himself to accomplish it as he might, wherefore, boarding her, as she held the mouth of the vat all closed up, in such wise as in the ample plains the unbridled stallions, afire with love, assail the mares of Parthia, he satisfied his juvenile ardor, the which enterprise was brought to perfection well nigh at the same moment as the scraping of the vat, whereupon he dismounted and Peronella withdrawing her head from the mouth of the vat, the husband came forth thereof* [pp. 328–329].

In the end the lover found the vat "well" and himself "satisfied" and gave the husband his seven florins.

Interpretation

Nothing less than an analysis of the story shows exactly why instead of being a tale in dubious taste it is a work of art. In performing this analysis, preliminary to dealing with symbolism in general, I must both apologize to the experienced for telling him not much that is new, and advise the inexperienced to prepare himself by studying Freud's (1900) remarks on "innocent" dreams (pp. 182–188), and on representation by symbols (pp. 350–384).

From the very onset the poet lets the sensitive reader know Peronella more intimately than does her insensitive husband. When the latter leaves in the morning, "the street (i.e., the vagina) where she abode" (i.e., which she had still cathected, or of which she had remained partial subject [see Glossary]) was "very solitary," (i.e., had not "incorporated" a penis); hence the lover should come to her house (enter her, the lonely woman). The fatuous mason, convinced of the chastity of his wife (the "locked door within") comes home early (is premature), proves incapable of foreplay ("Thou returnest home to me with hands a-dangle when thou shouldst be at work"), and is scolded elaborately by the young woman, already excited by Gianello (transformation of affect). The "knowing her husband by his way of knocking" if one considers the context and follows Freud (1900) [1] can only mean that Peronella, a normal girl, knew his ejaculatory convulsions by having felt them, although they had left her cold. The mode of representation calling for these last three interpretations is not, of course, symbolic; it employs allusion—hence my reference to Freud's "innocent" dreams.

The emboldened lover's "I want the woman with whom I made the bargain for this vat," in this context speaks for itself.

---

[1] Freud (1915a) interprets the alleged ticking of the clock in the sexual situation as a "knock or beat in [the] clitoris" (p. 270).

It is from then on that the juxtaposition mentioned above pervades the text. The reference to the mares and the stallions is allusive to such a degree that one may practically call it a direct representation, but it is at the same time symbolic: the horse symbolizes the parent, and the lovers act as though in imitation of a primal scene.

At this point I would suspend the translation of symbols and interpolate a remark about the self-contradiction in the narrator's words, so familiar to the analyst from his patient's associations. One the one hand he has Gianello engage in a "second best," i.e., do something that he does not really want but that circumstance forces upon him, and on the other he likens him to the stallions "afire with love," i.e., he presents him as being very intent on precisely what he has decided to do. The poet, as though to emphasize this contradiction, has it reverberate in the aftermath of his story when he tells how *"Filostrato [the narrator] had not known to speak so obscurely of the mares of Parthia but that the roguish ladies laughed thereat, making believe to laugh at otherwhat* (p. 329)." Why the artifice? Because the position in question entails perineal pressure and directs the man's frictions more strongly than the ordinary ones against the posterior wall: a normal though varying, anal erotic contribution to the drive is thus stimulated, felt, and discharged. Artistic balance and good taste demand that this be not simply admitted, but simultaneously emphasized and denied.

To return to the symbol translation and the remaining part of the story, told twice—once directly, and once symbolically—by the writer. By virtue of the adjunct anal or rectal erogeneity it already becomes clear why, of all the numerous symbols for the young woman's organ, a vat, and a dirty one needing scraping at that, was selected. Peronella thrusts, we are told, head and arm, shoulder and all, into the mouth of this vat, which was not "over-big," i.e., she offers her vagina to the lover in a suitable state of contraction. Transcending the purely symbolic expression, one may of course say that she transforms herself for him eagerly into a partial object. Yet the narrator is not satisfied with telling even this much; he tells all.

He at the same time symbolically employs the (husband's) "body as phallus" occupying the vat and doing the scraping, while he has the girl direct him and in so doing acquaint lover and reader with her need of the moment: "Scrape here, and there, and there also . . ." until the climax is reached, Gianello withdraws, and, symbolically, the mason comes out of the vat.

B. DREAM SYMBOLISM AND SYMBOLISM

What makes this story so perfect an introduction to a "General Theory of the Symbol"? In the first place, it is not a dream. Freud (1915–1917) maintained a distinction between dream symbolism and symbolism. He supposed dream symbolism to be more sexual than symbolism employed elsewhere (p. 166). Actually the distinction does not exist. The only two things from which symbolism in the analytic sense of the word—Freud here again chose an already existing term and gave it a new definition—must be distinguished are for one, linguistic, mathematical, musical, and all manner of scientific symbols (E for a certain vowel, 5 for a certain number, D# for a certain chromatic change in music, H_2 for the hydrogen molecule, etc.); and for another, emblems, often called symbols (the *lys de France*, the Stars and Stripes, the female figure with the blindfolded eyes and a scale in her hands, etc.). Our use of such symbols is *conscious and dependent upon having learned them;* the use of the analytic symbol is *unconscious and independent of learning.* Its employment in the dream is no different from that in free association, in fiction, in parapraxia, in symptomatic or symbolic action, in phobia, or in conversion. The distinction to be made is not, therefore, between dream symbol and symbol but between symbol in the ordinary and in the psychoanalytic sense of the term. The present chapter of course deals only with the psychoanalytic symbol.

C. WORD SYMBOLISM

The second reason Boccaccio serves one so well here is that

although the Italian story is given in English, its symbolism *rises through the translation intact*. Thus it offers the opportunity of deleting the term "word-symbolism" *(Wortsymbolik)* as obsolete. There is no "word-symbolism." All symbols are object-symbols, all symbolism object- or thing-symbolism, if you prefer. Words are very important in certain forms of unconscious representations, but their importance is nil if the representation is *symbolic*. It is the "street" and the "vat" that symbolize the vagina; it is the "body" that symbolizes the phallus, *and they do so by virtue of what they are, not by that of the word for them in whatever language*. The utilization of words on the strength of their ambiguity, their phonetic resemblance, their aptitude—even that of a syllable—for neologistic formation is frequent and has been thoroughly treated by Freud; *but it has nothing to do with symbolic representation*.

No, the old term "word-symbolism" is misleading and must therefore be discarded. In saying this I evidently contradict Freud, yet I cannot conceive what he had in mind when he wrote in his very last work: ". . . Dreams make an unrestricted use of *linguistic* symbols [*sprachlichen Symbolen*], the meaning of which is for the most part unknown to the dreamer" (1940, p. 166; italics added). Nor does my own experience allow me to imagine a clinical observation justifying the term "linguistic symbol." Circumstances, by the way, happened to give me an object lesson in the matter: continuing my analytic career in America after having begun it abroad, I failed to find the change in language affecting even a single one of the symbols described by Freud.

D. WHAT IS A SYMBOL?

Boccaccio illustrated the correct answer to the question, "What is a symbol?" with absolute succinctness. *A symbol is a particular kind of unconscious representation of an element or a function of the pleasure-physiologic body ego* (II,* Chapter 3). In treating this subject extensively, I have stated that an element

* Roman numerals refer to previous volumes in this series.

of the pleasure-physiologic body ego is inseparable from its function. This fact accords well with Freud's enumeration of symbols, which shows at a glance that both elements and their functions are symbolically represented. It is one characteristic of these representations (although not an exclusive one) that an erogenic part of the body is represented by a part of the object world.

The cathexis of the symbolized element (i.e. vagina), most frequently that of a part of the pleasure-physiologic body ego, is a sexual one; the cathexis of the symbol, in most instances that of the representations of a part of the object world (i.e., street), is not. Symbolization, *the substitution of the latter for the former, gives therefore the appearance of a desexualization.* It is of crucial importance to realize the deceptive nature of this apparent desexualization and to know that while consciousness falls victim to the deception *the unconscious does not.* In other words, if someone expresses himself symbolically, he sexualizes the representation of an element of the environment, *but he does not know it.*

I remember a supervision of a case in which this was demonstrated dramatically. The evidently agoraphobic patient, married to a completely impotent man, came to analysis precisely because of that deception. She allowed herself therefore to be cured of her agoraphobia. A street, once the object of her phobia, was no longer a symbol for her vagina. The sexual cathexis had returned to the organ itself. The exchange, however, merely meant to this patient that an element of the environment had relinquished its sexual cathexis (of which she had been unaware) to an element of the pleasure-physiological body ego which, although aware of, she denied. Nor would she admit that her erstwhile fear of locomotion had become that of the motor action necessary for vaginal gratification, e.g., frictions—digital, penile, etc.[2] She proved increasingly insincere and evasive, suppressing associations; and the analysis which, in a manner of speaking, could only now have begun, had to be discontinued.

---

[2] This, of course, is only the narcissistic fundament of the agoraphobia. It omits all object-libidinal determinants, some of which were briefly mentioned above (II, Chapter 3).

It is the same with a pleasure-physiologic function. If a non-sexual function is really what it appears to be, its cathexis is one with desexualized libido and its performance is not interfered with. If it serves as a symbol, however it is unconsciously sexualized and its performance will suffer, although the individual will not know of the first, and, as to the second, either be intent on a spurious explanation or find himself simply baffled. Here again the symbolization has effected a deceptive desexualization of an actually sexual function.

Piano playing is as good an example as any. When the playing was not a symbol, a certain patient devoted herself to it and derived great enjoyment from it. When it became a symbol, the patient was, without knowing it, endangered by the "buoyancy of the repressed." Playing the piano was, to the unconscious, masturbating, in this particular instance, masturbating her mother, and about to precipitate not only a sexual affect but homosexual wishes and fantasies derivative of repressed events. She had fought against these for the better part of her life with the result of a painful neurosis. In order to remain unaware of them and to believe that she was merely "playing the piano," she had to resort to her favorite defense: the "hypnotic evasion" (Chapter Four below). Consequently, on these occasions she felt herself first "dopey," then sleepy, and finally she had to desist.

I know of no instance where symbolization does not effect this descriptive desexualization. In the case of the "displacement symbol," where a sexual part of the body is represented by an ordinarily nonsexual one, the patient does not know that the latter becomes unconsciously sexualized, but the analysis often can easily show it. This is no different with the symbolization of incest objects.

I think that the principle stated here admits of no exception.

To return to our definition: the fact that the great majority of symbols represent an element or a function of the pleasure-physiologic body ego explain a peculiarity that has not escaped Freud's attention: *the many symbols represent only a few symbolized elements.* Why should it not be so? The pleasure-physiologic body ego has only a relatively small number of elements compared to the object world which has so many.

I furthermore merely reiterate what is general knowledge if I state that *an erogenic part of the individual or of a cathected object may have a number, sometimes a large one, of symbols, yet their role with regard to the symbolized element remains constant.* If a steeple symbolizes the phallus, or a street the vagina, they do so always; correct symbol translation is monotonously the same. It is not different with a pleasure-physiologic function. Climbing stairs, when a symbol, always represents sexual intercourse; yet there are other symbols for the fact, and the choice of a particular symbol in preference to others cannot always be explained.

Nevertheless, just as not every object is eligible for serving as a symbol, neither is every erogenic part subject to symbolic representation. A dinner plate or a plain cannot, as far as is known at present, be used as a symbol, as may, for example, a knife, or a valley; while the mouth, the eye, and many other body parts, although contributing to the pleasure-physiologic body ego, have no symbolic representations. In other words, not every element of the pleasure-physiologic body ego is symbolizable, that is, allows for being substituted by an element of the outside world; and not every element of the outside world can become a symbol, that is, be employed as a substitute for an element of the pleasure physiologic body ego.

As do certain patients—Little Hans (Freud, 1909a), for one Boccaccio used the horse as a symbol for the parents. There are other symbols for the parents, such as the King and the Queen, or the racially foreign person (e.g., the Negro); and there is, for oneself as a child and one's siblings, the prince and the princess. *These are incest objects, not elements of the pleasure physiologic body ego.* Yet the two groups have one genetic characteristic in common: their original cathexis with primarily narcissistic libido by the child, precipitating what Freud has termed primary identifications. If one becomes acutely aware that no other person, not even a grandparent or an aunt, is symbolizable, one does not find it so strange that these earliest extensions of the incipient self are as fit for symbolization as are the similarly narcissistic erogenic parts of the body.[3]

There is, finally, the symbolization of death. I know of only two representations of death that could be called symbolic: Freud's *abreisen*, i.e., leaving by train (in our time, also by plane) for a lengthy or least far-reaching journey, and Abraham's falling out of a tooth. Can it possibly escape one's attention that *abreisen* is at the same time the symbol for *Verkehr* (the single German word for the three English nouns, transportation, traffic, and intercourse), representative of sexual activities —in particular sexual intercourse? And is not the falling out of teeth a symbol for masturbation? Death, in other words, can apparently be symbolized only in terms of a sexual function, which is in good accord with Freud's statement that we are incapable of consummating the idea of death. Or to express it differently, since all symbols are representative of an element or a function of the pleasure-physiologic body ego, death, not being such a function, must borrow, as it were, for the purpose of its symbolization.

I may finally quote Freud's (1911) remark with reference to the fact that the German word *selig* means both "dead" and "sensually happy": ". . . that the same word should be used in our language in two such different situations cannot be without significance" (p. 30n). And I may add that the French *feu*, as an adjective, means deceased, and if a noun, means fire, a symbol for (infantile sexual) urination.

In either instance, a language equates the expression for death with a pleasure-physiologic process. In the first case the equation is a direct one and the process is genital; in the second the equation is symbolic and the process is phallic.

---

[3] The only apparent exception to my statements that a symbol represents an element or a function of the pleasure-physiologic body ego is the symbolization, which Stekel (1910) was the first to observe, of "wrong" through "left," both as opposed to "right." It would appear that this representation obtains upon occasion. Yet it has been suggested to me that one should, on the very ground that it concerns no element of the pleasure-physiologic body ego and no pleasure-physiologic function, exclude it from the list of symbols.

E. SYMBOLIZATION OF THE PLEASURE-PHYSIOLOGIC DISCHARGE OF AGGRESSION

So far it would appear that all symbols are purely libidinal; they represent, in other words, sexual or infantile sexual parts or functions. However, inasmuch as Freud established symbolism long before he established the dualistic theory of the instincts (I, 3–8) the question arises as to *whether or not the aggressive instincts partake in symbolization.* Freud has, after all, stated that for the purpose of its discharge, aggression is regularly put in the service of the libido. With regard to the symbolized elements except that for death, the answer is simple. There are no symbols for either the cannibalistic mouth or the musculature, named by Freud as the organ (system) for the discharge of aggression. I have elsewhere (I, 3–8, 152–168, 272–276) cited Freud as to the simultaneity of discharge of aggression with libido and I have treated this phenomenon for the special case of the sexual act. It is astonishing that only a few of the symbols for the penis and for sexual intercourse, for masturbation, and for castration appear to reflect this discharge. There are the knife, dagger, the lance—"pointed weapons of any description" (Freud), shooting weapons, and the snake, symbolizing the male organ. Finally there is the symbolic representation of sexual intercourse through being run over.

To begin with the latter, Freud's uncanny ability to select material valid far beyond the particular case led him to present the dream (1900) of an AGORAPHOBIC woman in which she ". . . went in a train with her mother and saw her LITTLE ONE walk straight on to the rails so that she was bound to be run over. She heard the cracking of her bones. (This produced an uncomfortable feeling but no real horror). . . ." (p. 362; emphasis added). I have already referred (I, 109) to the fact that the "hearing the bones crack," i.e., the bones of people run over, is cannibalistic. In other words, it is the discharge of the oral sadistic component instinct in the act that the symbolization does not fail to supply.

The cannibalistic significance of the knife allows of no doubt.

It is with the knife that Shylock intends to kill Antonio by cutting a pound of flesh out of him near the heart (I, 80–91), and it is the knife and the sword of which Rashi comments, at the occasion of Abraham's sacrifice of his son, that they "devour flesh" (I, 100n). The shooting weapons act much as a knife from the distance, and that the snake kills through biting need hardly be mentioned. The aggression alluded to in this group of symbols is cannibalistic and agrees well with the "fantasy of the phallus equipped with a mouth" (I, 176–181).

Furthermore, some of the symbolic components in the symbol aggregate described by Freud's "dreams with a dental stimulus [4] (1900, pp. 385–392) reflect the same discharge of aggression simultaneous with that of libido. Masturbation, for instance, may be symbolized not only by the painless falling out of teeth but also by the forceful knocking or tearing out of them. This is, of course, strictly speaking, a "symbolically modified" symbol because tearing oneself one off *(sich einen herunterreissen)* or tearing something off something (e.g., a branch from a tree), is itself a symbol for the masturbatory act.

Other components of this aggregate, e.g., the extraction of teeth, belong to another group that contains a small number of symbols for castration: beheading and hair cutting. Here the axe and the scissors, relatives of the knife, are concerned; and one is reminded of many patients' material that makes one so frequently wonder whether castration is not in the last analysis conceived of as effected through biting.

The reader may naturally object to my stretching the concept of pleasure-physiology to the extent of including castration. It is self-evident that the shock of castration is a most painful, not a pleasurable, experience. If one considers it by itself, the child on whom it is inflicted becomes indeed the subject of pure aggression. But all amnesia removal that I have ever obtained did not allow me to consider it by itself. It invariably occurred in the context of a libidinal experience (scoptophilic or other-

---

[4] The subject is not as clear as it would be, were the resistance to the analysis of these dreams not as enormous as Freud was the first to describe. My treatment of it in the present context is consequently not as lucid as I would have desired.

wise) and was inflicted upon the child in a state of sexual excitation. The shock merely terminated the pleasure abruptly, replacing it by extreme "unpleasure." The neurotic sequelae of
the experience, numerous as they are, always reflect a fusion—or
should one say refusion?—of libido and aggression. It is thus that
I justify the inclusion.

F. SYMBOLIZATION OF A PLEASURE-PHYSIOLOGICAL PART OF AN OBJECT

There is no doubt that a pleasure-physiologic part of an object can also be subjected to symbolization. Boccaccio's Gianello's "I want the woman with whom I have made the bargain for
the vat" shows that the symbolized element may indeed be an
erogenic part of the object. Yet his case is not only fictitious,
but also normal. When we analysts observe the phenomenon it
is real but pathologic. Such symbolization has previously been
explained (II, 254) on the grounds of an intense identification
with the object, endowing the subject with much of the object's
pleasure-physiologic body ego. In the examples presented there
the identification is of the type "I am she" (the mother). It is
worth paralleling these examples with one contained in Freud
(1896), where the morbid identification is of the type "She is I,"
usually called projection. The reader who wishes to understand
my brief comment made in the interest of the general theory of
the symbol, should of course familiarize himself thoroughly with
Freud's account. In order to make my point I shall divide my
few excerpts from his case history into two parts.

1. Amongst the patient's incipient symptoms was a sudden sexual
feeling, in the presence of her maid, accompanied by the thought that
the latter "had now an improper idea." She had images of the genital
of a female with hair, coincident with an organ-sensation in her own
body. These pictures became very torturous for her because they occurred regularly whenever she was in the company of a woman and
were accompanied by the hallucination that she not only saw the
woman in indecent exposure, but also by the delusion that at the
same time the woman had the same picture of her.

2. She began to hear voices after having read a novel called *Die Heiterethei* whose heroine was a young woman with a name that is a playful neologism elaborative of the word *heiter*—joyfully serene. Immediately after reading the story and being much absorbed by it, Freud recounts, "she went for a walk along a country road and, as she was passing a small peasant's house, the voices suddenly said to her: 'That's what the *Heiterethei's* cottage looked like! There's the spring and there are the bushes! How happy she was in spite of all her poverty!'" (italics added). "My patient," Freud continues, "easily discovered the analogy with her own self. She, too, lived in a small place, met no one, and thought she was despised by her neighbors" (pp. 181–182).

The first paragraph of my excerpt, with its direct representation, interprets the second, with its symbolization. In the first, the patient is sexually aroused by the woman and fantasies her exposed, while the woman is delusorily thought of as aroused and fantasying the patient. The women, in other words, are objects, while simultaneously being carriers of, a projection. The second paragraph describes exactly the same, although in symbols. Here the projection is upon the fictional *Heiterethei*, who exhibits symbolically to the patient, showing her house, spring, and bushes, that is, genital, urethral-erotic organ, and pubic hair. The sexual interest of the *Heiterethei* in the patient is implied in her delusory exhibition.[5] The projection, however, is evident throughout the report.

In the case of a morbid identification, erogenic parts of the object of that identification can evidently become subject to symbolization.

This does not, however, answer the question, *can the normal individual also symbolize erogenic elements of an object.* Or to express it more comprehensively: if a normal individual were observed symbolizing erogenic parts of an object, could theory account for it? I believe that it could. Gianello's employment of the "vat" is arranged by Boccaccio so as to illustrate that em-

---

[5] This is no speculation. I remember several women patients to whom, at the time of their analyses, women friends made advances by taking them into the bathroom and urinating in their presence.

ployment in almost textbook fashion. When he says, "I want the woman with whom I have made the bargain for the vat," Peronella is absent. He cannot, therefore, cathect his object, but only the "object representation" (Freud). That representation, however, is narcissistic—no less narcissistic than is the pleasure-physiologic body ego. There is no difference as such between representing Peronella's erogenic parts in Gianello's mind, and representing his own. This, I believe, explains their symbolization. As though to make his case even more complete than it need be, the writer has added a further circumstance. Gianello is having a mutually gratifying affair with Peronella,—that is, the "zone equation" had been consummated "many times." This equation of the object's genital with the subject's makes it transitorily part of the latter's pleasure-physiologic body ego and, as such, narcissistic. All in all, the symbolization or erogenic parts of the object hardly poses a problem even for the case of the normal person.

Needless to add that this is equally valid for the "displacement symbol" to be discussed presently, which symbol overdetermines the "charms" of the love object and determines the choice of the fetish.

G. WHEN IS A POTENTIAL SYMBOL ACTUALLY A SYMBOL?

The next question to ask is, *when is a symbol a symbol?* Or, more explicitly, what characterizes the actual symbolic use of the representation of an element of the object world, which may potentially be so used? [6] This question has two answers: a clinical and a theoretic one. The first is elaborately implied in Freud's work. It is the context that dictates the answer: *if a sequence of thought contains gaps that can be closed only by reading certain elements in it symbolically, then these are symbols.* More subtle, but perhaps no less frequent, is the case of a thought without conspicuous gaps that nevertheless does not yield all that it actually expresses without the translation of

[6] Cf. Freud: "A [potential] symbol requires often enough . . . not a symbolic interpretation but is to be understood at its face value *(im eigentlichen Sinne)*."

symbols. It is this instance of which Boccaccio's story is an example. If the symbolic mode of expression employed in it were not—at least unconsciously—understood, we would find it banal and surely no work of art; we could not empathize deeply with the young woman whose picture would lack its third dimension. By the same token, many productions of our patients would remain incomprehensible or partially so if the symbolizations in them remained untranslated. Thought may finally on infrequent occasions—in certain obsessions, symptomatic actions, or in the manifest content of a short fragment of a dream—be expressed altogether in symbols. In such instances, nothing can, of course, be understood without translation. Unfortunately the question of whether a potentially symbolic element is in a given context actually a symbol, is rarely asked, although Freud has raised it. If you do ask it, however, your work becomes both more difficult and more reliable: it may sometimes take the better part of an analytic hour to find the answer; but once found, it rewards you with insight.

Having spoken in favor of taking one's time and liberally lending the analytic ear to as much associative content as is necessary to ascertain beyond doubt that a potential symbol is actually one, I must now add that on rare occasions this method does not apply. Here the decision must be made entirely by means of intuition.[7] In these instances one "simply knows" upon hearing it that the potential symbol is actually a symbol. If that sounds like a contradiction, I cannot help it; it is a faithful report of my experience. This is not the place to discuss intuition, which comes into play in many phases of the analyst's work. With reference to symbol translation, two remarks will suffice. For one thing, the intuitive grasp of a symbol must precipitate a conviction, not merely a suspicion. For another, the associations in response to the translation must contain the symbolized element as one without which they would not express a coherent and understandable thought.

---

[7] I once defined intuition as consisting "of a preconscious utilization of the totality of one's knowledge about species and individual as a frame of reference for the results of empathy with the latter."

There are, finally, instances in which the analyst finds that for him a symbol translation, not communicated to the patient, illuminates a previously meaningless series of association. Some kind of verification such as this is as indispensable for the intuitively recognized symbol as for the symbol ascertained by scrutiny of the patient's associations.

The second, the theoretical answer to the problem of symbolization of an erogenic part of an object, demands that the hypothesis of "refractory narcissism" (II, 307–317) be adopted. *If the representation of an element of the object world serves as symbol, the cathexis of the representation of that element is one not with object libido but with refractorily narcissistic libido.* Nothing else can explain its equation with an element of the object's pleasure-physiologic body ego. The symbolic exploitation of the object world is, in other words, "transitivistic"; where it occurs, the object representations of the two environments, body and object world, become one by virtue of their narcissistic cathexis. It is thus that Boccaccio can tell us what goes on *in* Peronella by telling us what goes on *around* her.

H. WHY IS A SYMBOL A SYMBOL?

The last fundamental question to be asked is *Why is a symbol a symbol?* More explicitly: what qualities of an element of the object world render it suitable for the symbolization of a particular element of the pleasure-physiologic body ego? To be blunt, this question cannot be answered. "We must admit," Freud wrote (1915–1917),

> . . . that the concept of a symbol cannot at present be sharply delimited: it shades off into such notions as those of a replacement or representation, and even approaches that of an allusion. With a number of symbols the comparison which underlies them is obvious. But again there are other symbols in regard to which we must ask ourselves where to look for the common element, the *tertium comparationis* of the supposed comparison. On further reflection we may afterwards discover it or it may definitely remain concealed [p. 152].

One would wish that Freud had emphasized *picturization* specifically where he spoke only in general of *representation;* for picturization is present in symbolization far more frequently than the other modes of unconscious indirect representation: allusion, the opposite, and the *pars pro toto*.[8] Think of all the elongated objects taking the place of the male genital, and all the indented ones taking that of the female—if you discount their pictorial representation, a *Gestalt* resemblance to the part they symbolize, there is practically nothing left. It appears that it is the form of the street, on which one walks or rides *(Verkehr)* and the form of the vat into which the mason descends *(immissio)* that makes possible their employment as symbols for the vagina. If a staircase (the vagina) located in the house (the woman) is climbed (body as phallus), the same conditions obtain except that the increasing shortness of breath adds, as Freud pointed out, an allusion to the dyspnea of the sexual act. There is no point in further illustration; examine the symbols listed by Freud and see what remains after picturization. You will eventually rely on the criteria mentioned above—the ubiquitous use of a symbolization, the constancy of the symbol equation, and its being born independent of learning and of any particular language. Yet, wherever you try to account for the suitability of a particular symbol for representing a particular part, you find yourself comparing that part most often to its picturization.[9]

There is, however, a small number of "pure" symbols lacking any admixture of other kinds of unconscious indirect representation. A few examples: wood symbolizing the mother (Freud), or female matter, suicide (Freud), and telephoning (this writer) symbolizing masturbation, dead-end (this writer)

---

[8] Accustomed to Freud's precision, I may here be splitting hairs. He probably employs representation *(Darstellung)* and picturization *(Verbildlichung)* synonymously—an employment consonant with German practice, which uses *Darstellung* for the *Verbildlichung,* e.g., of a subject by an artist or a writer.

[9] I imagine that this is the reason why Freud (1915–1917), who was as great a writer as he was a scientist, so often employs in his classic treatment of the subject the words "symbolize," or "being a symbol for" interchangeably with "represents," "describes," "signifies" or "is encountered."

the rectum, and blue, the quality anal. Freud originally expected such instances to illuminate the ultimate meaning of the symbolic relation, and believed that "Things that are symbolically connected today were probably united in prehistoric times *(in Urzeiten)* by conceptual and linguistic identity" (1900, p. 352).

I, for one, do not share in this expectation; but I have nothing to put in its stead. I simply reason as follows: if the mind of primal man resembled ours sufficiently for us to use empathy on its productions—and if it did not, the subject cannot be discussed—I do not recognize in the symbol relation a relic and a mark of former identity (Freud, 1900, p. 352). Or to be more specific, I cannot see why primal man should have regarded wood and the mother as the same; and if he both masturbated and committed suicide, I cannot imagine why he might have considered these two activities one. The color brown is, for obvious reasons, a frequent *picturization* of, or allusion to anal; [10] yet is is unintelligible why the same quality should be symbolized —as it undoubtedly is—by the color blue. All in all, it would seem that the pure symbols explain the symbolic relation no better than do the others.

It is superfluous—or it should be—to repeat that there is no psychic mechanism and no regressive condition known to us that produce a symbol. As Freud has shown in connection with the dream work, regressive conditions utilize only what already exists in the unconscious. If Little Hans (1909) transfers to a horse what he feels for his father, such a transference explains a convenience, not the symbolization. The child is able, as Freud has made clear, to avoid the horse, at the price of a phobia, while he could not avoid the father. Such, or any other utilization, never accounts for the origin of a symbol. I would not of course restate this had not some of Freud's early pupils erroneously posited all kinds of regressive states to explain symbolization.

---

[10] The sadistic Hitler, e.g., began with the *braune Haus* in Munich, headquarters for his brown-uniformed cohorts, and ended up marrying *Eva Braun*.

Yet there is another question to be answered—one which, as far as I know, has not even been asked. It allows for at least two formulations: (1) Are the criteria mentioned above—ubiquitous use, independence from learning and constancy of equation—sufficient to characterize an unconscious indirect representation as symbolic? (2) Because the symbol is so frequently overdetermined, particularly by picturization and allusion, how can one ever be certain that it is actually a symbol? The first question would, strictly speaking, have to be answered with: They are not; the second with: How can one, indeed? What these answers imply is the admission of a subjective factor in the recognition of an object as a symbol.

Take the representation of the parent through the horse: I am convinced that it is a symbolic one, although Freud, in Little Hans or elsewhere, has never said so. Or piano-playing as a symbol for masturbation (treated extensively toward the end of the present section). Freud was the first to equate the two, but he calls the former merely an "intimation, not a symbolization" of the latter. Or take, finally, the representation of the adult female genital through the number 4 (discussed in the clinical section below). It took me years of observation until I eventually found the courage to call it symbolic; and I could not even now argue conclusively with someone who insisted that it is but allusive.

Denying this subjective factor will not do. I can only hope that the reader who knows his Freud and studies the present chapter will have become a little more sure of himself in terming a representation symbolic than he had been before.

I. THE BEGINNING OF SYMBOLIZATION

No one has to my knowledge ever asked the question *at what stages in his development does the child become capable of symbolic expression.* Freud has reported upon one case of a girl whose unconscious mastered it between the ages of three and four (1920, p. 266), and of another at four (1900, p. 373). All I can do personally is speculate. Inasmuch as there are no symbols for the mouth and its adjunct, the eye, but there are for the rectum, for the quality anal, and for the pleasure-physiologic combination namable only by the vulgar word "arse," I am led to suspect that the child in the oral phase lacks the ability for symbolization, as it lacks a fully developed pleasure-physiologic body ego, and acquires it at some time during the anal-sadistic phases.

I owe two clinical confirmations to this speculation to a colleague (who does not wish to be thanked by name).

She told me of a little girl with two affectionate parents and a seven-month-old brother. The home contained no psychotic. The father did not at that time give the daughter any opportunity to see him in undress; about the mother in this regard nothing is known. It was evidently the baby brother who had aroused his sister's curiosity as to the difference between boys and girls, which led to her being more open than ever before in her overtures to the father.

One day the little girl sat on the bed in her nightgown and the mother recited to her, as she had done many times, the Mother Goose verse:

> Pussy *cat,* pussy *cat,*
> Where have you been?
> I've been to London
> To look at the Queen.
>
> Pussy *cat,* pussy *cat,*
> What did you there?
> I caught a little *mouse*
> Under a chair [italics added].

This time, the little girl, upon hearing the last two lines, put her hand under her nightgown, obviously on her *genital,* in a protective gesture.

Neither my colleague nor I had any doubt that the child, although not employing symbolization, certainly understood it. That, in fact, was the reason for her relating the story. I then asked: "Is the girl being toilet-trained?" "Oh yes! She has been in training for about three months and is usually continent.

"However," my colleague added, "shortly before the incident with
the pussy cat she had told me, 'Sometimes I do duty in my pants.' "

We know that the phases in the development of the child overlap.
The little girl's phallic development had been accelerated by the baby
brother's arrival, but her own words testify to the fact that she was
still in the second anal phase. It was thus that at once she unconsciously understood symbolization.

A little boy of two and a half was being put to sleep when he had
an erection. His mother had never seen him with one before. She
asked him if he had to go on the potty. He said no; then seemed to be
aware of his erection and said: *"It's like New York City."* For several
months he had been picturing New York City buildings which had
greatly impressed him one day when he had caught sight of the New
York skyline. He had been building towers of blocks and saying it was
New York. Any tall thing was likened to the city.

The child had been bowel trained for at least two or three months
and was almost completely trained for urination by the time of this
incident. ("I have no way of knowing," my conscientious colleague
ends her report, "if this was his first symbolic representation.")

The second example is even more instructive than the first. Besides
repeating the previous comment, one can point to the fact that symbolism here is not only understood but employed by the child. In addition, the symbolization pre-empts zone-equation (I, 275–281), and
the little boy expresses symbolically what another small child expressed directly when he said: "Mama, I am going to peepee in your
eye" (II, 29). In either instance the organ becomes potentially equated
with the phallic mother, and the eye to be "peeped into" is a bisexual symbol filling the "castrated" socket with the "phallic" eyeball.

Another little girl dreamt at about the time of her second birthday
that she played with *two kiddies*.[11] "Since she had previously always
specified children by name, I felt," my colleague told me, "that this
designation [through two categorically identical persons] represented,
symbolically, the *mother*."

At the age of two years and three months the girl became aware of
"castration." She told of it at first directly: "Dolly is broke," holding

[11] I am indebted to Dr. Beatrice Enson for these observations.

the doll upside down, looking and feeling the mould-seam at its bottom. Her "explanation" was also direct: "Mommy put dolly in the washing machine and broke her."

Four days later she commented symbolically on her problem. Dissatisfied generally, she wanted "something" all the time but could not tell what. Her mother scolded her finally, and she calmed down. She put on her *slippers* and sang to herself,

> Along came a spider
> Who sat down beside her
> And frightened Miss Muffet away.

Because the slippers are shoes they are a bisexual symbol; the spider (I, 180–181) symbolizes the phallic mother as well as her phallus (Abraham).

At about the same time, the child's interest in objects that we are wont to encounter as symbols: umbrellas, cars and things that would fit into other things increased substantially.

Her distress disappeared when she was able to identify with her mother by reverting to treating her dolls as children: they were diapered, patted affectionately, and elaborately put to sleep. The girl's own wetting herself had increased during the four weeks of her acute distress.

Two episodes, one accompanying and one concluding the period of anxiety, deserve to be briefly recounted; in the second of these a well-known displacement symbol is employed, while the first contains a variant of a well-known symbolization.

Because she was grieving over the "lack of a tail," the child was given a pair of indoor roller skates. After mastering their use, she proudly came across the room and shouted, "I am *skating* like boys!" I once analyzed a skater and learned from her that skating is but a variant of the phallic-erective symbol of flying, encountered in dreams.

The last episode may be told in my colleague's own words: "After an enjoyable bath, she was having a delightful time jumping on the bed with Daddy catching her, tossing her about, and tickling her. Suddenly she paused and said, 'My *foot* is gone.' She held up her leg as if to show us and pointed to the front door. This was done in a playful, teasing manner. (Oh, your foot is gone?) "Yes." (Where it went?—mimicking her own way of asking when she is looking for something.) "To Jack." (Jack has it?) "No, Dick has it."

Jack is the little boy she saw urinate standing up—an experience initiating the phallic phase. Dick is Jack's father; and the foot is a frequently employed displacement symbol for the phallus (II, 229).

It would appear that my speculation as to the ontogenetic onset of symbolization is clinically verifiable.

J. IS THE SYMBOL ARCHAIC?

A further complication of the insoluble problem of the nature of the symbol has but briefly been mentioned by Freud. "A number of symbols," he writes (1900), "are as old as language itself, while others (e.g. 'airplane,' 'Zeppelin') are being coined continuously down to the present time" (p. 352). This of course is true and, although unexplainable, deserves to be given some thought. That the symbol is both archaic and yet constantly formed anew appears perhaps less contradictory if one places its development in the context of the history of man. One recognizes then that at first only a very limited number of objects of his environment were available to him for their exploitation as symbols (e.g., a landscape, a tree, or a valley, a branch to tear off, the fish, the snake, and the bird). Most of the objects we see him use as symbols today are things that he has had to invent. He made knives and pots, boxes and rods; then ladders, hats, coats, and houses; and, eventually, firearms and complicated machines. Freud mentions the four-in-hand as a distinctly male symbol, referring to an article of fashion even younger than himself. Thus, while the choice of the symbol remains enigmatic, the increase of the number of symbols with that of the products of human invention is not in itself a problem; it is almost as old as is symbolization itself.

Some of the newly formed symbols are only variants of old ones; the airplane, for example cited by Freud with reference to the symbolization of erection through flying, is really but a twin to the bird; but others such as telephoning for masturbation do not point to an earlier model from which they have been derived. Thus the contradiction between the apparently archaic nature of the symbol and the symbolic exploitation of ever new inventions remains an enigma after all; and the problem does not admit of solution.

K. ARE THERE "INDIVIDUAL" SYMBOLS?

There is a passage in Freud (1900) that contains a misleading term. He states that "a dreamer may derive from his private memories the power to employ as sexual symbols all kinds of things which are not generally employed as such" (p. 352). Sexual *symbols?* No, sexual representations. One of the few incontrovertible characteristics of the symbol is its general use. An "individual symbol" would be a contradiction in terms.

The importance of this distinction and the fact that Boccaccio's story does not contain an individual representation, may justify the brief presentation of two examples. Both are taken from associations of patients, one to an experience, the other to a speech in a dream.

Under the influence of several drinks, a woman friend staying as house guest masturbates in her hostess's bed, occupying it alone but exhibiting to her freely *a tergo*. The hostess, my patient, reports this in all detail but declares herself uninterested and incapable of remembering the friend's arms. Instead, she recalls her own: she was vigorously scraping a dirty dish. Knowing that her sexual interest, had it been allowed to develop, was immense, I recognize in the dish her genital, and in the scraping the masturbatory discharge of her excitement. However, neither the incident in itself, nor the abundance of confirmatory material, make the dish or the scraping a symbol. They are merely individual representations.

The second example concerns a male who dreams of an unknown man at the foot of a flight of stairs whom he asks: "When is Passover?" The analysis had been a successful one and had entered its terminal phase. He remembered how his mother baked delicious things on such holidays, remarking, "The place smelled so good." This was easily followed by the removal of an amnesia for a series of sexual intimacies with a psychotic woman, stemming from the so-called latency period, that left no doubt as to the "place" and its characterization. Sweet things to eat *(Süssigkeiten)* symbolize sexual enjoyment (Freud), but "the place" is again merely an individual representation of the female genital, not a symbol. I do not, by the way, remember the patient having used this particular representation except on that one occasion.

L. THE EMPLOYMENT OF SYMBOLIZATION

It has already been stated that the employment of symbolization by the dream work does not differ from that in other psychic productions: symptomatic or symbolic actions, parapraxies, obsessions, fantasies, associations. Nor is it confined to any of these—a fact attested to by the story introducing the present chapter. The symbol, however, whether used in analysis by a patient, by anybody in daily life, or by a writer in fiction, will almost always take its place side by side with other forms of direct and indirect representation. Freud distinguishes symbolization from other modes of unconscious indirect representation: pictorization, allusion, representation through opposites, and of the whole through a part. That distinction must be remembered. For one thing, as was said above, these other modes are intelligible, and symbolization is not. For another, they may or may not be conscious, whereas symbolization is always unconscious.

The male, for instance, who after seeing a woman companion home, proverbially asks her, "May I come up to your room?" is conscious of employing allusion but unconscious of using symbolization (body = phallus; coming up; stair climbing = intercourse (Freud); room = vagina).

A patient will therefore unpredictably at one moment express himself directly, at the next indirectly, and symbolically at that. Thus the symbol may indeed prove the "mute element." Without its translation by the analyst the patient's thought remains incomprehensible or incomplete.

A patient begins her analytic hour by remarking that she saw two policemen sitting downstairs in the hall, which reminded her of a time when she witnessed police restraining a psychotic and assisting in his hospitalization. "But," she goes on, "I think I should go back to the scene with my mother and me on the bed." She refers to her traumatic defloration as an infant by her psychotic mother, the memory of which emerges from repression, becomes described in detail, and is accompanied by an adequate affect. Here the mother is first symbolized by two policemen—"two categorically identical persons" modified by an allusion to violence, but in the next breath she is named directly and the particular form of violence is remembered. With regard to the employment of symbolization, theoretically one has here the choice between considering the initial symbolization indicative of a transient resistance quickly overcome, or regarding it merely as a sign of intrusion of the primary process into free association. Practically, however, I do not know upon what grounds one could make that choice.

Most frequent perhaps is the case of an association that appears reasonable and not even abortive but nevertheless conceals the better part of its meaning through the employment of symbolization.

I shall exemplify this with the brief remark of the essayist La Bruyère, who in a period when ladies wore high shoes and high coiffures to make themselves appear taller, observes: *"Il faut juger des femmes depuis la chaussure jusqu'à la coiffure exclusivement à peu près comme on mesure le poisson entre queue et tête* (1688)." (One must judge women exclusively from the shoes to the hairdress about as one measures the fish between tail and head.)

It is reasonable to assume that all the man meant to say was: You must discount her two prostheses, the high shoes and the high coiffure, if you want to size up the girl who is in between them. The statement appears plain and complete, although not very meaningful; but then La Bruyère is not profound. But, if for the sake of the argument one imagined it were a patient's association, one must also imagine an analyst listening to it, trained to hear primary process thought no matter how well concealed and how tightly condensed. That would transform the plain statement into an elaborate one and entirely deprive the simile, the comparison of the girl with the fish, of its gratuitous appearance. Why? Because now allusion and symbolization are understood and, although indirect and unconscious, evaluated as equal to the direct and conscious expression of thought. It is the mouth-eye unit (I, 55–60) that connects the simile with the statement proper: appreciating the woman means disrobing her mentally and devouring her with the eye, as one does the fish with the mouth. The remainder testifies to the simultaneity of acknowledgment and denial of the woman's castration, which preoccupied Freud (1905, p. 155m) even while writing a posthumous fragment. Her body is equated with the (edible part of the) fish, about which clinical observation leaves no doubt that it symbolizes the female phallus. But head and tail are inedible, and they must be chopped off (beheading = castrating; cutting off the tail is self-explanatory). Thus, the woman, when shoes and high coiffure are removed, has a phallus, her body, and at the same time has none.

In addition, the smell of the fish has often been likened to that of the female organ. Freud (1905) and Abraham (1910) have both drawn attention to the strong odor of some of the objects employed by the fetishist for his gratification. I sometimes have the impression that the smell of the woman's genital is unconsciously conceived of in a fetishistic manner as a quasi-corporeal emanation from her organ, in other words, in the last analysis again as the phallus. At the same time, of course, the odor proves her castration as the male genital lacks it. This, then, would be a final element in the dichotomic thought, so extremely condensed.[12]

One could, of course, call the employment of symbolization illustrated here that of modifying the direct expression of thought. Such *symbolic modification* is not infrequent, although often much less elaborate than in the example. Its importance lies in the fact that the gap in the associative context to be filled by inserting the symbol, the "mute" element, is not the

[12] My interpretation is not genetic and does not, therefore, contradict Freud's and Abraham's derivation of the olfactory pleasure from an earlier coprophilic one.

only one. It is merely the simplest. There are others where one cannot speak of a gap, yet where one is no less constrained to adduce the symbol for the sake of elaboration of thought.

In analysis, the symbol is often employed, as was stated in the beginning, for the maintenance of repression.[13] Yet the clinical manifestations of such employment, i.e., the ever varying combinations of symbolization with other forms of indirect and direct expression, are so many that they defy enumeration. The present section contains, therefore, only a few characteristic examples.

However, no idea can remain in repression—Freud (1915) taught us—unless the affect-quantum adherent to it remains suppressed, i.e., prevented from being developed: in the case of an "unsuccessful" repression with its consequent neurotic manifestations the affect may undergo one of several vicissitudes, described by Freud. Yet, there is one that he has not described—at least not in general terms. Here the affect persists: it is neither suppressed nor altered, but, instead of being attached to the idea, it is attached to a symbol for the idea. In that condition it may but need not necessarily be developed.

Little Hans, an extreme case of this kind, enjoys an affectionate relation to his father because he has attached the affective terror of being eaten by him to a symbol for him, the horse.

By the same token, a patient of Ferenczi's a young woman who transferred her father upon the analyst, could excite herself by gratifying her infantile sexual curiosity on the horse urinating in the street. The shift from the transference object to the symbol was clearly shown in her dreams.

A woman patient who symbolized her father by a racially foreign person, a sheik, could by fantasying that he raped her develop great quantities of sexual affect in orgastic masturbation.

The same symbolization permitted a violently anti-Semitic patient to belatedly develop hate and rebellion against an imaginary Jewess instead of the mother. The replacement of the latter by the symbol was contained in her associations.

---

[13] It is not, however, always so used. In the case of the two policemen, for instance, the employment is in the service of the buoyancy of the repressed.

The principle even obtains, as in a case reported by Freud (1915a), where the homosexual affect has been transformed into paranoia. An attack of delusory fear of persecution is precipitated not by the sexual object, the mother, but by a symbol for her, i.e., "two categorically identical persons": in Freud's case, two men at the foot of the staircase who the patient is convinced photograph her for the purpose of blackmail.

This implies, of course, that the displacement from the symbolized element to the symbol is no protection against the development of affect. Nevertheless, it often assists either suppression or transformation of affect.

There is, finally, nothing (outside the dream) that tempts one more strongly to speak of a *function* of the symbol or of its failure than the attachment, or lack of attachment, respectively, of an affect to it.

A colleague has put the following written clinical illustration at my disposal. It concerns the "rotating symbol," representing ego disintegration to be discussed in Section II of this chapter.

A young man has recently suffered a transient terrifying break with reality and since then has been struggling against having another one. His language and thinking during this period has taken on a definitely primary process cast. The breakdown he refers to in a concrete, stereotyped manner as "going off the edge." The feelings that, for him, threaten to lead up to "going off the edge" he calls "gyrations." The latest example:

"Last night I was at a dance. Everybody else was dancing, and I was feeling so awful. I felt I wanted to break down and go to the hospital. I was tempted to do gyrating *things.*" I ask him what he means by these *things,* and he explains that he is not talking about things but about feelings that he had and that he described in terms appropriate to action. His expression here is apparently contaminated by the image of the dancing going on around him—gyrating things—that evoke his own internal gyrations. He was terrified with the specific fear of going off the edge. As he talks more about his feelings, he seems to be involved in the image of a *spinning record* (portraying both self and the environment); the mechanism of the record player may go out of control, and the needle will then go "off the edge." When he begins to feel better and the danger of ego disintegration recedes, this is described as feeling "in the groove again." The groove is pictured as a straight line, and the movement along it is slow and orderly.

The gyrations are described as oscillating feelings of derealization and depersonalization (rapid changes in the body feelings) together with an awareness of loss of control of his emotions with shifts from one intense feeling to another—sudden hatred, sexual arousal, and terrible anxiety. Everything, inner and outer world goes spinning wildly. . . . The appearance of the symbol is accompanied by anxiety—anxiety that specifically concerns the possibility of losing control in the sense of being swept from feeling into actions—doing *gyrating things.*

The brief report, a model of analytic writing; is as lucid as it is comprehensive and requires little comment. The patient, struggling with disintegrative attempts to suppress a variety of affects threatening the existence of his ego organization by projecting them, as it were, into the object world, where, were he successful, they would appear in disguise as the "rotating symbol." But he is not successful: the rotation returns to his body (insofar as it had not remained there in the first place), and the affects defy transmutation. They were about to enforce or accompany a psychotic break.

All in all, the successful displacement of affect from the symbolized element to the symbol is still another function of symbolization.

M. OVERDETERMINATIONS OF THE SYMBOL

The above example illustrates something in terms of the individual representation that is also true of the symbol: it may be overdetermined. Most frequent is the historic overdetermination. The "place," mentioned in a previous example, is not only a genital but also the apartment where the patient lived as a boy. By the same token the street in Boccaccio's story, besides being a symbol for the vagina, is also the street where the mason and Peronella dwell. Needless to say that the element street is in such instances considered twice, once at its face value and once as a symbol. In the first case, the analyst has the patient associate to the element and learns that it is memory material; in the second, he examines the context and decides it is at the same time a symbol.

If the symbol is *overdetermined as day residue* the procedure is naturally the same; one could, in fact, call the day residue with regard to such overdetermination simply a memory from the most recent past. There is hardly a symbol that does not allow for these two overdeterminations; they are as frequent as the one to be described hereinafter is rare. This is the *metaphorical overdetermination.*

A metaphorical interpretation is, in my opinion, not the analyst's but solely the patient's privilege; it will occasionally be found in the course of his associations. Freud has shown that it merely assists in the transformation of abstract thought into concrete pictorial expression. I think that the analyst should not ever employ it, because it is not part of a reliable method as is symbol-translation or interpretation.[14] The analyst who ascribes a metaphorical meaning to his patient's association has, for one thing, no means whatsoever of ascertaining whether or not such an interpretation is valid. He is led, for another, to pursue *his own thought instead of that of his patient.* If, however, the patient does it, the case is altogether different: the metaphorical meaning is one of this patient's associations, and the analyst listens to it and evaluates it as he does all others. He will then find that on occasion a metaphor may actually overdetermine a symbol, which in this case is not of course taken at face value, but understood figuratively instead of concretely.

---

[14] Some of Stekel's (1911) fantastic interpretations, mentioned and rejected by Freud (1900, p. 357) are examples of a *metaphoric* reading of analytic material. The "not catching up with a [moving] wagon [or car]" is, for example, supposed to be understood as the "regret over a difference in age with which one cannot catch up"; or the "baggage with which one travels" as the "burden of sins, pressing in on one", etc. If the reader compares these interpretative associations, subjective and unsupportable by any clinical evidence, with the symbol equations, constant and objectively requisite to the completion of thought, he will appreciate my warning.

An example, deliberately taken from unfinished current clinical work, supplies an instructive illustration. Amnesia removal is being gradually obtained for episodes representative of the mobilization of instinct components belonging to the puberty incest. In one of these the psychotic mother unclothed from the waist down had her 13-year-old son, recently matured, not only hook up her corset but also her garters, since an alleged backache prevented her from bending down. The exhibition, its impact upon the boy, and his defensive reactions are told convincingly as they emerge from repression, and have memory-quality for the patient. Needless to add that much symptomatology is reducible to the experience which was not a single but a repeated one. Its termination, as happens so frequently in the course of amnesia removal, is at present not clear.

So far, so good. Moreover, the associations contained recurrently the element "burning bush." He understands this as the mother's genital, represented through hair in a state of arousal ("burning" with passion). Beyond stating that the patient recalled the very words with which the mother confided her sexual need and frustration to him directly, I must refrain from presenting further material that lends ample support to this metaphoric interpretation, and confine myself to saying that the woman's husband, the patient's father, had for several years actually lost all sexual interest in her.

Nevertheless, the apparently gratuitous interpolation of the association burning bush into the others alien to it, caused me to suspect that it contained a symbolization. If it did, the patient's metaphorical interpretation—justified as it is—would prove but an overdetermination. Since the symbol equation is constant to the extent that a symbol has always the same meaning, I expected that if the analysis progressed, the deeper meaning of "burning" (urination) would emerge and take its place in a context. For those inclined to call such expectation a prejudice, I may name its source: the experience in puberty must repeat, although in modulation, traumatic experiences from the first five years of life (Freud). These had for long been remembered. The urinary discharge of sexual stimulation, described by Freud as the phallic precursor of genital ejaculation, was naturally not missing; but it was complicated by the fact that it occurred at times simultaneously with that of the climactically incontinent mother.[15]

---

[15] A climactic urethral-erotic discharge was once directly described to me by a psychotic woman patient. It had happened the night before her hour of treatment during intercourse with her husband.

Such was the reason for my expectation. However, because the present section is devoted to the role of the symbol in clinical work, I should perhaps reformulate this reason so as to adjust it to that topic.

Ordinarily when a potentially symbolic element appears in the patient's productions, the analyst has the choice of taking it at its face value or regarding it as a symbol. Which of these two alternatives he will decide upon, usually depends upon the context.

Yet it does not do so in the case of the "burning bush." That element, whether read directly or symbolically, did not fit into context, but remained a foreign body in the otherwise coherent associations. If it were read directly it would interject an actually burning bush, which is absurd; and if it were here to be understood symbolically it would introduce female (maternal) urination, which, however, did not appear to play any part in the puberty incest.

One cannot of course disregard the element because that would be disregarding a repeated association; the only solution is, therefore, to regard it as part of a different context. The latter is known and has been mentioned above; it preceded by 10 years the events reflected in the present associative context, but is bound to intrude into that context because it is closely allied to it in the timeless unconscious. Thus, if the element "burning bush" is understood metaphorically it is part of the present context; if it is understood as a symbol it is indicative of the intrusion.

Yet, to my surprise, I later learned through further amnesia removal that the symbolization had not only been expressive of the intrusion of infancy into puberty but had indeed foreshadowed a type of event directly representative of that intrusion. The event was still repressed at the time of the memory of the occurrences reported, but the symbolization "burning bush" had been predictive of the eventual memory of it.

The depraved mother had groomed her son for the eventual incest through a series of cunningly planned preparations. The first of these has been described; none of them could, however, be epitomized by a symbolic reading of "burning bush." Yet about four years later the adolescent young man became seriously interested in a girl whom he wanted to marry. It was then that the mother, besides trying to dissuade him, resumed her seductions, which caused the son much anguish but failed in their goal. *Her practices now included repeated urinary exhibitions.*

Coming home from high school, the son hung up hat and coat and went into the bathroom where he found the woman urinating, gratuitously exposed. The patient does not recall excitement or even curiosity, but only irritation. Why was the door unlocked? Well, she had "just forgotten" to lock it. Had she not heard him enter the house? No, of course not; how could she, being in the bathroom? The material permits no doubt that these were lies; the meeting had been carefully timed. Amongst the indications demanding the further inference that the boy's irritation was but the result of a defensive transformation of affect is the fact that he took no precautions (knocking at the door, calling out) against the subsequent repetitions of the encounter.

The example demonstrates that a symbolic element may on occasion allow for a pertinent metaphoric interpretation by the patient. It shows furthermore that the two, without being confused, may nevertheless prove compatible with each other. If they do, the symbol sustains a metaphorical overdetermination.

N. SYMBOLIC CONDENSATION

There are cases where one phase of the primary process symbolization assists another, condensation. I propose dealing with two different instances of this kind: the "modification" and the "aggregation" of symbols.

1. The "Modified" Symbol

It is profitable to introduce this term because it clarifies certain phenomena even if it does not explain them. The modified symbol, is the antithesis of the pure one which it outnumbers. Here, modified is employed in only one of its meanings as defined by Webster (1947) in formulating the distinction between modify and qualify; "to change in form or in certain qualities rather than materially or essentially." In other words, modification, if so understood, does not either decrease or alter the substance; it merely adds some qualities to it. Thus the vat in Boccaccio's tale "with dregs or the like therein" is pictorially modified: a vagina with certain qualities of the rectum. The street, serving as it does the *Verkehr*, is an allusively modified symbol. If one meets, as one sometimes will, with a "snowy road" in a patient's material, one may have encountered a symbolically modified symbol—a bloody vagina—since snow is a symbol for blood. By the same token the modification of a room through curtains (labia) and a door (aperture) is pictorial; that of a key with the capacity of opening it is allusive; while the modification of a bird able to fly is both allusive and symbolic (flying symbolizing erection).

If the concept of the modified symbol does no more than acquaint one with a typical instance of extreme condensation, it has served its purpose. For it focuses one's attention upon this condensation and makes one aware that in translating the symbol the condensation must be undone.

2. *The "Symbol Aggregate"*

La Bruyére's aphoristic remark, previously quoted and analyzed is an example. I shall add, however, at least one particularly instructive clinical illustration, which makes it possible to not only identify the symbolic constituents of the thought but to corroborate this identification though the memory of experiences past and present.

A woman patient reports having been with her husband in their car on the eve of her session. With them was a document, important for his career. *Riding* with him, she was surprised by a sudden impulse to *open* the *door, jump out* of the *car*, and *throw* the *document* into a nearby *river*. Completely mystified by the impulse, she was unable to furnish any associations. The following are the interpretations and the corroborative data. They demonstrate that the eight words essential to the patient's verbalization of her impulsion (and italicized in the text) contain, either directly or by implication, *six* different symbols.

(a) *Interpretation:* Riding *(Verkehr)*, traffic, transportation—sexual intercourse (Freud).

Corroboration: When I first suggested to the patient that she not allow herself to slide into hypnotic evasion during subway rides, she had two vestibular orgasms in one ride, unaccompanied by any fantasy whatsoever. She was, at point of writing, involved in a renewed, yet still unsuccessful attempt to recover a memory of the primal scene.

(b) *Interpretation:* In this case the car (a bisexual symbol) is the female genital that can be opened.

Corroboration: The patient, who in childhood and adolescence suffered severely from car sickness, was struggling with the fractioned removal of an amnesia; on her, as a child, lies a nude woman whose hairy genital is "LIKE A DEVOURING MOUTH." SEEING AN ORGAN upon entering a concert hall on the following night sent her into an incipient hypnotic evasion. Forgetful of the homonymous character of the word organ, she compared the instrument's pipes to teeth.

(c) *Interpretation:* Jumping out of the car, she would in order to reach the edge of the river have to walk through fast-moving traffic, i.e., to risk "suicide"—masturbation (Freud) by (4) being run over = sexual intercourse (Freud).

Corroboration: The patient, who had been warned of accident proneness, reported how she had found herself jay-walking in the middle of Madison Avenue, a two-way street, crossing it without even looking at opposing traffic to the right. The better part of her masturbatory activities and arrangements had remained concealed from me for an unduly long time, and the resultant excitement was definitely played down. During the organ concert, mentioned above, she was bored, felt fidgety, fantasied sexually about women, and finally became so hypnotic that she went to sleep.[16]

So far only four constituent symbols have been discussed: one for the genital, in this case—as the modifying picturization, i.e., the opening of it, shows—of the female; two for sexual intercourse, and one for masturbation. Yet the last three contain a "symbolic prediction" (below): they forecast that the woman, as yet still lying on the child, will, when the time comes, move. In the course of further amnesia removal this came true, and the woman was recognized as the patient's (psychotic) mother.

---

[16] Cf. II, 191, where Grotjahn's as yet unsurpassed essay on *Boredom* is discussed. Grotjahn thinks that boredom entails the unconscious temptation to masturbate. The patient could soon be made conscious of the meaning of playing the organ, not, however, without carefully crossing her legs on the couch.

(d) *Interpretation:* The potential suicide mentioned above implies "falling down"—"giving birth" (Freud).

Corroboration: One of the patient's most torturous neurotic symptoms had been the obsessive wish for another child—a wish whose strength she concealed from her husband by keeping silent about it most of the time and mentioning it only once or twice in an offhand manner. I came to believe that this compulsion was symptomatic of a persistence of the preoedipal passive wish for a baby from the mother; hence the symbolism of giving birth.[17]

(e) *Interpretation:* The document to be thrown away is a sheaf of paper = the mother (Freud): it is the mother that she wants to throw into the river. The intended symbolic action at this point reaches its greatest condensation and is accompanied by a nonsymbolic component.

The patient's mother identification was extreme; it was matched only by her excessive bondage to substitutes for the mother object. She had come to be cognizant of the damage wrought by this constellation and wanted to get rid of the mother once and for all. "Falling into water" = giving birth (Freud) is, however, another symbolic component. It represents a symbolic elimination modified by a nonsymbolic revenge.

Corroboration: In *The Interpretation of Dreams* (1900) Freud relates how a four-year-old child said to her father: "I wish Josefine [the nurse] was dead." Father: trying [to] calm [the child]: "Why dead? Wouldn't it do if she went away?" Child: "No [because] then she'd come back again." (p. 255n).

In my patient, the mother, who had died long ago from an illness, actually became a *"revenant,"* tying the daughter to her obsessions so that nothing short of actively killing the mother could free the patient. However, the particular form of the falling implies secondly a nonsymbolic revenge. As a child her face was forced into the maternal vulva and she was choked; as an adult she suffered when swimming, attacked by the fear of drowning; she wanted now at last to retaliate by drowning the mother.

Interpretation: Mental achievement represents the phallus; the dis-

---

[17] The inexperienced reader may be baffled by the coincidence of symbols for both masturbation and giving birth. He will be more at ease if he remembers that Freud has called masturbation quite generally the "sexual executive of the child," and learns that another patient recalled only recently her onetime idea that if either she or her mother masturbated the act would produce a child.

placement of so concrete a part upon so abstract a function is as easy to observe as it is difficult to understand. The wish to destroy the husband's document is, in other words, reducible to the penis envy of the patient.

Corroboration: I must confine myself to but two of the many symptoms of the woman's pseudostupidity: she combined a high degree of adroitness in playing an instrument with an almost phobic attitude to the understanding of music. One can imagine where this left the analyst, who so often has to address himself, preparatorily, to the intellect of his patient.

It is difficult to conceive of an instance of condensation more dense than that exemplified in this contemplated symbolic and symptomatic action.

Both the modified symbol and the symbolic aggregate are, as was said above, instances of extreme condensation. Yet it would seem that there is also a difference between them. Modification, or a tendency toward it, appears intrinsic to the complexion of many symbols, while aggregation does not. The enormous degree of condensation involved is characteristic of unconscious thought. It can therefore be found in other psychic productions devoid or nearly devoid of symbolization—in symptomatic actions (II, 229), in conversion symptoms, and in the neologistic speech in the dream (Chapter Two, below). Nevertheless, the aptitude of the symbol for the condensed expression of thought justifies treating the aggregate side by side with its modification.

O. THE "DISPLACEMENT" SYMBOL

I am not sure of the order in which the next two problems in the formulation of a General Theory of the Symbol should be treated. Freud has described a particular group of symbols that are very frequently used and has called them—or so I thought for years—"displacement symbols" *(Verschiebungs-symbole).* (I am vexed by the fact that in rereading his work on the subject I found their description without finding the term; yet I cannot persuade myself that I coined it.) These are the numerous symbolizations of one part of the body by another; more correctly, an erogenic part by a nonerogenic part; and still more correctly, of an element of the pleasure-physiologic body ego by an element of the body ego. Examples: the nose for the penis, the lips for the labia, or, as in Boccaccio's story, the whole body for the phallus. In attempting a theoretical orientation, one should of course begin with a reference to the fact that the pleasure-physiologic body ego (II, 206–284) is dominated by the primary process (II, 228–230) and thereby beset with displacements. Since the latter include the body ego proper they produce a perpetual overlapping between the two psychic formations, the body ego and the pleasure-physiologic body ego. Or, to express it differently, elements of the body ego proper are intermittently sexualized and become for the time of their sexualization elements of the pleasure-physiologic body ego II, 215. Yet even then they *are* symbols but possess none. They cannot, in other words, become symbolized elements because they lack, as do all parts of the body ego proper, the suitability for symbolization.

The sex appeal of a woman may for one thing be dependent upon these displacements as, for example, the portrait of Cressida, (Troilus and Cressida) drawn by Ulysses, suggests:

> There's language in her eye, her cheeke, her lip,
> Nay, her foote speakes; her wanton spirites looke out
> At every joint, and motive of her body: (IV, 5) [18]

The importance of these displacements for the morbid conversion symptom and their contributions, although limited to the analysis of the so-called psychosomatic conditions, are common knowledge. However, when one attempts a next step toward the theory of the displacement symbol, one is again confronted by the insoluble problem of the essence of the symbol after allusion and picturization are subtracted.

---

[18] My justification for using passages from Shakespeare as equivalent to clinical illustrations can be found in the Foreword to Volume I, p. xv. My preference for the text of the Folios (1623) especially their spelling, as reprinted by the Nonesuch Press in 1953, is explained in the same place.

The stunning half-line: "Nay, her foot speaks," permits clinical corroboration because the poet describes here what Freud has called organ language. The foot is not only an old sexual symbol, but a phallic one at that. To exhaust its meaning, a study of the subject of fetishism and Freud's writings about it (1905, 1927) is indispensable. The reader will learn that the foot symbolizes the delusory phallus, derivative of the clitoris with which the woman unconsciously equips herself in order to deny her "castration," and is so equipped by the unconsciously fetishistically oriented man. In our civilization the foot is shod; its swelling becomes, because of the unyielding leather, more easily conscious than that of any other part of the body. I remember clearly one instance, and vaguely another, where women while stripping a shoe off because it felt too tight reported feeling their genitals in a simultaneous state of turgescence. The sexual organ, in other words, "entered" the pleasure-physiologic body ego, modified through a displacement symbol.

It is also not difficult to observe clinically how often the ordinary action of a joint, such as bending or spreading, has for the patient a sexual "motive."

An example of the "pure" displacement symbol in contrast to the modified ones is the tooth. Freud (1900, p. 387) avers that although a displacement (from below to above) is at work there, the very fact that the tooth "affords no possibility of analogy" with the symbolized element, makes it suitable to serve as a representation. This sounds somewhat absurd until one recognizes that it can only mean that the tooth is a pure displacement symbol lacking all other kinds of unconscious indirect representation, and that the symbolization *cannot* therefore be "explained."

P. THE SYMBOLIC EQUATION

Rank and Sachs (1913) once wrote, "Symbolism thus appears as the unconscious precipitate of primitive means of adaptation to reality that have become superfluous and useless, a sort of lumber-room of civilization to which the adult readily flees in states of reduced or deficient capacity for adaption to reality, in order to regain his old, long-forgotten playthings of childhood (Jones, 1912, p. 109)." Unfortunately, except for the words "primitive means of adaptation to reality" everything in this sentence is the opposite of the truth. I prefer to speak of an *adaptation* to the environment and I propose to call this particular means of adaptation the *symbolic equation.*[19]

Such equation is neither superfluous, useless nor a plaything; it is necessary, useful, and we are in as constant need of it as was probably primitive man. We perform it, therefore, intermittently all the time, by *equating an element of the object world with an element of the pleasure-physiologic body ego, through a shift of quantities of narcissistic cathexis from the latter to the former and vice versa—a process requisite to our living in the world (II, 246–254).* Searl (1932) has stated, "But there . . . must also be that unconscious recognition, 'things' are familiar to me, they belong to my mental life, they are part of 'me', which forms *our narcissistic symbolic link with the material world* (p. 330)." Similar formulations may be found in Melanie Klein's article "The Importance of Symbol Formation in the Development of the Ego" (1930), and in the papers of several other authors. The last of these that came to my attention was by Peto (1959): "Symbolism in dreams and folklore indicates that finding and evaluating external reality is to a great extent determined *by refinding one's own body in the environment.* Thus the body image is of decisive importance in grasping the world around us" (p. 230; italics added).

In other words: the symbolic equation is to be defined as the cathectic equation of an element of the object world with an element of the pleasure-physiologic body ego. What enables the object to be equated with or, if you wish, partly substituted for the body is narcissistic cathexis for the object.

In order to understand this as fully as possible, one must remember:

1. The cathectic shift from pleasure-physiologic body ego to environment is reversible; we perpetually execute it and cancel

---

[19] To be distinguished from the "symbol equation," a term by which one could designate the unconscious equation of a symbolized element with a symbol.

it, just as we express ourselves at one moment symbolically and at the next moment directly. However, the difference in the oscillation between object libidinal and narcissistic cathexis in free association, for example, and the performance of the symbolic equation must be understood: in expressing ourselves we cathect the object *representation* (Freud); in performing the symbolic equation we cathect the *object*.

The cathexis of the object world, as far as it results from the displacement upon it of cathectic amounts originally attached to the pleasure-physiologic body ego, is one with *refractorily narcissistic libido* (II, 304–317). In other words, the libido cathecting an object, i.e., an element of the object world, in the service of the symbolic equation is *refractory* to being transformed into object libido and *remains therefore narcissistic*. Conversely, if, when, and insofar as an individual cathects an element of the object world with libido that in the process does become object libido, he has not, in so doing, performed the symbolic equation.

2. An element of the pleasure-physiologic body ego is inseparable from its functions; and the pleasure-physiologic body ego includes varying bodily functions in consequence of their temporary sexualization (II, Chapter 3).

3. If the body is a "second environment" (Freud), with the first environment being the object world, the symbolic equation identifies elements of the two environments oscillatorily with one another in the unconscious.

4. Since symbolization blends into other modes of unconscious indirect representation, in particular, picturization—the symbolic equation is not always purely symbolic.

5. The symbolic equation belongs, as does all symbolization, to the primary process. That does not, however, mean that it is necessarily regressive. It can be normal and can serve our adaptation to the environment; needless to emphasize, it is unconscious.[20]

---

[20] Cf. Freud's general remark (1915b) that the "unconscious is also affected by experiences originating from external perception . . ." and that "all the paths from perception to the *ucs.* remain open . . ." (p. 194).

6. Nevertheless, this adaptation is dependent upon one condition: the symbolic equation must be balanced, i.e., the cathectic shift from body to environment must be counterpoised. The inability to cathect the environment, or to cathect it properly, is easily observable in the confusion of certain schizophrenics; it is less easy to observe how an overburdening of the environment with refractorily narcissistic libido also decreases the adaptation to it and leads to different regressive conditions. Here are two examples taken from the reports of purely *neurotic patients.*

The subway train in which a male patient was riding got stuck, i.e., broke down, in one of the tunnels going into the city. This made him not want to go to the city at all, but go home, shirk his work, eat compulsively, and be despondent (moods and impulses that he had at the time otherwise relinquished).

Interpretation: He had been "stuck" in the maternal rectum, leading, as it were, to the mother, the city. In order to validate this interpretation, one must know that preceding hours had shown the libido to be entirely with the mother; it was she and she only whom he could cathect. The particular period in his analysis was one of working through of incestuous experiences in puberty, the amnesia for which had quite a while ago been removed. These experiences had been terminated abruptly after a rectal penetration with an orgastic result for both. The "getting stuck in the tubes" both affirms and denies the termination while regressively re-enacting the mood engendered by it at the time.

The interpretation surprised the patient, yet he furnished immediate confirmation. He remembered that when he came out of the subway a "loose, middle-aged woman, probably a prostitute," had stood next to him and he had felt an urge for rectal intercourse with her.

The example illustrates how the environment became overburdened through an untoward amount of narcissistic cathexis with regressive partial libido transforming it into a partial-object representation (cf. II, 94–97). It was this excess of cathexis that effected the swing of mood. The symbolic process, however, remained unconscious; its subsequent nonsymbolic duplication, the object-libidinal cathexis of the prostitute, became conscious, and was therefore readily remembered.

The second example is both more elaborate and more fragmentary because of the phase of the analysis in which the episode to be described and selected as illustration occurred. The example is nevertheless convincing to me, and a few preliminary remarks may perhaps contribute to make it convincing to others.

There exists occasionally an exchange between agoraphobic and claustrophobic fear, with the former concerning the patient and the latter the *Begleitperson*, the companion. Helene Deutsch (1932) was, to my knowledge, the first to present such a case, although unspecified and unexplained: a daughter who originally could only go out in the company of her mother became able to go out alone, but was now afraid that something would befall the mother at home.

The patient of whom I shall speak had never been either agoraphobic or claustrophobic, but not infrequently had the fear that her apartment with her family in it might burn up while she was away. She also had an abundance of autohypnotic states which, as the analysis showed, evaded clitoral and vestibular excitations accompanying sexual fantasies about women. If and when the analysis made her aware of these sensations, no hypnosis occurred. She experienced "mild" hypnosis often merely as "exhaustion"; a typical setting for that was the climbing of a long flight of stairs. It had become demonstrable that such a transient hypnotic state depended upon the symbolic exploitation of climbing stairs—sexual intercourse (Freud). The hypnosis evaded external stimulation with its unconscious homosexual connotation, the conflict over which accounted in part for her difficulties with the sexual act.

In the analytic hour under consideration, the patient recounted how two days ago she climbed a long staircase in the company of her husband and did very well except for one moment when she "felt like an old woman." This was equivalent to a brief autohypnotic state, due to a transient symbolic overburdening of the environment in the sense mentioned above. Its overdetermination was an identification with her mother. That much was clear. Now one wanted to know the reason. I suspected the precipitate and transitorily becoming preconscious of an unconscious fantasy, which I actually succeeded in making conscious.

The couple had originally intended to take with them their adolescent daughter, who, however, had school work to do and had therefore stayed home. The fantasy presented itself at first as qualms over the girl's being alone in the house and fears of burglars or attackers. Without mentioning Deutsch's contribution, although that would have been to the point, I acquainted the patient with Freud's interpretation of claustrophobia and obtained confirmation: shortly before the parents left, the daughter had been in the toilet, and the mother, wondering what took her so long, had fleetingly thought that she might be engaged in masturbation.

This hour's sexual fantasy—by no means the only one the patient occasionally had about her daughter—was object libidinal and conscious. The later one on the stairs was narcissistic and unconscious: it exploited symbolically not only the "climbing of stairs" but also the daughter as "the little one"—an overburdening of the object world with narcissistic cathexis that engendered again a regressive, this time an autohypnotic, state.[21]

The cathectic imbalance between (pleasure-physiologic) body ego and environment in both these examples led to a relative failure of the symbolic equation, engendering in each case a different regressive state: in the first, despondency and a compulsive urge to overeat; in the second, an autohypnotic condition. It may, of course, produce other regressive states. Some of these have remained nameless; one of them will be discussed in a subsequent section.

Of the normal performance of the symbolic equation I can only repeat that it is oscillatory: elements of the object world, animate and inanimate, are alternately and unpredictably cathected first with refractorily narcissistic libido and then with object libido. In the first instance they become symbols, in the second objects.

[21] The "alone in the house," by the way, found its historic determinant in the very same hour. The patient "discovered" masturbation in adolescence when she was home alone because her mother had gone out—a situation now duplicated with the mother having gone out and her daughter staying home alone.

Q. THE SIGNIFICANCE OF SYMBOLIZATION FOR CLINICAL ANALYTIC WORK

Symbolic expression is one aspect of the primary process. The "quality" of this process is unconscious. Ideas that became unconscious through repression are indistinguishable, as Freud has shown, from those that are unconscious without ever having been repressed. There is, in other words, only one kind of unconscious ideation. If any of that is to become conscious, it must at first be permitted to express itself through the also unconscious primary process. Freud chose free association as the means to obtain the patient's unconscious thought because it allows for a much greater degree of intrusion of primary process than does any other form of communication. Yet the patient's associations are but the first step to securing his unconscious thought.

The next step is the analyst's interpretation which transforms primary into secondary process thought. The term interpretation, however, has two different meanings: the transformation proper, which occurs in the analyst's mind, and the act of imparting it to the patient. In dealing with symbolization I must speak of the former.

For one thing, although it is obvious, it appears to be sometimes overlooked that a symbol translation acquaints one only with an unconscious *thought element,* never with an unconscious *thought.* In terms of grammar, it yields a noun or a verb, never a sentence. Its value therefore, invariably depends, on a context, in which it can take its place in a thought—grammatically, in a sentence.[22]

For another thing, unconscious indirect representation, symbolization in particular, is employed by the patient long before the analysis has progressed sufficiently to inform the analyst through amnesia removal, reconstruction, etc., of traumatic

---

[22] The language of symbolism knows . . . no grammar; it is an extreme case of a language of infinitives, and even the active and passive are represented by one and the same image" (Freud, 1922, p. 212).

events in the patient's life. This initial employment of symbolization, usually in conjunction with other forms of unconscious
and conscious representation, may reflect these events, or essentials of them, in an extremely condensed form. Thus it is that
such symbolization when it first occurs has for the analyst on
occasion almost the value of a *prediction*.

1. Symbolic Prediction

A typical example for the symbolic prediction that I have learned
to understand is the conflict in the beginning of an analysis, overt or
latent, over telephoning the mother. I know of no instance where,
when this conflict was present, the mother was not psychotic and
where amnesia removal years later did not establish beyond any doubt
that she had exploited the patient in childhood, sexually, by having
him or her masturbate her. (Telephoning, a symbol for masturbation.)
Conversely, in cases where sexual exploitation took place but this particular phase, i.e., the child's masturbating the mother, was lacking,
the patient had no conflict over speaking to her on the phone. In
other words, the ever-astonishing accuracy of the unconscious extends
to symbolization.

An example of a symbolic prediction, that I failed to interpret exhaustively when it occurred and which I recognized only much later,
had, combined with allusion and picturization, foretold subsequent
traumatic material, requires further exposition. The onset of the patient's neurosis was acute. Her symptomatology included, at first, compulsive fantasying about the genital of a certain "fat, sloppy" mother,
spreading over to almost any woman she saw. Between the onset of
her neurosis and her analysis lay many years. During those years repression had not proven itself sufficiently effective, and I found her in
the grip of still another defense: (auto-) hypnotic evasion. She became
"groggy" and frequently fell asleep on a great variety of occasions. In
the beginning of her analysis the first of these hypnotic evasions occurred
at a certain meeting when two women, well dressed and obviously representative of the social class that had formed her own background,
got up in order to go to the toilet. This made her "dopey"—a feeling
that we had already learned to recognize as symptomatic of an hypnotic evasion. I was of course aware that two women in their role of
"two categorically identical persons" were a symbol for the mother.

Where I failed was in performing the following minute consideration which would have resulted in the prediction.[23] The knowledge of where the two women were going was conscious and, per se, taken by the patient in her stride. What then did she have to evade through hypnosis? It was obviously not the thought: the mother (symbolization) goes to the toilet (direct observation). It was a fantasy subsequent to this thought. The analysis, performed three years later, acquainted me with this fantasy in considerable detail and with the reason for its evasion. The detail was that of the women's subsequent actions: their partial undress, the position assumed by them, and the urination, to all of which the patient imagined herself as witness invited to an approach. The evasion was necessary because the better part of the fantasy quite accurately reproduced maternal seductions at the occasion of urination and, if conscious, would not have sufficiently protected the patient against the return of the repressed. Had I paid attention to the coincidence of the hypnotic evasion with what obviously had to be expected from the women, I would have obtained my prediction.

Yet, even later in an analysis, symbolization precedes or accompanies, either sporadically or throughout extended periods, the rest of the analytic material. At these times, whether predictive or not, it can aid the analyst by inducing in him a convincing expectation, help in dissolving a resistance, guide him in recognizing a memory as a screen memory or in distinguishing, at least preliminarily, associations expressing a fantasy from those indicative of a repressed event. Since I have never collected instances of this kind I must search my memory in order to furnish a few examples.

2. Symbolic Assistance to Interpretation

A man of limited education entered treatment. He had discussed his fear of verbalization with a friend. "Nothing to it," the friend told him, "If you want to screw your grandmother hanging from a chande lier, you just say so!" This, however, evaded his problem; he harbored

---

[23] I doubt whether my failure had any delaying effect on the conduct of this analysis. It is described here merely as a complicated example of symbolic prediction.

no such intentions. Instead, very soon one heard that before coming to analysis he had discontinued seeing a woman whom he called Margaret. That, of course, signified nothing. Yet it was later learned that her name was not really Margaret but Marguerite. Because at the time the man proved so inhibited that he could not be asked any sexual questions, one was compelled to rely at first on this symbolic information. Anything French, when a symbol, stands for fellatio or cunnilingus. The former turned out to be not only a compulsive activity of the patient but also the clue to a subsequent dream containing his most traumatic childhood experience: a seduction in the phallic phase to that very performance

3. Symbolic Assistance to Management

A well-compensated intelligent schizophrenic female—one of the type that is analyzable after sufficient psychotherapeutic preparation —had, in a previous treatment, been tortured by being forced to report her elaborate masturbation fantasies in detail. It was easily recognizable that the therapist, a sadistic voyeur, had increased her masochism to such an extent that, although complaining about the coercion, she expected it to continue. In the beginning, therefore, she started every session with remembering these fantasies and struggling painfully to recount them. At first I told her I was not interested in them and that she had the right to keep to herself anything she wished. Subsequently when more of her masochism became demonstrable, I could show her that being tormented had been her purpose. After three years of psychotherapy permitted a gradual change into analysis, the fantasies were in due course verbalized and analyzed, although but incompletely, without any suffering for the patient. Having been worked through sufficiently, they disappeared, and with them practically all masturbation. The complexion of these fantasies had been unusual: although stereotyped, they resembled dreams rather than daydreams, and their analysis left no doubt that they represented repressed traumatic events. Had they been dreams, one would say that they contained much secondary elaboration but relatively little distortion and, of course, no suppression of (the sexual) affect. (This, however, occurs occasionally also in certain actual dreams.) The patient had been extremely unhappy with her regimen because it maintained the impact of a constant return of the [pathogenic] repressed.

I have tried to make this introduction to the symbolic episode as short as possible; with anything less, the episode could not be understood.

The patient had an affair with a man, characteriologically and intellectually her inferior, who maltreated her and who she idealized in the interest of masochistic gratifications. When this man finally threw her over, she appeared inconsolable and was quite vociferous about suicide as the only way out. I may sound like a simpleton when I report having told her that that was no way to behave, that one did not kill oneself in analysis, but analyzed, etc. However, my naïve response sufficed to continue the treatment and bring it eventually to a satisfactory termination. Actually I entertained the conviction that suicide here had merely the symbolic meaning discovered by Freud: masturbation. "I must kill myself" meant "I must return to and become wholly dependent upon masturbation and the fantasies that will overwhelm me with their memory content of the repressed, traumatic, incestuous past to the point of disintegration." The fear was, of course, one of those elements in the fantasies that had not been analyzed, or analyzed but incompletely.

A purely symbolic meaning of "suicide" naturally implies the absence of any serious self-destructive intent. It enables one, therefore, to dispense with any management extraneous to analysis and to continue the treatment. The patient's unconscious employment of the idea of suicide merely as a symbol explains why instead of at least attempting to kill herself she eagerly seized upon the analysis and in good time found herself an affectionate and benevolent lover.

4. Symbolic Assistance in Distinguishing Memory From Fantasy

Freud has taught us that a repressed traumatic event may relinquish its cathexis to the locale. The result: certain details of the place where the event occurred are remembered with great intensity while the event itself remains in amnesia.

The removal of such, as of all amnesia, is dependent upon a variety of factors, among them the veracity of the patient. I remember one whose relation to the truth was, in consequence of a deep-seated identification with a psychopathic psychotic mother, so tenuous that he had to use me—particularly my critical function—in a fashion that one can only call prosthetic. Such a use is, in the early phases of character analysis, sometimes necessary; yet it has limitations because only the patient's, not the analyst's, unconscious contains the memories of the events to be freed from amnesia. The analysis thus becomes particularly dependent upon the ability of the analyst to sort out memory from fantasy in associations.

The man I have in mind told of having been hypnotized at the height of the phallic phase by an amateur hypnotist who masturbated him in the process, inducing the boy to perform fellatio on him. The importance of an answer to the question, fantasy vs. memory, was crucial. Only if this episode had actually occurred could one believe that it had conditioned him for later ones of a similar kind. All of these had to be appreciated for what they were: a series of traumata, interfering with the patient's normal development. On the basis of his intense mother-identification, they would then explain the man's desperate struggle against his homosexuality and his fears that giving in to it would destroy him.

The episode had actually occurred. From the wealth of material that eventually convinced me, while the patient, imitating his psychopathic mother's mendacity, maintained a compulsive doubt preventing the recall from acquiring memory-quality, I select a single element in the interest of the present subject. The element was one of locale; he remembered it with the intensity cited above, and it never became subject to doubt. It was, in fact, the only piece of equipment in the small bare hall, bordered by four doors: a *telephone stand.* Since the telephone is an allusively conditioned symbol for masturbation, *stand* had to be understood as a concretization, descriptive of the hypnotist's erection.

When I later sent this brief illustration to the erstwhile patient in order to obtain his opinion as to its anonymity, he recalled that he had told me in good faith everything as recorded in the text. But he became aware that his report had contained several inaccuracies, two of which I shall mention because they illustrate the distortions to which such a memory, in the process of becoming conscious, is subjected; and because they are relevant to the present topic.

First, *the hall did not have four doors but five.* We are accustomed to consider a number (in a dream, associations, etc.) separately from the objects it is supposed to enumerate. Five not infrequently alludes to the five fingers of one hand and thereby to masturbation. Its attachment to all manner of objects is in such instances an effect of censorship; the falsification of five into four was in the patient's case a distortion in the service of the resistance against the eventual removal of an amnesia.

Second, *the telephone stand stood, not in the hall but in one of the adjoining rooms, and there was a chair that belonged to the stand.* The man had brought the chair into the hall for the occasion, and had told the boy to sit on it in order to hypnotize and seduce him. Naturally he did not fetch the telephone stand, for that obviously would not have furthered his purpose. Had the patient's report been accurate, the environment recalled so vividly *would have lacked any element employable as a symbol.* The distortion had therefore to furnish one by repressing the chair and erroneously, placing the telephone *stand* in the hall.

Freud has taught us to assume that the repressed unconscious has a "buoyancy," i.e., a tendency to emerge, but is prevented from doing so by a countercathexis that keeps it in repression. The antithetic nature of the two distortions described here accords well with this hypothetical orientation. The first is an effect of the counter cathexis: it deprives the memory of the allusion to a fragment of the repressed event. The second is an effect of the buoyancy: it alters the memory so that fragments of the event are expressed through allusion and symbolization.

The case of the patient who feels instinctively that direct expression might endanger the maintenance of his repression and speaks instead in symbols which are meaningless to him is not rare.

5. *Symbolic Assistance in Recognizing a Memory as a Screen Memory*

I have, in a different context (I, 225) mentioned an instance which in the present context requires a more explicit description. There the symbolism of telephoning assisted me in an entirely different way.

In the analysis of a young woman, a memory emerged from amnesia that had the mother lie nude on the bed and masturbate somewhat inconclusively while talking on the telephone with a woman. She attained no orgasm and none was evidently intended, but she did have that "funny" expression on her face. The patient added that when she herself spoke on the telephone she often found her hand "wandering" to the same region. I decided that this was not an instance of the usual oscillation between direct and symbolic expression but that both were simultaneously employed in the service of an unconscious purpose; the story as told directly, was incomplete and was only symbolically brought to completion. I was, therefore, prompted to regard the remembered episode as a screen memory and to postulate a full-fledged orgastic masturbation of the woman in front of the daughter. The symbolization, in other words, had assisted me *not only in recognizing the memory as a screen memory but also in reconstructing the memory that it screened.* I doubt that without such a reconstruction I would have been able to orient the patient sufficiently for her to be able to remember the traumatic event. As it was, the event eventually emerged from amnesia. It was told convincingly, with conviction, and in detail. The latter even included the apparently not infrequent terminal insertion of a finger into the distal end of the vagina, which I have stated (II, 272) is vestibular in its pleasure-physiologic nature. There was but one detail missing: the child's reaction to the mother's performance. Questioning brought forth a variety of answers, all of them unconvincing, until after further considerable lapse of time the true one could be remembered. You will not find it in Freud, and, although this kind of exhibition by psychotic mothers is frequent, I have not heard this particular answer at any other occasion. The woman had previously acquainted the child with the existence and the dimensions of the vagina in many different ways (douches, intercourse at close range, etc.), and the girl therefore saw everything as it was. She distorted nothing into a penis (-equivalent), as she had done on the occasion of an earlier urinary exhibition, nor did she indulge in the belief that the penis must be hidden inside. She also knew that the difference in the appearance of her mother's genital and her own was that between the adult's and the child's.

She reacted by becoming acutely despondent and said to herself: "Even if I grow up I will never have *that.*" She referred here evidently not to the anatomy but to the *pleasure-physiology* of the mother. I omit describing the serious consequences of this conviction of inferiority for almost all aspects of her life because they would not contribute to the present subject. I will mention instead one, never serious and with the successful conclusion of the analysis of no consequence whatsoever, because it supplies the finishing touch to the picture: however desperately craving relief at times when no partner was available, the patient was and continued to be incapable of manual masturbation. That had actually remained the prerogative solely of the mother.

6. *Symbolic Re-enactment of a Trauma*

The assistance of symbolization in cases of which the next example is paradigmatic is sometimes not so much an assistance to the analyst as to the patient. There are, in some analyses, extended periods where a wealth of repetitious material compels reconstructions, which although correct, fail to precipitate amnesia removal. Nevertheless, while the repressions are not undone, they are influenced by the reconstructions, although in a fashion for which theory cannot at present account. The effects of such influence are in typical cases twofold: the patient frequently wishes the analyst dead—i.e., *unable to analyze further,* and himself becomes *accident prone.* The different means employed by the patient to integrate these death wishes with his affectionate relation to the analyst do not belong in the present context, although they would make an interesting subject for study. I shall merely mention in passing how a very literate patient described his situation by saying, "If you died, I would mourn you. But I would mourn you with so much relief!"

What does belong to the present example is the accident-proneness. Naturally it represents a punishment for the death wishes; but that determinant is only superficial. The deeper ones are the desire to avoid the amnesia removal, felt as imminent, and to gratify the need for punishment engendered by the traumatic events. However, the particular form of such accident-proneness often reveals a fourth determinant, the repetition compulsion. It does so by symbolically re-enacting the trauma.

Abundant material in an analysis left no doubt that the patient's psychotic mother, besides arranging for him to observe her masturbating, partly seduced and partly coerced him at the height of the phallic phase to stimulating her on the toilet. Three details of the occurrence were known: she had him insert a finger into the vulva while urinating; she inflicted the shock of castration, laughing derisively at him when he showed terror; and she caught the boy between her knees as he tried to run away. The last detail I could for the time being only attempt to explain tentatively with the speculation that she still needed him for completing her sadistic orgastic gratification.

In this phase of the treatment the patient had an accident; he burned his right hand while reaching into an oven in order to light it. He experienced quite a shock and recognized how potentially serious such a mishap was, particularly since he had to confess that he must have arranged it. (He had evidently left the jet slightly open, allowing a mixture of gas and air to accumulate and explode when a match was put to it.) He had indeed symbolically re-enacted a trauma. Nothing in the re-enactment, however, indicated that the burning (urination) or the box (female genital), into which he had put his hand and from which he got a shock, was the mother's. Yet that woman entered the analysis without delay. My mere agreeing with him that this was undoubtedly an "arrangement" caused a precipitate transference of her upon me and made me the object of a sudden violent hate. "You are talking exactly like my mother. Whenever any of us got sick, she scolded us because she considered it our own fault!" It was not easy to show him that his mother had accused him with a delusory confabulation, while I did not accuse but pointed out a reality; that her judgment was, as it is in all delusion, *a priori* while mine was *a posteriori;* and that my only purpose was the prevention of future self-damage. He gained insight, saw the symbolic action as fitting into the jugsaw puzzle, and the analysis lost a certain coercive quality with which it had recently been endowed.

The conclusion of the episode is so instructive that I report it briefly, although it has no bearing upon symbolization. Traumata such as those reconstructed here leave their mark not only in disturbed object relations but also in morbid identifications. Some weeks later, when the burned hand began to flake, he felt that it resembled his mother's, whose hands were subject to an allergic skin lesion of which I had not been told before. This acute identification of his hand with the mother's made direct connection between the two types of events mentioned above: one where she had him use his hand on her, and the other where she used her own on herself in his presence.

7. Piano Playing as a Symbol

My final example differs from the others inasmuch as instead of illustrating one particular role played by a symbol in one analysis it exemplifies a variety of roles played by one symbol in different analytic treatments. The symbol in question was discovered by Freud, who recounts the short dream of a patient on which he comments but briefly. He restricts his remarks to the man's situation in his analysis at the time, and he shows that the dream elaborates upon that situation.

It is convenient to begin by quoting the dream together with Freud's comments (1900), and to add to the latter in the course of presenting further examples containing the symbol:

> One of my patients, a man whose sexual abstinence was imposed on him by a severe neurosis, and whose [unconscious] phantasies were fixed upon his mother, had repeated dreams of going upstairs in her company. I once remarked to him that a moderate amount of masturbation would probably do him less harm than his compulsive self-restraint, and this provoked the following dream:
>
> *His piano teacher reproached him for neglecting his piano-playing, and for not practicing Moscheles' Études and Clementi's Gradus ad Parnassum.*
>
> By way of comment, he pointed out that '*Gradus*' are 'steps'; and that the key-board itself is a staircase, since it contains scales [ladders).
>
> It is fair to say that there is no group of ideas that is incapable of representing sexual facts and wishes [pp. 371–372].

Everyone knows that puberty masturbation has, unconsciously, the oedipal mother as its object. Freud recommends this activity, divorced from the object, to his patient; but the dream supplies the punitive oedipal father, although in excessive attenuation ("reproaching") and the vagina ("modified staircase"), seemingly omits its owner, the mother.

Since Freud reports the dream and associations in a section devoted to representation through symbols, and since the day residue is his suggestion to the patient to replace abstinence with moderate masturbation, we can only understand him as implying that piano playing, when a symbol, represents masturbation.[24] In reporting his patient's associations, Freud draws attention to some of the different elements fused in this complicated symbolization: the patient himself is explicit about the scale as a staircase and his remark on the *Gradus* is a further element in the fusion. Some examples recorded below leave no doubt that it must be so understood, and I shall isolate still another element in a final discussion of the symbol.

Chance has acquainted me with the symbolism of playing the piano in a number of cases; yet wherever I have encountered it, I have invariably found it to represent specifically female masturbation. Freud's patient's remarks about the *Gradus* and the scale would appear to support this interpretation because the staircase, when a symbol, always represents the vagina. Conversely, Freud gives but little information about his patient and none about the possible morbid identification with his mother that one so frequently finds as the collateral to a fixation upon her as an object. He refrains, furthermore, from reporting the analysis of the dream, if there was one. My experience does not therefore necessarily contradict him.

Loss of Manual Inhibition in Piano Playing. The only male in whose analysis I encountered the symbol was more deeply and more extensively identified with his mother primarily (and secondarily with another female in his family) than anyone I have ever seen. Most of his excessive feeling of inferiority stemmed from the fact that he literally considered himself a woman. After the traumatic events initiating these identifications had come to light and been worked through, he reported that an (inhibitory) rigidity of his fingers had recently disappeared, enabling him now to play the piano to his satisfaction.

Phobic Avoidance of Playing the Piano. An analysand, as has been stated before, alternates constantly between direct and symbolic expression, for both have the identical meaning in his unconscious. The further question is which of the two bears the burden of and

---

[24] Even had he not later explicitly stated (1915–1917), "Satisfaction obtained from a person's own genitals is indicated by all kinds of *playing*, including *piano-playing*" (p. 156).

maintains the cathexis? The answer is, of course, obtainable only through clinical observation, which shows that it is sometimes one and sometimes the other (cf. Section I, above).

The analysis of a neurotic female frequently revives the masturbation struggle from the past. The patient's eventual indulgence usually occupies but a passing phase and serves the purpose of living down at least some of the fears attached to the activity in her childhood. When this happened in the analysis of a well-trained pianist, it was successful, and the drives thus discharged became transformed into the normal desire for foreplay; the clitoris, in other words, assumed its "kindling function," as Freud has called it. Neither before, during, or for some time after the transformation, however, did she dare play the piano. That had evidently remained symbolic and endowed with the representation of her activity during a particular phase when she had to discontinue it in order to enter a belated short latency period. I am not free to show that her avoidance of playing the piano during so extended a period of the treatment was certainly not the result of anything like a loss of interest in it, and must confine myself to remarking that it gave the impression of being distinctly phobic, i.e., a repetition of her avoidance, in the beginning of the analysis, of masturbation.

Her eventual return to the piano must, I think, be understood as an indication that the playing had finally lost all unconscious symbolic meaning. It was surely no accident that the resumption coincided with the restoration of a bit of identity, formerly covered by a morbid identification: she suddenly became able to trust her own judgment in certain musical matters and to feel adequate on certain occasions, where she had previously been as anxious and confused as was the object of that identification.

Delusive Fears While Playing: Inability to Use Metronome. Analysis enabled an evidently gifted female to resume in adulthood piano lessons that had been torture for her as a child, and to gain pleasure from playing. The latter appeared to have lost its symbolic meaning; yet certain restrictions, fears, and symptoms attached to it proved that the loss was but incomplete. The intelligent patient chose an inferior but benevolent teacher in order not to be scolded. She could not play in the presence of someone else, particularly her mother; and when she played by herself she frequently entertained the delusory fear of an imminent violent interference by some—invariably female—neighbor. The bestial mother, sexually exploiting her to the limit, had at the same time not only interfered punitively with the child's masturbation, but had, allegedly in response to mistakes in practicing, actually beaten her fingers. The perhaps most instructive symptom: the patient was unable to use the metronome because its beat persisted in representing to her a beating. (A conjecture that beating might at the same time allude to masturbation found no support in the analytic material.)

Inability to Use Metronome. Hallucinatory Endowment of Notes with a Third Dimension. I remember the same intolerance toward the metronome from the abortive analysis of a schizophrenic female who, besides, suffered occasionally from the frightening hallucination that the notes stuck out of the paper. I believe that the two symptoms belonged together: one represented the punishment for masturbation, and the other the erection of the clitoris in the act. Both of course had their origin in the repressed past; the patient's masturbatory activity at the time of her treatment was rare and dispensed with the use of the hand. In her case, my interpretation had, of course, to remain speculative; yet there were indications in her environment, her behavior, and her associations that lent it support.

Hypnotic Evasion While Playing; Inability to Read Ledger Notes Below Lower Staff. Another patient, who continued even in puberty to sit on her mother's lap, as an adult used the piano bench belonging to her mother, who had died long ago. At one time she went so far as to endow the bench hallucinatorily with a genital odor. Whenever the playing became symbolic for her, she practiced hypnotic evasion and consequently became so drowsy that she was forced to desist. She had the same response to being sexually stimulated through riding, in which case it frequently led to her falling asleep.

Once she produced a symptom whose interpretation the reader may find hard to believe. It occurred, fortunately, at the same time as did a more credible symptomatic action of which it was actually a duplication. The patient had fearfully descended the cellar stairs "to do that thing," as she called it, which actually consisted of no more than fetching a photograph of her mother as a young woman. She experienced a double surprise; she had anticipated "finding a monster," yet the mother looked pretty, and the cellar she had expected to find smelling musty did not. Here the house is, of course, a symbol for the woman—the mother; the stairs, the cellar, etc., are self-explanatory, and the surprise at seeing the pretty mother instead of the dreaded monster reflect the antithesis between "above" and "below"—those aspects of the mother that were not and those that were concerned in the child's sexual exploitation.

At the same time she was unable to practice a certain piece, one admittedly easier than others she had mastered long ago. In her lesson she must have behaved quite regressively because the teacher, who had always thought well of her, exclaimed: "You are acting like a child!" When her difficulty was examined she could easily be specific about it: as an experienced player, she was of course facile in reading ledger notes; but the facility proved now irrationally confined to those between the two staffs, and above the upper staff. She was unable to read ledger notes below the lower staff, and since these abounded in the piece under consideration she could not play it. She was well aware of the absurdity of her limitation; the counting of lines and spaces is the same, no matter where the location.

I termed it fortunate that this symptom appeared simultaneously with the symbolic action because the interpretation of one assisted that of the other. It certainly facilitated communicating the interpretation to the patient, and I hope it will aid in convincing the reader. One needs, actually, but to vary the words of Freud's patient, quoted above, by saying that the ledger notes represent, as do all notes, a (virtually chromatic) scale, and are therefore equivalent to a staircase. Their location below the lower staff makes them a cellar staircase, and consequently they had the same symbolic meaning to the patient's unconscious, namely that of a vagina, qualified by the previously mentioned "below." Once that meaning became conscious the ledger notes lost it, and the patient was able to practice the piece.

The amnesia for the symbolized element from the past had in this case produced a lack of familiarity with the symbol in the present.

Historical Considerations: It is of course impossible to disprove that in an indeterminate number of instances piano playing, when a symbol, simply represents female masturbation. I am also aware that the number of patients studied thoroughly by a single analyst is too small to permit necessarily valid generalizations. Nevertheless, I found myself struck by the following correlation: the player uses his hands on a wooden instrument; wood, as Freud found and every analyst has ample opportunity to confirm, symbolizes the mother. (As for picturization, the vernacular describes unduly heavy legs in a woman as piano legs.) In four of the five cases I know, the mother had actually exploited the child for manual stimulation. In the sixth, I could not ascertain this, but I suspected if not the mother, a certain mother figure. The child's own masturbation is often punitively interfered with by the very mother who by her sexual use of him has rendered it excessive and has become the object of the attendant fantasies, although these are in most instances unconscious. Sometimes even in adulthood the masturbation retains characteristics representative of these terms of object relation, in mirror masturbation, for example, where a woman's excitement is increased by watching another woman; in terms of identification, for example, where orgastic urethral-erotic discharge, otherwise confined to certain psychotics, is found in a neurotic.

I mentioned in the beginning that some of my clinical illustrations necessitate the inclusion of the music, i.e., the paper on which the notes are printed, in the symbolization of playing the piano. Paper, as mentioned above, Freud has shown to be but another symbol for the mother. Since the piano is played and the music read, one of these elements represents the tactile and the other the scoptophilic contact of the child with the mother. Their separate symbolization accords also with clinical obervation. In the first place, there is a certain type of behavior in which the child is seduced or coerced to participate manually and another where he is merely made to look on. In the second place, after the manual exploitation has ceased, the exhibition often continues, and the child, or the erstwhile child—now an adult—reacts to it with fascination—admitted to by certain patients and denied by others.

R. CONCLUSION, CLINICAL AND THEORETIC

Clinically, symbols will on some occasions assist the analyst merely by being what Freud has called them: the mute elements in the dream or associations, representative of an element of unconscious thought. The term mute denotes the typical lack of associations, on the patient's part, to the symbol. Actually the matter is not, of course, quite as simple as it may appear. The frequency of a historic overdetermination of the symbol has already been mentioned; a certain street in a dream may be a symbol for the vagina but may also be dream material if, for example, it is representative simultaneously of the street the patient remembers having lived on at a certain age. The case of overdetermination of a symbol as day residue is the same, and the existence of an occasional metaphorical overdetermination has already been illustrated. We obtain these overdeterminations only by asking the dreamer to associate to a symbolic element as though it were no different from any other. Furthermore, having once had a symbol translated for him, the analysand may naturally remember and associate the translation when the symbol appears to reoccur. In so doing, he will never pay attention to the question of whether or not the once symbolic element is symbolic again. Such is his privilege; it is not the analyst's, who must ask and answer that question by applying the proper criteria. There are, of course, other sources, such as reading or attending lectures from which the patient, in particular the analyst-patient, may have acquired the translation, with the result that certain symbols are no longer mute. Yet I have never found that such knowledge—almost always confined to a relatively small number of "popular" symbols—interferes with the analyst's work.

This is not surprising, nor is it confined to symbolization. Experience teaches one that the analysis of a psychoanalyst is no different from that of any other patient. Although he has passed his medical examinations, he still has retained those illusions about his body that are precipitates of his history; he has acquired analytic knowledge, but proves unable to apply it to himself. "Learning" does not influence symptoms, defenses, reaction formations, or any other sequelae of a repression. It does not, therefore, influence symbolization.

Recalling once more the distinction made above between the act of interpretation on the part of the analyst and the communication of its result to the patient, I may mention that the former was, of course, necessary in all the instances illustrating

the present chapter, but the latter frequently was not. To name
at least one such example, the woman who contemplated solv-
ing her problem by suicide was never told its symbolic meaning.

Finally, the interpretation or, as I prefer calling it, the translation of symbols can (as can anything useful) also be abused. At
the risk of being redundant, I repeat the threefold safeguard
against the misuse of a (potential) symbol in the analyst's work:
Ascertain that a potentially symbolic element is, in the context
before you, actually a symbol (Section D). If it is, do not overlook its frequent historic and its occasional metaphoric overdetermination (Section M). Know that the symbol equation is constant; it does not bear tampering with: the analytic symbol has
only one *symbolic* meaning. In other words, its correct translation is always the same. Practically the sole exceptions are the
few bisexual symbols which naturally have two meanings, a
male or a female genital, as the context requires; and some
elements of the symbol aggregate of the dreams with a dental
stimulus (Section P).

Theoretically, the above inquiries about the symbol have
yielded almost nothing. Knowing that in most cases it represents an element or a function of the pleasure-physiologic body
ego, we are still ignorant of its source. Freud has mentioned
explicitly that the dream work does not *produce* the symbol but
merely *employs* it. There are, of course, other employments,
known and unknown at present, one of which is the symbolic
equation. As to the *origin* of the symbol, one has to be satisfied
with the modest statement that symbolization is one aspect of
the primary process. Disregarding all admixture of picturization, allusion, etc., *one cannot "understand" why a particular
symbol represents a particular element;* and the pure symbol,
devoid of such admixture, is of no help. I have assumed that the
eye and its adjunct the mouth have no symbol because the child
develops the faculty of symbolization only subsequent to the
oral phase; there is otherwise no ordering principle for those
elements of the environment or the body that can and those
that cannot be employed as a symbol. The *contradiction,* finally,

PARTICULAR SYMBOLS

between the supposedly archaic character of the symbol and the constant formation of new ones remains unresolved.

Nevertheless, the mere knowledge of symbolization is invaluable to the analyst because every symbol—whether learned from Freud, from others, or found for himself—increases his powers of interpretation.

II. DISCUSSION OF SOME PARTICULAR SYMBOLS

Freud has credited more than half a dozen of his pupils with the discovery of certain symbols. Many of their findings have proven valid to this day. The landscape, for example, often indeed symbolizes the female sexual parts and the little one, the genital of either sex (Stekel); flying symbolizes erection (Federn), and the great man (Hitschman), the father, etc. If one works conscientiously over the years, the typical representation of something through something else will gradually impress itself on one's mind. At times one may only become convinced that something *is* a symbol while failing to find what it symbolizes, as happened to me with "snow" until a colleague told me that it stood for blood (I, 221), which I could subsequently confirm. In other instances it may take many years until the recognition of the symbolized element joins that of its symbol, as was my experience in the case of the "rotating symbol," to be discussed below.

All in all, it appears that Freud was justified in expecting his first brief presentation to "stimulate others to a more careful collecting of symbols." Naturally one cannot deliberately undertake such a collection; the observation of further symbols is, as is all original analytic observation, a by-product of one's therapeutic work. A small list of symbols that I have encountered is appended; it will be inhomogeneous, and of course incomplete. The amount of clinical material illustrative of a symbol will also vary, since I have never been systematic in making notes (of course, only after a session) on the subject. In some cases I am not the first to have observed a particular symbol; I merely feel that it requires discussion.

I shall enumerate these symbols according to the symbolized elements and subordinate these to some headings, merely for the sake of making the whole less disparate and more manageable than it might otherwise be.

A. INCEST OBJECTS

1. *Horse* = *parent*

For the student of Little Hans (Freud, 1909a) it takes only a very small step to arrive at the symbolization of the parent through the horse. In taking this step I wrote (I, 16): "The horse is not only, as Freud has found, a totemistic representation of the parent but, as one finds in analysis, a symbol for him or her: either parent can by symbolized by the horse." As for clinical illustrations, the case history of Little Hans is replete with them: the expectation of being bitten (castrated) by it modified the horse in terms of the father; while "the horse's gait [posture] of pregnant women . . . so proud that they [will] fall down," (so pregnant that they will give birth) modifies it in terms of the mother.

I doubt whether anyone can better these illustrations. Ferenczi, who was evidently ignorant of the symbolization, reports (1909) that coincident with the inception of a father transference upon him, he began to appear quite frequently in the dreams of a young woman in the "not very flattering figure of a composite person [*Mischperson*] put together of myself and—a horse" (p. 89). In one of the dreams the horse was clad in a night shirt; its analysis led to the observation of the primal scene, and "most important, of the father's urination." Ferenczi fails to mention that the patient's choice of this particular symbol must again have been determined or overdetermined by a convenience, although one different from that in the case of Little Hans. Horse-drawn wagons and carriages were in his time parked in the street as commonly as are cars today. Horses urinating could therefore be observed frequently. His patient's infantile sexual curiosity about the transference object could thus be easily gratified by the use of the symbol. Anyway, those who know of the representation will not consider it unflattering, but symbolic.

The reader of the first volume of the present series may remember a menstrual dream (I, 231) in which the cannibalistic libido, intrinsic to any "genital" function, is allusively discharged upon the mother, symbolized by a horse.

To repeat only the most salient points: a young woman buys on an afternoon some cold sliced roast beef for dinner; when she unwraps it, she feels inexplicably repelled. "It looked so rare and bloody," says her report, and she left it uneaten. The next morning she wakes up, feels that her period has started, inserts a tampax, and goes back to sleep; whereupon she dreams of slicing meat off the side of a dead horse. At the end of the dream she feels the same disgust at the horse that she had felt at dinner time at the roast beef. The disgust was, of course, a reaction formation, that is, a defense against the unconscious cannibalistic desire.

2. *The Racially Different Person* = *parent*

The symbolization of the parent through the Negro (I, 118) is simply a special instance of that through a racially foreign person. Whether the "race" in question is actually anthropological (Negro, Chinese) or merely psychological (Gentile, Jew) makes no difference in its symbolic employment.

A woman patient, A., is asked to make an adjustment in the time of her analytic session for the sake of another woman patient, B. She feels imposed upon, *"exactly as it was with my mother, where I had to do all the adjusting,"* and is convinced that B., whom she does not know, is "Jewish," because otherwise she would not have asked for the change. I explained B's exigency which actually, in view of the rest of my schedule, admitted of no other solution, but without effect. Only a "Jewish woman" could be so forward and importunate.

Besides the symbolization which is to be illustrated, it was here again as in Freud's "Innocent Dreams": the change of hour on behalf of the "Jewish" person was negligible and did not even inconvenience the patient, whereas the mother had exploited her sexually and had literally ruined her life.

A woman patient whose most frequent masturbation fantasy was the second beating fantasy described by Freud (1919a) and interpreted as being (regressively) loved sexually by the father, masturbated occasionally with another fantasy in which she was a harem girl of a sheik, a (fictional) oriental (i.e., again racially different) potentate who "raped" her.

This next clinical illustration is more elaborate and requires study. I have on another occasion (II, 106) presented the verbatim report of a patient who as a 12-year-old girl invented, together with her best friend of the same age, a name for their menstruation. I repeat the quote: ". . . When we both had started menstruating we used to call it CLARA CURSE. The idea was that we have to have a first name (a girl's since it was a feminine function) that started with the same letters—both C's. I at that time had a colored maid named Clara— which X. and I thought would be funny if we attached her name to Curse. I'm not sure now why we thought it was so humorous. . . . except that it was sort of malevolent humor. . . . We made fun of the maid. . . . and therefore she was no good and should be attached to menstruation. . . ."

In these lines the adult writer expresses her lack of grasp for herself as a child and gropes for an explanation. One could also say that she does not understand her own primary process thought. In translating the latter there are several steps to be taken. The first is facilitated by a close reading of the sentence: "We made fun of the maid . . . and *therefore* she was no good" (italics added). That the maid is no good is an *a priori* judgment, explainable only as the effect of a displacement. It was actually the neglectful and viciously punitive mother who was no good and became replaced by a symbol for her, the Negress. The next step consists in equating, following Freud, "funny" with "sexual." The psychotic mother had acquainted the child during the first five years of life with every one of her own sexual functions, barring none. Amongst these was her extremely untidy menstruation. When the patient entered analysis she had come to conceive unconsciously of her own normal menstruation delusorily as the mother's and had developed a reaction formation against it: she was frequently amenorrheic. The last step is more complicated than are the first and the second because it leads to the recognition of the Negro maid "Clara Curse" in this particular instance as a "symbolically modified symbol" (Section I, N).

The modification is indicative of the fact that in this case the mother herself is a symbol. I have formulated this previously (I, 216) by saying: "If in the body-ego, the 'womb' is the seat of the early mother who became located there by introjection, it is expectable that, under certain conditions, the mother will appear in projection as a symbolic representation of the 'womb.' This is indeed so: for instance, in menstrual dreams." The present instance concerns not a menstrual dream but a menstrual daydream as it were, e.g., a partly unconscious fantasy about menstruation. In the latter, the menstrual partial subject is named, not after the mother but after a symbol for her, the Negro.

3. *Two Categorically Identical Persons = mother*

I have earlier mentioned this symbolism (I, 18), stating, "The symbolization of the mother through two categorically identical individuals (two men, two women, two strangers, etc.) is rather common, and the knowledge of it not infrequently affords the immediate grasp of an unconscious idea." This is correct, but requires a specification. Two categorically identical people may be a symbol for the mother *only if the first reference to them designates them as such.* In other words, if the patient says that he had (or dreamt that he had) lunch with two salesmen from out of town, these may be a symbol; if he says that he had lunch with Mr. Smith and Mr. Jones, both of whom subsequently turn out to be salesmen, they may not.

A most impressive illustration is contained in Freud's "A Case of Paranoia Running Counter to the Psycho-Analytic Theory of the Disease" (1915a). The 11-page paper is a classic; it has no meaningless line, no superfluous word. It therefore defies condensation, and any reference to it will be understandable only to those who have studied it closely and more than once.

The patient it concerns was an attractive celibate female of 30 who lived with her mother and worked in a department headed by a white-haired woman who reminded her of the mother and whose favorite she considered herself.

Pursued by a male colleague of excellent character, she visited him twice at his house. The details of their intimacies are not reported, except for her being in semi-undress and for the absence of a genital union. After each of these visits she developed a paranoic delusion. The first: She sees the man talking to the department head and becomes immediately convinced that he is "telling on" her, that the elderly woman is his mistress and despises her for what she has done. The second: GOING DOWN THE STAIRS after leaving the lover, she encounters TWO MEN, one of whom carries a concealed object that looks "LIKE A SMALL BOX." The men whisper, and she hallucinates (or has earlier hallucinated) hearing a click (projection, Freud convinces us, of a clitoris contraction in the aroused and ungratified woman). She was now certain that the lover had hired the men in order to have her photographed in a sexual situation for the purpose of blackmail. She therefore consulted her lawyer who in turn consulted Freud.

Because Freud learned at first only of the second delusion, the general validity of his discovery that paranoia is a morbid elaboration upon unconscious homosexuality was for a while in doubt. After all, Freud gives us to understand, the mother did not appear in this delusion. We may, however, correct that statement: she is not represented directly, but symbolically through the "two men," in other words, through two categorically identical persons.

The symbolization of the mother through two categorically identical persons is frequent. The first part of the present chapter contains two further instances of it. In one, the mother is symbolized by two women, whose going to the toilet precipitated a hypnotic evasion in one patient; in the other example, through "two policemen" allusive to the mother's restricting the patient while deflorating her as a child.

There is, further, no doubt that two categorically identical animals may fulfil the same symbolic function. The two horses, which Little Hans fears will fall down (= give birth), were interpreted previously as symbolizing the mother (I, 17). I remember the analysis of a female who developed the fantasy that her sexual partner died, whereupon she would "get a dog—no," she corrected herself: "*two* dogs" for performing cunnilingus on her as the mother had done in her childhood.

With regard to inanimate objects, I recall one instance where a woman seized by a slight claustrophobic agitation soothed herself by eating *two* bars of chocolate. Claustrophobia, Freud discovered, is caused by an unconscious fear of (puberty) masturbation; and eating of sweets he found representative of sexual enjoyment. The patient's early history was replete with mutual masturbation and cunnilingus between her and her mother. If the episode were not the only one in my experience, I would not hesitate in interpreting the two chocolate bars in the same sense as the two animals or two persons.

A Speculation: No symbol can be explained; any attempt to adduce at least an ontogenetic model for a symbol, as I said before, concerns itself with its pictorial or allusive modification. It is with this reservation that I speculate upon a possible ontogenetic contribution to the representation of the mother through two categorically identical persons.

Analytic experience teaches us that the meanings of "mamma"—the Latin anatomical term for the breast and the child's name for the mother—are neither coincidental nor a designation of the whole through a part. They are vestiges from the first oral phase in which the child perceived the mother in terms of the "mouth-eye" unit (I, 55) as a single breast fused with the equally single face. At about the time of the incipient second oral phase the mother becomes known as a person and the breasts are perceived as a pair. I have previously described how the transformation of the single, preoedipal breast into the two oedipal breasts reflected itself in the analysis of a severely disturbed adult (II, 317–321). Yet I have not, as I should have, distinguished the perceptory transformation through the mouth from that through the eye. The latter progresses toward beholding and incorporating two breasts while the former remains confined to sucking and incorporating simply one. In other words, one can *see* the two breasts, but one cannot suck them both at one time.

This is also reflected in the analysis of adults; and it does so in certain instances of the symbol under consideration. Had I been aware of it earlier I could now do better than present only three clinical illustrations.

(a) There are cases in which the symbol appears as described above, but where subsequent associations, without negating the categorical identity of the two persons, equip them with individual characteristics that are not identical but in contrast to each other.

The instance most vivid in my memory is the dream of a patient in which in an UPPER STORY of a HOUSE *two uniformed men* are seated at a TABLE, a pictorially and symbolically qualified symbol for the mother. However the dreamer declared associatively that he recognized the men from newspaper photographs as a then famous dictator and his right hand man; and he elaborated on the fact that the former was slim while the latter was very fat.

Hearing this, I was seized by a perhaps unverifiable conviction. A symbolic overdetermination made the table the mother (wood = symbol for mother; board—allusion to bed, cf. "bed and board"—Freud), and the two men the breasts: one sucked breast looked empty; the one to be suckled looked full. Because I could not establish that the table alluded to a meal, the dream (or what was remembered of it) evidently represented in isolation the perception of the two breasts via the eye.

(b) The first, and as far as I am aware, the only description of the typical dream of the analytic hour (Feldman, 1945) mixes the bad with the good and fantasy with interpretation. One of the verifiable characteristics described there of this extremely variable dream is the occasional presence of two analysts instead of one; in other words, that of two categorically identical persons. However, the two are never the same: the first is the patient's analyst while the second is an invention, sometimes of the opposite sex, often younger, an apprentice of the first, or the like. Yet the description notes correctly that only one of them analyzes (in the experience, the first) while the other is mute.

Evidence to be reported later has convinced me that the dream as well as its companion described in the same place, represents the wish

to enter (sexually) the mother. Behind it is again the wish to repeat
the first "entry," the sucking of the maternal breast. This explains
why the analysts, that is, the two categorically identical persons cited
above are both seen while but one of them analyzes; that is, only one
of them *uses his mouth* on the dreamer, which is to be read in reverse: *on only one of them the dreamer uses his mouth.* Here both
modes of perception found their representations; the eye perceives
the two breasts, the mouth (through the sense of touch and the ensuing kinaesthetic impressions, both displaced upon the auditorily
perceptory sphere of the dreamer) perceives but one.

(c) The third example is convincing only in the light of the other
two. When I published it (I, 216–221) I was aware of the symbolic
meaning of the categorically identical two other persons but unaware
of their subsequent differentiation. The example contains the typical
pre- or postmenstrual dream that I have designated as Mother Comes
In. For the sake of the present discussion I must ask the reader to refer to it (cf. also Glossary). When the dreamer becomes orgastic, the
mother appears directly. ". . . And then his mother came into the
apartment . . ."; later on she is symbolized as entering her in the
fashion under discussion: ". . . We went to my ROOM but I shared it
with *two other people* . . ." However, I had overlooked the final
qualification of the two: ". . . and one of them was asleep," that is,
again *one was mute* while the other, by inference, was able to speak,
i.e., to use his mouth.

Here the penis's entry into the womb *(Gebärmutter)* mobilizes the
wish to enter the mother. This wish, by way of resonance as it were,
has the two breasts appear;[25] one allusive to suckling, the other not.
It is thus that the two categorically identical persons symbolizing the
mother become qualified subsequently as, in part, not identical but
antithetic.

I believe future experience will verify this last speculation.

B. ELEMENTS OF THE PLEASURE-PHYSIOLOGIC BODY EGO

1. *Glass* = *hymen*

I am convinced that the symbolization of the hymen through
glass is not an original observation. Nevertheless, I think that it

[25] In accord with my modification of Freud's formulation: ". . . what is refound in
the genital sexual union is the breast" (I, 273).

requires the following brief consideration. The hymen is not an element of the pleasure-physiologic body ego, that is, it has no mental representation, except while it is being broken in the act of defloration. Then, and then only, for that brief span of time, does it "enter" the pleasure-physiologic body ego. Consequently, wherever glass appears as a symbol for the hymen the glass is being broken as is the hymen in defloration.

The oldest example in analytic literature is Freud's description of the second of two fantasies of Little Hans (1909, p. 41). The first one is phallic: the child wished to squeeze himself into a forbidden space in *Schoenbrunn*. Freud interprets this, of course, as a symbolic fantasy of intercourse with the mother, but since he denies the female genital any beauty (II, 271–282) he is unable to exhaust it. The mother, of whom he reports that she granted the child certain intimacies, must have given him opportunity to watch her urinate: for *Schoen* means beautiful, and *brunn* is a shortened form of *Brunnen*, meaning fountain. The second fantasy of the five-year-old boy is inexplicably genital; I have therefore commented briefly on it in discussing phylogenetic inheritance (I, 17). Here Hans smashes a window in the city railroad. Freud's interpretation is the same as that of the first. However, the fantasy also contains the symbolism of *Verkehr*, the symbolic defloration of the virgin mother.

The wedding ceremonies of certain ethnic groups include the breaking of a glass; and from Shakespeare's *Pericles*,

> BAWD: Boult, take her away; use her at thy pleasure, *crack the glasse of her virginitie*, and make the rest maliable [IV, 6].

2. *Mother = womb*

With regard to symbolization, the mother occupies a position that, as far as I know, is unique. She can for one thing be *symbolized* (as a parent through the horse, the racially different person, or two categorically identical persons) and she can, for another, herself *be a symbol*. This is most easily recognizable in certain menstrual dreams—a subject with which I have dealt fairly extensively in another place (I, 216–221). There the mother's appearance in the dream symbolizes the entry of the womb into the pleasure-physiologic body ego. Yet the same symbolization is, of course, also sometimes observable in associations.

3. Rug = womb

I have observed that whenever the rug has a symbolic meaning it represented the *womb*. (It is always a rug, not a carpet; I doubt whether a carpet, understood as something that is not a unit in itself but simply a floor covering, is employable as a symbol.)

The dream recorded on p. 218 in the first volume of the present series, in which someone impregnates a woman by ejaculating "all over the rug" when her "mother" comes in, is a clinical illustration.

Unfortunately, I failed to make further notes of the symbolic exploitation of the rug and have therefore no other to present.

4. (Wooden) Furniture = (inside of) womb

The caption may appear enigmatic; its explanation, however, will show why it is impossible to reduce this particular symbolization to a simple equation of two terms. As a starting point for the discussion of it one does best to choose Freud's (1900) statement, " 'Wood' seems, from its linguistic connections, to stand in general for female 'material' " (p. 355). The next step consists in acknowledging that in the symbolization to be considered, function and element of the pleasure-physiologic body ego are inseparable indeed (II, 212–215). It is thus that wooden furniture symbolizes the inside of the womb, if the former is *moved* and the latter is subjected to a *cathectic increase, decrease, or displacement.*

(a) The first clinical illustration of these is abortive. I remember a severely compulsive patient, given to frequent "anal reversals" (I,

125–128). She made, for instance, a date with a friend at a place up-
town, waited for her at another place downtown, and was deeply ag-
grieved over "being stood up." When she had a dream of the analytic
hour, my office appeared in its true likeness except that the furniture
was reversed. As yet ignorant of the symbolism, I failed to inquire as to
what was going on at that time with regard to her period, and my
record therefore lacks the collateral data.

(b) Another patient tried to become *pregnant* at about the time she
described how *cluttered* with *furniture* her parent's apartment *recently had become* because of senseless *purchases* by her mother.

At the end of the fourth month of the pregnancy when she felt the
first movements of the foetus, she searched in two different regions for
a particular *wooden piece of furniture,* as a BIRTHDAY [26] GIFT for her
husband. Unsuccessful in finding it, she gave up, saying that she would
otherwise have to devote herself FULLTIME to searching the ANTIQUE
stores of the *city.*

The coincidence of the appearance of furniture in her associations with increases of the cathexis of the (inside of her)
womb is self-evident. The difference between the two para-
graphs is merely that in the first the mother is mentioned directly, in the second merely symbolically.

(c) A patient recalled in a session not coincident with any of her
menstrual periods but lying between them, how she attended twelve
years ago a (theatre) *performance for children during her period* and
felt a sudden spurt of blood which she mistook for a hemorrhage.
"I remember it very well," she went on, "because the performance was
given in the morning and in the afternoon we went *buying furniture*
for the new house . . ."

The analysis left no doubt that the children's performance
had the unconscious meaning of a menstrual exhibition repeating that with which her mother has inflicted the shock of "castration" upon her as a child. The associative proximity of
menses and furniture is manifest.

[26] In this report as in others symbols and symbolized elements are set in italics, while
the collateral nonsymbolic elements are set in capital letters.

(d) The report of a patient in a single analytic hour. *Preamble:* She was five minutes late, because *traffic* had been stopped unexpectedly, and she thought I would think that she had forgotten her session. Earlier she had to TELEPHONE a whole string of women for DINNER invitations, and also a Mrs. WOODHOLE about possible damage done by flood to someone's *(wooden)* house.

The patient recounts all this in a somewhat apologetic tone and volunteers explanations as though to defend herself against an accusation that I naturally had not made and did not intend to make. I recognized only later in the session that this was, at least in part, a displacement and actually belonged to the episode yet to be told.

Symbolization: She had been upset during the morning. Her WOODEN DINING ROOM furniture, which had taken "a lot of beating" because of its varied uses over the years, had lately been replaced and was now to be disposed of. She had considered the "Goodwill" organization but found herself unable to contact them, rationalizing her indecision by ignorance as to whether they would take furniture, forgetting that she had seen their big trucks—which made it probable that they would. She called, instead, first a friend who had recently disposed of old furniture with the American Legion. They had sent, the woman told her, "two goons" over to appraise it and subsequently a truck to haul it away. The patient did not like the idea of having "two big red-faced goons with their Legion caps" in her house. She thought secondly of the Hadassah organization but settled eventually on a Negress, whom she had previously described as a "big fat slob." Amongst her further associations was the remark that she could have looked in the "RED BOOK" for a secondhand furniture dealer. Finally there were two late memories, never repressed, and the mentioning of an intention.

The first memory: She is *dressed* up, aged 16, for a *week*-end visit with a girl friend, but becomes greatly frightened by producing during defecation a *red* stool, the result (as it later turned out) of eating beets.

The second memory: When she was 21 her mother suffered the same experience and, as the doctor found, for the same reason.

The intention: She will attend tonight, a performance of the opera "La Gioconda" with a woman friend. Knowing that the patient was menstruating at the time of the session, I asked her, on the strength of these associations, whether the day of the session coincided with the height of the flow. She confirmed that it did.

Interpretation: The cathectic increase of the womb with respect to its interior is here again symbolized through furniture to be moved. This is accompanied by the appearance of the mother, symbol for the womb, both directly, as in the second memory, and indirectly, e.g., symbolically, as in the mentioning of Mrs. Wood*h*ole, the *"Red Book"* and the "two redfaced goons." Collaterally, the associations are pervaded by a whole string of women: the nameless ones, she reported having to telephone after alluding through traffic to *Verkehr*, Hadassah (= Hebrew for Esther), the girl friend X, La Gioconda, and in between them the Negress to whom she finally felt compelled to give the furniture against her better judgment because she, too, was a mother symbol.[27] It was this submission to an instinctual demand disapproved of by her superego that had in displacement and in projection been reflected in the aforementioned apologetic tone.

5. *Knee = procreative female genital*

A displacement symbol for the female genital in its procreative aspect is the knee. I have said almost all I am able to say about it in treating the establishment of the pleasure-physiologic body ego (II, 218–228) and have therefore but little to add. I gave Groddeck credit for having been the first to recognize that the knee can so be used and to find significant that its Latin name *genu* derives from the Greek verb for "to procreate," which survives in such English words as genesis, generation and miscegenation.

I do not know whether or not it is clinically pertinent to the investigation of this symbolic displacement that while a woman can have intercourse with her legs stretched out, she cannot give birth without bending her knees. As medical students we were taught in obstetrics that this has been experimentally proven.

As to fiction, everyone knows the famous passage where Hamlet, rather gratuitously and growing somewhat verbose, assures Horatio that he does not flatter him.

[27] Unsubstantiated here for reasons of anonymity.

". . . No, let the Candied tongue, licke absurd pompe
And crook the pregnant Hindges of the Knee . . ." [*Hamlet:* Version in the Quartos 2–4].

Here the parts of the knee effecting its action as a joint are directly called "pregnant." "Candied tongue" can be taken as allusive to the ubiquitous infantile theory of oral impregnation, while being symbolic of "sexual enjoyment" (Freud).

As for *clinical* examples, I remember only two instances where the knee was so employed, although I am certain of having heard it more often. One is a patient's dream (II, 308) of coitus with "two men" (= the mother), the report of which closes by her stating: ". . . there were no genitals involved in the intercourse . . . I was experiencing an ecstatic thrill from this action with my knees." It is obvious that here the knee is a displacement symbol for the genital, yet I cannot demonstrate that it symbolizes the organ in its procreative aspect. I find only one record among my notes that permits such a demonstration.

The patient was a young married woman with a very strong urge for a child. Gratification, however, in the beginning of her analysis, had to be subjected to the abstinence rule because one could not doubt that it would at that time have been equivalent to an acting out of a preoedipal wish for a baby from the mother.

In one hour she reported visiting in the company of her best friend an older couple, who to her represented idealized parents, the accompanying friend being in the late stages of pregnancy. The couple had been very affectionate, and the man said that he felt a vicarious grandfatherly pleasure in seeing her.

In the next hour she remembered having fallen and bruised her knee several times between the ages of four and five to perhaps seven. She went on to wonder why this should occur to her *now*.

I translated the symbolism of the knee and tied it to her report in the previous hour. Yet I refrained, for a reason I do not remember, from interpreting that the emergence of her memory is equivalent to a symbolic action, particularly in the light of her spontaneous, although seemingly gratuitous, question. On the strength of her wish, she identifies with the friend who is close to giving birth by falling down.

This example does show the nature of the knee as a displacement symbol for the pregnant womb even if the falling down be at the same time considered symbolic for giving birth (Freud).

6. *Moon* = *pregnant womb*

Another symbol for the pregnant womb is the moon. Strange as it may sound, the most frequent form in which I clinically observed the appearance of the symbol is this: When a female patient becomes engrossed with the idea of pregnancy, some woman named Helen often enters her associations. Helen derives from the Greek *Selene* meaning moon.

I remember, for instance, a particular patient, strongly preoccupied with the wish to get pregnant, speaking elaborately and affectionately about a certain Helen. I told her what is stated above and even recalled for her the case of a patient whose own name was Helen and who, for organic reasons was unable to bear children, yet who found another Helen to talk about when the subject of pregnancy came to the fore.

The patient became quite indignant over these remarks: they really went too far; in fact she had never heard such nonsense. When she remembered in the same hour having been shown an eclipse of the sun at about two years of age, I merely said that such an eclipse is caused by the moon; but beyond that, although I knew of her interest in mythology, I let the matter rest, as one should when the resistance is too great.

A few days later, after the strong initial resistance had subsided, she remembered suddenly that she had heard of, or rather had read quite a bit of this "nonsense" in the course of her mythological studies but had repressed it completely. Subsequently the resistance gave way to cooperation, and in the end she brought me a whole page of excerpts from Robert Graves's *The Greek Myths*, dealing with the moon-goddess Helen, Helle, or Selene, and the different forms of fertility she represented.

The question naturally arises of why the moon when a symbol appears more often as a woman by the name of Helen than directly. I can answer this question only with a speculation. The observations I have in mind concern different aspects of female sexuality (discussed by Freud in 1931). The number of patients so observed is, however, too small to permit more than a speculation.

Every analyst can confirm Abraham's (1911) finding that in the unconscious the name stands for the person; however, I have had the impression that in a number of instances his statement requires a twofold qualification. For one thing it applies every so often to the first name in particular. This appears understandable because the first, not the family name, is owned by the person alone, and is usually indicative of his sex. For another it applies primarily to the physical person. This not only agrees with Freud's statement that "the ego is in the first place body ego," but also with the fact that we identify a person by his physical characteristics, i.e., his body. If I say or think "There is Mr. Smith," I do so because he looks like Mr. Smith. Only afterward may I complete the picture by thinking, for example, of his character or his achievements.

When I noticed a "Helen" appearing every so often in the associations of a patient occupied with the idea of pregnancy, I should have observed whether or not this contemplated pregnancy was unconsciously the result of her "active baby-wish," i.e., the wish to give the mother a baby, persisting so frequently in the neurotic. Were this so, speculation could give way to explanation: because inasmuch as the name represents in the unconscious the physical person, the "moonish" Helen would represent in part symbolically the pregnant mother.

It is only in order not to confuse the reader that I add recalling certain patients from more recent years in whom the active baby-wish played a prominent role, yet no Helen ever entered their associations. Here the explanation is simple: they did not express themselves symbolically but through picturization by being emphatic about remembering their mothers as extremely obese, particularly in the abdominal region. Where the patient is able to express herself directly because when the active baby-wish dominated her as a child, the mother was actually pregnant and the sibling became the wished-for baby, needs hardly be mentioned; it has been described by Freud (1931b).

Nevertheless, I should be explicit in stating that the symbol for the pregnant womb is the moon. Helen is not a symbol, but merely a woman qualified symbolically as pregnant.

It is the same qualification that Freud (1900) has unwittingly described in a deceptively simple but much overdetermined dream of one of his women patients: "At her summer holiday resort, by the Lake of —, she dove into the dark water *just where the pale moon was mirrored in it*" (p. 400; italics mine).

Knowing the symbol moon as well as, in this instance, the symbolically modified symbol of diving into [= coming out of] the water one will not be astonished at Freud's interpretation: the dream represents the wish to be (re-) born and to give birth to the analyst's child. With regard to the moon, Freud, ignorant of the symbol, points only to a pictorial overdetermination: it is ". . . the white bottom [*la lune*] which children are quick to guess that they came out of . . ."

Actually, however, the adult dreamer although pictorially alluding to the infantile fantasy of anal birth, expresses symbolically the wish both to be (re-) born and to give birth to a child from the womb.

I conclude with the poetic dialogue between Theseus and Hippolita, shortly to be married, at the opening of *A Midsummer Night's Dreame*:

> THESEUS. Now faire Hippolita, our nuptiall
> Drawes on apace; foure happy daies bring in
> Another *Moon:* but oh, methinkes, how slow
> This old *Moon* wanes; she lingers my desires
> Like to a Step-dance, or a dowager,
> Long withering out a young man's revennew.
> HIPPOLITA. Foure daies will quickly steep themselves in nights,
> Foure nights wil quickly dreame away the time:
> And then the *Moone,* like to a silver bow,
> New[28] bent in heaven, shall behold the night
> Of our solemnities (I, 1).

It would, of course, be absurd to try to account for the ineffable beauty of these lines in which the moon is spoken of three times. There is, for one thing, their music, which as far as I know, cannot be

---

[28] "Globe" Edition. The "Now" in the Folio is evidently a misprint.

adequately transcribed. If one hears this music while reading the text, Theseus comes to resemble in the last analysis an impatient little boy whom his loving mother consoles. One recalls Freud's saying that no marriage can really be a good one unless the wife becomes also the husband's mother. The impatience itself is cannibalistic (I, 107–110) in agreement with the fact that cannibalistic libido demands discharge in the sexual act (I, 273), concerning which Theseus is so impatient. In the course of the discharge, time, as everyone knows, becomes suspended. Theseus tries to defend himself against being prematurely overwhelmed by the sexual affect at first through structurizing the elusive time experience ("step-dance") as patients will do in the session by suddenly looking at the clock or asking whether it is not time to leave. (This resembles the action of the "click" in the watch, which rhythmically arrests and retards the otherwise ever faster unwinding of the spring: cf. II, 200.) [29]

Subsequently Theseus evades into the less regressive anal-sadistic phase (". . . long withering out a young man's revennew") as has been described by Abraham and myself (as a means of warding off ego disintegration (I, 123).

However, there is, with it all, the *moon*. I consider it overdetermined as a symbol. In remarking on the theory of coition, I have, besides commenting on the regression to the preoedipal phase during the performance, thought it "possible that the intent maintaining, if not initiating, the act is always, unconsciously at least, procreative" (I, 276). It appears to me now that this is observable beyond doubt in the female if she functions normally: in the male I have not been able to ascertain it. One more reason why Theseus is impatient and why Hippolita is content: *The moon must be "new," the womb empty when they embrace in order that it may be ready to grow* (picturization).

[29] I know that the Folios and other editions print "step-dame" in this passage. This, however, is nearly synonymous with "dowager" and does not fit the "to" that precedes it. It would not therefore stylistically represent the Shakespeare of the time of his major works, of which this is, of course, one. Genius does not gratuitously repeat itself: it has forever something new to say . . . If Shakespeare is repetitious, as e.g., in the threefold mentioning of the moon in the dialogue quoted above, one feels the intent and often discovers the significance. (Reading Freud, for instance, takes a lifetime because practically every line contains a new thought.) My difficulty lies with my memory which in this instance has failed me: I recall having read this correction years ago, and my wife remembers that I told her about it enthusiastically, because it was the first time that the complete passage made sense. The man in whose work I read that he considered "step-dame" a printer's error where "step-dance" had been intended was, of course, a Shakespearean scholar; unfortunately I cannot recall his name.

7. *Dead End* = *rectum*

If any element in the environment or any part of the body that one can characterize as a "dead end" is a symbol, it represents the rectum.

The most dramatic clinical illustration I remember is a patient's dream, as brief, as inconspicuous, and as poor in action as Freud's famous dream of the botanical monograph. The associations to it, however, were as elaborate as were Freud's, although it took a long time to get them. Yet I doubt whether I would have obtained any had I not been able first to translate the "dead end" symbol for the patient.

The manifest content merely had an unidentified man pulling into the driveway at the side of a (or her) house. The usual driveway, the kind that appeared in the dream, is, however, a dead-end road. In addition, the activity of the man in the dream lent itself to calling him by the name of a certain individual, to whom, I had previously learned, the patient was in bondage during puberty and adolescence.

It was the symbol translation combined with the interpretation of the pictorial identity of the man that enabled the patient gradually to supply a wealth of associations to the dream. They informed us in great detail of an extremely traumatic experience, sustained by her when she was 15 years old, and completely repressed. It culminated in the girl's allowing the man to perform rectal intercourse during which he went wild and inflicted excessive pain. The immediate consequence was a state of depersonalization that lasted for days.

Thus the analysis of a dream leading to amnesia removal proved the "dead end," a symbol for the rectum.

The symbolization of the rectum through "dead end" occurs also as a displacement symbol.

A patient, for instance, recalls, as she had before, her habit of reading with her hand between her legs, but adds a completely new bit of information: at times she used to suck on the inside of her elbow, causing little blood spots to appear. I interpret, prompted by the context of her associations and because I had observed it previously in another case, that parts of the body like this are a "dead end" and may become a displacement symbol for the rectum. This symbol translation, which for a reason unknown to me made sense to her, induced clitoral sensations, combined with anal and rectal squeezing.

In the next hour the patient reports having felt strong separation anxiety in defecation and having inspected her stool (I, 117).

Here the translation of the displacement symbol while undoing the displacement mobilized both the persisting infantile sexuality attached to the organ itself and the fear characteristic for the phase in childhood in which it is the dominant erogenic zone.

8. *Head* = *"arse"*

There are medical terms for the several parts—buttocks, perineum, anus, rectum—combining into a pleasure-physiologic element for which there is no medical, let alone a "printable" name. The only term for the combination is the vulgarism "arse," for which I have observed two symbols.

First, an example for the direct expression: I remember how, long ago, a patient belonging to the lower strata of society told of an evidently attractive girl passing a group of young men and moving one of them to exclaim: "Oh, if I could only have a whiff of her arse!" It would be wrong to understand him as wanting to smell her anus. His instinctual aim was directed towards the combination here under consideration, including even the external genital evidently conceived of as cloaca. I cannot, of course, explain his restriction to the olfactory sphere; but I suspect it had become overburdened with the functions of other spheres—a phenomenon observable on occasion in patients

Certain artists, from the sixteenth century to the present, have represented this pleasure-physiologic element prominently, and in addition to its sexual nature have brought out its aesthetic quality in women. (See, for example, Correggio's *Jupiter and Antiope;* Rubens' *Venus and Cupid with Bacchus and Areia;* Velasquez' the *Rokeby Venus;* Watteau's *Judgment of Paris; La Grande Odalisque* by Ingres; Renoir's *La Baigneuse Blonde;* Modigliani's *Nudo Sitting;* etc.)

Of the two symbols for it one is a displacement symbol: the head. This is significant clinically for certain instances where the head appears in the patient's associations and for the analysis of, for example, certain headaches.

Secondly, I recall an instance where the significance was crucial. The few memories emerging from amnesia in this analysis all had the same peculiarity: they stopped where they should have begun. In one of them the patient recalled her arousement as a child in the phallic phase at the mother's beckoning her to come to the toilet after the father had left the house in the morning. There was a wealth of material from different ages including the present, not only allowing for, but completing the reconstructive interpretation of the beckoning as sexual invitation. Yet the memory would not come forth. The mother's underdrawers, open at the bottom, invited much speculation; they disgusted the girl who eventually explained to herself that they were fashioned so as to have menstrual rags stuffed into them, a whole unwashed pile of which she had come upon. This appeared to me a mockery until I knew better. The only further scrap of memory, never doubted by the patient, was that of her enjoyment of the mother's strong genital odor.

There the matter stood, and it appeared as though there it would continue to stand.

It began to move in consequence of a single remark of the patient and its interpretation,[30] which illustrates the symbolism under discussion. (It matters not that the particular context in which "head" was employed in this instance is, in my experience, unique.) The preceding paragraph makes it evident that, besides the child's sexual excitation at the mother's beckoning, the element toilet leads one to expect a sexual exploitation. Without this element one cannot either tentatively reconstruct or even explain the excitement. Yet, when I subsequently attempted to collate the scanty information with some other material, that element was no longer remembered. The only explanation for this familiar selective lack of memory is that the patient in the hours in which the element had been recalled was, without knowing it in a state of hypnotic evasion (to be dealt with later). I launched, therefore, into a description of this phenomenon, called it "symptomless," etc. *"Yes,"* the patient agreed, *"it has no symptoms; just a little sick feeling in the head . . ."* I knew immediately, this time by intuition, that here "head" was a symbol. I proceeded conse-

---

[30] Conscientiousness bids me report a fragment of insight preceding the change, although I do not know what relation to it it has, if any. I was convinced that the patient followed the analytic rule; yet I discovered eventually that she made an exception: anything hostile to me was withheld. Working this through proved, of course, generally beneficial.

quently to describe the symbolized element as I have done above. This placed the element toilet again at the patient's disposal and made the memory move. "No pants," she said resolutely, and remembered how the mother sat down, clad only in a nightgown, exposing the whole of the pleasure-physiologic unit symbolized by the "head"; whereupon she took the child's hand and used it for masturbation.

The amnesia removal for this type of event was in short order followed by two others in which the same unit was prominantly displayed. One of these memories, concerning a bizarre masturbatory exhibition while fully attired, took the lead in suggesting that the woman did not wear any underdrawers except during menstruation, which altered my evaluation of the patient's remark, reported in the first paragraph of the example.

9. *Sky* = *"arse"*

The other symbolization of this pleasure-physiologic unit is a symbolically conditioned symbol, the *sky*. It is conditioned by the color symbolism for the quality anal—blue, and it is not free from picturization since we see the sky as resembling the symbolized element in its shape.

I do not know how convincing to the reader the one meager illustration I find in my notes will be. A male patient, whose identity was extensively encumbered by morbid identifications that made him consider himself a woman, begins the session with silence. When asked what is on his mind, he answers languidly that he was just looking out at the sky. He went on to recount visiting a woman friend in a hospital the day before, who declared herself loath to leave her hospital room because it afforded her a magnificent view of a great expanse of sky, whereas her own apartment had but little sun and no view. I obtain only two fragments of information about this woman: she is still fairly young, and given to unconventional talk. She had told him how a nurse woke her on the morning before the operation and gave her a pre-operative enema. Lying on one side, and looking out of the window, she found the sky "gorgeous," got very excited over it and called out to the nurse: "Look, look, how beautiful!" But, she added, the nurse was not interested and "all she looked at was my . . . hole."

The simultaneity of the young woman's being given an enema and her exclamation leads one to speculation. The exhibition to the nurse, aided perhaps by the stimulation of anus and rectum, may have caused excitation subject to a transformation of affect whose attempted discharge demanded symbolic expression. The alternative would be to consider both the coincidence of exhibition and aesthetic outburst in his friend, as well as the patient's preceding association, as devoid of meaning.

10. *Dog* = *anal-sadistic partial subject; sometimes partial object*

The next symbolism to be described, although representative of an element of the pleasure-physiologic body ego, nevertheless does not represent merely an erogenic zone. The symbolized elements are either the anal-sadistic partial subject, or partial object, and the symbol for them is the dog. Freud (1930) without speaking of symbolization regarded the adoption of upright gait as a prerequisite to civilization. He states that the upright gait led to the "organic repression" of anal-erotism, and he emphasized a "social factor" in this repression. The factor has many manifestations: the most subtle being the restriction, mentioned by him, of our revulsion to the smell of feces of others in contrast to the relative tolerance of that of our own. He speaks in this context of the dog and explains the paradox that we use the name of our most faithful friend amongst animals as an insult, with contempt for him on two counts: he is a *"Geruchstier"* [odor-animal], i.e., an animal orienting and exciting himself by smell without disgust for excrement, and an animal that shows no shame with regard to its sexual functions (pp. 99–100). Freud might have added what is common knowledge; the dog, resembling man to such a degree that Freud has even ascribed a superego to him, did not adopt upright gait; and his coitus, displayed so freely, is without exception interpreted by the child as sodomy.

This is vividly illustrated in Editha Sterba's excellent report on the analysis of a dog phobia of a seven-and-a-half-year-old girl (1940). The condition began after a long period of enema applications by the mother during a middle ear infection which made the child fearful of soiling. The phobia, under whose influence she hardly dared leave the house, kept her from observing the cohabitation of dogs in the street as well as from being assaulted by them olfactorily.

Socially, one inadvertently observes quite a few anal-regressive traits in dog fanciers. I shall, however, confine myself to the analytic observation of patients.

Although women may not infrequently attract dogs sexually by their genital odor, many of them are not conscious of how strongly they themselves are tempted to give in to the overtures of a dog. What interests the analyst is that in each and every case that has come to my knowledge, the genital was conceived of as a cloaca. The persistence of the anal-sadistic fantasy of the cloaca, however, furnishes as strong a contribution to the feeling of inferiority in the neurotic woman as does the phallic fantasy of her castration. They coexist, and it is often a difficult task to disentwine them.

The clinical illustrations to follow are concerned with the dog as a sexual partner, the fantasy of the cloaca, and the ensuing delusion of inferiority. The fantasy, and the consequences of the fantasy, of castration are deliberately disregarded.

(a) I remember the analysis of a patient who, as a girl, had for years played sexually with a dog and as an adult had preserved intact the fantasy of the cloaca. When it came to correcting her delusions about her body by inspecting herself with a mirror, she described what she had seen but omitted the perineum because by separating the genital from the anus its existence contradicts the fantasy of the cloaca. My attempts to induce her to acknowledge the perineum met with the greatest resistance. When she finally consorted with a man, she was not only frigid but cried bitterly after the act because she interpreted the latter as a sadistic attack. Her "cloaca" made her feel so inferior that in spite of great gifts she kept herself in a menial professional position that brought her day after day in physical contact with feces.

(b) Another case is the successful analysis of a homosexual woman who in puberty had a dog perform cunnilingus on her when she was on the toilet; I recall her description of the dog's ejaculating on the bathroom floor and of her cleaning up. When she left her analysis, happy and in love with a woman who gratified her residual masochistic needs, she had to obtain my permission on one point: her partner occasionally emitted gas in the course of their activities: was it all right to enjoy the odor? Nevertheless, she left the analysis convinced that she had no chance in her job; that there was no sense in attempting to achieve the highest rank in her profession. Two years after the termination of her treatment, she was promoted to that rank.

(c) I recall another patient who slept through most of the evening hours in her home. I recognized this as an hypnotic evasion, but I was ignorant for a long time of what she had to evade. Finally I obtained the answer: she evaded fantasies threatening her with strong excitation about a psychotic member of the household, who, obviously for sexual purposes, took the dog to the toilet with her. The patient had, of course, remained unaware of the intensity of the temptation in response to occasional overtures that the dog made to herself. I omit all further symptoms, including those indicative of her inferiority feelings. I also dispense with all history except for reporting that in puberty, when by maturing she acquired the mother's sexual characteristics: she kept herself so soiled as to be offensive to others. The mother who had abused her excessively as a child was possessed of a strong genital odor which she evidently did not remove, but belonged otherwise to the type, described by Abraham, that is outwardly clean.

(d) I conclude with some notes on a single analytic hour of a woman patient. She lay down on the couch before I had entered the office and experienced the most hallucinatory illusion that I stood watching her from the foyer, occupying the space taken up actually by a small mahogany chest of drawers. The evening before, she had masturbated, lying on her stomach and finding the genital well-moistened. But she had reached no climax and had instead fallen asleep. The fantasy which she resisted reporting was that of being licked by a dog. This had actually occurred repeatedly in the phallic phase as well as in her early twenties, when sometimes the mere sight of a dog's erection aroused her. It became evident that my taking the place of the chest of drawers gave me the height and color of the big dogs from her twenties, and that the masturbation had to remain inconclusive because a climax would have transformed a fantasy of the dog into one of me. Hers was the only case I know of where the mother once failed in concealing her sexual exploitation: the husband surprised her while she was performing cunnilingus on the seven-year-old child. At the end of the session the patient reported for the first time how the mother assisted her in perpetuating the fantasy of the cloaca: she called the whole region in herself and the daughter "one's toilet." ("Wash your 'toilet.'" "Take your hand away from your 'toilet.'" etc.) The patient regarded this at first as a common idiom and was astonished that I did not know it, yet she had finally to admit never having heard it herself from anyone but her mother.

A few general remarks about this patient may round out the clinical picture. Her inferiority feeling was excessive: for years she went every day in agony to her job, convinced that she "could not do it" and would be fired. Her relation to me had the complexion of a paranoia and it took me longer than it should have to recognize this as a homosexual transference of the mother. She struggled perpetually with constipation, and with a mistrust of her financial adviser (money), although she had dealt with him for many years and his honesty as well as his competence actually permitted of no doubt. She was, finally, extremely and incorrigibly anti-Semitic.

I do not, of course, intend to deal in this place with the complex problem of anti-Semitism, but I must state that the Jew, whom one calls "dirty" and with whom one refuses contact lest one be defiled, serves not infrequently as a symbol for the same symbolized element as does the dog: Shylock equates the two directly in his reply to Antonio, who wants to borrow from him, in the *Merchant of Venice:*

> You call me misbeleever, cut-throat *dog,*
> And spet upon my Jewish gaberdine,
> . . . .
> . . . you come to me, and you say;
> Shylocke, we would have moneys. . . .
> You that did voide your rume upon my beard,
> And foote me as you spurne a stranger *curre*
> Over your threshold. . . .
> . . . Should I not say,
> Hath a *dog* money? Is it possible
> A *curre* should lend three thousand ducats? (I, 3)

The symbolization of the anal-sadistic partial subject—in contrast to that of the partial object—is perhaps more clearly recognizable in the Jew than it is in the dog. The dog has certain qualities by virtue of which he is suitable for being used as that symbol; the Jew does not have them. He is furnished with them purely through the projection upon him of what the Gentile wants to disown in himself. One is therefore entitled to speak of an "anti-Semitic delusion."

I must request the reader to assist me in making my point. He can do so by rereading the last few pages and concentrating on the narcissistic aspect of the representation through the element dog. He will then come to recognize that this element is a symbol and that it symbolizes the anal-sadistic partial subject (or object), i.e., the subject in *either* the ego or in the object of anal-sadistic strivings (cf. Glossary or II, 80).

C. PLEASURE-PHYSIOLOGIC FUNCTIONS

1. *French = fellatio, cunnilingus*

"French," when a symbol, represents sexual activities using the mouth—chiefly fellatio or cunnilingus. For both, the term "Frenching" is a vulgarism in English. A *Dictionary of Slang and Unconventional English* (Partridge, 1960) lists "French tricks" as a term for "cunnilingus and penilingism in the colloquialism of the 1920's." *The Dictionary of American Slang* (Wentworth & Flexner, 1960) contains "French (since World War I)—sexual gratification given or received orally and French way (since World War I)—sexual intercourse accomplished orally by cunnilingus or fellatio." Whether or not the fact that the French *baiser* which up to fairly recently—I believe it was in my own youth—meant to kiss, has come to mean having intercourse is somehow pertinent to the subject, I do not know.

The symbolism is not too infrequent; but again the only clinical record I have made of it is the one to be found in the first Chapter. It concerns the man who falsified the name of the girl Marguerite, because she performed fellatio on him, into Margaret, and broke off with her lest he have to speak of the matter in his treatment.

2. *Funny = sexual; Silly = infantile sexual*

I do not know whether one is entitled to call the following two expressions symbolic; but since their interpretation originated with Freud, I include them lest they be lost.

Dr. Ruth Mack Brunswick once told me that Freud said to her: "Why do people always mean 'sexual' when they say 'funny'?" I do not, of course, know the answer, but I have often had occasion to confirm his observation (II, 265). The small addition that I was able to make is that when they say "silly," "infantile sexual" is meant.

The only recorded clinical illustration I find is contained in the first part of the present chapter, where a patient's mother plays with herself while telephoning and gets that *"funny* expression on her face." The expression is naturally one of sexual excitation.

The only example for my extension stems from a note on a female homosexual patient who repeatedly had remarked about the sparseness of her pubic hair. In one analytic session she voiced her envy of a woman friend who had much more of it, and went on to compare her own genital as a child with her mother's, emphasizing again the relative abundance of the latter's pubic hair. In the midst of these associations she interrupted herself with the apparently gratuitous expression: "That's silly."

I cannot, as I have said above, be certain that one has the right to term these two expressions symbolic; but in this case I disregard my doubts because I feel an obligation to preserve what has come down from Freud to me by word of mouth.

3. *Telephoning = masturbation*

This symbolization is easy to observe, but has not to my knowledge been recorded before. It is in fact so frequent that it had to be mentioned before its proper discussion several times in the first volume of this Series (I, 91, 225) and in the first part of the present chapter in different contexts. It belongs not only to the group of newly formed symbols, but to those in this group that have no earlier model (e.g., airplane = bird), because a new invention here found a symbolic employment. To explain that employment would mean to explain a symbolization of which it has categorically been stated that this can in no instance be done. What can and should be done is to draw the symbol equation more accurately in two of its aspects:

(a) I cannot simply telephone; I can only telephone *someone*. Therefore if and when this has the symbolic meaning mentioned above, it implies a mutual stimulation of two persons. Although affect may attach itself to the symbol instead of to the symbolized element as in the case of the woman who masturbated while telephoning (I, 225), such attachment appears to be rare: ordinarily telephoning in itself, even if one can be absolutely certain of its symbolic meaning, leads to no sexual excitation.

I have observed only a single exception. It concerned a woman patient who had been acquainted with the symbolism and whose regular telephone conversations with a particular female had been meaningfully interpreted, with the result that she could experience her friend as a homosexual object. Shortly thereafter a talkative woman called her in behalf of the friend, showering her with gratuitous and empty talk. The patient let her go on, relaxedly, and experienced a mounting excitation. She felt literally masturbated, and when the woman happened to use the word "tongue-lashing" she underwent the sensation of cunnilingus to the point of becoming almost orgastic.

(b) The two persons telephoning each other and thereby maintaining this symbolization have originally been the present person (i.e., the patient) as a child, and an adult of that period. The neurotic, in whom I observe the symbolism, has of course remained that child, by perpetuating, psychologically, his childhood; the adult is usually his mother, if she is still alive; if not, a person serving as a substitute for her.

I shall present three paradigmatic examples from clinical observation. In the first of these the mother is still alive, in the second she is not and a mother substitute takes her place while in the third the symbolism of telephoning fuses with another one (described in both the first [I, 216] and the second volumes [II, 60] of the Series). In all three of them the telephoning or the struggle against it or the submission to it is recognizable as but the last link, so to speak, of masturbatory exploitation by the mother of the child, perpetuated symbolically by the neurotic. The service to which such telephoning is put is, as I have called it earlier (I, 90–92) that of a "cannibalistic reincorporation" or (II, 60) a "telephonic reintrojection."

(1) The mother took the child, in the phallic phase, to the toilet with her when urinating. She sat with the exhibitorily exaggerated spread of her legs, so typical of certain psychotics (see also I, 225). I must assume that her clitoris was erected, for the little girl, curiously watching and touching the mother, soon found it. Being allowed to play with it she was told and shown that "she had that too," which initiated their mutual masturbation. The latter continued in different places and situations until at least the age of six. Somewhere around the age of seven the patient was demoted, as it were, to onlooker at the mother's own masturbation, and the severity of the tactile deprivation expressed itself in her analysis in several different ways, one of which was that, although highly trained as a pianist, she could, when my patient, no longer touch the piano (cf. above). The mother meanwhile became severely depressed, and the child wondered whether that was not a consequence of the cessation of their sexual play. Finally the mother suffered from a psychosomatic disease which made the daughter anxiously overprotective and watchful; she tiptoed, for instance, into the bedroom to be sure that the mother was still breathing. When the daughter was adolescent, she was told by her mother that they both had the same physique. The patient was thereupon induced to overeat in an effort to simulate the mother's figure, chafing as she did between the legs and imitating her urethral incontinence by means of genital discharge. She finally conquered this by herself, but so deep was her bondage to her pathological mother that when she entered analysis she suffered a severe compulsive struggle over telephoning the mother. On the one hand she wanted to get free, on the other she tortured herself with an imaginary obligation to alleviate the mother's complaints by listening to them with the telephone in the center of her conflict.

(2) Amnesia removal of a woman patient who lived alone, had clic-

ited that the mother performed cunnilingus on her at the age of seven and that she used her finger for strongly orgastic masturbations through her nightgown at the age of 14. The critical reader will not be satisfied with this information. The root of the neurosis, he will say to himself, lies, as Freud has discovered, in the first five years of life; if the author has obtained memories only from ages of seven and 14 he has not performed an analysis. I agree: I had not; and I eventually had to break off the treatment. For the present purpose it will, however, suffice to imagine what must have gone on earlier. I could in fact reconstruct a good deal, but obtained only a few insufficient scraps of corroborative evidence. It was clear that the mother exhibited on the toilet and that, besides whatever went on there, the volume of the stream fascinated the child. Yet the patient would only remember *hearing* the mother, which is always the heir to seeing, and that she found even this "obscene."

During her treatment she frequently received telephone calls in the evening from a friend of her own age, of whom it did not become intelligible why she should substitute for the mother. Yet the patient described how the friend would loosen an unending stream of words, meaningless and often continuing for an hour. The patient, however, was helpless against this attack; she could never, for instance, indicate that she had to ring off because she had a dish on the stove that needed attention or because she had to go out, or any of the dozen "white lies" one would ordinarily use in such a situation. All she could do was secretly to take the receiver off her ear for a while and then respond with a noncommittal interjection. Since I failed in converting her treatment into an analysis, I can but conjecture that the patient subjected herself to the verbal stream because the friend served as the mother. For the same reason the pattern of the calls did not change through the years. Only once did the patient report that she felt a nipple erect after such a telephone conversation.

(3) I conclude with an example where the mother had long been dead, yet the compulsive telephoning went on. It concerns the patient who as a child was made to masturbate her mother. As an adult she took a job that required her to telephone women much of the day—easily recognized in the analysis as an acting out in the service of the need to repeat.

The observation recorded here of the symbolism of telephoning may be concluded by a remark on technique. In cases where the mother is still alive the compulsive telephoning serves—as the first example with the adolescent's hypersymbiotic obesity shows so clearly—the maintenance of an identification with her. Morbid identification, however, precludes the development of identity, which is one of the main purposes of psychoanalytic treatment. I have therefore found myself constrained to subject the telephoning, together with other contact between the patient and his or her mother, to the abstinence rule at the proper time. Where the analysis was successful the later resumption of contact was by a patient no longer in bondage, one who has found his identity, and has in the process discontinued the symbolic employment of telephoning with the mother.

4. Week = menstruation

I had observed for at least a decade that when a patient associates "week" she more often than not means menstruation. Something "takes a week," occurs "weekly" or it involves the "week-end"; these are the most frequent forms of expression. Sometimes, as in the first example below, "week-end" is not even verbalized explicitly, but only implied.

I was finally forced to recognize that the idea "week" is a potential symbol for the "monthly period." This is of course as inexplicable as is any symbol; one might expect an allusion to "month," but instead one hears the unexpectable symbolization "week."

(a) A patient started to menstruate on a Saturday morning (week-end), feeling an irrational urge to telephone her (psychotic) mother. When I reminded her of the abstinence rule we had recently invoked against such contacts, she answered: "It makes no difference, my mother will call me anyhow." And indeed the woman promptly telephoned. (Both the intensity of the mother's interest and the accuracy of her unconscious sense of time are hard to believe; yet the former is but derivative of the sexual exploitation of her daughter as a child, and the latter becomes, on occasion, directly observable in a patient.)

(b) A patient begins her session with a number of, at first, inexpressive associations, amongst them the report that she had planned to attend a semi-official affair with her husband but when the time came to go, felt reluctant and told him: "Oh, I don't want to go upstairs and change my dress." The husband objected to her remonstrance and they went, enjoying themselves.

Her next association concerned a projected *week-end* visit in the country. This at once endowed the previous meaningless associations with a meaning: the going upstairs (house = woman, stairs = vagina) and the changing of the dress (= dressing) meant replacing Tampax and Kotex, both of which she was accustomed to wearing. Since we knew that all manipulation of the genital (e.g., the insertion of a pessary) renewed her struggle over masturbation, the reluctance became readily understood. None of this was, however, communicated to the patient in the hour under consideration.

The transformation, in other words, of the earlier insignificant associations into significant ones was the result of my having silently translated "week" into menstruation.[31]

As though to confirm the translation, the patient reported in the course of further associations upon the last week-end, when they had been invited to someone's house in the suburbs. She had at that occasion worried over her period which was about to begin, and, disliking to make the trip "with all the paraphernalia," had hoped to "get by" without them.

The coincidence with the week-end, in the first example of menstruation per se and in the second of prodromata (abdominal cramps) and menstruation respectively, lends, I think, particular cogency to these clinical illustrations. Such coincidence is, however, not requisite to the symbolization. Week symbolizes menstruation also at times when, as far as the patient's associations inform one, neither she nor any "object" is expecting or having her period.

---

[31] In addition, cf. my reference to Freud's *"Innocent Dreams"* (1900, pp. 182–188).

5. *The Rotating Symbol* = *ego disintegration*

The last of this group of symbols can hardly be regarded as representing a pleasure-physiologic element or a pleasure-physiologic function. I observed it for many years before finding out what it represents: it is the "rotating symbol," and it symbolizes ego disintegration.

The particular nature of the rotating object to which the patient refers in his associations is immaterial; it obtains its potentially symbolic meaning merely by spinning around. If my memory serves me right, the electric fan and the phonograph record are most frequent; but I believe I have heard patients use the roulette wheel, the dentist's drill and certain toys for children that turn on a nail driven into a wooden stick, as rotating symbols representative of ego disintegration. In one instance it was a "winding" mountain road, i.e., one with a spiral course (II, 326n).

The cause of the ego disintegration is also immaterial; in the case of Van Gogh it was the ego disintegration in consequence of the psychotic process that expressed itself in the many whorls of certain of his paintings (The Night Cafe, A Road in Provence, Starry Night etc.), as it was in the example from fiction quoted by Freud (1919b) where Nathaniel—a character in the *Tales of Hoffmann*—while suffering a renewed attack of insanity, screams, "Hurry up! Hurry up! Ring of fire! Spin about, ring of fire . . . lovely wooden doll, spin about!" (p. 229).

I have notes on only a few examples of a very inhomogeneous complexion.

(a) A transient ego disintegration is effected through general anaesthesia. In the years when relatively slow-working gases, such as ether, were used, many patients reported seeing rotating circles of light in front of their eyes while "going under," i.e., while experiencing the disintegration of ego. I myself still remember this from an ethyl chloride application given to me in my early twenties. Today, where the much faster sodium pentothal is employed, or employed initially, the opportunity for this observation no longer exists.

(b) A colleague[32] was kind enough to put the following notes at my disposal. They concern the psychotherapeutic hour of a male patient, of whom I am not permitted to say any more than that in my colleague's judgment he was subject to periods of severe ego regression.

Patient: Don't you have a *fan?* I've never noticed an air conditioner. I could have sworn you had a *fan.* It's so hard to talk here—even about inanimate objects. Yesterday I went to the ear doctor—he had no *fan* or air conditioner in his office, and it was terribly hot in there. Why should that be? He obviously has a busy practice.

Therapist: What did you think?

Patient: That he must be indifferent to the patients' welfare. Your couch—it's not my picture of an analyst's couch. Now that I really look at it, I notice that you can lie down on it and use it as one—never realized that.

Therapist: Were you afraid at the ear doctor's?

Patient: Yes—instruments poking on one's ear—fear of poking through the eardrum *if he loses control*—like the feeling I have had in a *dentist's chair with instruments poking in my mouth.*

Therapist: Your fear and trouble talking here—might it not be related to the picture of an indifferent doctor—or even one who might harm you in some way?

Patient: True—I think of the couch as if it were an operating table.

I suddenly think of two experiences I had when a child—I had to be given *anaesthesia* which was very poorly administered so that I had the feeling of suffocation—of being submerged—of imminent death. *The most frightening thing of all for some reason was that I was staring at the chandelier which began to spin around and kept rotating.* Then I felt as if I were looking at it at the end of a long tunnel.

Therapist: Rotating like the fan you imagined was in this office?

Patient: Yes! I was about four or maybe six years old. The second occasion was in a *dentist's* chair when I was nine. I remember the feeling of a tunnel of air again with sounds of the rushing of gas. It made me feel as if I were being catapulted into space.

---

[32] I regret being unable to thank him by name.

I think of the fear of looking at the stars as a child—fear of the idea of infinity—of losing myself in space.

Therapist: Of being swallowed up?

Patient: Yes, that's it. I remember being afraid of sitting on the toilet [because, my colleague explains, he anticipated the flushing of the toilet that involves the rotating swirling of the water]—I would get up repeatedly as a child and look into the bowl. That was another tube I was afraid of—as if the universe could rush in upon me this time through it.

I think these notes largely speak for themselves. The patient expects or perhaps already feels an abortive ego disintegration probably in consequence of transference fantasies that he does not express.

(c) Peto's description (1959) of extreme ego disintegration of psychotic patients occurring in the therapeutic session contains passages such as these: One patient hallucinated that her

> minute body, which had softened up to the same extent [as the therapist's, whose body had lost shape and had become jelly-like or even liquid] penetrated the therapist's body or merged with it. Everything seemed to be involved in *a tossing or turning whirlpool* [p. 225].
>
> [Another patient] . . . wallowed in the amorphous mass of excreta and sweat, which were hers and the analyst's as well . . . Different sensory experiences fused into one semi-fluid conglomerate of smell, taste, temperature, touch, and noises . . . Dizziness with *rotating* and undulating feelings permeated everything [p. 225; italics added].

(d) A colleague, whom again I can only thank but not by name, has allowed me to use his notes on two therapeutic sessions with two different patients.

(1) A young woman, after a year of analysis, has identified with a destructive and probably psychotic witch of a mother "who used to cut her father to ribbons" during the continual parental quarrels. For some time she has been expressing her spite against the analyst—in and out of the sessions—for not fulfilling her sexual

wishes. Her session has, as its theme, her destructive and cannibalistic wishes toward the various men in her life, especially the
analyst. She makes a slip: ('when I sit down to a *man*') (instead of
a meal)—that is followed by a rush of cannibalistic feeling, with
some insight. Suddenly she takes notice of a slight protuberance
on the white wall of the analyst's office—('It looks to me like a
breast, a nipple' . . . [with mounting anxiety] Now I see *moving
concentric whorls* around it. It is as if it is turning inside out,
becoming concave. It threatens to suck me in like a whirlpool."

Here the ego dissolution poses no problem; It is a consequence of a
regression to the first oral stage in which no ego exists.

(2) A male patient felt, in response to the sight at six years of
age of his mother masturbating in a fashion to make it undeniably
clear at the moment that she had an opening instead of a penis,
"that *the room began spinning around him.*" The overwhelming
excitement, the concomitant castration anxiety with incipient ego
disintegration was experienced many times in the transference,
especially in relation to fantasies of seeing me undressed that
involved both an identification and an object relation with his
mother. At these times, too, "the room would begin to spin" for
him. A homosexual, this type of anticipatory anxiety was warded
off in reality by the sight of his partner's penis. This would "stir
him up" anally—that is, in his own "room within." Here the spinning room obviously alludes to the mother's genitals and *hands in
motion,* as well as being a symbolization of the accompanying
ego-dissolution threat. This patient had, in the course of his seduction, been seized by the mother, his head pressed to her genitals, apparently with her climax. Thus a partial asphyxiation, or
the threat of this, was involved.

No one who has not studied and directly observed what
Freud calls "the shock of castration" can imagine the overwhelming strength of its impact. I am not surprised to hear that
it may precipitate fear of imminent ego dissolution, which the
threat of asphyxiation would naturally compound.

(e) Finally, I find a note on an analytic hour that I conducted with
a patient who in the phallic phase was seduced by an amateur hypno-

tist. He observed himself counting seconds while waiting downstairs for his session. His associations to this are the hypnotist's counting while hypnotizing (other) people during occasional drawing-room performances as well as his own counting of seconds while developing film in the darkroom, where in adolescence he and the hypnotist had had a sexual talk. Waiting downstairs, the patient had had an erection. Familiar with the hypnotic evasion, he remarks that he is not in it, yet has to admit soon thereafter that he is.

His perverse, psychopathic psychotic mother had exploited him excessively throughout childhood and puberty; at the latter time she finally and repeatedly seduced him to incest. These activities culminated in a far-reaching rectal penetration after which the woman, evidently having had a rectal orgasm—such as one will occasionally observe in psychotics—"came to," and exclaiming "No, No, No," rushed from the room. Later, nothing was ever mentioned; the event was treated by both as *non arrivé.*

I shall not speak of the many morbid effects of the mother's polymorphously perverse exploitations, nor of the various mechanisms, besides repression, employed by the patient in order either not to know what ailed him or to know it only temporarily and incompletely. I will make a single exception and preface it with a general remark. The effects of the traumata in the neurosis are always twofold: consequences of a morbid object relation to the incest object and a morbid identification with him. If one is at all justified in generalizing, I would name the latter more noxious and more resistive to correction than the former. One will therefore not be astonished to hear that the patient as a young man suffered agony from the fear of becoming a homosexual and from the conviction that this would destroy him. What he concealed from himself was the instinctual aim: passive sodomy precipitating a disintegration of ego.

To his counting the seconds while waiting, I remark interpretatively, that by virtue of its rhythm and its combination with an erection it reminded me of the previously mentioned "No, no, no . . ." He professes his ignorance of how often the mother had repeated the word at the time, but proceeds to associate the memory of a broken *record* in which a member of the family sang something and the mother said, "That was very nice." Whenever the record was subsequently put on, it got stuck at that point and repeated over and over: "Very nice, very nice, very nice. . . ." [33]

[33] Belated correction by the patient: "Better than ever, better than ever, better than ever . . ."

By thus introducing the "rotating symbol" the patient indicates that the erection while waiting downstairs had been produced by an unconscious homosexual fantasy in the transference accompanied by the fear of an ego disintegration. (He had had before and after this episode many such fantasies consciously with erections and an almost uncontrollable urge to masturbate during the session.)

I translate the rotating symbol, of which he was ignorant, and explain its meaning to him. His answer: "This is uncanny (!). I was just about to tell you a fantasy in which my mother has her finger in my rectum when I was a child, lifts me up, and *whirls me around.*

The mother's rectal penetrations, in the course of which she inflicted unbearable stimulations, are actual memories for which the amnesia had been removed; the lifting him up and whirling him around, are, of course, fantasies precipitated by the unconscious wish to tell me by means of their symbolic complexion of the concomitant ego disintegration.

To repeat: the rotating symbol is representative of the unconscious idea (experience, expectation) of disintegration or dissolution of ego. It is the only symbolization of this idea that I know. The importance of being familiar with it need hardly be stressed.

D. BISEXUAL SYMBOLS

Freud has discussed this subject exhaustively, in opposing Stekel's fantastic claim that almost every symbol has potentially a bisexual meaning, i.e., that it represents sometimes the male genital, sometimes the female. It need hardly be mentioned that Freud was right. My own observation has shown me only an extremely limited number of bisexual symbols, and, in one or two instances, has compelled me to differ with Freud.

The horse is but rarely modified as a male, or a mare; one has to guess whether it symbolizes the father or the mother in a certain context; it could therefore be called a bisexual symbol. Since in the gelding at least, the penis becomes extroverted to full length in urination, it is on the occasion of the child's fascinated observation of this act that one is most apt to encounter such modification.

The "faceless person" or "the Negro" is, in contrast to the horse, usually modified as a man or a woman although on occasion such modification is lacking. As for the rest, there is the "little one" (Freud), which may or may not be modified as a boy or a girl; and the "car," which is definitely a bisexual symbol, as is "suicide," symbolizing masturbation in either sex. The one case, finally, where my experience differs from Freud is that of the "shoe." Freud (1900) found it to symbolize only the genital of the female. I find it a bisexual symbol.

A patient with no analytic knowledge surprised me once by discovering this by herself. The following is a transcript of a dream and her associations:

> I dreamt that I went to my clothes closet to get out some shoes to wear. I discovered that all my shoes were in bad condition as though they had met with violence. Some were worn out and torn, and one which I picked up and held in my hand had had the heel ripped off and several nails were protruding where the heel had been. I experienced a sensation of repugnance and horror at this violence which had been perpetrated on my possession (my shoe) by persons unknown. I also had a sensation of grief at this injustice done to me.
>
> I awoke and went to the bathroom to urinate. Without any conscious thought, I suddenly realized that I was looking for some bleeding from the vagina.
>
> Although I do not know the symbolic significance of a shoe, it suggests a small boat, hollowed out in the center with curving out sides . . . actually like a female genital with labia spread; the foot to be inserted into a shoe enters like a penis entering a vagina. The leg is also part of this penis.
>
> As for the ripped-off heel, snatched from my shoe so violently and perhaps painfully (if the shoe had feeling), it is also the penis which was removed forcibly from my own female genital. I was looking for the blood which would accompany this tearing off of the male part of my body. [It should be noted that, at the time of the incident, the patient was nowhere near her menstrual period.]

The other instance is that of the *hat*. Freud is but tentative

about its bisexual nature; I have never seen it symbolize anything but the penis or the phallus. *Fire*, a frequent representation of infantile sexual urination (Freud) is, of course, a bisexual
symbol. So, for that matter, is *flying* when it symbolizes erection. The incessant *talking*, described by Abraham (1924a) as a
substitute for urethral-erotic discharge, could perhaps be called
a displacement symbol and a bisexual one at that. *Telephoning*,
which involves two persons, when a symbol, represents mutual
masturbation. In my experience it usually concerns two females;
but I remember one instance where it concerned a male and his
mother, who in his later childhood had seduced him to performing in that fashion. *French* may symbolize either fellatio or
cunnilingus, and the *painless falling out of teeth* (Freud) symbolizes masturbation in either sex. There is, finally, a bisexual displacement symbol: *the eye*.

The little girl who showed so much distress over her discovery of "castration" (see Section I, above) ended the period of
her acute anxiety with a sudden great interest in eyes. I again
quote the observations my colleague jotted down for me.[34]

> It began with the child's abruptly turning her attention to a
> photograph on the desk and asking, "Where daddy's eyes?" She
> looks at and gently feels her mother's eyes. She runs out of the
> room and soon comes back to play. We play a game of "cry" at
> her instigation. "Mommy cry." (I oblige with a crying face.) "You
> will not cry." (All right, I won't.)
> [After about five or six days, she] began drawing again, an oc-
> cupation she [had] neglected for quite some time. Early in the
> day she was "drawing" letters, or rather her squiggles which she
> calls letters. In the afternoon she drew a circle. "That Beth." In
> it she put a mouth (?) which she didn't identify, *eyes*, a forehead,
> and then *more eyes* and then began drawing *more eyes* on an-
> other part of the page. She then put a longer wiggly line by the
> eyes and called it by a nonsense word which she has recently
> used and which I feel sure represents phallus.

[34] I again thank Dr. Beatrice Enson for putting this account at my disposal.

When she played with dolls during the next days and weeks she would always touch the dolls' *eyes* and often asked about *eyes* [belonging to her parents] and others [italics added].

This assurance of the "hermaphroditic" complexion closely preceded the eventual termination of the little girl's acutely anxious state.

These are the few bisexual symbols I know; all others, in particular when they stand for an element of the pleasure-physiological body ego rather than for a function, represent, if they do, the genital of only one sex.

E. COLOR SYMBOLISM

The subject of color in dreams has lately produced a wealth of rather uninstructive articles in psychoanalytic journals. If one wishes to approach it properly one must make certain distinctions:

The *whole dream* may be in color. No one has proffered an explanation as to why this happens occasionally, and what it means if it happens. I myself have not the slightest idea.

Certain *elements* in a dream are colored. This poses no problem. If the dreamer associates to them, these elements are no different from any others in the manifest content; in most instances the color is dream material.

Color *symbolism*. I have observed only two colors which are not merely picturizations but potentially symbolic. Their actual symbolic employment is of course as is that of any symbol, not confined to the dream.

1. *Blue* = *anal*

The symbolization of the quality anal through the color blue is also an element, one must assume, in the symbol "sky" (cf. 9, above).

I reproduce at this point material stemming from two psychotherapeutic sessions of a young schizophrenic girl. In general, one need know no more about her than that for one thing she had a strong scoptophilic interest in my "backside"—an interest that came to the fore whenever I entered the office ahead of her or turned away from her to the window in order to close it. For another thing, although of average intelligence, she was obstinately incredulous, doubting whatever one told her.

In the first of these sessions she reports fantasying during defecation that I am present and watching. When it becomes evident that she wants to exhibit and "do it for me," as does a child for the mother, she reacts with distress. Subsequently she expresses a particular liking for a *blue* suit that she has seen me wear. (I doubt whether I even owned a blue suit at this time; unfortunately my notes are ambiguous on this point.)

The second session begins with the delusion that I have put on that blue suit for her because she had told me yesterday that she liked it. (Here my notes are precise: I was actually wearing a gray pepper and salt tweed which had some red flecks in it but no blue.) She, however, does wear for the first time during her treatment a combination of a blue sweater and skirt. She is given no actual symbolic translation but told sparingly that this signifies a mutual showing whereby the blue clothing substitutes for the "backside." She responds with an urge to defecate and the fantasy of having for my benefit a bowel movement on the couch "with a blue ribbon round it." It is this fantasy that removes her doubt as to the meaning of blue; she exclaims with obvious relief: "Now I am convinced."

Another woman patient was sexually aroused by a maid clad in a blue uniform and cleaning the floor on all fours. She reverted to the incident several times, never failing to mention that the uniform was a blue one. A subsequent dream affirmed her interest, while denying it by having the maid stand motionless next to a mop; yet the sponge on the mop was blue. I refrain from describing the excessive olfactory curiosity of this patient in matters cloacal and anal.

2. Green = pregnant

The symbolical use of this color is, as is all symbolization, unexplainable. One may merely mention a popular German saying, *Gruen is die Farbe der Hoffnung* ("Green is the color of hope") and explain that *Sie ist guter Hoffnung* is one way of stating "She is pregnant." I regret not having made any illustrative clinical notes.

I am not aware that the idiom exists in French. Yet the great Couperin, composer and observer of humanity without peer, divides one of his famous suites, *Les Folies Françaises, ou les Dominoes,* by coordinating a colored costume to the title of each of its parts while unifying them through the key of B minor.

La Virginité, sous le Domino couleur invisible
La Pudeur, sous le Domino couleur le rose
L'Ardeur, sous le Domino incarnat
L'esperance, sous le Domino vert, *etc.*

In other words, in a progression from virginity to shame, ardor, and hope, the latter is associated with green.

Needless to add that these two potentially symbolic colors may also be merely employed for the purpose of picturization.

I have never observed of any color other than blue and green that it had a symbolic meaning.

F. NUMBER SYMBOLISM

There are but a few remarks to be made on this subject because there are only two numbers known to have a symbolic meaning, to which I am possibly able to add a third. "The number three," writes Freud (1900) "has been confirmed from many sides as a symbol for the male genitals" (p. 358), and there is little doubt that two can signify the female. All other numbers, those treated by Freud in *The Interpretation of Dreams,* for example, are, although he does not directly say so, allusive. None of them are of course, limited to the dream.

A psychotic mother insists on stopping by at her married daughter's house at a time that is utterly inconvenient. Arguing over the phone, she says that it is "only a matter of five or 10 minutes," which the daughter denies although she is eventually compelled to accept her coming.

I felt, on the basis of previous amnesia removal, as well as on that of the mother's present behavior, entitled to remark in the patient's session that the mother actually does impose upon her and that five and 10—the number of fingers of one or both hands—are allusive to masturbation.

A short while later two events emerge from repression. In the first the mother exhibits on the toilet allowing the curious child to touch her clitoris to the point of masturbation, while masturbating the child herself. In the second the mother masturbates herself as well as the child on the bed. Because in doing so she inflicts painful overstimulation, the child tries to defend herself by pummeling the mother, who reacts by forcefully slapping her into submission.

One has the choice between calling the unconscious indirect mode of representation by the numbers five and 10 either allusion or conceivably even *pars par toto*, but one certainly cannot call it symbolic. Nevertheless, it bears closer scrutiny. I would consider the misleading application of these numbers to minutes as doubly determined: once through repression and once through the "return of the repressed." On the one hand it is the countercathexis, maintaining the repression that gives the numbers the deceptive entity "minute"; on the other it is the "buoyancy" of the repressed that does so because five or 10 minutes may actually be the space of time necessary to the stimulation ending in an orgastic reaction. I omit a description of the dramatic identification with this mother, collateral to the amnesia removal of the activities in which she is a sexual object.

I would not have mentioned any of this were it not in order to show that what I have learned from Freud's *The Interpretation of Dreams* is, as I stated above, for one thing, not confined to the dream and can, for another, if the allusive role played by number is interpreted at the right time, be extremely productive: any corporal violence by the mother toward the patient, for instance, had for years been steadfastly denied although I was convinced that it must have been used. The removal of the amnesia for the one instance of it, described above, opened the gates for further memories of an almost continuous punitive abuse of the child by the mother over an indeterminate period.

I close with the brief report on two clinical observations and one instance from fiction.

Circumstances forced on a young woman an unforeseen expense that she could not meet. She eventually called her well-to-do father, who spontaneously—as I, knowing him, had predicted—asked: "How much money do you need? I'll send you a check for $200 right away." In reporting this, she remarked: "But I can't bring myself to tell him that I need $400."

This observation should be discussed with regard to two of its aspects, entirely different from each other except that both are concerned with numbers.

I had for years noticed that the unconscious disregards zeros; we had therefore to deal here with two and four instead of 200 and 400. Since this is nowhere stated in the comprehensive German edition of Freud's writings, I considered it an original observation. In 1958, however, a small, rather strange, but it seems to me, very important book became available. It had been written in 1911 by Freud in collaboration with Professor Ernst Oppenheim, and was called *Dreams in Folklore* (1911). In it one finds a footnote, "Psycho-analytic experience shows that noughts appended to numbers in dreams can be ignored in interpretation" (Freud & Oppenheim, 1911, p. 186). Freud, in other words, knew this long ago, and I cannot imagine why he omitted it in his *Collected Works*. Needless to stress again that it is not confined to the dream.

It appears to me that in the female child's pleasure-physiological body ego only two labia—the labia majora—are represented, while the mature woman's represents four: the labia majora and the labia minora (II, 109).

The patient cited above, who asked her father on the telephone for money, had two psychotic parents: a mother, who besides innumerable sexual exploitations had deflorated her, and the father, who when she was five played with her on his lap. On these occasions she felt not only his erection but her own genital opening wide. The scene habitually ended with the man dropping her abruptly, leaving her in a state of arousement; whereupon he would rush upstairs to the toilet. It appeared probable that, unable to contain himself, he had masturbated in order to discharge his excitation; but one will, of course, never know.

Because the daughter had remained for him a sexual object, which I inferred from other data at the time of her analysis, I became convinced that although she did not want to ask for more money she could not present herself as mature even though only symbolically through the number four and on the telephone. For she would then have been able to complete the sexual act which would have meant incest. She was, of course, unable to enjoy any man. I believe that *the number four interpreted here is symbolic.*

The second example is more complicated; it requires the same perseverance in assembling and eventually coordinating scraps of material found in Freud's *The Interpretation of Dreams.*

It concerns the analysis of a woman who had finally realized being beset by homosexual fantasies practically all day long. Any remotely allusive apperception and any deflection of thought allowing for rumination could now, i.e., after enough analysis, stimulate these preconscious fantasies to the extent of their becoming conscious.[35] In the hour under consideration she reports having to choose a theatrical show for an evening out with her husband and their children. Her first choice was a musical with a young woman singer in the lead. This, however, would cost $40 for the four of them, and she rejected it as too expensive. She had previously led my attention to her childhood by saying: "Can I choose a show? Must I not ask 'Daddy' [her husband]?"

I ask: "Was there not a '40' in yesterday's hour?" (I knew there was, but I had forgotten the context.) She replies: "Of course; the boy in the supermarket." The patient had arrived very disturbed for her hour because the boy who counts up the purchases in the supermarket had, in totaling hers, cheated himself out of 40 cents, and she had been unable to bring herself to correct him. What if the market made the poor fellow pay? She meant to tell him, but her mouth "refused to open," she said, as it did in the beginning of her analysis whenever she held something against me. Amongst other things she had bought a certain food, although doubtful whether her husband would like it. This doubt, her exaggerated reaction to the episode with the boy, and the number 40, had struck me, but I could make nothing of them.

It was different in the next hour, to which this report is devoted.

---

[35] Cf. Freud (1909b): "During the progress of a psychoanalysis it is not only the patient who plucks up courage but his disease as well; it grows bold enough to speak more plainly than before (p. 223).

Here the 40, followed by four, is attached to seeing, and a woman at that. In addition there were further associations, all pertinent to the theme; it suffices however to mention but one. We knew that seeing a woman displaying herself on the stage was apt to greatly arouse her scoptophilic desire. The night before she had seen a woman singer on television, whom she described as tall, blond, and with a good figure; she had immediately felt compelled to undress her, in fantasy, to the waist. This repeated, by means of allusion, the breast play in adolescence with a friend. I had heard of the play before, but I learned only now that it had consisted actually in kissing each other's breasts; and that she had expected the friend, on the strength of her unusual voice, to become a professional singer.

The analyst reading this material, knows that it is full of displacement from "below" to "above" (Freud) even if he is ignorant of the symbolic meaning of four or if there had not been, one or two days before, a dream showing a nude woman with emphasis on the pubic hair, lying on a bed on a stage whose curtains (= labia) were drawn apart.

When I translated the symbolism for the patient, she remembered a particularly bizarre exhibition of her psychotic mother, acquainting the child unmistakably with the four labia of the adult. I asked her: "Weren't you four years old at the time?" And she answered: "Of course; we moved into that house only after I was three." As though another four had been needed!

The example from fiction demonstrates the meaning of two.

I have been able to show on more than one occasion that Shakespeare's writings convey a knowledge of the human mind, comparable in their accuracy and profundity only to Freud's. He has painted the picture of the 14-year-old Juliet in great detail. I will briefly examine one particular trait, which on the surface appears senseless.

> JULIET: . . . come civill night,
> Thou sobersuted Matron all in blacke,
> And learne me how to loose a winning matche,
> Plaid for a paire of stainlesse Maiden-heads [III, 2].

If this is taken at face value, the virginal Juliet would have two hymens—which is absurd. However, if it is remembered that the hymen is not represented in the pleasure-physiological body ego except in the act of defloration (cf. Section B, #1, above), the displacement onto the child's two labia becomes intelligible. Yet, what gives one the right to treat the matured 14-year-old as a child? The passage gives one the right. Juliet, although impatiently yearning for Romeo, does not appeal *to him* for her defloration but to the "sober suited Matron," the mother. It is, in other words, the *preoedipal* sexuality which persists behind the oedipal one and frequently extends on into the girl's puberty, that the writer intimates subtly. He reminds one of Freud's saying that the mother "teaches" the child to love.

Thus interpreted, the strange passage becomes understandable, which is the proof of the interpretation.

The present section, dealing with particular symbols cannot, as was the preceding one devoted to the theory of the symbol, be concluded. It can only be discontinued, and its cessation is bound to appear arbitrary as well as abrupt. It is actually abrupt although not arbitrary; because, while some of the symbols treated in it are commonly known but are more fully discussed than they have been before, most of them are described here for the first time. There is no principle in their selection; they are chance observations of one analyst during his clinical work. Their description can therefore be nothing more than an enumeration. Having said what symbols one has found there is nothing to do but stop. Yet, even with future additions, a list, I imagine, it will remain; for I cannot envisage either the explanation of a single symbol or a principle yielding a system of symbolization.

III. POSTSCRIPT: SOME RESULTS OF SYMBOL TRANSLATION

A brief postscript may be devoted to a few personal observations that have surprised me although they should probably have been expected. Since they were made—in contrast to almost all those reported in the present volume—outside of analysis, I shall in the interests of anonymity give them the complexion of small stories rather than of clinical illustrations.

Psychotics and children are known, as is the dreamer, to employ primary process thought with all its unconscious means of representation. *Amongst these, symbolization appears as a particularly potent means; at least if one allows* oneself to focus upon its secondary employment as a *mechanism of defense.*

This latent defense function becomes manifest when the symbol is translated by exchanging it for the symbolized element. There are a number of different effects of such translation: I have seen only three of them, which I shall attempt to describe.

A Certain Unintelligible Behavior Becomes Immediately Intelligible

(1) An elderly couple share a love of music. The husband, however, lacks musical literacy and all but the most rudimentary knowledge, whereas the wife is an amateur pianist. Yet she plays only when he cannot hear her, particularly at night, when he has gone upstairs. His occasional protests—"Why don't you ever let me hear you? I am not critical. Couldn't be, since I do not know the difference between good and bad."—have been of no avail.

In order to understand the woman's puzzling behavior (for the couple were otherwise devoted to each other) one needs merely to recall Freud's (1915–1917) words: "Satisfaction obtained from a person's own genitals is indicated by all kinds of *playing,* including piano-playing" (p. 156). In other words: she must not masturbate within earshot of her husband who is to be kept in ignorance of such activity.

(2) A man of advanced age began to take piano lessons from a gifted young man who came to the older man's house for the purpose, yet he was hardly ever on time. Once he was actually half an hour late (for an hour lesson). When pupil and teacher at this time sat down at the piano and the pupil expected the teacher to indicate what of the previous assignment he wished to hear first, the teacher suddenly got up and ignoring his utterly surprised pupil's question as to why he was leaving, went

out the door, got into his car, and drove away, saying over his shoulder only, "I'm not interested."

When I heard of this episode, my "analytic ear" told me that the otherwise incomprehensible story became comprehensible only if one assumed that the teacher, a bachelor, was psychotic and had hallucinated being "propositioned" by his pupil. Playing the piano together would then become mutual masturbation. This, of course, was pure speculation on my part. In order to validate it, I needed more, in particular something equivalent to the "proposition." I therefore asked to be told the whole story in detail. Here it is:

That day upon arriving, the teacher (who was also an organist) had come in saying cheerily: "I guess you thought I wasn't coming!" His excuse: the delivery of a new "organ" that he had been eagerly awaiting and that he could not refrain from *playing* to try it out. In so doing he had *lost track of time*, he said. The pupil asked mildly, without censure, if, should he be so late again, since waiting so long was tiring, he would be good enough to *telephone* him. Here again symbol translation renders the incomprehensible story intelligible and coherent. If telephoning symbolizes masturbation (cf. Section 3C, above), asking for it is asking for masturbation, that is, making a sexual proposition. The context in which the symbol is embedded leaves no doubt that the translation is correct. The teacher gets a new "organ" on which he "plays": his organ is "new" because it entered his pleasure-physiological body ego consequent to the proprioception of its excitation. He "plays" with it and loses track of time as one does in the climactic phase. Through the symbolic proposition, the telephoning, and sitting down in order to play the piano together also become symbolic, and the young man bolts, declaring himself "not interested [in being seduced]."

Certain Symbolic Actions Understood

A woman celebrity said to a newspaper interviewer: "I'm not put together right." This, in its briefest and most general form is a complaint with which certain patients familiarize us to express the fact that, although their bodies are normal, there is something wrong with their pleasure-physiologic body ego. Ordinarily the latter, a psychic formation, reflects the former, a physical one. In some psychotics, however, it does not: they perceive parts of themselves as disproportionate to the rest, as distorted or even as missing. Because the pleasure-physiologic body ego is projectable into the object world (II, 246-254), one may also hear of the strangest distortions of objects. These objects include clothes.

Add to the foregoing an observation, the source of which I am not free to name: no matter for whom a psychotic dressmaker works objectively, subjectively she makes clothing for herself. Having come this far, you are ready for the following brief report on the work of two psychotic seamstresses—a report which I, personally ignorant of the craft, had to borrow from an expert. I shall therefore quote it verbatim.

> Both dressmakers were professionals—experienced and manually dextrous. One of them, however, cut into the front facing of a very fine coat, in complete negation of the usual practices at this point, in such a way that the hemline could never be let down later. She, furthermore, on a woman's dress coat sewed as holds for outer buttons, tailored buttons such as are put only on men's heavy outdoor or sport coats.
>
> The inside belting hooks on a skirt were so placed that only another person could get them together easily. Hooks and eyes at the necklines of dresses were reversed, although neither of the sewers was left-handed. In the same skirt, of a delicate cotton known to the trade as "handkerchief thin," she placed a heavy and clumsy zipper such as would go on a boy's work pants, and a huge thick snap to match.
>
> The second dressmaker, although again a competent craftswoman, was unable to fit anything; everything was either misshapen or too large or too tight. All she could really do was alter hems. Oddly enough she could refit men's slacks or shorts perfectly, from simple measurements, without a fitting proper.

Here again the final elucidation depends upon symbol translation: clothes symbolize nudity (Freud). It is this translation that shows the symbolic actions or omissions of the two dressmakers to be the equivalent of the woman quoted at the beginning of this section, in their feeling of not being "put together right."

An Utterance Seemingly At Variance With Theory Becomes Reconciled With It

This example shows a result of symbol translation altogether different from the others. A girl of three or four had a newly-born baby brother. Since her mother was already working, two friends of the mother took the little girl, who knew them both well, home from nursery school. When the adults had dismounted from the bus and were helping the child down the steps, she said suddenly, in a faintly apologetic tone: "I wish Charlie (the baby) would fall down the stairs!"

This, except for the slightly self-excusing tone of voice, contradicts theory, inasmuch as a normal child in the phallic phase is supposed to be ambivalent, not almost purely aggressive. Yet a symbolic reading of the brief episode reconciles observation with theory by showing the libidinal complement to the aggressive wish: the two women friends, that is, two categorically identical persons, become the mother (cf. Section A, 3, above), and the stairs (of the bus) the vagina. Thus, while wishing the baby dead the child at the same times asks the mother to give it birth and proves indeed as ambivalent as theory wills it.

My reason for publishing the above examples, although their number is so lamentably small, is to stimulate others to investigate the results of symbol translation. I am sure that there is a considerable variety of such results and that it would profit psychoanalysis if they were known.

I expect the reader's resistance to the subject of ambulatory psychosis will fasten itself onto the fact that these observations are made outside of the analytic situation and therefore cannot be valid. I do not know that anyone might go so far as to extend his doubt to the absurd behavior of the piano teacher, but there remain the wife in the first example and the seamstresses in the third. Those refusing me credence may remember that from the standpoint of the present subject the diagnosis is not important because primary-process thought is not the prerogative of the psychotic. The creative writer shares in it (cf. Boccaccio, above) as do the nonpsychotic patients associating freely and—as Freud has found—individuals making a joke.

CHAPTER TWO

ON THE DREAM

In his Preface to the Third English Edition of *The Interpretation of Dreams* Freud wrote in 1931 that the original book, published in 1900, had remained "essentially unaltered. It contains," he goes on to say, "even according to my present-day judgment the most valuable of all the discoveries it has been my good fortune to make" (p. xxxii). If one considers further how voluminous and exhaustive *The Interpretation* has gradually become and that Freud in the course of time added 13 publications to the subject of the dream (only one of which is duplicative), one will surely expect any addenda to dream theory to be minor.

The present chapter contains four such addenda. The first two may definitely prove themselves addenda; the last two, abortive and often speculative as they are, may perhaps engage the interest of a few analytic observers for the sake of their own future work.

I. TOWARD A THEORY OF DREAM HALLUCINATION

This short section is devoted to a single speculative proposition based upon a number of premises, which, however, are not at all speculative.

(1) To begin with, Freud has reflected on the fact that imagination, however vivid, is never taken for reality; if it were, it would be hallucination. The problem is that it is so regularly

taken for reality by the dreamer that one must say the dreamer hallucinates. This of course was known before Freud. The question is: why does he?

(2) The next premise owes its existence entirely to Freud's genius: no dream can arise unless an unconscious infantile dream wish calls it into existence.

(3) This dream wish is bound to set erogenic or "pleasure-physiologic" processes into motion because otherwise it could not present itself as fulfilled, and its wish-fulfilling nature is the one indispensable factor for dream formation.

(4) In the manifest content the pleasure-physiologic processes often although by no means always reflect themselves as symbols, because by definition a symbol represents a pleasure-physiologic element of process.

(5) Since the dreamer perceives his experiences, his ego must, of course, have reintegratively possessed itself of his perceptory apparatus.

(6) In order to evaluate the hallucinating dreamer's situation fully, however, one must consider a revolutionary statement left us by Freud in his posthumous *Outline* (1940), a statement which has hitherto not been put to use. He is describing how we receive conscious information—from inside the body, from sense organs, and from the terminal organs—and he adds, ". . . *as regards the terminal organ of sensation* and feeling, the body itself would take the place of the external world" (p. 162; italics added).

(7) Freud has always made much of the fact that the sleeper relinquishes all cathexis of the environment and that the dreamer perpetuates this relinquishment. It is only on rare occasions that the environment will overcome the cathexis withdrawal and force itself upon the sleeper. In this case, if the latter is unable to ignore the potentially sleep-disturbing stimulation, he may react in one of two ways: he either succeeds in weaving into a dream the perception of the stimulus issuing from the object world and by so doing continues sleep, or he becomes overwhelmed by the perception and is forced to wake up.

For the first of these two alternatives Freud's own dream the Pope is dead (1900, p. 232) is paradigmatic. At the price of a dream he remains unaware of the nocturnal ringing of the church bells that endanger his sleep. In his dream he vents his annoyance on the head of the church, not of course without the assistance of an infantile dream wish: a death wish against the father *(Papa* = Latin for Pope).

For so intense and so persistent a stimulus from the environment that it enforces arousal, the three Hildebrandt dreams (1900, pp. 27–28) are paradigmatic. The irresistible stimulus is an alarm clock; but in each dream one sees the dreamer first trying Freud's technique by attempting to interpret the stimulus as compatible with the continuance of sleep; he weaves it into a dream until eventually the failure of his attempt compels his arousal.

(8) Throughout his work Freud's discussion of the sleeper's and dreamer's withdrawal of cathexis from the environment concerned but one environment, the object world. Yet his posthumous statement, quoted above, revolutionizes the discussion. There are now two environments to decathect: the object world and the body.

(9) The relinquishment of each of these must be investigated separately because the results are not in all points the same.

(10) To complete the picture as far as is possible at present, one must add that the dreamer's body ego proper is also decathected to the extent that, roughly speaking, only the pleasure-physiologic body ego remains subject to perception. Exempt from perception and therefore suspended are those functions in particular which in wakefulness would distinguish the second environment from the first, that is, the body from the object world.

Not only the visual but also the tactile and kinesthetic stimuli which make me know when awake that I am lying in bed remain unperceived and do not therefore interfere with my dreaming, for instance, that I roam the woods.

The dreamer's actual ego-boundaries, to use current analytic parlance, are decathected, and fantastic ones, more or less distinct, take their place in his dream. This decathexis, combined with that of the environment, prevents all perceptive feeling. Instead, ego and object world, both deceptive, are supplied by imagination. As to the pleasure-physiologic body ego, its perception is twofold: pleasure-physiology or its ultimate consequences may be perceived directly or indirectly. In the case of direct perception, an affect or a sensation arises exactly as it would were the dreamer awake. This instance, not confined to and consequently not specific for the dream, does not bear upon the present discussion, which centers entirely around the second instance, where a pleasure-physiologic process is perceived indirectly. Here certain elements in the imagined environment are representative not only of memory traces but of percepts. In other words, they are overdetermined by the indirect perception —in most cases pictorial or symbolic—of a pleasure-physiologic process. That process, however, is real and its perception concurrent.

It will have been noted that the above brief discussion of the withdrawal from the object world (cf. #7), centered almost exclusively around the wish to sleep. The wish could prevail or it could be frustrated; and when the stimulus impinging on the wish appeared in the dream, it did so in consequence of an attempt, successful or unsuccessful, to guard sleep against it. Such a disturbing stimulus can also issue from the body and be elaborated upon in the dream; successfully if sleep continues, or unsuccessfully if the dreamer wakes up.

Freud's grandiose denial of an extremely painful perineal abscess in his dream of riding on a horse (1900, pp. 229–230), which shows him riding horseback unimpaired and looking down on a colleague, is an impressive example for a successful elaboration. Failures where pain, a bodily need, or an uncontrollable affect arouses the dreamer are too well known to require exemplification.

However, the dreamer's withdrawal from the second environment, his body, while rarely impeded by pain, is regularly interfered with by pleasure-physiologic processes consequent to the unconscious infantile dream wish. These pleasure-physiologic processes are as ubiquitous as is the wish that precipitates them—a fact leading to the recognition that it is much more difficult to decathect the second environment than the first. The sleeper's withdrawal from the object world has found its classic and complete description by Freud; clinically one can say that it is usually successful. In trying to describe the cathexis withdrawal from the body, one must acknowledge that one's body stays with one and that the slightest stimuli issuing from it are able to enter the dream. A discussion of the dreamer's cathexis withdrawal from his body will therefore appear paradoxical when compared with Freud's discussion of the cathexis withdrawal from the object world: it parallels Freud's description inasmuch as there is, in effect, also only one environment with which the dreamer has to contend, yet deviates from Freud's because that single environment is not the first one, the object world, but the second, the body. In it the unconscious infantile dream wish will—as was said before—precipitate pleasure-physiologic processes, many of which will be represented in the dream. The predominant mode of such representation is—as has also been said—the symbol.

If the dream consisted only of representations of pleasure-physiologic processes, symbolic or otherwise, the question of why the dreamer, in contrast to the awake individual, is convinced of the reality of the products of his imagination, would allow for a simple answer. *The subjective quality "real" that distinguishes hallucination from imagination, reflects the objective quality "real" of the pleasure-physiologic process—a quality that attaches itself to the representation of the process in the dream.* This is possible because the body is practically the dreamer's sole environment, which he (unlike the nondreaming sleeper who succeeds where the dreamer fails) is unable to decathect.

Naturally the dream does not consist only of representations of pleasure-physiologic processes. Nevertheless, *I hold the answer to be valid for all of the dreamer's hallucinations.* I do so because the dream is pervaded by condensation, a term denoting an aspect of the primary process, the effects of which Freud has described as "enormous." The analytic reader, familiar with the phenomenon, is perhaps less so with Freud's theory for it. He may at any rate be reminded of a short passage in Freud's systematic treatment of the dream work that has become meaningful to this writer only recently, and in the present context.

"But although condensation makes the dream obscure," Freud (1916–1917) writes, "it does not give one the impression of being an effect of the dream-censorship. It seems traceable to some *mechanical*[1] or economic factor . . ." (p. 173; italics added). What could such a "mechanical" factor conceivably be but a pleasure-physiologic process? Or, to rephrase the question: why should the dreamer react differently to the intrusion of pleasure-physiologic "affectivity" (Freud)—of a motor (secretory, vessel regulatory) discharge—into his dream than to the obviously mechanical ringing of a bell?[1]

> ROMEO: I dreampt a dreame to night.
> MERCUTIO: And so did I.
> ROMEO: Well what was yours?
> MERCUTIO: That dreamers often lye.
> ROMEO: In bed a sleepe while they do *dreame things true.*
> MERCUTIO: *O then I see Queene Mab hath beene with you:* she is the Fairies Midwife, & she comes in shape no bigger than agat-stone on the forefinger of an Alderman . . . she *gallops night by night* . . . on Courtiers knees, that dreame on Curtsies strait; ore Lawyers fingers, who strait dreamt on Fees, ore Ladies lips, who strait on kisses dreame, which oft the angry Mab with blisters plagues, because their breath with Sweet meats tainted are. Sometimes she gallops ore a Courtiers nose, & then dreames he of smelling out a suite: & sometime comes she with Tith pigs tale, tickling a Parsons nose as a lies asleepe, then he dreames of

---

[1] Shakespeare must have thought as much, for in Marcutio's tale of Queen Mab the, in this case external, "mechanical" stimulation (by the "Faries Midwife") of an erogenic zone produces dreams fulfilling a wish attached to the day residue. The tale is placed in a discussion of "truth" in dreams, in other words, of hallucination.

Here the mechanical stimulation of an erogenic zone is, as in sexual foreplay, an external one: The touch of the Fairy Queen Mab. But it explains, as the italicized fragment of dialogue shows, why sleepers "do dreame things true," in other words, why they believe their hallucinatory wish fulfillment.

another Benefice. Sometimes she driveth ore a Souldiers necke, &
then dreams he of cutting Forraine throats, of Breaches, Ambus-
cados, Spanish Blades: Of Healths five Fadome deepe, and then
anon drums in his eares, at which he startes and wakes; and
being thus frighted, sweares a prayer or two & sleepes againe
. . . [*Romeo and Juliet:* I, iv; italics added].

A theory of dream hallucination is not, however, dependent
upon the above interpretation of Freud's "mechanical" factor.
If the theory is correct, pleasure-physiology may contribute to
condensation; if it is not, the two merely co-exist. In either case
condensation could be credited with extending the hallucinatory effect of a single pleasure-physiologic process over an indeterminate stretch of manifest content, and by so doing explain the often apparent continuity of hallucination in the face
of the discontinuous pleasure-physiologic stimulation.

The hypothesis presented here would gain credibility if it
could be shown that the pleasure-physiologic stimulus is not
only objectively but also subjectively real. I believe this can be
done.

Freud opposed "affectivity," causing internal alteration of the
individual's own body without relation to the environment, to
"motility," finding its expression in actions destined to accomplish the alteration of the environment. His discovery of the
two environments necessitates reformulation to the extent that
affectivity alters the second environment, the body, and motility alters the first, the object world. Of motility Freud has explained that it is instrumental in reality testing. "The system
Cs," he writes (1917),

must have at its disposal a motor innervation which determines
whether the perception can be made to disappear or whether it
proves resistant. Reality-testing need be nothing more than this
contrivance [p. 233]. A perception which is made to disappear
by an action is recognized as external, as reality; where such an
action makes no difference, the perception originates within the
subject's own body—it is real. . . . [p. 232].

In other words, we judge an object in the first environment to be real if the ego is able to employ motility toward an alteration of that environment in such a way that the object is no longer perceived; if motility fails in effecting such alteration, it is something in the second environment, the individual's body, that initiated and maintains the perception. If an alarm clock arouses me prematurely and I am able to turn it off to continue sleep, I am convinced that the ringing was real; had it been in my head I could not have turned it off. Motility has, in other words, eliminated a stimulation issuing from the first environment, the object world, and in so doing made the objectively real stimulus also subjectively real.

Can one escape the conclusion that with regard to pleasure-physiologic stimulation affectivity plays exactly the role for the body, the second environment, that motility plays for the first? It supplies a reality testing by effecting discharge: the body is altered to the extent that the stimulus disappears and, with it, the perception to which it had given rise. It is thus that the objectively real pleasure-physiologic process becomes subjectively real.

The economic advantage for the dreamer of the reality testing through discharge over that through motility lies, of course, in the fact that he can perform discharge without waking. He may, therefore, compelled by the wish to sleep, even attempt to transform a stimulus from the first environment into one from the second. He does so by interpreting the perception of a stimulation, issuing from the object world, as that of a pleasure-physiologic process in his body. This would seem to occur in certain arousal dreams.

I am unfortunately not able to illustrate such a reinterpretation with dream material; and neither was Freud, who chose instead a series of humorous drawings, in which—as he expresses it (1900)—an "ingenious artist has . . . cleverly depicted the struggle between an obstinate craving for sleep and an inexhaustible stimulus towards waking" (p. 368).

With regard to the present subject the "dream" does much more than merely depict this struggle. The drawings transcribe graphically a sequence of symbols and picturizations, expressive of a pleasure-physiologic sequence; and they show at the same time the reality testing mentioned above: the dreamer's (in this instance unsuccessful) attempts to abolish the pleasure-physiologic stimulation through discharge. They illustrate, in other words, the objective as well as the subjective reality of a complicated pleasure-physiologic process. It is to this reality, both objective and subjective, that the dream owes the quality "real," which transforms the dreamer's imagination into hallucination.

The reader will do well to open at this point *The Interpretation of Dreams* (Freud, 1900, p. 368), where the drawings are reproduced; for without looking at them he will not understand either Freud's comment on the page before, or mine. The pictures represent a French nurse's dream. She tries to continue sleeping in spite of the increasingly louder screaming of the little boy under her care who wants to be taken up and assisted in urination. What the drawings depict is "the struggle between an obstinate craving for sleep and an inexhaustible stimulus towards waking" (p. 367). Freud's comment, which the reader is asked to study in full, treats the dream essentially as one "of convenience": the more insistently the boy demands the nurse's arousal, the more emphatically the dream assures her that she is already complying with his demand and therefore need not wake up. Yet in so doing, the dream, as Freud expresses it, *"translates the increasing stimulus into the increasing dimensions of its symbol"* (p. 367; italics added). The boy's stream floods the scene, carries first a rowboat and eventually a steamship, until at last the prolongation of sleep through dreaming reaches its end: the nurse awakens and perceives the actual stimulus and its source.

In saying that the dream translates the arousal stimulus into the dimensions of the symbol Freud unwittingly implies that it transforms the stimulus originating in the first environment, the object world, into one issuing from the second, the dreamer's body. He does so because a symbol by definition represents a pleasure-physiologic process and because pleasure-physiological stimulation issuing from the boy offers the chance of being abolished and thereby allowing sleep to continue, in contrast to the persisting perception of stimulation issuing from the object world that enforces arousal.

The nurse's dream (reproduced by Freud under the heading of Urinary Symbolism) also allows for a more detailed comment, to be rendered below.

Freud (1900) himself has made a general comment on arousal dreams upon actual bodily stimulation that implies at least one more important detail. "Such dreams," he writes, "exhibit not only the tendency to wish fulfillment and the character [as dreams] of convenience quite openly but very often also a perfectly transparent symbolism as well; for it is not infrequent that what leads to the arousal is a stimulus *whose gratification under symbolic disguise had already been attempted in vain* in the dream" (p. 402; translation mine). He follows this with a brief discussion of dreams of emission or orgasm and dreams precipitated by urinary or defecatory urges.

Elsewhere (Freud & Oppenheim, 1911), while interpreting two particular arousal dreams, he expresses himself explicitly in what must be regarded as support of my general thesis. In the first instance he writes: "When [or "if": the German *wenn* allows for either] the sleeper feels a need to defecate, he dreams of gold, or treasure . . ." (p. 187); and in the second: "The sleeper is overcome by a strong erotic need which is indicated in fairly clear symbols in the beginning of the dream. (He had heard that wheat—probably equivalent to semen—was standing at a high price. He charged forward in order to drive with horse and cart—genital symbols—into the open gates of Heaven.)" (p. 194).[2] In conclusion Freud admits furthermore that "a group of dreams" is reducible "to [as his examples show, sexual or infantile sexual] needs and wishes *which have become immediate*" (p. 203; italics added).

Freud's remarks leave no doubt about the actual presence of pleasure-physiology concomitant with its symbolization. Where he confined himself to the arousal dream, I have merely sup-

---

[2] Correction: Wheat is not a symbol for semen; but the high price (*Vermoegen*) represents potency, and the "standing" may be allusive. The charging forward with horse and cart is a pictorially modified symbol for the forceful *Verkehr*; the gate of Heaven is an obvious picturization.

plied the data compelling one to suppose simultaneity of pleasure-physiologic process and symbolization (or other indirect
representation) in all dreams or dream parts containing hallucination. The simultaneity need not exist throughout; but there
must be enough of it in a dream to cause, with the assistance of
condensation, the hallucinatory effect.

Returning to the fictitious nurse's dream the *first* picture illustrates
the dream of convenience: the nurse takes a walk with the child
whose wish can be gratified without the inconvenience of waking up.[3]

In the *second* picture the transformation begins because the boy,
while being the child, is also "the little one," i.e., the genital of the
nurse (Freud) who gratifies her own need while assuming a quasi-
urinary posture. That the nurse's performance is phallic conforms to
the regressive character of the dream.

The *third* picture bears this out by increasing the child's stream to
the extent that it could only be understood as the nurse's.

In the *fourth* picture the urethral-erotic nature of the nurse's activity (in contrast to a purely urinary one) becomes evident through the
inclusion of "the boy in the boat." In American slang this denotes the
clitoris, whose quasi-symbolic appearance in the manifest content pic-
turizes the entry of the organ into the pleasure-physiologic body ego
of the dreamer (II, 238–240; cf. also I, 170). At the same time it becomes clear that the dreamer's attempt to prolong her sleep is enuretic, which again agrees with the regressive nature of the dream. She
floods with increasing vigor not the street (vagina—Freud) but the
roadway *(Verkehr* symbolism—Freud) so that the water supports an
ever heavier boat.[4]

In the *fifth* picture the boy in the boat is replaced by a man in a
gondola: the girl's clitoris erected and her vulva became turgescent.
At the same time she appears small and distant, while the symbols for
the organs involved in the pleasure-physiologic process occupy all
available space: partial subject formation (II, 80–81; cf. also my remarks on Priapus, I, 271).

[3] I remember a psychotic patient who wet the bed while dreaming that she was on
the toilet; and a neurotic one, whose need, which she did not gratify, made her dream
of several locales where she could have done so: a bathroom, a protected outdoor area,
etc.

[4] Realistically, walking is of course also a form of *Verkehr* (= transportation or
traffic); yet in most instances where I have encountered the symbolism, it employed
vehicular traffic of some sort: trains, cars, elevators or—boats.

In the *sixth and seventh* pictures where the stream carries a sail-boat and a steamship respectively, the water has distinct waves—a possible indication that adult sexuality begins to partake in the excitation (cf. my remarks on the Wave Dream, I, 221–230 and on The Wave Dream and the Fear of Waves II, 359–364).

In the *eighth* and last picture the dream has failed to prolong sleep any further: the nurse has awakened, has perceived the screaming boy, and is getting up.

I have included the analysis of this arousal dream because it is paradigmatic for the *economic* failure mentioned above, to which, beside the mechanical ones, Freud has traced condensation. If the nurse interprets the stimulus issuing from the object world as a pleasure-physiologic one confined to her body, she does so for economic reasons. The abolishment of the first through motility requires arousal; the abolishment of the second through affectivity is often compatible with the continuation of sleep.[5] One can say that she is at first successful because she actually prolongs her sleep and that she fails in the end. Affectivity cannot master the stimulus because it is not pleasure-physiologic.[6]

Needless to add that affectivity may not always succeed in canceling even an actually pleasure-physiologic stimulation; there are dreams that do not awaken the dreamer and dreams that do. Yet these instances are extreme; it happens frequently that a patient does not know whether or not he woke up from a certain dream. In these cases it is of course impossible to ascertain whether affectivity was successful in abolishing all pleasure-physiologic stimulation.

I have omitted the arousal through the anxiety affect because the

[5] The motility available to the sleeper is essentially postural: he may stretch, bend, or turn. More motility and all locomotility are dependent upon waking up. Sleep-walking, for example is a misnomer: it occurs only after the sleeper has awakened into an auto-hypnotic state (in. Chapter Four).

[6] C.f. the dream of the burning child (1900, p. 509). Freud's analysis of this dream is incomplete in one point: it is true that it fulfills both the wish that the child be alive and the wish to sleep; but the father's arousal is essentially the same as the nurse's and distinguished from the latter only by the fact that the child's demand is hallucinated, not real, and expressed symbolically, not directly (burning = urination—Freud).

latter is merely the effect of a transformation of libido which the dreamer could not contain. Freud, who discovered this transformation, has never described in what way it occurs. A particularly vivid example of arousal through untransformed sexual affect that I have also neglected is the awakening of the dreamer of either sex in consequence of a nocturnal emission. Neither instance would have contributed to the discussion.

Remaining is my attempt to establish a theory of dream hallucination in comparison with that of Freud. He explains (1917) dream hallucination as occurring through the dreamer's regression to an early stage at which the nurseling, lacking as yet coordinated motility and unable therefore to test reality in the object world, hallucinated the object from whom he craved gratification. Yet, as has been said above, Freud himself calls the positing of such a stage an indulgence in "fiction." He thus explains hallucination with hallucination, and with a fictitious one at that. My attempt, in contrast to Freud's, does not account for dream hallucination with hallucination and it does not resort to fiction. The body, the dreamer's environment, with which in the interest of the preservation of sleep he must try to cope by means other than decathexis, is real. And so is the pleasure-physiologic process. In other words, none of my premises are fictitious. The only hypothetical element is the conclusion, which in the last analysis has the dreamer perceive the (mostly indirect) representation of something as real that actually is real.

The reader to whom my argument may have appeared convincing might want to expand the theory of dream hallucination developed here into a general theory of hallucination. Freud's recognition of the dream as our "nocturnal psychosis," as well as the psychotic's cathexis withdrawal from the object world and its replacement by a fantastic one, may indeed increase the temptation. I withstand it, however, because for one thing the present chapter is devoted exclusively to the dream, and for another what characterizes the ego of the psychotic is still practically unknown. An assumption, therefore, to the extent that the perception of pleasure-physiology is responsible for his hallucinations—as is the dreamer's—would be unsupportable at this time.

II. ON THE SPOKEN WORD IN THE DREAM

A. FREUD'S CONTRIBUTIONS

There is no point in attempting to add, however little, to Freud's work before quoting or abstracting Freud first. This is nowhere more true than in dealing with the dream speech. Freud has treated the subject twice: once extensively in *The Interpretation of Dreams* (1900), and once briefly in the "Metapsychological Supplement to the Theory of Dreams" (1917). I believe he has contributed even more. Without meaning to do so, he has laid the foundation for a theory of speech in the dream in other works: in *The Ego and the Id* (1923a) and in his "Remarks on the Theory and Practice of Dream Interpretation" (1923b). I have abstracted Freud's contributions under three different headings: (1) Direct Speech in the Dream, (2) Auditory Perception, and (3) Superego and Dream.

Direct Speech in the Dream

(a) *The Interpretation of Dreams:*

(i) The raw material for the dream speech can be found in the waking life of the dreamer. This raw material, however, is not only fragmented, slightly altered, and deprived of its content in order to yield spoken words in the dream; it may also be subjected to a process of selection. If it is, the speech, by virtue of displacement, appears in the dream in place of another speech. It is the latter that should have entered the dream; it is the former that did so. Both were associated in waking life; the one excluded from entry into the dream must, in analysis, be separately recalled and interpretatively put in place of the other if the thought expressed through the spoken word is to be understood. Freud's example is the "I don't recognize that" in the market dream (1900, p. 183). "The dreamer," he writes, "had on the previous day . . . reproved her cook with the words: 'Behave yourself properly! I don't recognize that!' " (1900, p. 668). Of the two phrases, she had taken the meaningless one into the dream; but only the suppressed one tallies with the rest of the dream content.

(ii) Dream speeches are definable as speeches in the dream that own something of the sensory character of speech and are described by the dreamer as speeches. They are felt to be quasi-heard or said; i.e., they own an acoustic or a motor emphasis collateral to their occurrence in the dream *("akustische oder motorische Mitbetonung im Traum")*.

(iii) When conspicuously prominent as a speech, the dream speech is reducible to one spoken or heard in reality by the dreamer. When not so prominent, reading matter is apparently a source that flows abundantly but is difficult to pursue.

(iv) The dream speech may be fragmentary and its coherence deceptive; under analysis it may fall apart and reveal that the raw material besides having been broken up in the manner described above, has also been joined anew. Thus the product, the speech in the dream, although containing the words, does not contain the meaning of the speech in the waking life.

(v) Close inspection shows the dream speech to be composed of two kinds of elements, one "thorough and compact" and the other merely holding the first together after having been supplied in the manner in which a reader will substitute missing letters and syllables.

(vi) The dream speech need not be meaningful in itself, but may instead be merely allusive to an event coincident with the speech in waking life.

(vii) The speech must be conscious in waking life in order to be reproduced in the dream. Only the reproduction of unconscious compulsive thoughts in a dream speech is an "exception."

(b) *"Metapsychological Supplement to the Theory of Dreams":*

Here the dream speech is treated in but a few lines that may be quoted:

> Only where the word-presentations occurring in the day's resi-
> dues are recent and current residues of *perceptions,* and not the
> expression of *thoughts,* are they themselves treated like thing-
> presentations, and subjected to the influence of condensation and
> displacement. Hence the rule laid down in *The Interpretation of
> Dreams,* and since confirmed beyond all doubt, that words and
> speeches in the dream-content are not freshly formed, but are
> modelled on speeches from the day preceding the dream (or on
> some other recent impressions, such as something that has been
> read). It is very noteworthy how little the dream-work keeps to
> the word-presentations; it is always ready to exchange one word
> for another till it finds the expression most handy for plastic rep-
> resentation [1917, p. 228].

The passage includes the following tenets:

(i) The raw material is a *day residue.* the speech in waking life was either spoken, heard, read, or thought on the day before it is reproduced as a dream speech.

(ii) The principle guiding the dream work on a speech in the dream is the regard for *plastic representation.*

(iii) For the purposes of the dream speech the dreamer treats verbal day residues in the manner not of a dreamer but of a schizophrenic: a word image in the speech of the day before is not conceived as representative of a thought element or of an object, but as an object itself. It is not, therefore, reduced to the object image denoted by it, but it is instead, as are object im ages, *subjected directly to displacement and condensation.* The dream work does not, in other words, deal with the word as intermediary between thought and idea, but as idea, it does not succeed in laying hold of the idea represented verbally, but it seizes upon and exhausts itself on the word.

The other two contributions are fundamental to a theory of

the spoken word, although Freud made them without having the dream speech in mind. They will, as were the previous ones, be summarized without comment. (All discussion is reserved for the second, the original part of the present chapter.) Nevertheless, their inclusion seems plausible, for the first deals with verbal images and the second deals with the dream.

Auditory Perception: The Origin of the Superego
The Ego and the Id:

Freud's formulation of auditory perception as the origin of the superego is the first and so far still the most comprehensive because it accounts simultaneously for superego, ego, and id. In attempting a sensory allocation of the superego he remains aware that the latter is by virtue of its definition partly ego and partly id; and in assigning its origin to "word remainders," i.e., acoustic memory traces of words, he remembers that this sensory territory had already been occupied by the ego. Thus when any part of the superego becomes conscious, it appears joined auditorily to the ego; when unconscious, it remains as does all id, indescribable except in terms of cathectic energy without known substratum. It is, Freud (1923a) writes, with regard

> to the importance we have ascribed to preconscious verbal residues in the ego, [that] the question arises whether it can be the case that the super-ego, in so far as it is *Ucs*, consists in such word-presentations and, if it does not, what else it consists in. Our tentative answer will be that it is as impossible for the super-ego as for the ego to disclaim its origins from things heard; for it is a part of the ego and remains accessible to consciousness by way of these word-presentations (concepts, abstractions). But the *cathectic energy* does not reach these contents of the super-ego from auditory perception (instruction or reading) but from sources in the id" [pp. 52–53].

Superego and Dream

"Remarks on the Theory and Practice of Dream Interpretation":

The superego, shrunk ordinarily to the dream censor, may occasionally expand reintegratively to the extent of being completely re-established in the dream. This occurs when the dreamer's attempt toward an unconscious infantile wish-fulfillment has the effect of invoking the superego against it. The dreamer, who ordinarily complies with the censor by modifying the wish, complies in this instance with the superego by replacing it with a reaction formation. He thus excludes the original wish from the dream and with it much latent thought from the manifest content. But he does not furnish us with an exception to the wish-fulfilling tendency of the dream, for he supplants the dream wish with the wish for punishment and in so doing merely exchanges one form of gratification for another.

This description of the "punishment dream" implies that the dream is brought about jointly by ego and superego. It is thus a special case of the general "need for punishment," defined by Freud (1930) as "an instinctual manifestation on the part of the ego, which has become masochistic under the influence of a sadistic super-ego; it is a portion . . . of the instinct towards internal destruction present in the ego, employed for forming an erotic attachment to the super-ego" (p. 136). It is, in fact, this masochistic compliance that enables the ego to preserve sleep through dreaming instead of undergoing arousal—the alternative designated by Freud in the case of objection to a dream wish by the re-established superego.

The above quotation is applicable to all phenomena caused by a need for punishment, including the punishment dream. I have appended it because it is explicit about the interaction of superego and ego.

D. DISCUSSION AND A FEW FURTHER CONTRIBUTIONS

The Dream Speech—a Day Residue

This is often verifiable, even easily so; but frequently it is not. Freud (1909b) admits what he calls an exception. "The speeches in his [the Rat Man's] dreams," he writes, "need not be related to real speeches. His Ucs. ideas—as being internal voices—have the value of real speeches which he hears only in his dreams" (p. 274). I believe this is not an exception but applies to an indeterminate number of instances of the spoken word. I can see no theoretical reason why a preconscious or even an unconscious thought could not be the day residue and appear as speech in the dream. Clinical observation would seem to bear this out, inasmuch as the patient often cannot account for the thought, although circumstances suggest that he had it.

For example, a patient was requested to write down a dream containing three speeches after she had reported it in her hour. I quote her transcript in full and verbatim. I have italicized the spoken words.

> I was lying on the couch and at the end of the hour, when I picked myself up to go, you said *"You can stay here if you'd like"* . . . I was delighted, said nothing but went over to a phonograph on the other side of the room and played some records. I sat on the floor and listened. You remained seated in your chair and read a newspaper. I felt wonderful, relaxed, secure, and most of all, at home. Then the door opened [not the door through which I enter, a private one], and your wife walked in. . . . She looked around at me several times as if to say *"Beat it . . ."* She then said to you, *"I think Miss X. ought to go."* You said nothing, stood up and I was suddenly aware of what you were wearing—a navy blue pin-striped suit with a white shirt. I felt no hostility toward you, but I hated your wife. I walked out. I still felt as though you loved me, but that there was always someone to break up any of my love feelings. I was not surprised at your wife kicking me out. It felt familiar. (I didn't wake up from this dream.)

I could not ascertain and had no reason to assume that the patient had spoken, heard, or read these words, or words resembling them the day before. Yet there was every reason to believe that she had, probably without knowing it, thought them. They represented, in other words, a descriptively unconscious thought.[7]

---

[7] I use this noncommittal expression because of my ignorance of the essence of the quality "preconscious." The latter stems from the *Outline* (1940), where Freud declares

This is demonstrable in a measure because the patient is fortunately no stranger to the reader of the *Psychoanalytic Series*. She has previously been described (I, 73–75) as someone to whom the end of each session was extremely traumatic because her transference was regressive to such a degree that the analyst represented to her the breast, which, in Freud's (1900) words, "is part of me." Terminating an analytic hour amounted, therefore, to a severe mutilation to which she reacted with dizziness and marked postural disorientation. It accords well with her extreme regression that the young woman was able to dream, like a child, hallucinating undistorted wish fulfillment. In the very beginning of her treatment, for instance, when an explanation of the analytic rule interfered with her utter disinclination to talk, she dreamt of being in analysis and of the analyst's demanding, "Don't say another word." The first speech in the dream under consideration is of the same kind: it expresses the wish to be permitted to stay on after the end of the hour. With Freud's tenet in mind, one is led to assume that the preconscious thought, representative of the wish, had occurred to the patient the day before she dreamt the dream; but there is of course no way to prove it.

An analysis of the other two speeches requires additional general information. The patient's father adored her, shared an interest in music with her but, in consequence of his obvious sexual interest, was inhibited in their dealings and often disappointed her by reading the paper when she wanted to chat. It was he, not I, who actually owned a navy blue pin-striped suit. The mother, a vicious psychotic, admitted without qualms to having beaten the patient as a child and interfered with the overtly harmless intercourse between father and adult daughter by admonitions to the latter as absurd as, "Remember he is my husband." When the patient came to analysis she still lived with her parents; a year later she moved away.

Two particular preoccupations of the patient at the time of the dream are known. For one thing, she expected her period and was suffering from prodromata: swollen and aching breasts and a bloated stomach causing unpleasant sensations. In addition, identified as she was with her mother, she had until recently regarded menstruation as injurious (II, 52). For still another thing, her frequent intercourse with the mother over the telephone had become subject to the abstinence

---

himself dissatisfied with his definition of preconscious and promises that he will revise it. Death, however, intervened.

I am inclined to consider the day residue for the first speech in the patient's dream preconscious and those for the second and third unconscious.

rule (II, 8). This, it turned out, was the real moving away from the mother: the abstention from telephoning imposed an incomparably greater hardship than the original change of domicile which had been effected practically without emotion.

I shall, in the interest of economy, omit all but one of the oedipal determinants of the dream and focus upon the preoedipal ones. Of the first of these—the impending menstrual period—it is known that it was on the patient's mind the day before the dream: her discomfort reminded her of it. Of the second—the abstinence—one can only say that it occupied her at the time of the dream. Had my notes been more accurate, I might here have been able also to narrow the time down to the day before. Inasmuch as no associations to the speeches could be obtained, I am dependent upon speculation. The latter suggests that each of the two speeches is overdetermined by both the premenstrual state and the abstinence from intercourse with the mother.

The reader familiar with the subject will recognize the second part of the dream as a typical one. I have described it as in most cases premenstrual and have termed it "mother comes in," because the mother's entry into the room symbolizes the entry of the womb into the pleasure-physiological body ego (I, 216–221; II, 238–240). Both speeches contained in this part verbalize the intent of eliminating the dreamer. It is fortunate, lest my speculation appear *ad hoc,* that I reported long ago and in a totally different context the "regressive identification of the adult with his excrement as a hated object" (I, 117). In the present instance, the partly oral-sadistic, partly anal-sadistic interpretation of the menstrual product is known and has previously been described (II, 52). It appears therefore plausible that the wish to rid herself of the discomfort does not appear in the speeches as the wish for the product to leave the vagina, but, instead, for the dreamer to leave the "room." The analysis of the second of the two speeches is, with regard to the menstrual problem, the same.[8]

[8] Except for a further bit of speculation that I relegate to a footnote because although it appears to me to have a good chance of being valid I doubt whether it will appear so

With regard to the second determinant, the abstinence rule which proved so difficult for the patient to follow, it would fit her passivity that the dream, instead of detaching her from the mother, has the latter throw her out. It is therefore in this sense both a dream of convenience and an example of the case where the day residue contains an (unconscious) wish. There is, of course, no lack of historical overdetermination: the instance in which she had cruelly been dismissed by the hateful, violent mother would make a small treatise. I single out one because it illustrates Freud's tenet that the speech—here the first of the two—may appear in the dream instead of another speech. The mother had intercourse in front of the four-year-old under circumstances allowing detailed observation (II, 223). Only when all was over did she turn to the child, who was quite beside herself, and command abruptly: "Get out!"

The unconscious nature of the day residue, together with several of its vicissitudes in the course of its tranformation into the spoken word, described by Freud, sometimes make it difficult—as the example shows—to find the former behind the latter.

Secondary Elaboration

The strongest contrast to the type of case described in the previous section, where a verbal day residue, and sometimes an unconscious one at that, undergoes an elaborate processing in order to become dream speech, is the instance wherein a con-

---

to the reader. It is based on the "schizophrenic treatment of verbal day residues where the word is treated as an object" abstracted above under (j). It is supported, furthermore, by my knowledge of Freud's uncanny way of presenting general truths under the guise of casuistics. The difficulty of demonstrating this for the case of the dream speech is compounded by the fact that it can only be shown in German. In the second part of the third speech in the market dream (cf. [a], above) ". . . I do not take that" appeared in the dream, Freud explains, instead of the day residue: "Behave decently." In English the two speeches lack any resemblance; yet they are assonant in the original German. The first: "Das nehme ich nicht"; "Benehmen Sie sich anständig," the second. On the strength of both the "schizophrenic" treatment of the verbal day residues in producing a speech in the dream and the occasional assonance between dream speech and speech in waking life, I venture to translate the former into the latter as: "I think Miss X. ought to flow," instead of "go." Before rejecting this interpretation, remember again that the dream is premenstrual and that the words are spoken by the mother, symbol for the womb.

scious speech from waking life is taken verbatim into the dream.

The example for this is as short and simple as the other was complicated and long. A dreamer sees a recumbent nude woman who says to him: "I have no milk." He has difficulty in identifying the speech, although he had heard it shortly before retiring when his wife had opened the icebox, noticed that there was no milk, and had spoken these very words. The analysis proved the woman to be the mother, of whom it had been said she had no milk and therefore could not breast-feed her children.

This deceptively simple dream actually illustrates several tenets original with this writer. For the present, only one of these is singled out: the insertion into the dream of words actually spoken, i.e., spoken day residues. (The dream will be quoted again.)

By reproducing a speech from waking life without altering it, the dreamer saves himself one particular phase of dream work: secondary elaboration. Spoken when awake, the speech has already been subjected to secondary elaboration, which therefore need not be repeated in the dream. Because the day residue is purely verbal, it is self-evident that the same words when occurring as dream speech are apt to convey an entirely different meaning.

Sensory Qualities

The sensory qualities of the spoken word are immaterial. Whether a dream speech is spoken, thought, heard, or seen does not alter its meaning. Sometimes it even lacks all quality and is merely remembered as what we have become accustomed to calling a "verbal dream." The analysis is in all these cases the same. In this respect the speech resembles the day residue from which it derives.

Freud, without meaning to, gave an example by way of an error on the occasion of his analysis of the *"Non vixit"* (1900, p. 421). The re-

port of the dream contains the passage, "But what I actually *said*
(italics added)—and I myself noticed the mistake—was *Non vixit.*"
But in the analysis of the dream, one reads on the very next page: "It
was a long time, however, before I succeeded in tracing the origin of
the *'Non vixit'* . . . at last it occurred to me that these two words possessed their high degree of clarity in the dream, not as words heard or
spoken, but as words *seen.*" Thus confusing speech, where the words
were *spoken,* and day residue, where they were *seen* on a monument,
is obviously a mistake; yet one can look upon it as an unwitting illustration of the fact that the mode of perception of the spoken word is
immaterial.

Needless to add that the sensory qualities of the day residue
and the dream speech may but need not be the same.

Position in the Manifest Content

The first part of the dream in which the patient wanted to
stay with me is, as has been pointed out, a "child's dream," although the dreamer was an adult. Since these dreams are relatively undistorted it is not, as far as the speech is concerned, an
effect of displacement that the analyst (father) speaks it. With
regard to the speech in the next dream, I am not convinced
that the words "I have no milk" actually belong to the recumbent nude woman, but am inclined to believe it was dream
work that put them into her mouth. However, since the analysis
of the dream remained incomplete, I am unable to prove it. I
save for the next section an example in which the speech is
demonstrably spoken by the wrong speaker and for the present
limit myself to the consideration of the effects upon the spoken
word of one aspect of the dream work: displacement. These
effects, in addition to attaching the dream speech to a person
to whom it does not belong, also on certain occasions shift the
speech altogether to a wrong place in the dream. To understand this one must acknowledge that the dream work may dis-
place the spoken word as it displaces affect. The similarity of
dream speech and affect with regard to such displaceability is
not, I believe, accidental. I shall attempt to account for it in

the next section. At the moment I confine myself to abstracting a technical rule: the spoken word is in most cases a foreign body in the dream. Its place in the manifest content is as immaterial as are its sensory qualities (cf. above). *In order to analyze it, one must therefore, if it appears displaced, restore it to its proper position* (indicated in the examples to follow by "[Sp.]"), *after which one must lift it out of the dream and consider it by itself.* Only when one has undone that much dream work is it sensible to ask the dreamer to associate separately to the speech and to expect his associations to be instructive. Two examples,

(a) The dream of a patient in the last phase of his analysis, dreamt after the death of his mother.

> I was seated at a large table in a large, white, well-lighted room. My aunt was seated beside me. It was after my mother's funeral. Before me on the table lay a large round pie with choco-late frosting and some sort of creamy filling. I had apparently eaten a chunk of it. [*Sp.*] I then remembered that my mother was dead and began to cry uncontrollably. My aunt murmured wordlessly in a comforting way. I then began to eat at the pie—that is, pick it up and put a corner of it into my mouth. I felt very full and almost nauseated. *"I am making myself sick,"* I thought as I tasted the pie.

The patient spontaneously attached to the transcript of the dream the following associations:

> After writing this, I recalled the story of fellow students eating lunch at the autopsy table in our very well-lighted anatomy lab-oratory with white sheets covering the cadavers. Also a bit of a poem by Gertrude Stein (a Lesbian), "Toasted Susie is my ice cream." It seems to me that the introjection of my mother in this dream must have an especial cannibalistic import because I never chewed at the pie—indeed, it seems to me now that I had few or no teeth. My mother and my aunt have false teeth.

The dream is a typical one: it deals with the cannibalistic introjec-tion of the lost object, discovered by Freud and treated extensively by

Abraham (1924b, pp. 433–442). I must expect the reader to be familiar with this subject.) The dream admits the introjection and expends a tremendous amount of dream work to deny it, and the patient repeats both admission and denial in his associations. I will have to enumerate and explain the different means of denial because one of them is the displacement of the speech in the manifest content.

The first explanation requires a short preamble containing a small addendum to the theory of the dream. Freud has observed that many dreams contain elements that have "escaped the transformation into pictures," but he has failed to state that these elements are expressive of delusions. Yet they are. They complement the dreamer's sensory experience with a "knowledge" that must be called delusory for the same reason that the sensory experience is called hallucinatory—because of the "irreality" (i.e., psychic reality only) of the dream.

In the present case the dream abruptly replaces hallucination with a delusion, containing the only direct admission of the cannibalistic introjection of the mother (in a "vegetarian mode of expression," II, 322): "*I had apparently eaten a chunk of it*" (the pie). In so doing it not only deceives the censor but almost succeeds in deceiving the patient, who in his associations denies the introjection: ". . . I never chewed at the pie—indeed it seems to me now that I had few or no teeth." The second part of this sentence reinforces the denial by saying in effect: "I *could not* have eaten the pie," although the dreamer does not fail to preface the whole sentence with the conviction that so strong a denial connotes an "especial . . . import." The first part of the sentence shows the patient deceived to the same degree and by the same means as the censor had been in the dream. Undeceived, he would instead have expressed himself to the extent that he never *experienced* chewing the pie (hallucination) but merely *knew* that he had eaten a chunk of it (delusion).

With the foregoing in mind, the briefest reflection upon the obvious fact that no food can make one sick unless one eats it illuminates the displacement of the speech in the manifest content. The displacement puts the speech at the end of the dream where it follows a denial of eating, whereas it actually belongs in the place marked [Sp.] where it would have followed the admission.

Further dream work need not be pointed out to the analytic reader and is not meant to be illustrated by the example; it consists mainly in allusions. They reverberate, as it were, in the second association, which represents the attempt to attenuate the libido of the second oral stage by exchanging it for that of the first: if "Susie" is to be toasted, she can only be eaten; if ice cream, she can also be sucked.

I conclude this example by admitting that I do not at this point expect the reader to be particularly impressed. Supposing, he may say to himself, that there is an apparent displacement of the speech in the manifest content of certain dreams, and supposing it can be undone. What is gained? How does restoring the spoken word to its proper position assist its interpretation? The question is justified; it shall be answered after the presentation of the second example.

(b) A patient reports the following dream:

> I was lying on a very large black leather couch—as large as a double bed. The analyst was behind me, seated in a chair. Between us was a huge black leather bolster that made seeing the analyst impossible unless I peered back around it. The proportions of the couch and bolster suggested a greatly exaggerated version of your couch. [Sp.]
>
> I was talking—something about numbers and mistakes involving, numbers [Sp.]. A janitor walked into the room. He was redfaced, rather poorly and dirtily dressed. His expression was one of arrogance. Without looking at us he sullenly emptied a wastebasket into a sack. This was repeated two or three times. You let this happen and said nothing. I felt angry but with an assumed naïveté asked—as if it were merely a point of interest—*"Is he allowed to come in here?"*

I select several of his spontaneous associations: to *double bed:* incest with psychotic mother in adolescence (coitus and fellatio). To *bolster:* prevented any mutual inspection between analyst and patient. If I were to have an erection, it could not be seen. Also a barrier to sexual activity with the analyst (fellatio). To *numbers:* his ages at the times of intimacies with the mother. To *janitor:* Provocative—his arrogance and sullenness obviously seemed to despise analyst, and patient and analysis; provocative taunting leer with which I envisioned looking around at the analyst—my father's despising me. Memory of provoking and defying him when he was weak and very sick. (Circumlocution: the patient named the father's sickness.)

He had no associations to the speech, which is understandable since its displacement in the manifest content had rendered it harmless to such an extent that, ignorant of the rule enunciated above, one would not even be curious about it. However, it was on the very strength of the rule that I asked the patient whether, in view of his associations, the speech might not be a soliloquy indicative of his feeling of guilt. The thought compressed in it could then be expanded as follows: "*Is he* [i.e., the patient], who has committed all these transgressions and wants to repeat many of them with the analyst, worthy of being *allowed to come in here* in order to be treated with compassion and assisted in getting well?"

The patient confirmed this emphatically and at once: "I immediately felt," he reported, in transcribing dream and associations, "that this was so—that especially in this session I felt that I ought not be tolerated by you, had no right to your sympathy and your care."

In other words, the analysis of the speech makes it clear that the speaker is not the janitor but the dreamer, and that the speech is not spoken but *thought*. It enables one, furthermore, to undo the displacement: the speech does not belong at the end of the dream but at one of the two places marked with the brackets in the transcript, preferably the second. For it is here that, as the associations to them show, the preceding dream elements allude to events causing the feeling of guilt and verbalized in the spoken word.

What is the *raison d'être* for the technical rule enunciated above? One must first, the rule says, undo the displacement if it has occurred. Is this not merely performing a sleight-of-hand? Decidedly not; because by relegating the speech to the wrong place the dream work has prejudiced the interpreter against it, if it has not directly misled him. In both examples it has rendered the speech insignificant; in the first, it has in addition suggested a wrong interpretation. The defensive devaluation of the speech through the displacement is most easily seen in the second example where the speech in reaction to the janitor's

intrusion is made equivalent to the commonplace assumption
that the analytic situation excludes the presence of a third person. Hardly something to dream! Yet how different is the complexion of the spoken word when restored to its proper position! It becomes expressive of a searching of the soul, resulting
in the acknowledgment of the results of amnesia removal (with
which the patient had great difficulty over a protracted period
of time), of a suffering from the effects of the repetition-com-
pulsion, and of a strong feeling of guilt. Subsequently, the rule
prescribes, one must lift the speech out of the manifest content
and consider it separately from the rest of the dream. This
transforms it in the second example into a soliloquy, i.e., weighty
thoughts full of affect, pondered by the patient, yet expressible
only in answer to the analyst's question.

Applying the rule to the spoken word is so often such a *sine
qua non* for its interpretation that it seems worth demonstrating
this once again by analyzing the speech in the first of the two
examples. With the displacement intact the speech appears to
have little meaning: food disagrees with someone because eating has unconsciously a cannibalistic meaning; on occasion this
becomes observable, and there is of course no reason why it
could not also be dreamt. The displacement of the speech has it
appear at the end, where the eating is represented allusively,
while its effects are directly and explicitly named in a hallucinatory part of the dream. The interpreter in accepting this position of the spoken word is not only prejudiced by the dream
work but outright deceived. For the manifest content preceding
the speech is a commentary on it, declaring that "sick" is to be
understood as "physically sick."

In order to contrast the truth with the deception by undoing
the displacement, one must hold the dream speech against its
background, to be found in the patient's analysis previous to the
dream. When the extremely psychopathic mother suffered from
a protracted terminal illness, the analyst, on a mere "hunch"
and without being specific about the matter even in his own
mind, expressed the hope that she die before the analysis
reached its end. He did so because he was convinced that the

patient, now close to full health, would without analysis relapse severely. Fate complied, and the analysis appeared successful.

If one undoes the displacement and examines that part of the manifest content which should have preceded the speech, one finds it not only representative of the kind of dream described by Abraham (1924b) as requisite to the process of mourning, but one notices that it connects the pie with the mother by placing it on a twice-named symbol for her, the table. What is more, one fails to detect any comment whatsoever on "sick." One is thus free to recognize the speech for what it is, an introspective soliloquy, as precise as the analyst's notion had been vague: "[If I eat from and thereby introject, that is identify with, my mother] *I am making myself* [mentally] *sick* [again]." One could not indeed epitomize the deepest determinant of the patient's condition and character disorder more cogently than by calling it an identification with his mother. The example is an unusual one, inasmuch as the restoration of the spoken word to its proper position not only assists its correct interpretation but changes the complexion of the dream, which reveals itself against all expectation as a dream of getting well.

I hope I have not only established, but also shown the necessity for establishing, a technical rule for the interpreting of the spoken word.

The Topography of the Spoken Word

The foregoing considerations have shown the spoken word, subjectable to all manner and all degrees of dream work, to be a soliloquy—either plainly so or overdetermined as such. If it is put in someone else's mouth, dream work placed it there. If it has sensory qualities for the dreamer, these can be disregarded interpretively because they are also effects of the dream work. With all dream work undone, and all overdetermination acknowledged, the dreamer is left—in most instances, if not all—speaking silently to himself.

The identification of the dream speech as a soliloquy raises the theoretical question: who is, as far as topography is concerned, speaking to whom? The answer, besides returning one to familiar ground, would justify including the abstracts on auditory perception and the superego and dream in the present section as well as in the previous one (see A, 2). In the first of these Freud (1923a) explains that the superego, no less than the ego, is derived from auditory impressions and "remains accessible to consciousness by way of these word-presentations (concepts, abstractions)" (p. 52). In the second he asserts that the superego, shrunk ordinarily to the dream censor, expands reintegratively in the punishment dream, to the extent of being completely reestablished.

The question, who, topographically, speaks to whom? is answerable if one has convinced oneself that the re-establishment in the dream of the superego is not confined to the punishment dream but obtains also, at least temporarily, in the case of the spoken word. What Freud describes is the highest degree of topographical differentiation compatible with the continuation of sleep. Since everyone has on occasion heard a sleeper speaking a few words aloud, one is certainly justified in endowing him with a silent speech.[9] The examples cited above, however, show the spoken word as expressive of self-observation. The latter is either plain or critical, as has been shown before (II, 85–86, 116). In the first case the introject observes the partial subject alone, in the second in conjunction with the superego. It is the second of the two cases where the superego, again to quote Freud (1923a), ". . . appears joined auditorily to the ego."

---

[9] I believe that this extreme topographical redifferentiation obtains equally for the partial liberation of affect which as everyone knows also permits the perpetuation of sleep. I imagine there a reintegration of ego to the extent of a re-establishment of a partial subject, and of an introject opposing instinctual discharge in the service of the superego (and the wish to sleep). The opposition, however, has only a limited success: hence the partial liberation. The dream work resorts at this point, if I may claim the license of anthropomorphic expression, to a last desperate measure: displacement of affect. That it takes this measure both in the case of the liberation of affect and the occurrence of the spoken word, I consider due to the fact that in both the excessive redifferentiation poses the threat of arousal.

It is in this way that I account, as I promised to do, for the displacement common to both, which without such accounting would appear accidental. If I omit the punishment dream, which is naturally the third case, I do so only in the interest of simplification.

Abiding for the time being by my examples: the speech, "I have no milk" is uncritically introspective and can therefore only represent an observation by the introject of the partial subject.[10] In the extremely self-critical speech, "Is he allowed to come in here?" the partial subject in conjunction with the superego is observed by the introject.

Common knowledge affirms that certain self-observations, critical or uncritical, when endowed with sufficient affect may have a person address himself to himself in a silent speech when awake. It is the high degree of reintegrative topographical differentiation that compels one to consider the dream speech in the last analysis but another instance of the same kind.

C. SUMMARY

In concluding the present chapter it appears convenient to summarize briefly the contributions to the theory of the spoken word developed in the foregoing discussion.

1. The day residue for the dream speech, that is, the verbalization of a thought on the day before dreaming its transformation into the spoken word, may but need not have been conscious.

2. The sensory qualities of the day residue are, of course, accidental; those of the dream speech are effects of the dream work and therefore not pertinent to the interpretation of the spoken word.

3. The speech may be displaced in the manifest content. Such a displacement may impede the correct interpretation of the spoken word in more ways than one. It may prejudice the interpreter or deceive him by having the speech appear in the wrong context; it may give the erroneous impression that an actually weighty thought expressed in the speech is of but little importance; it may have the speech spoken by someone to whom it does not belong. Undoing the displacement and restor-

---

[10] What causes the dreamer to identify with his mother could of course only be explored in an analysis of the dream. It is, however, not pertinent to the point under consideration.

ing the speech to its proper position in the manifest content is therefore prerequisite to its interpretation. The interpreter must lift the dream speech, undoing displacement, if present, out of the manifest content, and consider it by itself. This entails obtaining from the patient, if possible, separate associations to the spoken word.

4. The spoken word in the dream is a soliloquy, either solely or overdetermined as such.

5. The soliloquy is expressive of self-observation, either unaffective or critical; its topography is the same as that of all self-observative thought: if the introject alone observes the partial subject, uncritical self-observation results; if the partial subject is observed by the introject fused with the superego, the effect is critical self-observation.

III. ON TYPICAL DREAMS

Owing to the disparity between their respective subject matters, the contrast between this chapter and the preceding one could hardly be sharper. The spoken word lent itself to a definitive treatment; it is improbable that anything essential will be added to it as long as Freud's theory of the dream remains valid. The very opposite holds true for an attempt to add to his discourse on typical dreams (1900, pp. 241–276, 384–404). Here one engages in spade work, labors much for little, and cannot in most instances be sure of the actual value of any apparent result. In writing the present chapter I have more than once hesitated and wondered whether I should continue; it was only the hope that a future investigator possessing a wealth of new observation might make use of my modest contribution that made me go on.

Specifically what I have tried to do is (1) to extend and elaborate on Freud's (1900) discussion of typical dreams; (2) add to the interpretation of one of these dreams, and (3) contribute two typical dreams not hitherto described.

A. ADDENDA TO FREUD'S DISCUSSION OF TYPICAL DREAMS

Freud's discussion of typical dreams needs amplification and reordering. For one thing it is disjunct. Reviewing the material in 1909 and 1911, he felt a need to interpolate a discussion of dream work (Ch. VI) into *The Interpretation of Dreams* before concluding the subject. Taking up the original subject, he seems to disregard his original definition of this kind of dream. Thus on two counts the subject asks for clarification.

Freud begins by postulating that only such dreams be called "typical" "which almost everyone has dreamt alike and . . . have the same meaning for everyone" (1900, p. 241). He describes the embarrassing dream of being naked, dreams of the death of beloved persons, of flying or falling, and of examination. He acknowledges the occurrence of two typical dream themes in one dream, citing his own staircase dream as an example. He then deals, systematically with the subjects of dream work and symbolization, and only after this describes and interprets a second group of typical dreams. But how radical the difference between the first and second groups! In 1900 dreams having a similarity of manifest content "have the same meaning for everyone" (p. 241); in 1909 they must "nevertheless be interpreted in the greatest variety of ways" (p. 385). One of the two distinguishing characteristics of typical dreams is constancy (or similarity) of affect; the other is similarity of manifest content. Both are relinquished in Freud's discussion of "new" typical dreams.

Any affect, or none, may appear in a dream of this second group; and the resemblance of dreams representative of one of its members is due entirely to the prevalence of a certain symbolization. These are the "harmless" dreams where sexuality is disguised, masked oedipal dreams, those containing a *déjà vu*, dreams of water, of rescue, and dreams upon bodily stimulation. (Dreams of missing the train, although mentioned here by Freud, do not belong to the second group but to the first.) *The "typicality" of these dreams is simply that of the symbol; noth-*

ing is to be said about them that Freud has not said while interpreting them or while dealing with symbolization.

Since it is nevertheless the similarity of manifest content that both groups share with each other, it appears advisable to retain Freud's term "typical dreams" for both, while clarifying the subject of *"symbolically typical dreams."*

With regard to this second group, the initial section of the first chapter of the present volume contains the statement that there is no "dream-symbolism" as distinguished from symbolism in other psychic acts; conversely, any symbol observed outside of the dream may therefore enter the latter and by so doing increase the number of symbolically typical dreams.

Not so with those of the first group—the "truly typical dreams"—although they may also include symbolizations. What renders these dreams typical is not the employment of symbols but a *basic similarity of their manifest content, regularly combined with a constancy of affect,* and that they are dreamed by a great many people.

Dreams of missing the train, for instance, are typical not because they contain the departing train, i.e., a vehicle employed in this instance to symbolize death. Were it so, this would be a *symbolically typical dream*. It is a *truly typical dream* because, for one thing, the train is always missed and, for another, the affect is always a feeling of disappointment.

The distinction, therefore, of the *truly* typical dream from the symbolically typical one is the first step toward clarifying the subject.

Next a word upon *method*. "If we attempt to interpret a typical dream," Freud (1900) writes, "the dreamer fails as a rule to produce the associations which would in other cases have led us to understand it, or else his associations become obscure and insufficient so that we cannot solve our problem with their help" (p. 241). What is left? The translation of symbols to which Freud alludes, and, we must add, divination. The former method is insufficient, and the latter, prerogative of a genius, is unemployable by the average worker. Yet I believe that there are two more methods, one used by Freud simply in passing while interpreting a particular typical dream, and the other employed extensively by him for the interpretation of certain other typical dreams.

The *first* of these two additional methods of interpretation is *the comparison of the typical dream with a clinical picture.* Freud's (1900) single cursory use of this method, where he compares the dream of nudity with the paranoid delusion of being observed while undressing or dressing and with the exhibitionistic perversion, fails to do justice to its importance and calls for an elaborate clinical illustration.

One may exemplify by comparing the dream of the death of beloved persons (1900, p. 248) with a certain clinical observation. In discussing the dream, Freud makes clear that the infantile concept of death is synonymous with "away" or "gone," and that the wish that someone be gone is directed against anyone who interferes with the "absolutely egotistical" we would now say highly narcissistic—child.

The analytic procedure on the one hand adapts itself to the narcissistic needs of the patient, for it occupies itself exclusively with him, bases itself entirely on his associations, and attaches importance to his minutest experience. In thus giving it room, it lets his narcissism expand. On the other hand, by insisting on abstinence, by undoing countercathexes, by striving toward amnesia-removal and, where necessary, for characterological changes, the analyst interferes with those narcissistic demands of his patient that are incompatible with eventually attaining health. He impinges upon his narcissism perhaps most strongly both by knowing what the patient wants to keep to himself and by insisting on knowing what the patient wishes to leave unknown.

One typical reaction to these restrictions is the death wish directed against the analyst, in my personal experience most frequently expressed by the patient through a silent "drop

dead" when he announces himself, or the daily and hopeful
perusal by him of the obituary column in the paper. The analysis of these responses to analytic frustrations shows that, in contrast to others also belonging to the transference, they are
either affectless or lack the appropriate affect not merely
through being compulsive but largely by expressing the infantile death wish of Freud's description. The analyst is, in other
words, not meant to suffer a cruel fate but merely to be gone
from the patient's life. Here the death wish is exactly as Freud
has shown for many a dream of death: it is not a wish for destruction but only for elimination. Thus the clinical observations
mentioned here confirm Freud's interpretation of a typical
dream.

If I have shown that the interpretation of a typical dream
may be the same as that of an observable symptom, the reader
may follow me in employing generally the analysis of clinical
phenomena as auxiliary to the analysis of a typical dream.

The *second* of the two additional methods is applicable only
to the combination, mentioned above, of two typical dream
themes. *It consists of the interpretation of one typical dream
theme with the help of another.* Freud has illustrated it elaborately enough by interpreting the dream of inhibition on the
staircase in part as a dream of nudity because of . . . "very incomplete dress." Freud's attempt to adduce infantile exhibitions
met, however, with an unexpected result whose significance
escaped him. I shall return to this shortly. But in order to do so
I must first contribute in however small a measure to the theory
of the dream; and not only to that of the typical dream but to
that of dreams generally.

Freud has discovered that the dream is our nocturnal psychosis, distinguished by hallucination, delusion and, at times,
schizophrenic speech. He explained the compatibility of this
periodic regression with mental health through two factors:
its dependence upon a (psychic) motor paralysis and its relinquishment on arousal by the dreamer. We do not, in other
words, act while dreaming. This is true, and it was known

in its essence even to Plato (I, 269); but it is not the whole truth. Actually the motor paralysis is not confined to action but must also include those muscles, striped and smooth, instrumental in elimination. The dreamer, in other words, although under the impact of an unconscious *infantile* wish, must, in contrast to the psychotic, preserve continence: he is not allowed the very excretory instinctual discharge that his regression to childhood demands. This, of course, is valid only for the adult. Children in general are known to dream before being continent; and neurotic children, continent during the day, may be enuretic at night. Yet, if an adult sleeper wets or soils, he is, with negligible exceptions, psychotic. That the normal "nocturnal psychotic" must remain continent or, to rephrase, that maintaining continence is a condition for dreaming, Freud has not pointed out.

How completely the significance of this fact has escaped him is testified to in his essay "Dreams in Folklore" (Freud & Oppenheim, 1911) which deals almost exclusively with incontinent sleepers whose arousal dreams show a preference for ending in defecation. Freud points to the libido regression, interprets both primary and secondary gain, but apparently does not recognize to what these tales of dreams, which he treats throughout as he would real dreams, owe their existence. Actually, if the common man derived pleasure from these products of a coarse and artless imagination, he could in the last analysis, I believe, do so only because they permitted him to identify with a dreamer to whom the story allows an indulgence that reality does not allow: *the incontinence to which the dream moves him.*

The conflict forced upon the dreamer consists, in other words, in the antithetic demands to abandon himself to an unconscious infantile dream wish while opposing the excretory libidinal and aggressive discharge that the wish demands. He must do one in order to be able to dream, and the other not only in order to preserve sleep, but also to limit the disintegration of ego caused by the "psychotic" dream. It stands to reason that this dilemma finds its expression occasionally in certain dreams, and I believe that at least one or two "truly typical dreams" represent it. They appear to me to be *continence dreams*—a supposition not easy to support. The reader, who I must naturally assume to be familiar with Freud's interpretations, should not, therefore, expect proof for my thesis; the inadequacy of method, discussed above, rules that out. I can at best make it appear reasonable to look upon some truly typical dreams as representative of a successful struggle for continence in the dreamer.

To avoid any possible misunderstanding, it may finally be pointed out that the compatibility with preservation of ego of a nocturnal emission—the only "excretory" discharge occasionally allowed the normal dreamer—does not contradict the observations made above. The reason is obvious: ejaculation, unavailable to the child, is not regressive; it is genital, not pregenital: it discharges sexual libido in the adult, which the toilet functions no longer do. It is the one form of nocturnal "incontinence" that leaves the ego intact. Where a dream shows the dreamer struggling against it, his motive is neither preservation of sleep nor concern for his ego but the fear of fulfilling an incestuous wish against the censor's proscription.

A Dream Combining Nudity with Inhibition

Freud considered his own dream of running upstairs (1900, p. 238) a dream of inhibition as well as of nudity. Dream of inhibition is correctly named; dream of nudity is a misnomer. In my experience the dreamer is hardly ever nude; his attire is, however, more or less incomplete or in disarray; sometimes he is only worried lest it be so. The lack in his clothing may be distinct or indistinct; the only constant characteristic of the dream is that it manages to disclose directly or by allusion which part of his body the dreamer, if I may use Freud's words, feels "ashamed and embarrassed" to show. The part is sometimes represented directly; more often it is displaced.

Freud's dream is indeed a mixture of the two typical dreams of motor inhibition and nudity, if his term is to be retained. I venture now to extend the interpretation of that dream.

His comment (1900) on his mounting the stairs by skipping two or three at a time alludes to the symbol of "flying," representative of erection (p. 238). Yet he here fails to apply the symbolization described by him only some 25 pages later: "Steps, ladders or staircases, or, as the case may be, walking up or down them, are representations of the sexual act" (p. 355); supplemented by the remark that ". . . the rhythmical pattern of copulation is reproduced in going upstairs" (p. 355n). His omission is evidently due to the fact that in the light of the rest of his associations the symbolism unmasks the dream as depicting an attempt to enter the mother sexually. The staircase is doubly determined as his own—leading from the downstairs office to the upstairs bedroom, and as that in another house—leading from the entrance to the apartment of an old lady to whom he twice daily gives injections. Yet the dream represents more than an attempt. Through the symbolization of the phallus by the body and the vagina by the staircase, it confirms that the wish is fulfilled, and only at the point where the mother (partial object? See Glossary), complies by meeting him do inhibition and shame appear.

So far no support for my contention that this typical dream is a continence dream has been gained. Actually, I have presented only the background for two further associations of Freud to his "continence" dream, in both of which incontinence is the subject. One of them belongs to the present, the other leads from a day residue to the past. The first: visiting the old lady in the morning, he is regularly seized on the stairs by a desire to clear his throat and expectorates on the stairs. He is satisfied with explaining this by the absence of a spittoon: the report gives no thought either to the alternative of a handkerchief or to the question why the urge always befalls him then and there. This is again understandable as a defense. Had he asked himself: "Why am I almost always compelled to spit on the stairs while approaching the old lady?," he would hardly have avoided understanding his dream. The picture so far is best epitomized by stating that if one incorporates the dreamer's associative commissions and omissions into the manifest content the result bears resemblance to a dream with nocturnal emission.

The second association communicates a day residue. Visiting the old lady on the day before, he had in the anteroom been confronted by her maid and blamed for soiling her floor: "You've made the red carpet all dirty again with your feet" (p. 239). Freud associates to this that, according to information recently acquired from his mother, from early infancy until he was two and a half he had been under the care of a nurse, as old and as ugly as the maid, whom he probably loved, although she scolded and possibly beat him during his toilet training.

The analysis of the dream is incomplete; resistances got the better of Freud. This is evident in the illogical sequence of his thought. To the day residue he makes the defensive remark, "This [the maid's scolding the visitor] was the only claim the staircase and maid-servant had to appearing in my dream" (p. 239). Whereupon he proceeds (pp. 247–248) with the associations quoted above which show unmistakably that the day residue, far from being the "only claim," is actually the bridge to the experiences from early childhood. Furthermore, a colleague reminds me that Freud (1887–1902, p. 220) expressed the suspicion that the maid played with him sexually. This might well have led the child to urethral-erotic discharge.

This abortive analysis and the lack of amnesia removal make it impossible for me to suggest convincingly that the dreamer combats incontinence. It must be satisfied with pointing out that each and every one of his associations lead to the subject of incontinence—ejaculation and toilet functions, specifically— although there is no direct sign of it in the manifest content.

The Embarrassment Dream of Partial Undress

Freud's dream mixing inhibition with nudity is paradigmatic only for the dream of inhibition. With regard to the dream of nudity it presents but a variant, because the "many strangers" described by Freud, "with their features left indeterminate" (1900, p. 243) are missing. In his associations, expectoration and soiling each occur in front of a single observer. The latter is distinguished from those of whom the dreamer of nudity is ashamed in three different respects: she is critical, identifiable, and alone. Nevertheless, if this is at variance with the typical dream, it is not so with a certain clinical picture. The female paranoiac of Freud's observation (cited earlier), for instance, whenever in the company of a woman, felt tortured by the delusion of an active as well as passive scoptophilic experience in which the (mutual) observers were single. The moral: one has to follow Freud in adapting to what he once called the "peculiar plasticity of the psychic material," if one studies typical dreams.

However, there is another characteristic of all typical dreams for which the one previously discussed is paradigmatic: the lack in the manifest content of direct representation of incontinence or, frequently, even of any urge for elimination. In other words, *the incontinence dream of the continent dreamer is in most instances continent in appearance.*

I suggest renaming the dream of nudity the typical *embarrassment dream of partial undress,* and I shall comment separately on the three essential elements of this dream.

(1) *The dreamer is never nude, but only somehow dressed incompletely.* Freud's interpretation implies that he considers the incomplete dress an allusion in the sense of a part for the whole. Had he not, he could not have named the dream as he did. He assumes that the dreamer's infantile wish is to show himself in the nude, but the censor allows only a small part of the intended total undressing. However, what forbids the assumption that the wish aims at no more than partial undress? The contribution of the dream work would in this case be limited to a displacement. Freud, for instance, could have reached his aim with the same amount of undressing that he describes associatively, had it concerned another part of his clothing. This applies, of course, to the initial function referred to in his associations.

I remember the dream of a patient in which the displacement appears missing. She walks among many well-dressed people on Fifth Avenue in bright sunshine. She is "clad in a long, completely transparent white ruffled chiffon nightgown"—which seems absolutely in order. (She is not being looked at.) "Suddenly," however, she "notices with terror, that the gown has a square window exactly over the rear end, so that is completely bare. The material is cut on three sides, and folded down."

A few data pertinent to a fragmentary analysis of this dream:

(a) The psychotic father undressed the child many times to the same extent as did the dream, beating her while displaying an erection. With regard to this type of determinant, the dream element representing the site of the partial undress is to be read "directly," that is, back = back. The "flap" was a common part of children's night- and underclothing of the period.

(b) Frequent mutual masturbation with a psychotic sister at the height of the phallic period was accompanied by the telling of uncanny fantastic stories. The sister imposed the condition that neither must show arousal and berated the patient when she did. With regard to this and the other determinants, the same element is to be read in reverse (back = front). That, of course, is equivalent to a displacement.

(c) The repetition compulsion had previously forced the patient into a treatment that amounted to little more than a sado-masochistic acting out of daily exhibition and beatings. She consequently began her analytic hour with me by remembering masturbation fantasies and, in attempting to verbalize them as she had been accustomed to doing, experienced extreme degradation and shame. How that was technically dealt with lies outside the present context (cf. Chapter Seven, below).

(d) It is, however, this very context that compels me to add that prior to the unsuccessful treatment mentioned above the unfortunate woman had been exploited sexually by an evidently psychotic psychopath under the guise of a psychological therapy on the couch.

I have adduced these occurrences because they are all concerned with partial undress. The latter is not therefore a concession to the censor, but *is an undistorted element in the representation of the unconscious infantile dream wish and its successors from subsequent ages, i.e., actual experiences involving not total but partial undress.*

It is strange that Freud overlooked this possibility, because he compared the dream to the exhibitionistic perversion where the aim obviously entails only partial undress.

(2) The second and third essential elements of the typical embarrassment dream of partial undress: *the dreamer feels shame, but (3) the many strangers present are completely uninterested in his exhibition.* Freud's ingenious interpretation that "many people" symbolize a secret is, I believe, to the point. But it does not fit Freud's own description of the child's carefree and "promiscuous" exhibition. The symbolization is fairly frequent and by no means confined to the dream, typical or otherwise: a good deal of symptomatology cannot, in fact, be understood without it. Yet I have less often found it utilized by the repressing forces, which in the dream would mean by the censor, than by the "return of the repressed."

The element "many strange people" is overdetermined. With respect to its next determinant Freud writes,

> I know of no instance in which the actual spectators of the infantile scene of exhibiting have appeared in the dream . . . What takes their place in dreams—'a lot of strangers' who take no notice of the spectacle that is offered—is nothing more nor less than the wishful contrary of the single familiar individual before whom the dreamer exposed himself [1900, p. 245].

True, but not always so. If it were, Freud could not have called his own dream a dream of nudity and the unappealing elderly maid in it a representative of his old, ugly nurse.

All in all, if one limits oneself to Freud's interpretations, does not the censor emerge as literally draconic? The child's wish to show himself is not only reduced to a partial undress frequently so arranged that it actually shows nothing, but the "onlookers" do not even look on. To be sure, there are dreams which remove infantile wishes to the extent that only a thorough analysis reveals an attempt at fulfillment. Nevertheless, is it to be doubted that the innocuous early childhood wish under consideration should regularly—in the paradigmatic form of the typical dream—suffer that thorough an eradication? I think not.

However, if this be a misconception, I can at least account for its origin in three clinical observations.

The first concerned the patient whose dream of nudity on Fifth Avenue has been reported above. Her enuretic episodes in puberty and adolescence were often accompanied by the same dream in which she felt the need, held back anxiously, but eventually dreamt that she was on the toilet, where, greatly relieved, she performed the requisite partial undress and let go. The same was true of a second patient who wet her bed regularly from between the ages of three or four until she was 10. The third patient, instead, experienced an arousal preceded by an arousal dream in which the urge was also felt and caused the dreamer to scurry anxiously from place to place for its gratification. The scene was always outdoors (the patient lived as a child in a rural area), and she squatted each time, beginning the necessary removal of clothing until she found that the bush or fence which had promised privacy did not grant it, and eventually woke up.

I believe observations such as these entitle one to view the partial undress in the misnamed dream of nudity as serving the drive, not the interference with it by the censor. This becomes the more convincing because it is possible to subject the third typical element in the dream, *the disinterestedness of the many strangers,* to a reinterpretation overdetermining it. This can be done by comparing it to the clinical picture of the recovery from delusions of observation through the undoing of a morbid split in the ego. In describing this (II, 115–118), I have stressed the fact that the malevolently critical "observers" do not in the course of recovery from the delusion become benevolent but merely cease to observe. And I adduced the tremendous relief experienced by a patient whom the erstwhile "observers" had changed into an uninterested crowd—a crowd exactly as the one appearing in the dream.

Shame and partial undress then, would allude to an infantile sexual excretory drive mobilized by the unconscious infantile dream wish. However, the drive must be conquered; continence must be maintained in the interest of the wish to sleep and the preservation of the dreamer's ego organization. The manifest incongruence between shame and the disinterestedness of the crowd is due, it would appear, to the general lack of grammar in the dream. The antithetic juxtaposition (primary process) should therefore interpretatively be replaced with the adversative conjunction *but* (secondary process). The latent thought would then read as follows: I am under the impact of an excretory drive (partial subject formation), *but* I am suppressing it (most often apparently by means of an transient ego split allowing the introject to inhibit the development of the partial subject) and thus remain intact and asleep.

Since the partial undress is only allusive, it is impossible to specify the exact nature of the drive alluded to by the undress, although I personally am left with the impression that the drive is most frequently urethral-erotic and subject to Freud's explanation of the enuresis of the child.

A critic once accused me of "manipulating" my patients' material. I assume that the man was ignorant of the difference between manipulation and interpretation, and I hope the reader will not share his confusion if I present a dream of the same patient that seems at first sight to contradict my thesis, inasmuch as here the dreamer is actually in the nude.

Dream: she is in complete undress on the street but well tanned and again free from anxiety until eventually she encounters a Mr. X., a man in authority who, perceiving her, is shocked and says: "Well, this is really going too far." Whereupon first she gets down on her knees, then squats on her heels and puts her hands in a "graceful pose" over her lap and an abdominal scar, at the same time covering her bosom with her hands. She believes she looks beautiful and hopes that it is not too bad . . . . The telephone rings (on a little table in the street), and he is too busy and forgets about her.

The interpretation rests on several fragments of information, some derived from Freud, others not, and one never published before.

To begin with the last: "tan," in my experience, always alludes to the "uncastrated constitution" (cf. I, 171–181), illustrated by the sculptors of antiquity who omit the female genital by joining the abdomen to the thighs. The insurance of continence (I, 176) is the fundamental determinant for the primal fantasy of this constitution.

Yet the whole of the dream and, in particular, the dreamer's squatting and covering her genitals with her hand make it quite clear that she is *not* possessed of an uncastrated constitution. Is it fantastic to say that she is clad in her "tan" and that in this instance only her genital represents the partial undress? Those who think it is ought to know that she was an incontinent adolescent girl who resumed in the first two years of analysis a certain measure of urinary incontinence collateral to the fantasy of a "vaginal" urination. She called her protection against it through closing the vulva by means of femoral pressure, "making it all skin." This direct mode of expression was accompanied by a symbolic one: she appeared for her hour invariably carrying a stiff pigskin purse with brass edges and a clanking brass ring—a veritable small piece of luggage—which she closed noisily and placed firmly on the floor next to the couch before lying down. It was long after the incontinence had been relinquished, the urethra ascertained, and the struggle for the appropriation of a genital started, that she began leaving the pocketbook in the hall. Later still, when her previous symbolic action was interpreted, she promptly associated [bell-] "ringing" to the pocketbook ring.

This association suggests commenting next on the telephone ringing in the end of the dream. It appears an "arousal dream upon external stimulation," yet it is not. No telephone actually rang, and the patient never wound her alarm clock to strike. The ringing was merely dreamt, and the stimulation was altogether internal. Interpretatively one has only to follow Freud's (1900) original comment on the dream with the neologism *"tutelrein"* (p. 297) to know that the stimulus is urethral-erotic, even if one were disinclined to consider the squatting allusively. Whether or not street, table, and telephone are symbols is a moot question, in spite of the fact that the patient at the time of the dream still indulged in vaginal masturbation. The "disinterested onlookers," finally, are here not hallucinated but merely implied.

In conclusion, the affect: It is lacking—at first she has no anxiety and later only the slightest doubt—but the lack allows for a ready explanation. It lies in the occurrence of a spoken word in the dream. The latter testifies, as was explained in the preceding chapter, to a transient reintegrative superego formation by which a soliloquy is produced, expressing a critical self-observation. One is led to imagine that the "free" energy, requisite to the liberation of the anxiety, is bound by the institutions (and demi-institutions) opposing each other as a result of the reintegration. Thus interpreted, the dream no longer appears to contradict my thesis.

Freud once apologized for the complexity of his presentation with the remark that the complexity is not of his doing but inherent in the subject matter described. I hope the reader remembers this if he recalls a dream of nudity previously reported (I, 219). I repeat the text in order to add a few essential fragments to my earlier interpretation:

> Company, all male, is gathered in the patient's room; father among them. She is clad only in pajamas and begins to menstruate; blood is running down her leg and foot. She asks her father to reach into a cupboard and hand her her bathrobe, which he does.

Typical elements present: partial undress, disinterestedness of the onlookers; element missing: the affect (embarrassment). The complexity of the subject forces one to append the contradictory statement: while embarrassment is requisite to this particular dream, it may nevertheless be lacking if the censor has succeeded in his task of suppressing all affect. This may not, however, necessarily alter the otherwise "truly typical" nature of the dream. Finally, my impression rendered above concerning the urethral-erotic stimulus, elaborated upon in the dream, is supported by a clinical observation concerning menstruation. Menstruation, in particular its inception, is not seldom subject to a regressive interpretation by patients, who thus reveal their fear of incontinence which may hitherto and in other contexts have gone unnoticed. Upon perceiving what should be clearly recognized as the beginning of their period, they have to inspect themselves in order to make certain that the percept is blood. Conversely, in the case of the menstrual dream repeated above, the dreamer's correct apperception of the actual onset of her menstruation may have assisted the censor in sparing her the affect of embarrassment otherwise typical for the dream of partial undress.

It was only after the manuscript of the present section had been finished, that looking over old notes I came upon a long forgotten transcript of the most instructive embarrassment dream of partial undress in my possession. If this dream were paradigmatic it could have saved much argument, because the dreamer while dreaming it actually felt in need of urination. Unfortunately it is not paradigmatic; on the contrary it is the only one of its kind I have. However, it must have unconsciously guided me in my attempt to unravel the others.

The dreamer, a schizophrenic female, reports a long, confused, and unanalyzable dream, the locale of which shifts from a restaurant to a skating rink and then to the room of an unidentifiable man, before it ends on the street, where the dreamer finds herself in the company of this man.

From the end of the transcript I excerpt the pertinent parts: . . . I was only wearing my nightgown . . . and I think . . . a dark blue coat over my shoulders . . . I had to go to the bathroom, and I asked him where the ladies' room was. He said there wasn't any and told me we would have to go to a large public street toilet.

We were walking (rather we were running), it was freezing out, and I was still wearing my nightgown. We had to wait for the light to change and were standing on a small street island. I felt very embarrassed standing there on the street in my night-gown . . . But nobody paid any attention to me, people were rushing on with that "get-home-at-five-o'clock-look" on their faces . . .

She wakes up, finds her bedroom actually cold and herself in urgent need of the toilet.

This is, except for its very end, an absolutely typical embarrassment dream of partial undress: the undress is undisplaced, and the embarrassment is not only felt but directly contrasted with the disinterestedness of the crowd. (That such occurs so late in the dream is evidently owing to a displacement of affect [Freud] which really belongs to the beginning.) What distinguishes this particular dream from so many of its kind is the direct expression of the urethral-erotic drive. In the others it was merely my contention that they represent it, although indirectly. The dream is an arousal dream, as was the one quoted two dreams earlier in this section; yet if anyone would hold that against my rendition of the latent thought, which has the urge conquered and the disturbance removed, he would only prove himself unfamiliar with the tenacity of the wish to sleep.

What actually happened is this: The dreamer is stimulated by the urge and is suitably clad for its gratification. However, the wish to sleep forces her to engage in two different gambits, both of which are well known. The first is the production of an embarrassment dream of partial undress. The second is the attempt to hallucinate finding a place that affords the opportunity for relief. Both attempts are at first successful: sleep is actually prolonged. Both fail in the end. Nevertheless, how insistent the wish to sleep! It compels the dreamer to try a third gambit, projection: it is now no longer she that rushes but the people who urgently have to get home. Only after the failure of this last attempt to rid herself of the urge does the wish to sleep finally give way to arousal.

Lacking the opportunity for experiment, the analyst cannot investigate which particular constellation caused the drive represented indirectly in the usual embarrassment dream of partial undress to represent itself in this one directly. He can only substitute a few reflections. I have become accustomed to ask myself on the occasion of any dream I thought I had understood: why does he or she dream that? The answer given *above* for the typical dream under consideration was: because she is forced to remain continent in the face of a drive demanding phallic urethral-erotic discharge. The reader has probably noticed the feminine pronoun employed in the reply: I, for one, have never encountered this dream in a man. This jibes, for one thing, with the fantasy equating castration with incontinence (I, 171) and, for another, with the fact known to everyone that the boy may flaunt his performance while the girl will seek cover. Standing or squatting, respectively, as the shibboleth for a phallic or a castrated make-up has been described before (II, 214).

In view of these considerations, I am satisfied with my interpretation, quite in contrast to the few abortive interpretive remarks to follow concerning the other typical dreams described by Freud.

Freud's Other Typical Dreams

Is the interpretation suggested here for the embarrassment dream of partial undress basically applicable to any other truly typical dream: the examination dream, the dream of missing the train, or the dream of the death of beloved persons?

The question must be answered with the admission that the evidence available at this time does not suffice to support such a supposition. If I mention it, nevertheless, I do so merely because it might whet the curiosity of a future worker free to investigate where I am dependent upon abortive and inconclusive speculation.

The two antithetic elements directly juxtaposed in the dream of undress—the urinary exhibition and the disinterestedness of the onlookers, representing the drive and its suppression by the dreamer—are recognizable, although more obscurely, in both the examination dream and that of missing the train. The examination is feared, yet it should not be, for it has previously been passed; the train is approached with the intent to board, but it is missed. Clinically, the sexual meaning of examination is difficult to overlook. The fear is originally that of the doctor's examination that will uncover the almost ubiquitously imagined damage through masturbation; it survives in the neurotic woman who palpitates in the waiting room without knowing why, or is afraid the gynecologist will not find her clean enough; but it may also spread onto any kind of examination. Thus an infantile drive to masturbate and its suppression, if more evidence were adduced, might possibly be found alluded to in the examination dream.

Riding in trains is, as was first shown by Freud (1909), a *Verkehr* symbol (*Verkehr* being a single German word for three English ones: transportation, traffic, = intercourse) and equated in the unconscious with activity of a sexual nature. This is observable clinically in certain women (and, in my experience, one man) who become aroused—the women even orgastic—riding in trains, subways, or cars.[11] Missing the train would be equivalent to not embarking upon the sexual "ride"; that is, to suppressing the drive in the interest of the continuation of sleep. So far the situation is understandable, since the "wet dream," in either sex, is apt to lead to arousal. The concurrent motive, the preservation of ego, is less easy to understand. It is intimated by Freud, who at that time unaware of the *Verkehr* symbolism, interprets leaving by train (*abreisen*) as symbolic of dying. He consequently calls the dream one of consolation, expressing the assurance, "you will not die." Here one would have to adduce the relatively frequent unconscious equation of orgasm with death, which I have observed but never understood.

There remains the typical dream of the death of beloved persons, with which I personally am not clinically acquainted, and to the interpretation of which I cannot therefore contribute.

A variant of Freud's dream of inhibition: In the typical dream described by Freud in *The Interpretation of Dreams*

---

[11] A colleague has been kind enough to write me that he has seen it in two men patients and was furthermore able to elicit their concomitant fantasy—one of "passivity in relation to being excited by the 'hot' seat of the bus or subway," the contact with which meant contact with the mother (phallic parent). He also reminds me that Lincoln Steffens in his *Autobiography* tells of his first ejaculation coming from the stimulation of riding a horse (parent symbol) without a saddle.

(1900, p. 238) the restraint is muscular, and the dreamer, try as he may, cannot get off the spot; the inhibition, in other words, is felt in the body. In the variant to be reported here, it is not so felt but is projected upon the environment: in particular upon vehicles and the clock. The affect is the same in variant and original: an often anxious feeling of frustration.

Three examples:

Perhaps the oldest example is to be found in *The Interpretation of Dreams,* although it is not recognized there as a typical dream. Freud's patient wanted to give a supper-party, but

> I had nothing in the house but a little smoked salmon. I thought I would go out and buy something, but remembered then that it was Sunday afternoon and all the shops would be shut. Next I tried to ring up some caterers, but the telephone was out of order. So I had to abandon my wish to give a supper-party (p. 147).

Although an affect is not reported, the shops being closed and the telephone out of order resemble the vehicles and the clock inasmuch as they are elements of the object world requisite to the fulfillment of an intent which they foil.[12]

A patient who was a figure skater had this dream:

> I took my skates down to Rockefeller Plaza to show off for my family. I put on my skates and, feeling very confident and anxious to fly out across the ice, I stepped onto the rink. My feet just crunched down—the ice had turned to sand—I couldn't glide at all. I awoke and was miserable. It would have been such a satisfactory dream if I could have performed for these people.

The third example comes from yet another patient.

Preamble. She reports that she had intended to go to the premiere of a performance, in which the lead was to be played by a woman upon whom it was known that the patient had transferred her mother. Several

---

[12] A study of Freud's ingenious analysis is most rewarding, although he does not elucidate the intent as such or why the smoked salmon escapes the "no" expressed in all dreams of inhibition.

hours before the beginning of the performance she found herself in the grip of a mounting anxiety which she promptly allayed by a bit of self-analysis. She recognized the scoptophilic nature of the impending experience: a premiere is an "opening" performance, and the curtains to be drawn aside symbolize the labia while at the same time representing the open underdrawers, worn and drawn aside by her exhibiting mother. The leading lady, actually her junior, is thus symbolically and historically equipped as her (psychotic) mother. She connects this correctly and in detail with the earliest sexual seduction by the latter, that had a while ago come out of amnesia.

Her next association is a dream she had the night before the premier.

> She comes to the performance a day late, to the second performance instead of the premiere, and is very disappointed. The auditorium has half of the seats facing one way, sideways, and the other half facing in the other direction. Only one row faces the stage. On the left side of the stage (the side seen to the right) there is a huge wooden pulpit or lectern obscuring much of that side. Behind it is the leading lady "performing" . . . The dreamer wore a blue sweater but was not sure whether she had it on. She therefore looked down on herself making sure that she did. But she saw that her dress had no belt.

Comment: I omit the analysis of the dream because the preamble contains all that is pertinent to the present subject. I confine myself to pointing out that it represents the variant of the dream of inhibition described above. Again the inhibition is not felt in the body but projected onto the object world: it is a day late (clock), and the better part of the seats in the auditorium face away from the stage, that is, only a few of them allow for seeing. (In addition, what the dreamer sees is not what she came to see.) The typical affect: a feeling of strong disappointment.

Yet the dream is not purely a dream of inhibition, but a mixture of it with the dream of partial undress: she is not sure whether she wears her sweater (displacement from below to above), she has to inspect herself, and she finds that she lacks her belt. This element, expressive of an identification with the exhibiting mother testifies to the aforementioned tendency of typical dream themes to combine with each other.

B. THE SYMBOLICALLY TYPICAL DREAM OF THE ANALYTIC HOUR

This difficult subject is perhaps best treated against the background of two examples wherein the analytic session is dreamt of, without, however, either dream being a "typical dream of the analytic hour."

The first of these is a so-called "child's dream" (Freud), that is, one representative of an undisguised wish-fulfillment from the present. The dreamer is an adult beginning her treatment, but loath to comply with the analytic rule, and a paradigm for "oral-erotic silence" (I, 293–298).

Dream: She finds herself late in the evening in the analyst's office, feels "warm and cozy," and while speaking is aware of her leg having slipped off the couch and hanging down from the side, without a shoe. "You knelt next to me," her report continues, "put your hand between my legs . . . etc. . . . It felt good." Whereupon the analyst walks back to his chair and addresses the patient: "Don't say another word!" Then in undress he resumes his approach.

The wish-fulfillment is twofold and has both times escaped dream work: sexual gratification instead of analysis, and interdiction of verbalization instead of the demand for it. The locale, however, portrays accurately that of the session, which it never does in the typical dream to be discussed shortly.

The second dream, here only summarized, stems from the so-called reanalysis of a patient who had previously been with someone untouched by analytic knowledge. The locale is again portrayed correctly, and the dreamer tells the present analyst a dream concerning which the analyst gives him an absolute gibberish of an interpretation.

The dream was not difficult to interpret: it represented the wish that the first analyst be refound in the second. This was easy to understand, for the latter had acquainted the patient with a most troublesome life situation, difficult to resolve—a situation of which the former had left him completely unaware.

It will be noted that in both dreams not only the locale is represented correctly but even the action is possible—at least as seen from the standpoint of the dreamer. In the first case the patient, unacquainted with analysis, may well have conceived of the analyst's ceasing to insist upon verbalization and instead doing her bidding. In the second, the analyst could have proved himself—was in fact at least preconsciously expected to—as ignorant as his predecessor.

None of this is ever so in the particular typical dream of the analytic hour under discussion here, where the manifest content is always completely absurd. A comprehensive description of the manifest content is almost impossible because of its great variety from dream to dream. Almost impossible, but not quite. There are a few features, more or less distinct, that lend to all of these dreams a basically typical complexion:

(1) The privacy of the analytic session is always replaced by its opposite in the dream through the presence or the intrusion of a person or persons more often than not unknown. One gathers the impression that with regard to the present this is a defense against a wish arising in consequence of the transference, and with regard to the past a wish-fulfillment because the dream often shows an indeterminate number of persons in the locale, representative, one must conclude, of the symbolization through many persons of a secret (Freud).

(2) In the second place the locale may or may not be the actual office, and if it is it need not stay so throughout the dream. Even the couch may change its characteristics.

(3) In the third place the analysis either does not take place or soon "peters out"; what patient and analyst say is hardly ever known. Sometimes the analyst "has no time," at other times he has an assistant ("two people" = mother?) or he may refer the patient to someone else of the opposite sex. (I remember a paranoid woman patient who tried to rid herself of her painful mother transference by the expectation voiced many a time in the actual session that "someone else, perhaps a woman" might be able to help her.)

(4) And lastly, is the constant symbolism of the (analyst's) "room," to be discussed below.

The original description of the dream of the analytic hour by Feldman (1945) contains, I believe, many errors; I select two to assist in clarification. For one thing, the dreamer is supposed to react with "resentment" to the intrusion. I have never heard this from patients, which, without excluding it, shows the lack of a constant affect and proves that one deals here not with a true but with a symbolically typical dream.

The second point is much more subtle. The original interpreter saw in the dream the fulfillment of a wish for the mother, a desire to be "in perfect fusion with her," and to change his relation to the analyst into that between mother and child. This quite evades the sexual nature of the wish. In order to show that the wish is one for a *sexual* "fusion," I shall quote the report on a dream of the analytic hour and its interpretation, given to me by a colleague who was altogether unbiased because of the lack of any knowledge whatever of the subject.

> I was to be analyzed by a different analyst who looked like Dr. X. [Someone else's analyst, sharing an office with others.] There was a couch or some similar hospital equipment. The analysis was to take place in the open air. It was raining, so we had to go somewhere else for the analysis—to a garden or something—I had the thought "It's like being analyzed by a friend." Then I woke, sexually aroused.

Here again are all the hallmarks: the "different" analyst, a defense against the one upon whom the patient has tranferred and by whom he is therefore threatened; the other analysts, by implication, and their patients, i.e., the presence of many people; the transformation of the couch, the negation of the analyst's "room," the symbolic object of the unconscious infantile dream wish and, in spite of the reassuring spoken word, the undisguised sexuality upon arousal.

In the interest of preserving anonymity I will not reproduce the expert analysis of the dream which, of course, took its cues conscientiously from the patient's associations. I can only quote the final interpretation by the analyst who, as I mentioned, was unprejudiced by any knowledge of the typical meaning of the dream: "The patient's associations to the dream show the latter reflecting an intense homosexual transference to the analyst, who represents for the patient chiefly the phallic mother."

The symbol dominating this symbolically typical dream is, of course, the [treatment] "room" that the dreamer wishes to enter; that is, the vagina (womb, "mother's belly"), to be entered sexually as a part of the analyst upon whom the mother (essentially the maternal partial object) has been transferred. Yet the dream is particularly graphic in showing the interplay between wish and censor: the instinctual aim is foiled in the very process of being at least implicitly fulfilled.

This, then, is the interpretation; what has been described above are the constant features of the manifest content of the symbolically typical dream of the analytic hour. They define a portion of its otherwise infinite variety of content.

C. THE TRULY TYPICAL DREAM OF THE MISSED ANALYTIC HOUR

The furnishing of an analyzable transcript of this dream is complicated by the tendency mentioned above of typical dreams to combine with each other. It is consequently a conglomerate of two typical dreams, that of the analytic hour and the variant of the dream of inhibition. It is in view of this complication that I precede its description with an example:

> My watch read 2:45—I had 15 minutes to get to you. Leisurely I got into a bus, and as I looked out the window I passed a clock which read 4:30. I was panicked and very furious with myself. My watch had stopped, and I had missed my appointment with you. I decided to forget the appointment—not to call you, but turn around and return home.
>
> I woke feeling terribly frustrated and sad. When I realized I had only been dreaming, I was overjoyed. Tomorrow I could see you on time as usual.

> [*Associations:*] This dream reminded me of dreams I had as a child. One, in particular, where I was walking up the steps to school and the bell rang. I was late, and as I tried to run, my legs froze. I couldn't budge. The frustration was similar to that in the recent dream, although it was not actually I that caused the frustration—my legs moved freely—it was my watch that had stopped.

It is convenient to comment upon this material in reverse order because the associations place one on familiar ground and thus supply a starting point for the analysis of the dream. The first association consists of the memory of another dream, dreamt at six years of age, a dream not only typical but well known—the dream of inhibition, the analysis of which has been amended above.

The adult patient's dream is the variant of the dream of inhibition described toward the end of Section A, above. As has been said before, in the dream Freud described, as in the childhood dream of the patient, the inhibition is felt in the body; it is muscular. In the variant, it is not so felt but is projected upon the environment: vehicles and the clock.

A more comprehensive account of this type of dream would therefore have to state that in the dream of the missed analytic hour the dreamer *tries to come to the session but fails because each attempt is met by an obstacle of one sort or another: trolleys and buses reverse their course, streets have altered their location, elevators refuse to stop at the office floor, clocks change their time; and the hour is missed in the course of interminable endeavour.* In this dream the *affect* is constant; the experience of failure is accompanied by a mixture of anxiety and disappointment, often condensed to a more or less pronounced feeling of frustration.

This, of course, is a "truly typical" dream *since it is always accompanied by the same affect.* In contrast to the symbolically typical dream of the analytic hour, it depicts traveling to the session instead of the session itself. Yet the traveling is of no avail; the environment foils the dreamer's attempts to reach the analyst's office.

The pressure of the resistance against the work of interpretation has, in my experience, invariably been so great that I have never succeeded in learning the meaning of this typical and not too infrequent dream. I cannot, therefore be definitive in interpreting the dream in this case, I can only speculate. Instances where elements of the analyst's domicile are exploited symbolically for the transference of the mother upon the male analyst are not rare. Nor is the reason for such exploitation obscure: the house, the staircase, the vestibule, the (treatment) room are all female symbols representing the transference object's sexual parts. So much for the object of the dreamer's drive. As for the aim, it is introjective; she wants to enter the mother—a particular kind of identification that is distinctive for the psychology of the pregnant woman (I, 213–215).

In the ordinary dream of the missed analytic hour none of this is discernible because, while the object is known, the aim is not reached and lacks all, even indirect, representation. Yet the childhood dream associated to the dream, quoted at the beginning of the section, does represent the aim, and the aim is the same: the dreamer freezes on the STAIRS of the (school) HOUSE which she is eager to ENTER.

This is as far as I am able to go toward an interpretation. One could, in addition, bring forth two more reflections and questions.

In the first place, one should articulate a characteristic of the typical dreams Freud illustrated in his staircase dream but never described: the aforementioned tendency of these dreams to combine. In the last clinical illustration, for example, only the first part of the dream is actually a dream of the missed analytic hour; the second part is an abortive dream of the analytic hour.

If it could be shown that the typical dream actually represented the dreamer's *struggle for continence* in the face of the incontinent unconscious infantile dream wish, the frequent fusion of several typical dreams could be understood.

To be specific: the dream of the missed analytic hour resembles Freud's typical dream of missing the train (1900, p. 385) so closely that one is tempted to borrow his ingenious interpretation for the rendition of an overdetermination. Both train departure and analytic hour are precisely scheduled events; the dream quoted at the beginning of this section emphasizes time and the clock.

Of the symbolization of death in the dream of missing the train it was previously explained that it is a sexual process. However, the process is a different one and so, consequently, is the symbolization. Here death is symbolized, if at all, as the return to the mother's womb (Freud, 1933). It is the *Mutterleib* fantasy consummated in the symbolically typical dream of the analytic hour that may well lend itself to the representation of death and force the dream of the missed analytic hour to devote itself to its negation. Both "missing trains" and "missing the session" are inhibition dreams *(Hemmungstraeume)*; and in both the latent negation is manifested as a failure of action. It may be true of both that the dream, as Freud has expressed it, "says in a consoling way 'Don't worry, you won't die." ("leave by train" in the present instance = return to the womb); and to both these dreams his remark may apply that the difficulty in understanding them stems from "the fact that the feeling of anxiety is attached precisely to the expression of consolation" (p. 385).

Two further typical dreams have been adquately described and interpreted in the previous volumes of this series; in the present one they need be merely recalled. The first is the pre- (sometimes post-) menstrual dream "Mother Comes In" (I, 216–221). It is of course a symbolically typical dream because no constant affect accompanies it, and it is typical only by reason of the employment of a symbol (mother = womb).

The "Wave Dream" was described and interpreted partly in the first volume (221–230) and partly in the second (359–364). It is a truly typical dream, for the affect in paradigmatic wave dreams is always terror inducing arousal. In some instances a diurnal fear may evidently replace the nocturnal one; the patient is then afraid of waves when awake but does not dream about them.

D. POSTSCRIPT

I have more than once given voice to my frustration over the fragmentary and often speculative character of the preceding text. But, after all, I have not promised more than that at the outset; and, as the saying goes, "only a scoundrel gives more than he has . . ." My justification in writing it has been the hope that a future analyst interested in the subject might, in spite of its shortcomings, find it useful. The kindness of a colleague enables me to demonstrate in a postscript that even the present-day analyst may profit from it. My colleague was good enough to study the manuscript, to make some editorial suggestions which I have followed, and to send me some pertinent material that I shall quote verbatim before appending a brief comment of my own.

Dream of a Missed Analytic Session:

Basic Situation: A young man in analysis who later went on to have a psychotic break has become increasingly provocative toward a sadistic boss at his job—being late, making errors, etc. It was interpreted that he was provoking punishment and being fired—provoking the very anger and disapproval he complained of. He has been bringing up homosexual feelings with great resistance. These feelings in relation to the analyst have just been inflamed (by way of anal eroticism) after a discussion about raising his analytic fee which made him very angry, distrustful toward the analyst in a mild paranoid fashion.

Dream: "A vivid dream. I overslept and missed a complete period. I woke up and pictured you here waiting for me the whole time. I felt overpowering anxiety. It was inexcusable. Then I really woke up."

Associations: "Fear of your hatred of me [projection of his anal rage, and retaliatory expectations in relation to it]. Lately I have been going back to sleep after the alarm clock rings and have been late to work every day this week. I'm really provoking being knocked down."

This is the patient's characteristic expression for his provocation at work. The boss is very close to his father, who hears all about his son's conduct.

Missing a period: "Sounds like a woman—I don't think that is significant."

Here the provoking "being knocked down" (symbolic of pregnancy and allusive to being the woman in intercourse would be associated with provoking being "knocked up" (= pregnant). The pregnancy fantasy is unconscious, and the path to it is repudiated. The associations went on to fear of being made fun of in relation to saying the wrong thing at work; fear of being mocked and criticized for the way he expresses himself, here, the fear of doing something wrong with his mouth. This was related to "it was inexcusable." There is at work a wish for intercourse with and becoming pregnant by the analyst. His feeling of doing wrong would seem to refer primarily to this. But it turns out also to refer to incontinence—perhaps the incontinence of the castrated woman.

The next day he again woke up late and got to work very late. He was yelled at for his lateness and for "messing things up." He discovered that he had *forgotten* (missed) putting on his belt and that his pants kept falling down. During the intervening night he had another dream—a dream of partial undress [!].

"I was throwing a hand grenade, everybody ducked and turned their backs. I thought I was OK but discovered that I had no shirt on. I got some holes in my back that seemed to be OK, but my little finger was bleeding."

Associations: "It's like a war at work, with all the quarreling that goes on." He has always had a fascination and fear for war novels and war movies. "I throw bombs at work by messing up and making mistakes and coming late." He has a real abrasion on his hand. As a child, he hurt his finger in the *back* of his father's car; it bled so badly he fainted. Part of his finger was lost in an accident as a child.

Here the anal-erogeneity is predominant, and the libidinal wishes are passive and feminine, with fluctuations back and forth throughout all the libidinal levels. The sadistic destructiveness certainly goes back to wishes associated with incontinence. Incontinence = losing control of his anus (messing things up)— being penetrated and impregnated and castrated.

My comment is not intended to correct any of my colleague's intepretations, all of which I find convincing, but to confirm and amend them. His communication should be entitled A

Dream of the Missed Analytic Session *Followed* by an Embarrassment Dream of Partial Undress. The reason why in this instance the two typical dreams do not, as is their common tendency, combine but follow each other I would seek in the peculiar situation of the dreamer. He is a psychotic under the exigency of an imminent break. Observation has shown me that many psychotics defend themselves, with or without success, against breaking down. In the present case it would appear that almost everything atypical in the two typical dreams is explainable, speculatively I admit, in light of the dreamer's make-up and situation. In other words, as far as the dreams are typical they are interpretable along the lines laid down in this chapter, while the atypical elements in them reflect defenses against the psychotic break.

Before demonstrating this, a few general preliminary remarks. The nocturnal psychosis of the normal individual is sharply delimited: it begins with the inception of dreaming and ends with arousal. Once awake he is no longer psychotic, and the primary process prevails only in daydreaming and parapraxia. The failure of the censor to suppress affect is the only common characteristic of his typical dreams. Anxiety is observable in these dreams only as an admixture of a fully developed affect. The immersion, finally, into primary process is harmless; where it would not be, dream work makes it so under the watchful eyes of the censor; and where the censor fails the sleeper, he has, in consequence of the ready changeability of the depth sleep, still two further safety valves at his disposal: interpolation of dreamless sleep and arousal.

All this is different in the patient under consideration. He enters his nocturnal psychosis not from normality but from a diurnal psychosis, recently aggravated by the transformation through treatment into a transference psychosis. This has mobilized both anal erogeneity and the common defense against it: (strong) anger and (mild) paranoid distrust. Thus agitated, he has an atypical "typical dream." Atypical in three respects: there is for one thing no attempt to reach the office, and for another no affect connoting disappointment or frustration; only severe anxiety and implied fear of punishment. ("It was inexcusable.") The arousal, finally, is preceded by a "waking up" in the dream. I would for all three of these divagations imagine only one reason: the inability, inherent in paranoia, to admit love. The dreamer's attempts to approach the analyst implies being attracted by him, as does the disappointment when he fails to reach the office. By the same token this particular patient's arousal has to occur in the dream, that is, with the censor's assistance in suppressing the affect of frustration which would testify to the attraction. That eventually the actual waking up is devoid of affect ("Then I really woke up.") would accord with this explanation. Only in the associations is the sexual love (in anal-sadistic terms with phallic-castrated overtones) permitted to be expressed and understood by the analyst, although not by the patient.

Much of the same reasoning applies to the atypical features of the second typical dream, which in contrast to the first, revolving around the instinctual *object,* concerns itself with the instinctual *aim.* This dream is again entered not from normality but from a psychotic state. The patient's omitting his belt, for instance, so that his trousers kept falling down can surely be called a parapraxis. (One must not forget that Freud was only interested in interpreting this phenomenon and in demonstrating its applicability to everyone—hence the title of his treatise *Psychopathology of Everyday Life* [1901].) It devolves upon us to draw the line between a normal and a psychotic parapraxis. I am convinced that a normal white-collar office worker could never go so far as to actually forget his belt, but would relegate such a degree of partial undress to the dream. (Cf. the nonpsychotic patient discussed above who *dreamt* that she was in the theatre without her dress belt.)

The dream itself is again an atypical form of a typical dream, that is an embarrassment dream of partial undress with the affect—the embarrassment—missing. Instead, the assurance: "that seemed to be OK." My colleague's interpretation follows mine in interpreting the partial undress while implying why the embarrassment is not allowed to arise: it would add the inadmissible libidinal instinct component (penetration, impregnation) to the destructive one, regressive in terms of the first anal stage.

IV. ON THE TOPOGRAPHICAL ANALYSIS OF THE DREAM

A. THE PROBLEM AND THE TECHNIQUE

The "Topographical Analysis of The Dream" is another bit of pioneer labor with results as fragmentary as with the analysis of the typical dream. However, there is a fundamental difference between the two: the procedure applied to typical dreams is still analysis, pure if not simple; the topographical analysis is not psychoanalysis in the accurate sense of the word. Instead of occupying itself with interpreting a dream, it attempts to trace the alterations in the dreamer's ego during the course of dreaming. It investigates predominantly, although not exclusively, causes as well as effects of the dreamer's varying depth of sleep.

Sleep research notwithstanding, with very few exceptions only "arousal dreams" are subject to a topographical analysis at the present time. This is true because for one thing the very arousal furnishes a bit of "vertical" reference for the depth of sleep, and for another such dreams frequently contain "ready-made fantasies" (Freud). One has, of course, studied these fantasies thoroughly in the dreamer's analysis, and therefore possesses much more information about them than the interpretation of a single dream could supply. Finally one is apt to be acquainted, either in or after the dream, with the stimulus that has compelled the arousal.

Technically, a transcript of the dream is required; a mere recital will not suffice, and the time for attempting a topographical analysis is *never* the analytic hour. The method is best described while presenting the few results obtainable so far.

A starting point is easily found in one of Freud's writings. In the fifth of his *Introductory Lectures* (1915–17) he gives a vivid description of how the dreamer experiences different dreams or parts of dreams.

> We might try to account for these many variations in dreams by supposing that they correspond to different intermediate stages between sleeping and waking, different degrees of incomplete sleep. Yes, but if this were so, the value, content and clarity of a dream's product—and the awareness, too, of its being a dream—would have to increase in dreams in which the mind was coming near to waking; and it would not be possible for a clear and rational fragment of dream to be immediately followed by one that was senseless and obscure and for this in turn to be followed by another good piece. The mind could certainly not alter the depth of its sleep so quickly as that. So this explanation is of no help: there can be no short cut out of the difficulty [1915–1917, p. 91].

As a whole, this argument is of course correct; the assumption of different intermediate stages between dreaming and wakefulness cannot explain a dream: everything else contained in *The Interpretation of Dreams* is needed for such explanation.

However, if one disregards the argument as a whole and examines separately the statements that make it up, one finds two that are incorrect. One of these tenets states that shallow sleep, that is, sleep close to wakefulness, should be accompanied by a relatively clear awareness that the experience is a dream. The other is that the mind could not that rapidly vary the depth of sleep.

With reference to the first statement, it takes but a cursory glance at the arousal dreams upon external stimulation, quoted in *The Interpretation of Dreams* to show that this is not so. Because the stimulus is obstinately reinterpreted in the interest of the wish to sleep, it *must* be perceived by the dreamer; and because it is perceived, the ego must reintegratively have possessed itself of the faculty of perception—a fact *testifying to a relatively shallow sleep.* Someone deeply asleep might not have heard the alarm clock at all. However, there is not the slightest awareness on the part of the dreamer that the experience, Hildebrandt's sleighride, for instance (Freud, 1900, p. 28), is only dreamt. In some of these dreams the ringing even becomes progressively louder—the perception approximates that of wakefulness—yet again there is no lessening of the dreamer's conviction of the reality of his hallucination.

One can pursue this argument still further if one studies a certain phenomenon which has apparently not engaged Freud's attention. It is the *aftermath* of some dreams. Most dreams lack aftermath: the erstwhile dreamer is fully awake upon arousal; he perceives his environment and may remember his dream with detachment as a dream. Affectively he may regret that a beautiful dream had to end or feel relieved that a nightmare is over. A certain number of dreamers, however, have on occasion a very different experience upon arousal. They are awake inasmuch as they are aware of no longer sleeping or dreaming. Yet they find themselves under the impact of a carryover from the dream—in the instance I could observe, a delusion coupled with intense fear—which they succeed in dispelling only after a noticeable lapse of time.

I remember a paradigmatic instance of aftermath where the dreamer maintained that it took her "two or three minutes" to realize that the fearful experience had actually only been dreamt and that there was really nothing to be afraid of. I do not know of course how accurately she gauged the time interval, but I do not have to; her description tells definitely of an aftermath as compared with the ordinary arousal.

To revert to contradicting Freud's thesis: in the case of the aftermath, sleep is not only shallow but altogether relinquished, and there is still no distinct awareness that the experience is only a dream.

B. THE CEILING OF THE DREAM

I have pursued the argument this far, not in order to run it into the ground, but to establish the concept of a "ceiling" for the dream. This ceiling, which separates sleep from wakefulness, has a point of bifurcation from which a short, direct time leads the dreamer immediately to complete arousal while a longer, indirect one has him first wake up into a hypnopompic state,[13] reaching wakefulness eventually from there unless he returns to sleep. The same bifurcation becomes evident in falling asleep: one may pass from wakefulness into sleep either directly or through a hypnagogic state.

There is no doubt that both the hypnagogic and hypnopompic states (the aftermath is an impressive example of the latter) are autohypnotic.[14] In the case of the aftermath the reader may illustrate this for himself by comparing the erstwhile dreamer's condition with that of a hypnotist's subject. The latter's affect and ideation are reactive to his environment not as it is but *as the hypnotist says it is*. In the aftermath one merely exchanges hypnotist for the dream and reacts according to what has been put into it by the sleeper. "*Sleep*walking" is thus recognizable as a misnomer: it is not during sleep but during a *hypnopompic* (i.e., autohypnotic) state that the walking occurs.

C. THE FLOOR OF THE DREAM

By the same token, the dream also has a "floor." If the ceiling is adjacent to wakefulness, the floor abuts on the sleeper's reflex apparatus operative in dreamless sleep.[15] Since reflexes, as Freud has expressed it, lie outside of the realm of anything psychic *(ausserhalb des Psychischen gelegen)*, the ego in dream-

---

[13] This intermediate state between sleeping and wakefulness is called hypnopompic if traversed in the course of arousal and hypnagogic if traversed while falling asleep.

[14] Cf. Freud (1900), speaking of the condition requisite for free association: "What is in question, evidently, is the establishment of a psychical state which, in its distribution of psychical energy . . . bears some analogy to the state before falling asleep—and no doubt also to hypnosis" (p. 102).

[15] I feel that those who deny the existence of dreamless sleep do not rate an elaborate refutation. They can naturally oppose any experience of dreamless sleep with the argument that the dreaming is not remembered. However, the theory of the dream describes the latter as a *disturbance*, caused by the resistance to decathexis by a combination of day residue and infantile wish, and a relative failure of the wish to sleep. To assume that sleep is always disturbed is no more sensible than to postulate a disturbance for every instance of any other natural function. The fact that some people limp because their gait is subject to a disturbance will induce no one to postulate that all people walk with a limp.

less sleep is completely dissolved. The clinical observation to be introduced at this point is the "ellipsis" in the manifest content of the dream. It is indicative of a breaking through the floor and *of the consequent transitory interpolation of dreamless sleep*. The ellipsis, marked with the symbol [E] in the dream text below, indicates the incongruity between an implied continuity of dream action and a break in the dream text. This, I am firmly convinced, is indicative of a temporary suspension of hallucination in consequence of a sinking of the depth of sleep below the "floor" of the dream state.

Example: The dream (as transcribed by the patient):

> I dreamed I was in a semi-dark room. There was a mirror. I was naked and looked at my left side in the mirror. I wanted to pull up my left breast and suck the nipple. At first I hesitated, thinking about having to report it to Dr. F. Also it would be acting out instead of waiting for the analysis. But I couldn't resist the temptation [E_1]. After sucking the nipple I noticed I had a piece of nipple in my mouth. I wondered what to do with this little piece of flesh in my mouth [E_2].[16]
>
> Then I was standing in line waiting to get into the hairdresser's. I was the first one. A woman came and tried to sidle in in front of me. I pushed her away, telling her I was first. Then the beauty parlor opened. To amuse the customers and hairdressers I gave an imitation of Miss (Mrs.) Bell, the proprietress, who is very bossy and won't allow anyone to loaf a second.
>
> [*Postscript:*] I woke up needing to urinate very much. When I went to the bathroom I suddenly noticed (after sitting on the toilet for several moments) that no urine was coming out—or very little. I looked at the clitoris to see what had happened. [The stream of urine was not normal until after breakfast.]

At the point marked [E_1] there is an ellipsis: the actual sucking and, as is shown by its result, the biting of the nipple is not experienced. The dreamer's employment of the interpolation of dreamless sleep is not difficult to understand, if the demand for

[16] Threshold symbolism (see Section D below) occurs at this point.

continence, distinguishing dream from psychosis is remembered. In the present instance the urethral-erotic discharge of her cannibalistic desire (I, 152–158), of which one learns only in her postscript, *threatened the dreamer with incontinence:* in the words of the postscript she "had to urinate very much" on awakening. Only a breakthrough of the depth of sleep through the floor afforded her the twofold benefit of keeping the drive from becoming conscious and making it possible for her to rely upon a continuously unimpaired reflex closure of the sphincter.

An inspection of the text contiguous to the ellipsis shows the latter's abrupt appearance between two passages devoted to hallucination and rumination. This precipitate interpolation of dreamless sleep in the midst of a depth of sleep sufficiently shallow for dreaming contradicts the second statement made by Freud and cited in the introduction to this section. "The mind could certainly . . . not alter the depth of sleep so quickly as that." The opposite is the case: the depth of sleep can be *subject to the most precipitate alteration;* in fact, there are instances of the arousal dream that appear to exhibit a number of rapid oscillations between ceiling and floor prior to waking up.

While floor and ceiling correspond to each other topographically, their description is historically not of the same order. They occupy, in other words, a different position in the development of analytic thought. The description of the ceiling given above may recommend itself though its economy of rendition, its designation by a name, and its devotion to the clinical phenomenon of the aftermath. Nevertheless, there is hardly anything in it that was not previously known. The acknowledgment of the floor, on the other hand, is new because it derives from a new clinical observation: the interpolation of dreamless sleep into the dream. I may therefore divagate briefly by reporting upon the only other form in which I was clinically presented with the existence of the floor.

A mother (an analyst), whose three-year-old girl kept fairly dry by day, could not understand why she wet at night when everything pointed to the fact that she was dreaming, whereas in apparently dreamless sleep she did not. If it be true, she argued, that *"un rêve est un reveil qui commence,"* sleep should be shallower in the dreamer, causing more reintegration and therefore furnishing more control. I do not have to repeat all the arguments which I opposed to hers, except for the ultimate one: the reliance of the dreamlessly sleeping child on the reflex apparatus situated, in terms of the depth of sleep, "beneath" the floor. Again it was here, during dreamless sleep, that is, when, having broken through the floor, the child could be dry, whereas when dreaming, that is, in more shallow sleep, she was incontinent.

It is not possible to enter into an exhaustive examination of the position and the uses of the ellipsis. The latter is preceded by a "ready-made" fantasy of Freud's description. In the particular instance of the patient whose dream is transcribed above, it is a masturbation fantasy: the patient whenever awake and engaging in clitoris stimulation to the point of orgasm was actually in the habit of doing as far as anatomy would allow what she proposes to do in the dream. Although she could not, of course, reach the breast with the mouth, she could with the eye ("eye-mouth unit": I, 101–104), and did so as the dream depicts, scoptophilically in a mirror. This had eventually become her sexual life after the relinquishment of vaginal sensitivity and the dissolution of her marriage in the course of the worsening of her neurosis. I believe that it was long after the dream that the goal of this regressive course became known through amnesia removal: the severely psychotic mother seduced the child (in both phallic phase and puberty) by taking her breast out and having the girl suck it forcefully with an orgastic result, subsequently mounting a wooden bucket, exhibiting, sighing, and, in the patient's words, "taking a big piss."

Prior to the ellipsis, dream and fantasy are in agreement except for the one detail that makes the regressive object "mamma" (nipple) directly accessible to the mouth. (It may have been for the sake of this detail, which is a wish-fulfillment, that this part of the dream had to be dreamt.) How different the result of the same comparison after the occurrence of the ellipsis! Here the dream, while retaining the object, changes the aim to a cannibalistic one; in so doing it represents purely unconscious thought which could never have entered a fantasy while the subject was awake.

The two cannibalistic component instincts are typically subject to different vicissitudes (I, 86–92), in this case by the dream work: the biting is represented by a simple allusion (if a portion of nipple remains in the mouth it must have been bitten off), and the devouring by an ambiguously allusive rumination. The latter is allowed to remain inconclusive because it is but preliminary to a second ellipsis.

The dreamer is no newcomer to the pages of the *Psychoanalytic Series:* what she expressed here in a dream she expressed at another time through conversion (cf I, 112–114). There, a syndrome combining pain and secretion suddenly reappeared in spite of the previous successful removal of a fistula recti. It disappeared in the next analytic hour, and I have reported the material of the two hours as well as my interpretation, which, of course, was the same as that of the part of the dream in question. The coincidence would appear to confirm the above dream interpretation, and in so doing corroborate the description of the topographical uses of the recurring ellipsis rendered above.

The investigation recorded here has, I think, made it clear that a break through the "floor" serves the wish to sleep as effectively as does a break through the ceiling. Freud's (1900) classic account of the latter fits the former practically verbatim. "Experience shows," he writes, "that dreaming is compatible with sleeping, even if it interrupts sleep several times during the night. One wakes up for an instant and then falls asleep again at once. It is like brushing away a fly in one's sleep: a case of *ad hoc* awakening. If one falls asleep again, the interruption has been disposed of" (p. 557). This passage, describing a break through the ceiling, requires but a few alterations, such as the "interruption of dreaming" instead of "sleep," the "transient submersion in dreamless sleep" instead of "awakening," and the resumption of "dreaming" instead of "sleeping,"—if one wishes to adapt it to the description of a break through the floor of the dream.

Second Example: I owe this example to the kindness of a colleague, who after reading the present section put it at my disposal.

A dream in which the experience of falling—symbolizing female identification and involving incontinence—is evaded via an ellipsis. This dream was experienced by a young man with severe obsessive-compulsive character traits who has been in analysis for several years because of potency difficulties and premature ejaculation. There has been very little progress up to recently; he is really just starting to be able to associate. He habitually suppresses great rage, which is intense enough to be noticed by others, although his actions are usually "correct" and fair. His mother, a vicious psychotic woman, habitually deprived him and teased him. There has been almost no amnesia removal so far. His initial description of her is relevant to the dream, I feel: "My mother, when she menstruated, refused to use Kotex. She would keep crunched up bunches of toilet tissue between her legs. The floor was always covered with piles of bloody toilet paper."

Setting of the dream: He had been quarreling with his fiancée, whom he had not seen for several days following an unsuccessful attempt at intercourse. They had had a phone conversation the night before the dream. She had said that she didn't want to see him and had responded to his statements with hostile silence. This made him furious, but he was unable to express it to her adequately.

DREAM: "I was backing a car on some land near a river bank. I stopped. I was hit in the rear by another car driven by two women. Or maybe it was by a man. (Ellipsis.) Then, *as if a part about still being on land had been left out* [italics added], I found I was in the water. They had pushed me in. I impressed on the two women that they were responsible. They didn't deny it and said they would call a derrick."

Associations: "When I awoke, I found I had pushed the pillow onto the floor. I'm holding onto the pillow of the couch right now. It disturbs me when I push off the pillow. I feel now as if this pillow [on couch] is going to be swept out from under me."

Two women or one man: "Mother and my girl; or mother, father and my sister [entire family group]."

"The night before I had threatened to hang up on her. She

didn't want to see me and I felt completely rejected—I suppressed my anger, and then I felt dizzy, as if someone were banging my head. I felt like hitting someone. I feel empty and lonely. I feel as if I had been whipped and ready to *fall*. [colleague's italics.] I was constipated—I didn't move my bowels all day—it's unusual for me. After I spoke to D. [fiancée], I tried but couldn't move my bowels. The dream *woke me up very scared*, [italics added], yet my sleep was restful and the next morning I had no trouble moving my bowels."

Dream was on Sunday. Friday he had tried intercourse but ejaculated prematurely. He says of Sunday: "I felt like doing something sexual, but it was as if my body didn't want me to. My penis couldn't erect and I couldn't even masturbate. [This inhibition, greater than usual, comes with a change in the relationship with his fiancée who seems now to be trying to get rid of him; and his anger and sadistic impulses are increasing under this pressure.] "That night I felt beaten, battered, and without strength. This weekend she was menstruating, so I felt I couldn't try again anyway. Besides she felt sick with her menstruation."

In this dream the ellipsis follows *being hit* in the rear and the *falling off* the bank into the water is hereby left out. The feminine identification with its implications of incontinence is avoided —by retreating from the dream via the floor?

My comment: I agree with all of my colleague's remarks and interpretations. There are only two comments I have to add. One of them simplifies understanding the dream and the other complicates it.

(1) In contrast to mine, this dreamer is aware of the ellipsis while dreaming. Hence the report, "Then, *as if a part about still being on land had been left out,* I found I was in the water." There is no clearer proof for the existence of the ellipsis, that is, of the transient interpolation of dreamless sleep in a dream, than that awareness. Yet I did not know it occurred before I read this report.

(2) Freud has discovered that if an affect arises in dreaming, that is, if the censor has failed in his task of suppressing all affect, that affect is displaced. The displacement is, of course,

part of the dream work, and must interpretatively be undone. My colleague's patient teaches one something new and entirely unexpected: the affect prevented by the ellipsis from arising, arises nevertheless in another place where it makes no sense: during arousal. To put it plainly and naïvely in terms of the manifest content: why should the women's promise to call a derrick in order to rescue him frighten the dreamer? The answer lies, of course, in the fact that the affect does not belong to the manifest content *but to the latent thought,* at which one arrives of course only by means of interpretation. Part of the latter is obviously the symbolization of birth through rescue, which represents to the patient, to use his analyst's words, "the experience of falling—female identification and incurring incontinence." It is evidently this element in the dream, suppressed by the ellipsis, that intuitively caused my colleague to include the mother's menstrual habits in his report.

D. THRESHOLD SYMBOLISM

The next element that becomes evident if one attempts the topographical analysis of a dream has long ago been observed and named "threshold symbolism," but has never been adequately described. The word, coined by Silberer and adopted by Freud, is a misnomer; symbolism is either not at all or not essentially a part of the phenomenon. It is economical to reduce one's interest in the literature on the subject to Freud's treatment of it in *The Interpretation of Dreams* (1900, pp. 504-506). The latter has two distinctly separate parts. The first part is reportorial and treats "threshold symbolism" as a part of Silberer's "functional phenomenon"; every word of it is, in this writer's opinion, in error. The second part is original; in it Freud hazards a query as to what that so-called threshold symbolism might really be. In so doing he exercises the utmost caution, but it would appear that he is in every one of his suppositions correct. He certainly adumbrates the ideas to be entertained hereinafter when he writes:

> It is by no means unthinkable or improbable that this threshold symbolism might throw light upon some elements in the middle of the texture of dreams—in places, for instance, where there is a question of oscillations in the depth of sleep and of an inclination to break off the dream. Convincing instances of this, however, have not been produced. What seem to occur more frequently are cases of overdetermination, in which a part of a dream which has derived its material content from the nexus of dream thoughts is employed to represent *in addition* some state of mental activity (pp. 504–505).

If we assume—postponing justification—that the patient marks the threshold symbolism in her dream by a paragraph in its transcript (see footnote 16, above), Freud is already borne out: the "threshold symbolism" does illuminate an element in the midst of the context of the dream, and it occurs in the present instance in a place distinguished by an oscillation of the depth of sleep. (The wish for incorporation of the mamma is exchanged for that of entering the mother [-figure's room].) With regard to the dreamer's inclination to terminate her dream abruptly at this point, one must note that she actually follows that inclination if but briefly by interpolating dreamless sleep.

The above considerations make it possible to take a step beyond Freud by describing the nature of threshold symbolism more specifically than he was prepared to do.

Threshold Symbolism indicates the for the most part abrupt transition from one erogenic zone (of which the dreamer's ego is the executive) to another. In the first paragraph of the paradigmatic transcript, where the "mamma" is to be sucked and bitten, the zone is oral; in the second, where the mother is to be entered, it is phallic. There is no indication, however, that such an exchange of regressively dominant erogenic zones, per se, effects any alteration in the depth of sleep. That alteration is recorded in the dream under consideration not by the process named threshold symbolism but by the accompanying ellipsis. Without the latter, i.e., without a brief interpolation of dreamless sleep, the forbidden biting would have had to enter the manifest content of the dream.

There is, otherwise, nothing to say about the second paragraph that would be new to the analytic reader. The postscript, however, makes it obvious that compliance with the wish to sleep, recognizable in the dream, fell short of its purpose. The dreamer was in addition compelled to so vigorous a sphincter closure that it became spastic and could not be relinquished at will, even when after arousal it was no longer needed. Only after breakfast did the stream become normal, that is, did the spasm subside. (One observes occasionally that a particular meal has an unconsciously cannibalistic meaning[17] for a patient, and one is therefore entitled to suppose that an instinctual discharge partook in the restoration.) When this particular patient entered analysis she had to confine herself to a breakfast of liquids only. The fantasy that makes the clitoris the seat of the anuria has been dealt with in another place (I, 170–171): the not infrequent "fantasy of clitoris urination."

E. CONCLUSION

In concluding this fragmentary treatment of the topographical analysis of the dream, there are two more observations to be made, neither of which is, however, illustrable with the dream employed above. If it is true that the spoken word may appear as a soliloquy but is actually a dialogue between introject and partial subject (see Section II, above), one is led to assume that the two demi-institutions of the ego may at times be reintegratively established in the dreamer without precipitating arousal. Yet it is reasonable to believe that sleep at the time of such topographical reintegration is less deep than when the two demi-institutions are dissolved and therefore are not traceable. Strictly speaking this applies only to the noncritical, that is, the purely self-observative, dream speech. If the speech is self-critical, a still higher degree of reintegration, including an at least partial establishment of the superego (which ordinarily shrinks disintegratively to but a remnant, the censor) must be

---

[17] The assassination of President Kennedy, for example, in the assassin's unconscious was part of his luncheon. The murderer pulled the trigger at lunch time, and his abandoned perch was described as strewn with chicken bones.

imagined; for it is the superego that serves as "critical institution." Needless to say that this higher degree of reintegration would make for a comparatively still shallower sleep. There is, however, the case of the complete re-establishment of the superego in sleep, described by Freud as causing the punishment dream. Here, as he has found, the ego avoids arousal only by employing the desperate means of relinquishing the unconscious infantile dream wish and, in deference to the superego, replacing it with the wish to be punished. In the present context it must be observed that *the punishment dream indicates almost the shallowest possible depth of sleep in a dreamer.*

Clinical observation enables one to extend Freud's description of the punishment dream for certain, perhaps infrequent, yet typical cases. Here the dream invades if not all at least the better part of sleep, and the dreamer, due to the shallow depth of such dreams, is only remotely aware of having dreamt. He is therefore apt at times to complain of a torturous night almost devoid of sleep rather than of a disturbing dream.[18]

In concluding, it may be repeated that the criteria so far known as indicative of alterations of the dreamer's ego are but few. Some of them are and others are not dependent on oscillations of the depth of sleep. To the first group belong the interpolation of dreamless sleep (the ellipsis), the self-observative

---

[18] Cf. The Jail Scene in Shakespeare's *Richard the Third.*
KEEPER. Why lookes your Grace so heavily today?
CLARENCE. O, I have past a miserable night,
So full of fearefull dreames, of ugly sights.
That . . . I would not spend another such a night. . . .
So full of dismal terror was the time (I, IV).
Clarence's answer is characteristic: he first complains of the night and mentions his dreams as if he were not quite sure that all was but dreamt, for he adds "ugly sights," and "dismal terror." Nevertheless he goes on to tell the keeper a long, compound, fairly analyzable dream. My few comments on it shall be confined strictly to the subject under consideration.

(1) Freud in describing the punishment dream writes: "It [that is, the critical institution] *might have reacted to the undesirable content of the dream by waking up* [italics added]; but it has found a means, by the construction of the punishment dream, of avoiding an interruption of sleep" (1923b, p. 118). Shakespeare uses almost the identical words. At the point in the recital where Clarence's dream becomes a nightmare that has him choke beyond endurance, denying him even the peace of death that he seeks in order to end his suffering, the jailkeeper interrupts the Duke: [italics added.]

dream speech, the reappearance of introject and partial subject, the self-critical dream speech (the additional reappearance of the superego fused with the introject), and aftermath (hypnopompic condition). To the second group belongs the exchange of one dominant erogenic zone for another (threshold symbolism).

Two of Freud's ideas were shown to be invalid: first, shallow—even extremely shallow—sleep does not engender awareness in the dreamer that he dreams. (Freud knew that such awareness may on rare occasions exist, but neither he nor we have explained it.) Second, the oscillations may be rapid, that is, the depth of the dreamer's sleep is sometimes quick to vary.

V. DELUSION IN DREAMS

The following short section is the only one in this monograph that contains nothing original, but is merely didactic. I am motivated to include it because of a certain ellipsis in Freud's work on the subject. That ellipsis may confuse the serious student of psychoanalysis, and I wish to spare him this confusion.

In *The Interpretation of Dreams* Freud has pointed out that certain elements of the dream thoughts do not partake in the transformation into visual pictures, but that is as far as he went. In his "Metapsychological Supplement to the Theory of Dreams" (1917) he discusses the vicissitudes of the preconscious dream wish, suggesting that one of three paths it might take would be

KEEPER. *Awak'd* you not in this sore Agony?
CLARENCE. *No, no*, my dreams was lengthened after life.
　　O then began the Tempest to my Soule . . . etc.
2) The dreamer has an evidently long aftermath to which everything applies that has earlier been said about it:
CLARENCE. . . . I (trembling) wak'd, and for a season after,
　　Could not believe, but that I was in Hell,
　　Such terrible impression made my dreame.
With regard to the relatively shallow depth of sleep, Clarence's sleep was so shallow that he conceives of it as no sleep at all, and expresses the wish to sleep now instead.
CLARENCE. . . . Keeper, I prythee sit by me a-while
　　My soul is heavy, and I faine would sleepe.
KEEPER. I will my Lord, God give your Grace good rest.
One cannot imagine a more ingenious illustration.

"the path which would be the normal one in waking life, by pressing from the *Pcs.* to consciousness; . . . but in the state of sleep this *never* happens" (pp. 226–227; final italics added).

In discussing this passage with colleagues I have for years maintained that instead of "never" he should have said "always." Eventually, in 1937, Freud published his article on constructions (1937b). Even this paper does not contain an acknowledgment of delusions in dreams, but speaks instead of the hallucinations of normal individuals (for which I have postulated an unobserved autohypnotic state—cf. Chapter Four of this volume) and mentions "the delusion formations into which these hallucinations are so constantly incorporated . . ."

Is this not confusing? Does it not cry for elucidation? It is so easy to clear up when one recognizes the simple fact that many of the thoughts expressed in the manifest content of the dream resist their transformation into visual pictures and thereby the transformation into hallucinations. Instead they become delusions. I hope to have sufficiently convinced the reader of my integrity to the extent that he believes me when I state that, in order to illustrate this tenet, I have opened *The Interpretation of Dreams* literally at random. In so doing, I chanced upon page 205 of the German Edition (page 199, Standard Edition), and found the following short dream of a woman patient: "In a dream *she is to visit her woman friend; her mother told her to ride but she runs and hence constantly falls down*" (Freud's italics; my translation).

Is it not obvious that the conjunction "but" divides the manifest content into two parts, the first of which contains delusions and the second hallucinations? Neither part reflects the reality, which would show her in bed and asleep. Both express something else. The first part contains two thoughts so much at variance with the reality that one can only call them delusions: "She [knows that] she should visit her woman friend, [and she knows that] she should ride, not walk." Only the second part contains a hallucination: ". . . she [experiences, that is, sees and feels that she] runs and [while running] constantly falls down."

This admixture of delusion with hallucination occurs more or less in all dreams. The reader may ascertain it for himself. I can only, for good measure, repeat myself by pointing to the famous dream of Irma's injection (1900, p. 107) with which Freud begins his subject because he considers it paradigmatic. Here the sequence is simply reversed: "A big hall—many guests that we receive. Amongst them Irma [the patient] whom I immediately take aside, etc., etc. . . ." Hallucination, obviously. At the end of the seventieth line of the German text: ". . . I think, in the end [that] there I am overlooking something organic . . ." Delusion, obviously. From there on the two alternate: ". . . I take her to the window and look into her throat, etc. . . ." ". . . I think, she [really] does not need it . . ." Next again the long hallucinatory passage in which Irma is elaborately examined by several doctors and a dream speech followed by the delusory: ". . . We also know immediately the origin of the infection, etc. . . ." And so it goes to the end: hallucination alternating with delusion (my translations).

It is impossible to imagine that Freud never recognized this: yet all his later descriptions of the dream (1933, 1940) lack acknowledgment of it. There is only one single sentence, and in his posthumous writings at that, which contains at least the belated admission of the existence of delusions in dreams. The opening sentence of Chapter Six in the *Outline* (1940) reads: "The dream, then, is a psychosis, with all the contradictions *(Ungereimtheiten)*, delusions and perceptive descriptions of the former" (p. 172, my translation).

It is the implicit character of this admission, its brevity, and the fact that it might easily be overlooked, which have prompted me to be explicit about the subject.

CHAPTER THREE

THE AMBULATORY PSYCHOSIS:
A PARTICULAR TYPE

". . . childhood experience, repressed yet so extremely significant."
Freud: THE ACQUISITION AND CONTROL OF FIRE

In the two earlier volumes of this series I indicated that my methods had brought me face to face with material which was undoubtedly authentic, but which, on the face of it, was "unbelievable." If originally I had held the hope that my findings would be subjected to competent examination, I have gradually become aware that this expectation has on several counts been unjustifiably naïve. For one thing, from what I have heard and read, few analysts master Freud's method to the degree that would enable them to confirm my findings. Since this holds true for their teachers as well, the average analyst thus remains ignorant of his own psychotic parent, should he have one, and hence is not equipped for patients who confront him with fragments that are replicas of his own history—fragments that should, were he properly "trained," no longer be traumatic but actually still are.

I must not, at this point, neglect to mention that I personally started my analytic work no less blind or more skilled than my colleagues, and suffering from the same preconceptions. It took me many years to acquire the technique requisite for obtaining amnesia removal for the earliest years. The same holds true for my diagnostic ability: I recall the cases of two intelligent patients who assured me they were psychotic, which was true, but which I stoutly denied.

The average analyst, therefore, even one who has attained highly prestigious (scientific and/or administrative) positions, is bound to respond to his patient's associations with a number of powerful resistances (cf. II, Introduction). The resistance I have termed the hypnotic evasion, which the analyst shares with the patient at times, is amplified in Chapter Five. The most important, the denial of the ambulatory psychosis in the patient's family will be discussed in the beginning of this chapter. The reasons for my own freedom to accept what my patients proffer (or could be induced to proffer), was documented as early as Volume I (Foreword, xviii, fn.).

The particular type of psychotic to be described in this section is the unknown psychotic. He neither suffers nor seeks help, living the life of his class to all outward appearances like a normal, respectable person. He therefore remains undiagnosed. Should anyone acquainted with him call him abnormal, it would appear altogether absurd. It is only the psychoanalyst who, by chance as it were, comes upon his secret life, often when the subject is no longer living, and for one reason only: this psychotic makes the child the partner to his highly abnormal sexual life and the victim of his brutal aggression.

The child as he grows up "forgets," i.e., represses this, and in the process becomes severely neurotic. If he ends up in analysis and undergoes sufficient amnesia removal, the strange picture of his psychotic parent or parent-substitute, preserved intact in repression, will see the light. I formulated this more than a decade and a half ago in the first of these volumes (I, xvii):

> . . . amnesia removal uncovers much more frequently than Freud's writings lead one to expect, *memories* of which there can be no doubt as to their authenticity, yet which are of so bizarre a nature that, if one followed the general trend in these writings, one would declare them—erroneously—as *fantasies* of the polymorphously perverse child. Finding this, I found also the cause. It lies in the unbelievable frequency of the (undiagnosed) ambulatory psychosis. When one is able to diagnose it, one sees relatively few families of one's patients that are entirely free of it; and one recognizes that the patient in need of a long and thorough analysis would appear to be, by and large, someone who had been damaged by and has identified with a psychotic parent.
>
> There is no place here [I continued] to deal with the inex-

haustible subject of the psychosis; I can therefore say only in passing that the child of such a parent becomes the object of substantially defused aggression (maltreated and beaten almost to within an inch of his life), and of a perverse sexuality that hardly knows an incest barrier (is seduced in the most bizarre ways by the parent and, at his or her instigation, by others). . . .

It is the importance for the etiology of the severe neurosis that now makes mandatory a discussion of the type I call the "unknown psychotic." Time has passed. My notes have accumulated. And my conviction regarding the importance to our field of this type of psychotic has only deepened.

My contentions in the excerpts cited above might be separated into three:

1. The neurotic seriously in need of analysis is apt to have at least one psychotic parent.
2. He has been victimized by the bizarre sexuality of this parent.
3. He has suffered the (largely defused) aggression of which this parent has made him the object.

Such is, I am convinced, the environmental etiology of the neurosis when a sufficiently susceptible "constitution" (in the sense of Freud's "complementary series" [1905, pp. 239–240] between environment and constitution) is present.

I. PERTINENT LITERATURE

Does it not stand to reason, however, that if my statement is correct it would have somewhere found both adumbration and confirmation in print? The answer is both yes and no. As a whole, consisting in its entirety of the three indivisible parts mentioned, I have nowhere seen it either anticipated or confirmed. One or two of these parts have nevertheless been described in isolation both long before I wrote the lines quoted above as well as after their publication. I shall therefore begin by reviewing the literature on the subject.

Freud's Original Discovery and His Subsequent Denial of It

The first place to look for an anticipation of at least two parts of my thesis is, of course, in the work of Freud.

All Freud's technical papers are without exception the work of a genius. Stretching over his lifetime as they do, they are classics describing the psychoanalytic method with an acuity matched by few writers in the history of the written word. This method, correctly applied to suitable individuals, is extremely potent. It is this very potency of the technique invented by the genius that led eventually to the denial of its results by the man. He was of course totally unprepared for them. Self-analysis, even if practiced by a Freud, cannot possibly have the result that a competent analyst working with a flexible and intelligent patient or student-patient may obtain. Yet self-analysis was the only way open to him to prepare himself, and he used it with great success. What seems to have happened could, with the benefit of hindsight, therefore be foreseen. In the beginning, the conclusive results gained by the technique of his own invention must have brought Freud face to face with the truth. This is attested to by a few early letters from which I will quote some excerpts. The first was written in October of 1895: "Note that among other things I suspect the following: that hysteria is conditioned by a primary sexual *experience (before puberty)* accompanied by revulsion and fright; and that obsessional neurosis is conditioned by the same accompanied by pleasure. . . . later transformed into guilt" (1887–1902, pp. 126–127; italics added).

(I have italicized the words "experience (before puberty)" because they make my point. With regard to that point, it is immaterial that the generalization about the difference between hysteria and obsessional neurosis is premature.)

Follows a letter written a little over a year later in January 1897 (characterized by the editors as "the first attempt to verify a psycho-analytic reconstruction"):

Everything now points more and more to the *first three years of life* [italics added]. This year I have had no further news of my patient with obsessional neurosis, whom I treated only for seven months. Yesterday I heard from F. that he went back to his birthplace to check the genuineness of his memories for himself, and that he got the fullest confirmation from his seducer, who is still alive (she was his nurse, now an old woman). . . . New valuable evidence of the soundness of my material is provided by its agreement with the perversions described by Krafft [pp. 183–184].

That the excerpt implies an experience, not "fantasy," need hardly be pointed out. In April, 1897 Freud writes, "In my analyses I find it's the closest relatives, fathers or brothers, who are the guilty men" (p. 195).[1] "Guilty" again implies the actuality of the abuse.

Freud's honeymoon with this truth, however, was brief. The next excerpt (September, 1897) already shows the infringement of defenses upon the reasoning of the great man:

Then there was the astonishing thing that in every case . . . blame was laid on perverse acts by the father . . . though it was hardly credible that perverted acts against children were so general. (Perversion would have to be immeasurably more frequent than hysteria, as the illness can only arise where the events have accumulated and one of the factors which weaken defence is present.) Thirdly, there was the definite realization that there is no "indication of reality" in the unconscious, so that it is impossible to distinguish between truth and emotionally-charged fiction. (This leaves open the possible explanation that sexual phantasy regularly makes use of the theme of the parents.) [pp. 215–216].

The quotation contains two gross errors. The pioneer who

---

[1] Freud was frequently unreceptive to the importance of the role of the mother in the lives of his patients. I have always refused to regard it as a coincidence that he discovered the preoedipal phase only after the death of his own mother when he himself was 72. It accords with my tentative notion that only this particular paper "Female Sexuality" (1931b) contains the belated admission that much of the earliest instinctual stirrings and fears appear transferred onto the father while actually often belonging to the mother.

founded a natural science and whose work reveals him as a consummate epistemologist remarks: ". . . it was hardly *credible* that perverted acts against children were so general . . ." [italics mine]. What place has "creed" in a science? And is the scientist allowed *a priori* statements? The frequency of perverted acts against children is a subject for scientific exploration; and if they exceed, as they do, one's naïve expectation, that is a fact of no more than quasibiographical value to the explorer.

Secondly, "there is no 'indication of reality' in the unconscious," distinguished as it is by primary process thought. But its very timelessness would, since occurrence in time is the ultimate criterion of reality, preclude such an indication. Not so, however, when one interprets, since interpretation represents a translation of the unconscious with its primary process thought into consciousness dominated by secondary process. Here, as Freud himself pointed out in a later technical paper, one may, if one continues to interpret patiently and correctly, expect conclusive indications for or against the reality of an alleged occurrence. In other words, memory in the long run is separable from fantasy in the course of the analytic work.[2]

That Freud was still assailed by doubt with regard to memories and fantasies is attested to by a letter he wrote shortly afterward. Two weeks later (October 3, 4, 1897), referring to his old nurse whom he terms "my instructress in sexual matters," he adds,

> A severe critic might say that all *this* was phantasy projected into the past instead *of being determined by* the past [italics added]. The *experimenta crucis* would decide the matter *against* him. The reddish water seems a point of this kind. *Where do all patients derive the horrible perverse details which are often as alien to their experience as to their knowledge?* [italics added, pp. 220–221].

I have italicized "against." The "reddish water" stems from a dream in which the nurse washed first herself and then him, and

---

[2] See this Volume, Chapter Six, for a discussion of "detail," "memory quality," "feeling of continuity of self."

of which Freud remarks: "not very difficult to interpret" (p. 220). The *cri du coeur* in the last sentence is only too understandable, coming from one who is forced to descend so deeply and to dwell so long in the psychotic world without recognizing where he is.

It is unnecessary to try to document what must have been years of increasingly strong doubt on Freud's part concerning the memories of his patients. It suffices to quote from his writings after doubt had reached the proportions of denial. He expressed categoric negation of the ubiquitous, originally repressed, pathogenic experiences from infancy in 1914 (S.E. 14, pp. 17–19), and repeated it in 1925. I find the first of these passages deeply regrettable and the second outright pathetic. To avoid redundancy I shall quote only from the second one. There Freud (1925) reminisces as though he originally believed what his patients told him, and consequently supposed he had "discovered the roots of the subsequent neurosis in these experiences of sexual seduction in childhood. My confidence," he goes on to say,

> was strengthened by a few cases in which relations of this kind with a father, uncle, or elder brother had continued up to an age when memory could be trusted. *If the reader feels inclined to shake his head at my credulity, I cannot altogether blame him; though I may plead that this was at a time when I was intentionally keeping my critical faculty in abeyance so as to preserve an unprejudiced and receptive attitude towards the many novelties which were coming to my notice every day* [italics added]. When, however, I was at last obliged to recognize that these scenes of seduction had never taken place, and that they were only phantasies which my patients had made up or which I myself had perhaps forced on them, I was for some time completely at a loss. My confidence in my technique as well as in its results suffered a severe blow; it could not be disputed that I had arrived at these scenes by a technical method which I considered correct, and their subject-matter was unquestionably related to the symptoms from which my investigation had started. When I had pulled myself together, I was able to draw the right conclu-

sions from my discovery: namely, that the neurotic symptoms were not related directly to actual events but to wishful phantasies, and that as far as the neurosis was concerned psychical reality was of more importance than material reality.

He lamely concludes with the remark that "seduction during childhood retained a certain share, though a humbler one, in the aetiology of neurosis. But the seducers turned out as a rule to have been older children" (pp. 34–35).

I have to explain why I find this passage pathetic. It is for this purpose that I took the liberty of italicizing a few lines. In these Freud, under the impact of what the patient tells him, apologizes for nothing else but his "free-floating attention": in other words, for an attitude he has demanded the analyst adopt in every analytic session. Compare this passage with one deliberately describing "free-floating attention" (1912), and you will recognize the latter as hardly more than a circumlocution of the former. "The psychoanalytic technique," he writes

> rejects the use of any special expedient (even that of taking notes). It consists simply in *not directing one's notice to anything in particular and in maintaining the same 'evenly-suspended attention' (as I have called it) in the face of all that one hears.* In this way we spare ourselves a strain on our attention which could not in any case be kept up for several hours daily, and we avoid a danger which is inseparable from the exercise of deliberate attention. *For as soon as anyone deliberately concentrates his attention to a certain degree, he begins to select from the material before him;* one point will be fixed in his mind with particular clearness and some other will be correspondingly disregarded, and in making this selection, he will be following his expectations or inclinations. This, however, is precisely what must not be done. In making the selection, if he follows his expectations he is in danger of never finding anything but what he already knows; and if he follows his inclinations *he will certainly falsify what he may perceive.* It must not be forgotten that *the things one hears are for the most part things whose meaning is only recognized later on* [1912, pp. 111–112; italics added].

In comparing the two passages, in particular the parts I have italicized, it is immediately evident that they describe the same mental attitude of the analyst: only once it is called "credulity" and apologized for, while the other time it is called "evenly-suspended attention" and described not simply as desirable but as the *sine qua non* that it is for the correct perception and evaluation of the patient's communications.

At this point I am ready to reverse myself with regard to a previous statement. In the Foreword to Volume I wrote that it was my "impression" that Freud "went too far in *favoring fantasy on the cost of memory . . .*" (p. xvii). I would now contradict him head on: *no one is ever made sick by his fantasies.* Only traumatic *memories* in repression can cause the neurosis. This fact alone is sufficient reason for discounting Freud's later "denial." Fantasies, in particular compulsive ones, *are a symptom of the disease,* never its cause.

Ferenczi's Comprehensive Anticipation of Two Parts of My Thesis: the Parental Sexual and Aggressive Abuse of the Child

Sandor Ferenczi wrote a series of papers (1930, 1931, 1933) advocating certain changes in technique. It is in these papers, dealing mainly with other matters, that Ferenczi anticipated two of the three parts of my statement, through his stark acknowledgement of the sexual and aggressive exploitation of the child by adults, including his parents. In the last of them (1933) he speaks of the confirmation of his suspicions

> that the trauma, especially the sexual trauma, as the pathogenic factor cannot be valued highly enough. Even children of very respectable, sincerely puritanical families, fall victim to real violence or rape much more often than one had dared to suppose. Either it is the parents who try to find a substitute gratification in this pathological way for their frustration, or it is people thought to be trustworthy such as relatives (uncles, aunts, grandparents), governesses or servants, who misuse the ignorance and the innocence of the child. The immediate explanation—that these are

only sexual phantasies of the child, a kind of hysterical lying—is unfortunately made invalid by the *number of such confessions,* e.g., of assaults upon children, committed by patients actually in analysis [p. 227; italics added].

I have italicized the end of this part of Ferenczi's report *because his experiences there are not dependent upon the removal of any amnesia.* My personal knowledge of such confessions is restricted to two instances: a psychotic mother told me in a short treatment how she masturbated both of her small children, a boy and a girl; and a psychotic bachelor with ejaculatory impotence reported playing sexually with an infant girl. Neither of my informants showed even the slightest feeling of guilt.

Ferenczi continues,

It is not so, however, with pathological adults, especially if they have been disturbed in their balance and self-control by some misfortune or by the use of intoxicating drugs. They mistake the play of children for the desires of a sexually mature person or even allow themselves—irrespective of any consequences—to be carried away. The real rape of girls who have hardly grown out of the age of infants, similar sexual acts of mature women with boys, and also enforced homosexual acts, are *more frequent occurrences* than has hitherto been assumed [ibid.; italics added].

The report is followed with a classic description of the painful overstimulation experienced by the child, his vain attempt at rebellion, his helplessness, and his eventual complete submission to the destructive adult.

Ferenczi also speaks of the abnormal, senseless, whimsical, tactless, even cruel treatment of the children by these adults, and of the "reproduction [in analysis] of the mental and physical agony produced [originally] by incomprehensible and intolerable woe" (1931, p. 478).

All in all it is evident that Ferenczi, by anticipating them, confirms two parts of my three-part statement without, however, confirming the third—my conclusion. Instead of diagnosing these parents as psychotic, he explains their extremely abnormal behavior through a lack of sexual gratification, an untoward fate, addiction. One or more of these factors may naturally at times be present, but they are not the common denominator characterizing these inhuman parents or their substitutes. The common denominator is their psychotic make-up. This is why Ferenczi speaks of "the introjection by the child of the guilt feeling of the adult" who exploits him, while I said (I, xvii–xviii) that "it appears as though the child takes over all of the feelings of guilt over incest that the parent *should have had,* but being psychotic, *did not."* I have never had the slightest indication that the exploiter felt guilty, but merely that he was afraid of being found out. This he forestalls so effectively that I have encountered only two single instances where he failed. In one of them, a mother performing cunnilingus on her seven-year-old daughter was evidently so carried away that she did not hear her husband entering the house and the room; in the other, a mother surprised the maid in sexual play with the child. One is quite generally reminded of the almost daily reports in newspapers where someone, after having committed a crime so bizarre that it fairly shouts out the psychosis, faces an outraged judge without showing the slightest feeling of guilt.

The "Battered Child Syndrome," Confirming One Part: the Aggressive Abuse

Some years ago a pediatrician, an X-ray man, and a psychiatrist jointly published an article (Kempe et al., 1962) devoted to the description of what the authors called "The Battered Child Syndrome." The subject has since become common knowledge: a child with a fresh fracture is X-rayed, and the picture reveals a number of former fractures. I have forgotten how the investigators found out that the parents, maltreating the child severely, had caused the fractures; but I recall the tremendous resistance to the discovery. One pediatrician present at the discussion being reported illogically exclaimed, "This cannot be true because if it were, I could not go on practicing pediatrics." I also recall why this "battering" had not been earlier ascertained: the parents, afraid of being found out, with each new fracture took the child to a different clinic.

Needless to say that this confirms merely one part of my statement: the parental aggression toward his child, but only when it causes a lesion demonstrable in an Xray. (Amongst all the victims I have personally encountered, there was only one who had suffered such a demonstrable one: the mother had broken the child's wrist.

WEDNESDAY'S CHILDREN *Leontine Young—Confirming One Part: The Aggressive Parental Abuse of the Child and Hinting Strongly at Another: The Parents' Psychotic Make-up*

A much more comprehensive confirmation of parental aggression is contained in the book *Wednesday's Children: A Study of Child Neglect and Abuse* by Leontine Young (1964). Her account is hair-raising; her method—the study of case records written by different social workers connected with organizations of which she was either director or staff member. Here again no amnesia removal is involved. The author distinguishes, as the subtitle suggests, the "neglecting" from the "abusing" parents of the child-victims who are her concern. The former deprive their children of food, reducing them to skeletons— many times actually starving them to death. The latter flog them, strike them with heavy objects over the head, fracture their limbs, burn them with lighted matches, and in severe cases succeed in murdering them in the process. It is as though one were reading medieval history over again, only this time the victims are not adults but tiny children, often mere infants!

Dr. Young, whose report is much more moving than that of the physicians referred to above, describes how in reading records in a midwestern city she discovered that she had happened upon a "nightmare world within the world" she already knew, but had assumed, tragic though it was, to be rare. "Here were children who huddled in cold rooms alone at night, who never had enough to eat, who lived in terror of the unexpected blow, who even in their sleep never knew when [parental] violence might hurl them from dream into a living nightmare" (p. 4). These parents act with cold deliberation, exhibiting what the author so aptly calls that "refinement of cruelty," reminiscent of the horrifying reports from the death camps of the Nazis. (One father had his son look on while destroying the lad's pet dog by forcing it into a blazing stove.) Dr. Young makes it very clear—and here her insight exceeds Ferenczi's—that the flogging of the child "is not the impetuous blow of the ha-rassed parent nor even the transient brutality of an indifferent parent expressing with violence the immediate frustrations of his life. It is not the too severe discipline nor the physical roughness of ignorance. It is perverse fascination with punish-ment as an entity in itself . . . the cold calculation of destruc-tion which . . . requires neither provocation nor rationale" (p. 44).[3] One man, for instance, described in detail to the social worker, the agonizing pain and terror he inflicted upon his helpless son.

According to Dr. Young, the parents themselves did not see any family problem requiring a request for service. The neglect-ing parents were indifferent or withdrew to the point of deser-tion. The abusive parents had one single consistent characteris-tic: ". . . the urge to destroy, and this was an end in itself . . ." Until receiving criticism from the outside, they were open about this destructiveness. There was an almost boastful quality to their accounts. This candor revealed a lack of awareness that there was anything reprehensible or even unusual about their behavior towards their children. In other words, none of those parents gave any evidence of guilt, and there is no evidence

---

[3] These are the parents I discuss in an addendum to the libido theory (II, 308–312). Almost all available aggression appears to take the child as its object. I have termed the quality "Refractory Narcissism," for it appears to be a *residual narcissistic libido*, resist-ing the only vicissitude ordinarily undergone by narcissistic libido—its transformation into object libido. And for a discussion of the damage wrought, e.g., inhibition of thought, motor restriction etc., from distortions of body ego and ego see II, 48–62.

that the children at any time were seen as persons by the parents. They saw persons as objects rather than as people, and the objects were divided between those who can be controlled and those who cannot. Toward the former they are destructive. Toward the latter, if with authority, they are ". . . either appeasing or respectful; and toward everyone else they are indifferent. . . ."

As to the sexual use of the child by the parents, one common factor is apparently the sexual use of the children. The evidence of incest appears over and over in these families. Because it was rarely explored or clarified, the extent of incestuous relationships could not be determined from the material. However, it was reported in a number of cases by the children themselves, nearly always *after removal from the home.* In several other cases one of the parents reported an incestuous relation between the other parent and one of the children. Sometimes these reports were made in anger, but many of them were part of the general admission that "something ought to be done." One father stated that he knew the mother had been abusing her small daughter sexually for some time. He felt there was nothing he could do, but he hoped "someone would do something about it." In another case the mother reported that the father had been sleeping with his pre-adolescent daughter for some time, and as she aptly pointed out, "it doesn't look nice." In this case the father defended himself by pointing out that the mother had been sleeping with the son.

The children of all these families were damaged emotionally. Those who had remained in their own homes when the parents were either severely neglecting of them or both abusive and neglecting, were almost without exception severely disturbed. While precise information is lacking on many of them, there is sufficient recorded material to show [subsequent] results are delinquency, mental illness, chronic dependence, marital failure, desertion of their own families and abuse of their own children.

I found the similarity of the findings of social worker and analyst, particularly in view of the dissimilarity of their methods, significant.

One can only marvel, with Dr. Young, at the ignorance of the judge who—as he so frequently does—returns the fearfully mal-treated child to the parent simply because this bestial specimen of mankind "promises" to improve.

A few statistics cited by Dr. Young are also worth quoting. A recent report of the American Humane Association found "662 cases of excessive cruelty reported in the papers, from January through December of 1962. They came from all but two of the fifty states. These 662 children came from 557 families" (p. 55). Age range: infancy through 17; barely 10% over 10; 55% under four. (Note: Freud made it the shibboleth of analysis that it suc-ceeds in recalling these early years.) Of the children mentioned here, 178 or one in every four *died* from the injuries inflicted by the parent. And again, over 80% of the dead were *under four years of age.*

In other words, the majority of the often fatal injuries were sustained by the child at those very ages when the exploitation of the child, sexual and aggressive, are pathognomonic for the development of his later neurosis. (Compare this with Freud's original report, quoted above: "Everything points more and more to the first three years of life.")

Dr. Young ponders the causes of these excesses in abnormal parental behavior. Psychosis? she asks herself. Of the figures so diagnosing a certain percentage of parents in her study, she feels that they certainly err on the low side because neither psychiatric study of, nor consultation for most of the subjects of her report were available. Yet again, in another place, she ex-presses the opinion that there are "many more psychotics [amongst the parents] than officially listed." This certainly goes as far as a social worker can go in confirming my three-part statement.

My own results, I must reiterate, were all gained by and within the limits of the strictest analytic procedure. This proce-dure, whose goal is of course therapeutic, has thus yielded an important secondary result in the thorough knowledge of the secret life of a certain type of ambulatory psychotic.

The etiology of the severe neurosis lies, I am convinced, in the traumata suffered at home and in the earliest years. In addition: the guilt the parent (or parent-substitute) did *not* feel appears to be borne by the victim, for I have not failed to note the consequent precipitation of an unconscionable amount of it. This, coupled with the unconscious need for punishment, may often vitiate our analytic endeavor.

II. REFINEMENTS IN TECHNIQUE OF AMNESIA REMOVAL

Here I must interrupt myself to underscore that in order to recover material of the sort under discussion from a patient's childhood, the analyst must possess some rarely found qualifications: he must be able to remove amnesia; and he must be able to disown Freud's denial which has amnesia removal producing fantasies instead of the truth, that is, yielding memories of past events (in Macbeth's poignant prophetic words: ". . . Plucke from the Memory a rooted Sorrow," a line that could serve as a motto for the goal of amnesia removal).

To the two qualifications I have cited, the analyst studying the ambulatory psychosis through amnesia removal in his patient, the erstwhile witness of or partner to the parent's secret life, I must add a third that I have never heard mentioned. The psychologically endowed and sufficiently analyzed analyst will be able to employ empathy for a wide range of behavior. The qualification of which I now speak, however, is the ability to *suspend* this empathy. Such a stricture goes "against the grain" of all of our past experience and training. We have become habituated through the use of empathy to significantly accommodate ourselves to human experience. Suddenly something appears in the patient's associations that is "incredible." It literally is beyond our understanding. Where is our "empathic grasp?" It must be put in abeyance; there is much psychotic behavior that simply does not lend itself to empathic grasp. *We must therefore renounce it* rather than make the mistake of *denying the behavior,* e.g., by calling it "fantasy" because one cannot "understand" it. To repeat: the analyst must be endowed with empathy, increase it through training, and at the same time be able to renounce it completely when evaluating psychotic behavior.

III. SYMPTOMATOLOGY

I expect, as I said at the beginning of this chapter, to arouse strong resistances in the reader. The reason? While meaning to report upon someone in the patient's home when he was a child, I may unwittingly describe someone in that of the reader's—someone with whom he had dealings in infancy that have remained in repression. The patient's analysis will then parallel too closely what the analyst's should have been. In this case it is likely that the analyst, unable to withstand a mobilization of the repressed instead of its dissolution, will be forced into a denial. He cannot be blamed: insufficient amnesia removal in his own analysis, again as I have earlier indicated, would leave him unequipped to perform it on others and thus unable to check and confirm my results.

Furthermore, it must not be forgotten that one is generally prepared to accept the psychotic behind the walls of an institution while rejecting the notion that he walks in one's midst. The particular type to be accounted for here is perverse but not "sick"; the occasion for meeting him is therefore not his treatment but in the analysis of his offspring.

A. THE WISH TO CONCEAL

We know that the psychotic ego is overwhelmed by the id and consequently compelled to abandon the environment. In the type of *ambulatory* psychotic that is the subject of the present chapter such breaks with reality although, of course, present are not characteristic. On the contrary, he is distinguished by such an excellent contact with reality that he is able to keep secret his psychotic life. No one but the analyst is in a position to study him, and he can do so only because of that one evidently frequent characteristic: he makes his child, sometimes his grandchild, or the child of someone else, witness to or participant in his secret psychotic life.

As I said in the beginning of this chapter, if such a child as an adult has a successful analysis, the removal of his amnesias for traumatic events will portray most accurately and in great detail the secret life of his ambulatorily psychotic parent. This portrait will frequently be as terrifying as it is pornographic. Such should not cause surprise. The psychotic works with largely defused aggression, and his sexuality is often extremely regressive. His solid contact with reality, however, makes the psychotic parent aware that his secret partner may also betray him. The perpetrator—in the early years it is most often but by no means always the mother—has therefore "to insure herself against the child's informing anyone of her sexual and aggressive exploitations. She does this sometimes through blandishments: in most cases, however, by threats (II, 16)." One mother who had "battered" the child by breaking her wrist seduced her at the age of three by masturbating in front of her, displaying her clitoris, telling the daughter, "You have that too," and instructing her in its use. She furnished one of the relatively rare examples of entreaty instead of threats to silence the child: "That," she said to her sweetly, "is our secret." In most cases the child is, as I have reported,

. . . promised severe beatings if he "lets on"; occasionally the intimidation is accompanied by a sample punishment where the child is mercilessly slapped around. (This may, of course, at the same time relieve the mother of an excess amount of aggression that the sexual act could not discharge.) [Years later,] *that injunction "not to tell" is obeyed by the patient in his analysis where it becomes, eventually, one of "not to remember."* The resistance is in some cases difficult to overcome; at the same time it takes its place amongst the phenomena that make one wonder why hate welds a bond as strong as or even stronger than affection [II, 16].

It appears didactically useful to insert here a brief episode told to me by a patient. I choose it because the occurrence has the "advantage" of not being obtained through amnesia removal. The episode consists of an observation and two remarks that concern persons of whom I had never heard before and was never to hear again. Here then is the story:

My patient's baby sitter one day seems pensive and is holding her head in her hand. The alert three-year-old girl for whom she sits becomes aware of her absorption and asks what she is thinking. The sitter replies: "Nothing." However, the child keeps urging her and insists she must be thinking of something. My patient, on her way out, overhears and questions. The sitter proceeds to unburden herself about her last baby-sitting experience.

She is taking care of a three-year-old boy. The mother returns home, and the child rushes to greet her. She responds by flinging him against a sharp-edged piece of furniture so furiously that he suffers a considerable gash in his scalp. The sitter, concerned, says she had better get him to a hospital because something must be done. The mother: How could she? What would she tell as to how it happened? Later the (divorced) father telephones the child, who tells him he has hurt his head "while he was falling." The sitter finishes her recountal to my patient by saying: "With that mother threatening him, the boy would never dare to tell the truth to anyone. Nor would his brother (a nine-year-old who was present).

This is a direct glimpse at that inhuman, psychotic parent who in analysis emerges with such tragic frequency from repression most often in the shape of the patient's mother. The typical features of this portrait, as far as I was able to observe, are enumerated and exemplified in the subsequent sections. Note that this method of observation of the ambulatory psychotic—supplementary as it is to direct observation—is as new as it is unique; the patient as a child, to say it once again, was the only one intimately acquainted with the psychotic's secret life. He repressed almost all of it, but the lifting of his repressions open numerous windows—keyholes if you wish—

through which the analyst can behold what the world was never allowed to see.

By way of contrast, an example that shows the successful dissimulation of the ambulatory psychotic, yet again where amnesia removal is not involved: I remember a case where special circumstances had necessitated my obtaining permission to discuss with a colleague, known to me as a good analytic observer and well informed on the subject, the analysis of a patient, who in the present was tormented by an ambulatorily psychotic wife. The colleague reacted to my description of the wife with utter surprise. He had on at least one occasion an extended social contact with her. His impression was that of a fine, tastefully clothed, and well-mannered young woman with an unusual interest in literature and art. He could not, even in retrospect, recall the slightest oddity that might reconcile the person he knew with the one upon whom I was reporting. He did not doubt my word, but it was nevertheless inconceivable to him that she maltreated and underfed her children, withdrew from them and her husband by simply going to bed whenever she felt like it, and as to her "interest" in literature—that for many years she had read only trash.

B. THE SEXUAL ABUSE OF THE CHILD

Here is an example leading straight to the heart of the problem. A mother, on one of many occasions of sexual and aggressive abuse, performed fellatio on her little boy and slapped him mercilessly when his excitement made him urinate into her mouth.

On another occasion she took the five-year-old to a horror movie that terrified both of them and caused her to exclaim repeatedly, "Ma . . ." (= Mama?). At the same time, in the dark of the movie house, she managed to initiate mutual masturbation with the boy which eventually led to his wetting.

I seriously doubt my ability to persuade the reader to consider these reports to be what they are, namely, results of amnesia removal, even if I add that as such, they enabled the patient to see the mother for what she was. For example, after a visit from her on the day before a session, he remarked to a close friend who had known the family for a long time that he found the old lady's extreme décolletage rather shocking. The friend answered that she always dressed that way. The patient then added, in his session, a vivid description of the overtly sexual nature of the supposedly social maternal embrace.

Should the reader refusing credence to the above example go so far as to ask himself *why,* he could easily find the answer. There is in it practically not a single element that allows for empathic grasp: neither the abuse and punishment of the child, nor the excitation through fictional horror and the "invocation" (if that is what it was) of the woman's own mother, nor the mutual masturbation with an immature child—and one's own at that. If the woman had taken a lover of either sex, or if she had merely gratified herself, one could understand. As it is, her actions are completely beyond any empathic comprehension.

Nevertheless, if you remove the amnesia for early traumata in your patients who come from different walks of life and have never so much as seen each other, you are told over and over by each of them, to the point of tragic monotony, of their abuse as a child.

What, then, are the other features, besides the ability to conceal his psychosis from the world at large, in the portrait of the ambulatory psychotic, as contained in his partner's memory and becoming discernible upon being lifted out of repression? There are several that are fairly constant.

C. THE DEPENDENCE UPON MASTURBATION

In the first place there is the psychotic's dependence upon excessive masturbation, already known to Karl Abraham (1908) and shared by the type we are discussing. His terse statement, however, requires elaboration. This dependence is by no means the result of a lack of "normal" gratification. Authentic primal-scene observations by children of varying ages who had been made knowledgeable through much seduction show many an ambulatorily psychotic mother fully responsive to her husband. That applies, for instance, to a woman who masturbated or had the child masturbate her at least once, at certain times probably twice, a day. I can parallel these results of amnesia removal by the direct observation of one psychotic woman patient, who, without abstaining from intercourse and the exercise of perversions, indulged herself masturbatorily in a violent fit of nymphomania (unconscious mother transference) at least once a day.[4]

The few instances that made me suspect—although I was never certain—that some of the masturbation was a sequela of intercourse are best illustrated through a report given outside of the exercise of my profession.

An acquaintance once told me of her extremely promiscuous woman friend, who, as she expressed it, "really took chances with strangers." After such episodes, the young woman often visited my informant and masturbated in front of her. Cunnilingus, for which she asked on occasion, was refused her because her genital was unclean. Here it is obvious that intercourse stimulated clitoral sexuality, which then required a separate gratification. I cannot, for evident reasons, assume responsibility for the diagnosis, but such excessive promiscuity combined with a gross lack of hygiene leads me to suspect that the girl was an ambulatory psychotic.

The ambulatory psychotic I am reporting on confronts one, however, in the matter of his sexual regime, with an apparently paradoxical attitude, widespread, yet again defying any empathic grasp; and it is again shared with other types. He prefers masturbation, enjoys it greatly, becomes fully orgastic, and yet is forced to repeat himself in short order. One may venture to call this behavior pathognomonic.

---

[4] I will at times illustrate certain characteristics of the type under discussion from observation of other types—my patients or their reports.

D. THE NEED TO EXHIBIT

The next feature is the imperative need to exhibit. The mother indulging herself insists on being watched by her child. This leads, on the one hand, to the mother sooner or later having the child masturbate her, often mutually. It is, on the other hand, not confined to actual masturbation. I have described in another place (II, 253) and for another purpose how such a mother "scratched herself, stooped and spread her labia, examined her breasts and beckoned the little daughter to join her in her inspection."

To again confront these results of amnesia removal with direct observation, I remember a young woman patient who described to me how her mother, during the time of the analysis, performed "beauty exercises" in complete undress and in knee-elbow position in front of her children, two of whom were about four and five years of age. I recall, furthermore, a charming, intelligent married woman patient whose two psychotic parents were still alive at the time of the analysis. She told me what happened on the occasion of her mother's visits to the couple. Repeatedly the old lady would call her into her bedroom for an evening chat. There, the mother, clad in nightgown, would put her legs up and spread them, while the daughter, sitting at the foot of the bed, "figured desperately where *not* to look."

In her childhood this patient's respectable middle-class family were nudists. But they were nudists only at home. The psychotic father used to explain that the body was such a beautiful thing that it should not be hidden. On Sundays he regaled his progeny with a special treat: he led them, boys and girls, into the bedroom, where the psychotic mother lay stripped to the waist, to admire her "lovely" breasts.

None of this, by the way, had been repressed by the patient. (I know now, of course, why. Because it served as a screen for her early repressed experiences with the mother. It was suitable for this role through restricting itself to being scoptophilic, by displacing "from below to above," and by employing the "whole family" to symbolize "a secret.") I was at that time not able to obtain amnesia removal for the experiences that this memory screened.

Another young woman patient told me how an old friend of long standing in the family at the time of her analysis asked her psychotic mother: "Edith, why do you always sit so that one can see your vagina?" (In my experience, when the layman says "vagina" he means "vulva.") Further examples would not teach more. *In re* "secret life" I shall only mention that when I once saw the person called Edith in a consultation she seated herself demurely in full accord with convention.

Theoretically I can only conclude that the relation to the "object" of the exhibition—in most cases the child—is partly, more often altogether, refractorily narcissistic (II, 304–317 and Glossary, below). This might explain the two questions put by the masturbating "verbal" mother to the child, "Do you see it?" and "Do you like it?" At their object-libidinal face value these questions are senseless: the questioner knows from a multiplicity of previous experiences that they could only elicit a positive answer. They become meaningful only if one considers them expressive of the woman's narcissistic proprioceptive experience. The first question then signifies the entry of the genital into her pleasure-physiologic body ego (II, 238) and the second the proprioception of pleasure issuing from the organ in excitation. The whole performance is thus analogous to the mirror-masturbation, clitoridian and vaginal, described to me as indulged in prior to their analyses, and for a while during it, by two childless women patients, both of whom were ambulatory psychotics.

E. THE PRIMAL SCENE WITH PSYCHOTICS

The analytic conception of the ontogeny of the primal scene is, as Freud has found, based upon a typical misunderstanding of the child by pre-Freudian parents. The latter err in assuming that the small child lacks sexuality and, consequently, a sexual interest, and perform before him unaware of the significance of his reactions. When the child later shows unmistakable signs of sexual interest, they resort to privacy, and exclude the witness. The behavior of the ambulatory psychotic is different. Whether both parents are psychotic or only one of them is immaterial, for if one is, the other is living with him or her in a *folie à deux.* In the first place, the parent who has seduced his child cannot possibly believe in the child's sexual "innocence"; in the second place he continues to exploit the child as a witness at ages so late that he could not possibly be believed by anyone to be without sexual interest. One can only assume that being watched is as stimulating to intercourse and to the exercise of perversions as it is to masturbation.

The mother who has been quoted several times, on at least one occasion, took the child during the phallic phase out of her crib, putting her into the parental bed prior to having intercourse with her husband. When the girl finally wet the bed, she was roughly shoved onto the floor.

I have reported in another place (II, 223) on a psychotic couple who performed in broad daylight with the mother slouching in a chair and their five-year-old daughter standing by and observing everything in detail. When it was all over—but only then—the mother looked straight at the child and commanded: "Get out!"

The mother previously mentioned as the only one, in my experience, who ever got caught, had perhaps aroused her husband's suspicions, for on this occasion he came home for luncheon, omitting the customary whistle announcing his arrival. The child heard his footsteps; the mother, evidently too far carried away, remained unaware of them until he entered the room and surprised her in the performance of cunnilingus on their seven-year-old daughter. Did that induce him to discontinue having the child sleep only one foot away from the parental bed? It did not. The patient went on sleeping there and recalled hearing him apologize for having forced intercourse on the frigid woman, saying that he "could not contain himself"; on other occasions he was irate and jumped out of bed in the nude, turned the light on, etc. In the case of psychotics many a primal scene would often appear more like pandemonium than the primal scene as we know it.

Whether enacted by psychotics or by normal parents, the primal scene has in common the fact that the witnessing of it does not concern the parents so much as it does the child. The latter, as Freud has shown, interprets the scene on the basis of his own sexual organization. The child mentioned above, as yet ignorant of the vagina, was convinced that the apologetic father had punctured and murdered the mother and was therefore greatly astonished to find her alive in the morning. Another patient who as a seven-year-old saw her parents having intercourse in broad daylight in front of a wide-open door, exclaimed in analysis: "There was that big ape killing my mother!" This patient was by then frigid and lacked even sexual actuation. When I pointed out that her memory of the mother's happy countenance and jaunty behavior after the act testified to her gratification, she argued with me, taking it as feigned and intended only for "cover-up."

The difference between the primal scene with normal and with psychotic parents is, as has been said above, that the latter arrange to be stimulated by observation on the part of an older child of whose interest they are fully aware. Whether they make certain of the child's presence from the beginning, or plan to be "surprised" by the child, is immaterial.

F. REGRESSIVE SEXUALITY

The next feature in the portrait of the ambulatory psychotic is his regressive sexuality. His excessive masturbation is certainly a regressive trait; and the regression goes further. (To preclude any possible misunderstanding, I add the truism that perversion must not be equated with psychosis.)

A woman reacted to anal stimulation with sexual pleasure and when orgastic emitted flatus. At an earlier time the same mother, after masturbating and stimulating the child on the toilet and becoming orgastic, pushed the daughter away, took her place, and simultaneously urinated and had diarrhoea while the child, by now facing her, wet the floor (II, 260.) It is quite typical in at least two general aspects, to be mentioned later on, that this woman took laxatives for her diarrhoea.

Another mother lay down on the bed and made what the patient called a "tent" with the bedsheet for her little daughter, whereupon she started a slow and gradually increasing masturbation. I suspected at first no more than the inordinate urge to exhibit at close range. However, when the patient again mentioned the episode she recalled in addition that the mother bade her insert her finger into her (the mother's) rectum; and still later she recalled being admonished to perform violent motions in the organ, while the mother gradually came to a climax. From about the same period a memory emerged from repression that had the parents perform coitus *in anum* during the mother's menstrual period. There was no room for doubt: the woman was not one to lend herself to something she did not enjoy, and the scene was replete with detail. Besides, the two memories substantiate each other.

I can parallel the memories mentioned here with a direct report from the psychotherapy of a young schizophrenic. The young woman told me once that her (psychotic) husband, suggesting "a change," performed sodomy to which she reacted with a full-fledged, highly pleasurable rectal orgasm. Unfortunately, she did so at the price of an acute worsening of her condition.

Another direct observation made long ago is that of a man patient, psychotic, alcoholic, wealthy, and a member of one of the town's most exclusive clubs. (His intelligence was superior to mine, and he rightly reproached me for not making the diagnosis of which he was fully aware.) It was his custom every so often to go to a Harlem bordello, where a colored man performed sodomy on him.

It became evident in the analysis of a patient that she had at the age of five been seduced by a maid. The latter appeared at first as fully dressed, but soon changed to being nude. This was puzzling, but one could not dismiss it because of one very distinct detail: the naked girl wore a crucifix on a chain about her neck. She had the child masturbate her and reacted to it with "shivers," indicative, one was allowed to assume, of incomplete climax. From then on the story progressed without, however, making much sense. It had the maid crawling on all fours with her genitals over the face of the child. I was dissatisfied with these reports and their several versions because, for one thing, I know the seducer demands end pleasure from his victim, and for another, the nudity remained without explanation. Nevertheless, a particular symptom of the patient at the time underwent a certain change, far from easy to describe. She had for a long time shown a compulsive interest in the genitals of women chosen at random. And she always faced the object of her curiosity head on. Suddenly this was no longer so. I recall, for instance, that she attended a fashion show while her scoptophilic interest had, as it were, reversed its axis. The genitals of the models were now fantasied as seen from the rear. I demonstrated this change repeatedly to the patient, eventually obtaining a totally unexpected result: she remembered the maid as squatting and engaged simultaneously in manual masturbation and defecation. The patient also recalled the details of the subsequent removal of the product in newspaper and its deposition in the toilet. After this bit of amnesia removal, the patient's fantasies about women promptly resumed their previous complexion.

I have described a psychotic mother[5] who, when her daughter confessed to having played with herself, cuffed the child, beat her on the head and kicked her—by then on the floor—at random. Through these sadistic ministrations she excited herself sexually to such a degree that she eventually had to reach a climax through masturbation. This, moreover, she did under conditions that allowed the daughter to "observe." An obvious admission is overdue at this point. In evaluating human behavior as pathologic we have no other way than to compare it with the "norm." Yet the norm varies from civilization to civilization, limiting the validity of our conclusions to a place and a time. Notwithstanding the cruelty of our wars, we in the western world could not either execute persons by disemboweling, or by quartering them alive; nor could we make public spectacles of such procedures. Yet Shakespeare's England, and France—even up to the time of the Great Revolution—did so, and people flocked to see. I have forgotten the source (Memoirs of the Sansons?), but I recall reading long ago how many a French lady, leaning forward to get a closer look at the slaughter, became so aroused by it that she had to offer herself to her escort a posteriori. To conclude that all who did this must have been psychotic, I would naturally consider invalid.

[5] For a discussion of the hypersymbiotic mother, see Volume II, pp. 48–62 and 304–317.

I conclude this subsection with a few observations that do not strictly belong here, but although one cannot necessarily call them "regressive," they are pertinent to a discussion of the sexuality of the psychotic.

Two of my analytic patients, of whom I am not sure that they had so much as a speaking acquaintance with each other, mentioned the same old lady, an octogenarian, give or take a few years, at the time of their treatment. One gave me ample proof that the woman, whom she called "crazy as a coot," was actually psychotic, and the other quoted her as telling a group of women friends that every so often she became orgastic without doing anything at all. I have no reason to doubt the reports and am ignorant of what fantasies, if any, were had on these occasions. It did not sound as though conscious fantasies were entertained.

If I search my memory for observations with which to parallel this report, the subject becomes confusing. The psychotic patient (I, 151) who was seized unexpectedly by a violent orgasm after having pressed out an inverted nipple during hours of housework is unsuitable as a parallel because her case shows physical stimulation, although not of the genital, still of an erogenic zone. The closest parallel is, surprisingly, offered by a purely neurotic woman who reacted with a strong excitation leading to a subdued orgasm in the session. The occasion was amnesia removal for scoptophilic experience as an older child, concerning her mother. For the case of the male, there is of course the "nocturnal emission," but in the waking state.

I have not observed any man directly gaining "end pleasure" without physical stimulation and do not know whether or not he exists. The only positive testimony at my disposal is indirect, and dependent on a surmise. A friend of a patient had to watch a guard flogging an inmate in a torture camp. She witnessed so strong and increasingly loud and peculiar a vocalization by the guard that she became convinced it accompanied an ejaculation.

The problem occasionally becomes important for "constructing" correctly after memory fragments have escaped amnesia. The above discussion shows that it is doubtful whether the question of presence or absence of direct physical stimulation should be treated under the heading of *regressive sexuality* as I have done.

G. INCONTINENCE

Urinary Incontinence

Incontinence is by contrast quite obviously regressive. Urethral incontinence seems to be rather frequent in the ambulatory psychotic and has a number of different manifestations.

To prevent certain forms of acting out and to channel a maximum of unconscious mental content into verbalization, I found it effective to have no bathroom available to analytic patients. In two cases I had, however, to make an exception: the patient mentioned before, who "could urinate all day long," in many a session suffered from urinary urges strong enough to absorb her in a severe continence struggle that precluded free association. While she used the toilet I always busied myself at my desk and was separated from her through two closed doors. This did not, however, prevent her from entertaining the delusory fantasy of being watched. Nor did the apparent relief often preclude an almost immediate return of the urge. The other case was that of the adolescent girl whose incontinence dream is described at the end of the chapter on Typical Dreams in this volume. Of the nature of the urethral-*erotic* aspect of her incontinence, she gave without knowing it a vivid description. Wiping herself after having urinated led to more urination, which necessitated more wiping, which, in turn, stimulated more flow, and so on in an unending sequence. However, she was unaware that the wiping had this effect because it furnished a clitoral stimulation. After she had relinquished her incontinence through analytic work, she described with a charmingly expressive little gesture, "How nice it is simply to wipe oneself, and that is all."

There are, of course, other examples making the same point, except that in them the sexual nature of their incontinence is conscious because they wet while being strongly aroused. The woman who had her child masturbate her to the point of orgasm on the toilet accompanied by copious urination is illustrative of this point. Another patient distinctly recalled the preorgastic urination trickling down the mother's leg during masturbation. From the analysis of a male patient I find the following note: "Mother seducing him during attack of 'psychotic' headache. He remembers her genital throbbing and a urinary release, to which he responded with one of his own. Age circa four." The note conceals the nature of the seduction, and I do not recall it.

All in all, the sexual nature of psychotic incontinence is in some cases demonstrable, while in others it is not. The mother just described, for instance, wore no underwear in order not to have to remove it upon reaching the toilet. This, however, did not prevent her from also wetting the floor. The report cited shows her being masturbated in the bathtub to the point of an orgasm accompanied by flatus. When she finally stepped out of the tub "like a gazelle" (the patient's words—to my ear's indicative of an infatuation) she was observed several times emitting small quantities of urine. Another woman seated herself in such a fashion that the flood sprayed the bathroom floor; one can ponder the question of whether the wish to exhibit or to soil was the stronger.

Here are three additional examples of the occasions for incontinence in the ambulatory psychotic.

The pubescent psychotic playmate of a neurotic patient (II, 107) urinated wherever she found herself—in the movies or on the street. My mischievous patient could make her incontinent at any time by making her laugh. Another patient had to urinate whenever she was surrounded by water (bath, shower, a swim). The third one, an attractive young divorcée who was enjoying a highly gratifying affair at the time, suffered frequent attacks of incontinence on the street without any conscious provocation. She had to press her hand on the urethral region and take refuge in a telephone booth in order not to be seen. Here the pressure aroused her; she masturbated in the booth, and the climax abolished the urge. In the first two instances there was no awareness of the drive's being urethral-*erotic*, in the third it made itself felt as such only after changing complexion from a urinary to a sexual urge.

I recall two psychotic women patients who reported a single attack of urethral incontinence in their first therapeutic session, evidently caused by the impact of a transference. One woke up finding she had copiously wet her bed, which she was not in the habit of doing. The other wet during intercourse, sending a protracted stream upward while on her back. The first of these women was puzzled, the second distinctly amused.

If the reader should remember the report concerning the mother who wet herself conspicuously during a meal in a public restaurant (II, 53), he will be impressed by the ability of the incontinent ambulatory psychotic to avoid attracting attention. Another psychotic mother, for instance, occasionally stopped in the street and urinated standing still. This was done, however, only when it was raining and she could thereby avoid detection. The women already mentioned who wet while orgastic were invariably dry when they masturbated in places other than on the toilet.

Rectal Incontinence

My experience with rectal incontinence in the ambulatory psychotic is not extensive. One woman assisted it, as was mentioned earlier, by her habitual use of laxatives. In another instance the analysis came to postulate it, I forget how, and the patient eventually remembered his mother's grossly soiled underdrawers. The psychotic male patient who had sodomy performed on him, experienced his incontinence only as an "inability to wipe himself clean" after defecation. Actually his performance was the anal-erotic equivalent of the urethral-erotic incontinence of the girl described above. He was as unaware as she had been that in his case the wiping was a regressively sexual anal stimulation causing a defecatory response. Finally, I recall an ambulatory schizophrenic whose treatment, an "analysis" in name only, helped him a good deal. He was married to an ambulatory schizophrenic woman, young, attractive, and evidently with a superior background. I had seen her a few times, at the husband's request, and had obtained the impression that she might have been able to profit from psychotherapy. Yet a strong jealousy, of which the husband was totally unaware, compelled him to keep her away. She was sent instead to a young man without qualifications who even failed to make the diagnosis, obvious as it was. One day the husband, whose treatment had meanwhile been discontinued, called me sounding quite upset and asked urgently for an appointment because his wife had suddenly defecated into her clothes. However, when he appeared two weeks later (because that was the time of my first free hour), the occurrence that had so disturbed him was never mentioned.

Incontinence Equivalents

Abraham (1924a) was the first to discover compulsive talking to be an equivalent of urethral-erotic incontinence. It seems there are others. One of them is excessive promiscuity.

The incontinent adolescent friend of the neurotic patient mentioned above later became promiscuous. My patient told me of some of the friend's experiences in the park, indicative of both lack of discrimination and inability to support delay. In one instance a man friend drove the girl to a meeting with her fiancé. On the way she "propositioned" the man. My patient, close to her since childhood, described her as a good, warm-hearted person who did not in the least regard this as infidelity and could not, in fact, be made to understand that her behavior had been wrong in any respect. One is forced to explain it as an example of regression to the earliest stage of pure "need cathexis" (I, 56, fn. 2) prior to the cathexis of even parts of an object.

The patient described in Volume I (p. 288) as paradigmatic for the incontinence type of urethral-erotic language, who reacted to the inception of her treatment with an attack of urinary incontinence during coition, was an ambulatory psychotic. She was married to a sadistic psychotic, who had given her an electric vibrating gadget to take his place when he was out of town. After overcoming her religious scruples, she eventually divorced him and from then on became quite promiscuous. Her reports of these occasions were distinguished by an utter lack of detail with regard both to what had gone on and the individuality of the partner.

The analytically-trained reader will bring this clinical picture into focus if he compares it with that presented by a neurotic young woman patient. The latter also for a while became fairly promiscuous; but her partners entered her associations meaningfully long before her relation to them became a sexual one; her intimacies with them showed a human complexion, and her reports were by no means without detail.

The woman mentioned previously who had been victimized by a psychotherapist told me that the "incontinent" man victimized all his women patients. What causes these women, by the way, to lend themselves to the exploitations is not their sexual appetite, but their masochistic desires. My own patient was extremely masochistic; I have learned of another one who eventually "escaped" into a marriage with a husband who beat her.

In suggesting one more possible equivalent I merely follow a "hunch" and must leave its validation to others who have the requisite analytic material at their disposal. The equivalent I suggest is verbal indiscretion.

Another example: a psychotic young woman began her treatment by accusing me of passing gas several times during the session. The occasions were those when I made a small sound, such as leaning forward or back in the chair, taking a cigarette, or the like. The interpretation by the patient was, of course, due to her own impulses of which she was not aware. They were therefore allowed to manifest themselves only in projection. This is certainly a regressive response, yet the extent of the regression becomes recognizable only if I add that this is the schizophrenic young woman who later proved capable of a complete rectal orgasm in response to her husband's performing sodomy on her.

Because rectal incontinence is more regressive than urethral incontinence, the question presents itself of whether it is accompanied by a more thorough destruction of the incest barrier in the psychotic. Neither of the mothers mentioned above desisted from exploiting their children at the customary age of seven or thereabouts, but went on into puberty. One performed fellatio on the boy when he was capable of ejaculation and thus seduced him to incest. The other indulged in sadistic attacks on the genital of the pubescent but now, of course, completely helpless girl.

Two cases are not enough for an answer, but the questions pile up, and I ask them again for the benefit of future observers with more material.

II. THE RETENTION OF DIRT

It is hardly necessary to say that the student of the ambulatory psychotic will not be pleased by his findings, and when he lays them out he will often displease his reader. The following short section may be found particularly repugnant because it deals with the psychotic patient's defective disgust barrier.

Whether the defect is a regressive one or the result of an arrested development is unknown. The psychotic parent allows himself to be closely observed by our informant—his child, now our patient—for only a few years; and the direct observation of the ambulatory psychotic patient is fragmentary because he is analyzable, if at all, only up to a point.

Furthermore, at the risk of being repetitious, one can not generalize about the retention of dirt. It is here as with any symptom: it may often be lacking. Certain psychotics are immaculate, and their surroundings are in perfect order. And again, one can treat the symptom only against the background of place, time, and social stratum. Freud's comment on the general lack of personal hygiene in the French aristocracy of the 17th century will be remembered at this point. Conversely, I recall a patient, in whose profession the daily shower is a matter of course, reporting that he bathed only about once a week—a report that should have made me suspicious of his diagnosis, one I actually made much too late. And I recall the unforgettable Aichhorn presenting the case of a scrubwoman who washed her hands six times daily and exclaiming in his homely Austrian: "A scrub woman? Six times? Why, she has a washing compulsion!"

My previous examples contain many illustrations of the retention of dirt in the psychotic: women neglecting their genitals, others not wiping themselves after urination, two who retained fecal matter in their underwear, another who never cleaned herself during her period and repelled her child (whose hair she kept unwashed) with the display of menstrual blood clots. I could add still another one with a chronic nasal catarrh, who exhibited an unspeakably soiled handkerchief for days on end.

The psychotic housewife not infrequently keeps in her icebox spoiled food that anyone else would long since have thrown out. I recall one who in the midst of a meal commanded the family to stop eating while she sniffed delusorily "spoilt" food on the table. Still another actually kept urine in bottles in her kitchen, and at least once served it, instead of vinegar, with red cabbage. I have more than once heard of the psychotic's failure to flush the toilet after urination or even defecation. To all this one must add the many instances in which "dirt" is equivalent to "worn," "torn," "ragged," and "in disorder." When I once saw a patient's (psychotic) mother in consultation and commented to the patient on her immaculate appearance, I was answered: "You should see what she wears underneath. Everything is torn, held together with safety pins, and such."

One patient told me how her psychotic husband strewed used handkerchiefs and socks around their apartment; and several others described the bathroom floor as littered with bloody napkins at the time of their psychotic mothers' periods.

Such actually is not surprising. Because the pleasure-physiologic body ego is projectable into the environment (II, 246–254), one will every so often find the retention of dirt or its equivalent there instead of on the person.

I. PERCEPTORY ABERRATIONS

There are, as far as I could observe, two different types of perceptory aberrations in certain psychotics. I have never read about them, know no name for them, and my only justification for calling them two different types is that, while I have no understanding at all for the first group, I can as to the second make at least one or two orientative statements.

A few examples that will acquaint the reader with the first group:

(a) A neurotic, quite underweight college girl entered analysis with, amongst other symptoms, a severe anorexia. After a year of analysis she had the normal appetite of the adolescent, ate as she said "like a horse," and filled out. Her psychotic mother spent the last three months of that year abroad, returned, and greeted her daughter at the pier with: "You look awful!" What is this? Hallucination? That phenomenon describes the individual who sees something that is not there. Yet the mother sees and recognizes her daughter, who certainly is there. But she sees her altered. Hallucinatory alteration?

(b) A patient upon entering analysis reports of scars on his late psychotic mother's breast which, she had told him, stemmed from abscesses contracted while she was nursing him. In the course of his analysis he recalls how inadequately she nursed him and how often she kept him hungry. A severe weaning trauma leaves no doubt as to the precipitation of violent cannibalistic impulses in the child. But with all that, there actually never were any scars! Amnesia removal attested definitely to their absence. This example resembles the first one, except that here the alteration by the psychotic patient is supported by the mother's statement.

(c) An older boy to whose profession accurate functioning of the hands is indispensable, in the psychotic mother's absence puts one of them through a glass door. The nonpsychotic father is present and rationally concerned. He rushes his son to the doctor who examines, stitches, and bandages the injured hand, stating that he has not the slightest doubt with regard to an eventually complete restitution. (This was subsequently confirmed.) When the mother comes back, her husband immediately reassures her with particular emphasis on the doctor's unqualifiedly favorable prognosis. Yet when she sees the bandages, she throws her pocketbook on the floor, becomes desperate, and bewails the irreparable damage. Can one, unable to call this a hallucinatory alteration, speak of it as a *"delusory* alteration?"

I have discussed the matter with an analytically trained, experienced psychiatrist who told me that the textbooks disregard these phenomena, which consequently have no name. I do not disregard them, but cannot name them and am unable to make even the slightest theoretical contribution to their understanding.

The second group of perceptory aberrations contains proprioceptive as well as exteroceptive anomalies with regard either to the body or to an element of the outside world. Some of these are at least descriptively understandable; others are even descriptively obscure. I have heard them from two different patients; unfortunately I was, at the time of the treatment of the first of these, relatively inexperienced.

This patient complained that every so often the environment had only two dimensions instead of three (which, if my memory serves me, occurs also in dreams), that one or more of her limbs had vanished, or that her body had cavities (similar to those in Henry Moore's sculptures). I am ignorant of whether or not the literature describes these complaints, but I recall that colleagues told me of them with regard to their own patients. Examples of the obscure psychotic complaints mentioned above are: "I am airy," "I have that black-and-white feeling," or "Time has a gap."

The last is from the second patient, who often perceived the environment in distortion: in school the chemistry room was all out of shape; on the street a certain house with a candy store stood askew, etc. While walking, her steps sounded loud and fast; both she and the city had "a hot rhythm"; the volume of the ticking of her wristwatch had increased out of all proportion, and while playing the piano the notes suddenly stood out from the page. (Here, by the way, an element of the object world is endowed with, not deprived of, a third dimension.) Finally: "I am decomposing." (After the fashion of Rouault's paintings, in which an imitation of the leading of Gothic church windows is evidently attempted.)

The sensitivity, intelligence, and analyzability of this patient, combined with the increase of my technical skill, enables me to state that all these complaints were removable in the course of treatment and that at least some of them were exchangeable for an affect whose place they had evidently taken.

When the girl told me that both she and the city had "a hot rhythm," she also reported for the first time her masturbation and the technique employed by her, adding that she had been firmly convinced that she would never be able to tell this to anyone. I responded briefly to the extent that none of it was new to me, and I may have added that the need for an outlet was natural. In the next hour the city still had the "rhythm" but the patient was able to "hold her own," and no longer compelled to join the city in it.

One cannot and should not avoid reading such a report "symbolically" with the proviso, however, that the expectations furnished by such a reading with regard to a particular future amnesia removal are purely tentative and do not prevent one from keeping an open mind. ("Hot rhythm" = sexual pulsations; "city" = mother, etc. For brevity's sake, here I am call-

ing all forms of unconscious indirect representation "symbolic.")
After the patient had her first petting session one no longer
heard of the notes standing out from the music score
(picturization of projected clitoris erection was no longer necessary after its direct proprioceptive and exteroceptive experience). The affect covered by the schizophrenic experience with
the notes was the sexual affect. Correct "timing" forbids, by the
way, the analyst's going into any of this with the patient at such
a time. Even the mystifying "I am black-and-white" could
eventually be understood. An excessive urinary urge that could
not be delayed had compelled the patient to urinate squatting
behind a tree. The shame over this exhibition was conscious, the
wish to exhibit was not. The two made a compromise in the
unconscious fantasy of exhibiting by simply standing up in undress. She should then have shown only her *black* pubic hair and
her *white* skin, both of which she actually possessed, without
the addition of the pink vulva and the yellow urinary stream
which represented a colorful display of her "castration." Here
the psychotic experience of being "black-and-white" covers a
conglomeration of affects: the sexual affect consequent to a discharge of a partial drive, exhibition, fear of castration, and
shame.

For the next small illustration I cannot account because it stems
from daily life and not analysis. A patient reports that a schizophrenic
maid left a note in the lavatory saying: "This [the toilet] appears to
be out-of-order. Did not use." Actually the toilet was in perfect order,
so that it could only have been her genital (cloaca) that was "out-of-
order" and had not been used. (The name "toilet" for the organ was
known to me from another patient whose psychotic mother used it
as a matter of course: "Wash your toilet." . . . "Take your hands off
your toilet." . . . etc.) The maid, for reasons of her own, evidently
felt impelled to inform my patient of the distortion, probably delusory, of an element in her pleasure-physiologic body ego in projection
—a distortion that made it temporarily unfit for urinary and/or masturbatory employment.

Sometimes schizophrenic symptoms change by acquiring detail that
rarely fails to point to the traumatic past. Another patient, for in-

stance, was often and for a long time disturbed by hearing a constant "noise" of which I could make nothing. Eventually she recognized the hallucinated "noise" as that made by two people fighting and shouting angrily at one another. There was no doubt in my mind that this was preparatory to a potential amnesia removal of the repressed past, and that the two persons as well as the subject of their quarrel could be identified in the course of further analytic work.

In conclusion, I must declare myself negligent for not having made a note of an incident where schizophrenic symptomatology was in the end actually exchanged for an affect. I do not therefore recall the circumstances except that they were of a sort that had repeatedly caused experiences of the kind related above. This time, however, the patient in the same situation reported instead that she was "so afraid"; and I answered, knowing that she would not misunderstand me: "Congratulations! At least you can be afraid instead of experiencing all these funny things." And she did indeed understand.

IV. THE AGGRESSIVE ABUSE OF THE CHILD

FUSED AND DEFUSED AGGRESSION

For only one reason this is a difficult subject. Freud, at the end of his life, admitted not knowing whether or not the discharge of pure (i.e., completely defused) aggression furnishes pleasure. Nor have I obtained a final answer; but observations have allowed me to study the question clinically.

Since the course of my discussion of the question is a circuitous one, I shall attempt to facilitate following it by charting it at the outset. I begin by comparing sadistic abuse of the child where the parent's libido is not defused because his aggression effects sexual arousal, with a few instances suggesting that he derives pleasure of a nonsexual nature from the aggressive abuse. I then comment on a perversion and finally return to the analytic observation of the ambulatory psychotic via the amnesia removal of his victim, the child, concluding that aggressive abuse is in most instances not of a defused nature but one where aggression and regressive libido are fused. It is, in other words, in most cases simply sadistic, and occurs frequently but not always in the course of the sexual exploitation of the child.

In some of my illustrations the objects are not children. I nevertheless include them because they lend themselves to a discussion about the fused and defused aggression respectively.

An example, for the sake of comparison, where the abuse is not defused:

The sadistic father (mentioned above), who beat his little girl on her nude buttocks in the psychotic mother's presence while displaying an erection (the child in a nightgown, the man in open pajamas), does not of course exemplify almost total defusion. Another father who beat his son with his belt so that the metal buckle bit into the child's flesh, gave no sign of sexual arousement, although it is naturally impossible to exclude it. Here the primal scene was such as I had never heard: in the foreplay he and his psychotic wife enjoyed each other's anus olfactorily, on all fours, in daylight, and in the boy's presence.

I have several times referred to a mother (II, 55) who aroused herself by cruelly maltreating the child to the point of having to masturbate—an instance which here needs no comment. However, the same psychotic woman has been described (II, 55) as beating the one-year-old in the face with the soiled diaper because the baby showed signs of nursling masturbation, and years later (II, 53) on the occasion of washing the child's hair, of knocking her head against the washbowl, rubbing soap into her eyes and pulling her hair. This, for all I could ascertain, did not lead to masturbation; it lacked in fact any sign of sexual arousal, and yet it could not but have given the woman some kind of pleasure because she continued it into a time when the daughter was fully able to take care of herself. I cannot help suspecting defusion, and considering the pleasure a nonsexual one.[6] In her digital attacks upon the genital of the daughter in the beginning of puberty (II, 56), no sexual arousal was evident, and circumstances, while of course not categorically excluding it, were extremely unsuitable for an indulgence.

[6] What induced me to give credence to *the memory from age one* is, for one thing, the hardly describable yet so typical way it came out in her associations; and for another, the recollection of the occurrences' continuing into later years.

Furthermore, the woman was one of the two psychotic mothers who tortured their daughters when out walking by dragging them at a rate almost beyond endurance. Holding the child by the hand in a department store, she rushed at a pace so fast that the patient remembered herself practically "flying" in a horizontal position. Another psychotic mother has been mentioned before as doing the same on the street with the result of breaking the daughter's wrist. In these instances it would be approaching the fantastic to assume that the torture yielded sexual excitation.

I am now prepared to draw from the other source I mentioned, the newspapers that report a horror story almost every day. They present facts, some of which analytic experience enables one to understand. I shall comment upon a few I have retained, and I advise the reader to throw the psychotic deviations into relief by holding them against my exposition of the theory of coition (I, 272–276) where a normal simultaneous discharge of libido and of aggression is described. In the case of the psychotics under consideration here, libido and aggression are discharged not simultaneously but separately.

Two society matrons are raped in their car by two Negro boys. One may suppose that in this case it is not necessarily the libido that was defective because what marks the act as psychotic is the defective discharge of the aggressive instinct-component. After the deed was done, one perpetrator said to the other: "I guess we better kill them or they will tell on us"—a pure rationalization, for the youths were promptly apprehended anyway. But they had in the meantime run their cars over the victims because they needed to kill. It was a biphasic discharge of libido and of extremely regressive aggression.[7]

When a female septuagenarian is raped, one must suspect the absence of incest barrier in the psychotic, whose mother may have reached that age at the time of the crime. The papers, of course, never give the background; but what else could endow the victim with any appeal?

---

[7] I recently found the reverse sequence of the discharge of libido and aggression described in a saying attributed to Genghis Khan. The Mongol chieftain is said to have exclaimed, "A man's greatest joy is to conquer his enemies, to drive them before him, to rob them of their possessions, to see their loved ones in tears, to ride their horses and to sleep on the white bellies of the wives and daughters!" [Heissig, 1964].

He who clubs to death an invalid woman seated in a wheel chair, he who brutally kills an aged storekeeper, must be assumed to be psychotic even though not a patient, and the act to be an example of the discharge of pure aggression. If the woman carries some coins on her person, if the store has a till with some money, the theft appears to be purely incidental.

I am writing this chapter in a spot so idyllic and peaceful that I would not exchange it for any other. But our house although far from the road and open to a garden of ineffable beauty is nevertheless part of a village. The latter was not too long ago rocked to its core by tragedy. A local young man had one night killed a young girl by inches, slowly crushing her head with a rock. That is all I heard at first, but a friend, one who knew the village from many years of residence, was more than eager to supply me with every detail, many of which I omit. The girl's underwear showed a rent, but she had not been raped. The murderer, soon apprehended, was 23 years of age and had three months before been dismissed from a military mental institution and returned to the community. Under questioning by the authorities he said: "Oh, *I knew I had to kill* someone tonight." This is, at least, an authentic confession of an imperative drive and its discharge. Brief as it is, it implies relief although not necessarily pleasure. The young murderer must have desisted from violence in the hospital, possibly from mere lack of opportunity, for he had been adjudged cured and dismissed.

Finally, one more newspaper account that appeared several years ago. Both perpetrator and victim were boys and had barely reached adolescence. One boy fatally stabbed the other without any provocation and, while the latter died, thanked him profusely for having let him experience hearing and feeling the bones crack and the tissues tear. Here again there is definite pleasure, yet of a nonsexual kind.

Circumstances have arisen that allow me now to be explicit about a certain form of abuse that I could only allude to briefly before (II, 304–317). My example is as good as any, and it reveals at least one instance of a certain morbid condition as psychosomatic that I have never heard so named.

Long, long ago when I was as yet completely ignorant of the neurotic patient's so often psychotic parent, an unhappy woman sought analytic help, and I had the good fortune to be able to supply it. The analysis literally unearthed a very rare human being who in due course became happy, productive, and loved. She entered her treatment with a "lupus erythematosus," a chronic symmetrical skin eruption on either cheek next to the nose which the dermatologists of that time could not cure. Of the parents not much became known: an affectionate, outgoing father had died, and an unsympathetic, bigoted mother was still alive. The patient was slow in developing the relation to me that is prerequisite to amnesia removal because she obstinately transferred the mother, against which I was of too little assistance because of my ignorance then of the true nature of transference. Yet she eventually established the relation, and amnesias were removed. One of them told of the sexual exploitation by a maid who choked the child (at age five?) by pressing the little girl's face into her vulva until she became orgastic; another one told of a sort of "transformation into activity" [Freud] when the 12-year-old had their dog perform cunnilingus on her while she sat on the toilet. The first of these memories was of course pathogenic: the patient was "crushed" when the maid became orgastic. The second I considered indicative of a favorable prognosis, as I always do when puberty allows for a few healthy years before the onset of the neurosis. The child was guiltless, determined, and felt that the pleasure was due her. When the memory of the abuse by the maid was worked through, the lupus erythematosus disappeared; the repression had evidently maintained it: the maid's vulva had "come off" onto the face of her victim.

The "second beating fantasy," so termed by Freud in his famous article "A Child Is Being Beaten" (1919a), has the wording: "I am being beaten by my father." He remarks upon it: "This second phase is the most important and the most momentous of all. But we may say of it in a certain sense that it has never had a real existence. It is never remembered; it has never succeeded in becoming conscious. It is a construction of analysis, but it is no less a necessity on that account" (p. 185).

I was therefore greatly surprised when I saw a severely neurotic woman, vaginally insensitive, and altogether dependent sexually upon clitoris masturbation, with an elaborate fantasy of being beaten by "a man." Her analysis, of long duration, unfinished, yet very successful, left hardly any doubt that she had never been beaten by her neurotic, inhibited, but devoted father. Instead, a pathogenic scene emerged from repression, often repeated and taking place in the phallic phase as well as the first years of latency, which in spite of a fair amount of authentic detail does not readily lend itself to a complete description because one crucial detail could not be obtained. Locale: the empty house in the afternoon; cast: the little girl and her bestial psychotic mother. Both the psychosis of the mother and her extreme sadism were ascertained without the help of amnesia removal: close friends of the patient in the later phases of her analysis when they met the old lady were struck by her extreme withdrawal; and the patient had never repressed the fact that a switch hung on a hook in the kitchen with which the mother used to whip the bare legs of the growing girl to the point of producing big welts. In the scene mentioned above, the mother took the daughter into a bedroom, had her lie down on the bed, bared her buttocks and informed her that she could cry all she wanted to because no one would hear her. Whereupon she began flogging her to excess. There was no room for doubt about the fact that she became orgastic in the process: her peculiar tone of voice in commanding the child, her admonition, her attire, her earlier sexual abuses, the absence of even a pretended punishment, and the contrast with her subsequent actions, still to be described, all testify to the exercise of her perversion. (The patient came to and left her analysis afflicted with a painful and incurable skin disease.) The one detail that would not relinquish its repression: had the woman required any physical stimulation? The patient clung to the excuse that she could not see what went on behind her back—obviously an evasion, because in the earlier abuse where the mother also wore a nightgown the same question remained unanswered, although here the child was approached from the front.

With the flogging done because it had achieved its purpose, the depraved woman slowly regained her "persona": she got herself completely and conventionally dressed and went visiting neighbors and friends with the daughter. Here she looked normal, said exactly the right things in the appropriate tone of voice, and observed the amenities so meticulously that the child was unable to reconcile the two "worlds" she was made to inhabit in so short a succession. She decided eventually upon the first one as having been but a "dream." It was tragic to hear that the performance continued into an age when the daughter would have been physically able to get away, outrun the mother, and so foil her. Nevertheless, psychologically she could not: the patient clearly recalled how as a child, upon hearing the mother say "Come here . . ." in that certain tone of voice she could never reproduce for me, she was literally "hypnotized" like the proverbial rabbit by the snake, glued to the spot until compelled to enter the torture chamber.

The question raised above remained almost throughout the analysis merely a subject for speculation. The man in her fantasy furnished a running commentary while he beat the patient, using exactly the tone of voice of the mother. He commented on the reddening and increasing turgor of the buttocks, obviously exciting himself coincident with the patient's own digital stimulation. This, of course, copied the sadistic phallic mother who might possibly have used the man's words on the masochistic child. The most distinct of these words, the patient said, were so obscene that for a long time she could not bring herself to repeat them. When she finally did, they were not obscene at all, but merely characterized the buttocks as becoming "red as a brick." In my experience, words accompanying such beatings are hardly ever invented, but represent a single ruin that has escaped the apparent destruction of the rest of the past events. I had, furthermore, no doubt that one was entitled to apply the comment simultaneously to the genital of the increasingly excited mother.

There the matter stood; I felt frustrated by the patient's unconquerable fear of castration because I simply did not believe that this was a case of a psychotic gaining end pleasure without masturbatory assistance.

Toward the very end of this incomplete analysis an event occurred that I shall merely report, letting the reader decide whether or not it answers the question. The patient invited her mother for a visit and was alone with her in the house for the first time since entering analysis, watching television. Suddenly she became aware of a "scraping" noise that she remembered having heard as a child, although it had never entered her associations. Looking around she saw the 70-year-old woman masturbate by sliding one thigh back and forth over the other.

I conclude the example with two fragments of information.

In the first place, I had learned long before that "seeing"—any seeing, for example, the social "seeing" synonym for visiting, or seeing something on television regardless of what is shown on the screen—can acquire the meaning of sexual, scoptophilic seeing. In the second place, unbelievable as it may sound, *I would not have been told the episode,* although it had happened only the night before the session, had I not first expressed the "hunch" that the mother utilized her being alone with her daughter for indulging herself while "sleeping" in the next room. The patient reported it only as a confirmation of my "hunch." In other words, in spite of her improvement, spectacular as it was, proximity without witness made her regress into masochistic dependence and obey the command "not to talk."

In discussing the question raised but not answered by Freud of whether or not the discharge of pure aggression yields pleasure, I shall simply sum up. The flagrant and never-missing aggression against the child is—amnesia removal has convinced me—by and large not defused but *sadistic.* In many cases it is inflicted in the course of the sexual abuse of the child, whose suffering only heightens the abuser's pleasure.

FURTHER CONSIDERATIONS

A few more remarks to be made upon the aggressive abuse of the child are not connected, and I shall restrict myself to their enumeration.

(1) *The Psychotic Mother as Procuress*

There is no reason to assume that the mother in one of my examples had any knowledge of the seduction of her daughter by the maid until she surprised them, let alone that she arranged the seduction. Yet there is every reason to be practically certain that the mother in another example did arrange for the rape of her adolescent daughter. She knew as well as did her husband what a certain psychopathic evangelist could be counted on to do to a young girl if left alone with her. And she knew that the girl would give in to him because she herself had prepared her for it through her flogging. The reader will confirm this for himself if I tell him that she was the woman in the example just related. I must have encountered this type of behavior several times, because why did I write more than 10 years ago that the child "is seduced in the most bizarre ways by the parent and, at his or her instigation, by others. . . .?" (I, xvii). But I have no records, and my memory fails me; the only other instances that I recall stem from an analysis that had not yet begun when I wrote the sentence just quoted. It concerns the amnesia removal of a boy's seduction by his uncle. The patient told of performing fellatio on the uncle and added, "My mother knew nothing of this, you understand!" Further amnesia removal proved this to be a "negation" (in Freud's classic sense): the psychotic mother had arranged it and was looking on.

(2) The Girl's Defloration by the Psychotic Mother

I have already dealt so exhaustively with this topic (II, 73, 325, 363) that there is little to add. The ages at which this occurs vary in my experience from one to four. The procedure also varies: one mother first masturbated the child in order to make her accessible; another did it abruptly without any preliminaries; a third (the "verbal" mother) said eagerly to the three-year-old: "But don't you see, Mary, we *have* to do this!" And the child implored her fearfully: "Mother, don't hurt me!" I have also described how the defloration mobilizes the normally dormant vagina as well as the "spot" (see I, 212), which the girl in the phallic phase may use for masturbation, and how these premature elements of the pleasure-physiologic elements enter the body ego, causing their symbolization in dreams.

The memories of the defloration are as detailed as are any true memories; their most astonishing characteristic is that while the child experiences great pain, the mother shows no signs of pleasure so familiar to other forms of exploitation. Her motive is completely unknown.

This is the most mystifying aspect of the act. It is obviously aggressive, yet one cannot explain why it takes this particular form; and since all the familiar signs of climactic arousal otherwise so distinctly recalled are missing, one is left totally in the dark as to what precipitates the impulsion.

The repression of the event entails a "scotoma" in the adult; the patient readily admits that she did not bleed when she first had intercourse with a man, or if she did, hardly at all; but previous to that admission she had never been struck by the fact, although bleeding upon defloration is common knowledge.

Nevertheless there are certain conscious derivatives of the repressed defloration experience in the adult. Most of them are fantasies, such as that athletic activity or bicycling is responsible for the broken hymen; some of these fantasies have acquired a deceptive "memory quality."

One patient believed that she had been thrown on a picket fence as a child (the alleged circumstances were not "remembered"), and another had the screen memory, probably true, that as a little girl she used to sit on a sharp-edged piece of furniture which she considered the cause of her not bleeding at her first, and very little at her second, cohabitation. Another one had a premarital examination at the age of 22 by a woman gynecologist whom the family had known "all her life." Nevertheless the mother accompanied her, and she recalled the "slyly gloating" look on the mother's face when the doctor mentioned that the hymen was broken.

In two other cases a remnant had persisted for a long time both before and during the analysis, prior to the amnesia removal for the defloration. In one of them it concerned herself; in the other it concerned the husband, who in the end proved a duplicate of the mother. Although the remnant to be described had for many years caused resentment in one patient and rage in the other, each was reported only after the repressed defloration was recalled. One might call it the "syndrome of the outstretched forefinger," stemming originally from the (cannibalistic) defloration performance. In the case of the first patient, the mother used this exaggeratedly outstretched index finger in ordering more potatoes or the like in a restaurant. In the case of the second, the husband had previous to the session orated about a certain object, using the same outstretched forefinger to draw imaginary diagonals, point out the identity of certain parts of the object, etc. I now heard for the first time in her long treatment, that this finger gesture of her husband had irritated her for many years and had frequently dampened her affection. Subsequently in her associations, the finger moved promptly into the restaurant where it was used to write in the air for the benefit of the waiter. Some of them understood the pantomimic command, others did not; but the patient was always annoyed out of all proportion. *It is in this same session that we obtained the verbal details from the episode of the defloration.*

In the normal heterosexual woman, the "spot" is increasingly stimulated by penile frictions; it furnishes what we are accustomed to call "deep vaginal sensitivity," and one can if the woman becomes completely orgastic call it the very site of the climax. It has the strange property of being excitable not only from inside but also from outside, that is, through manipulation or of pressure upon the abdominal integument above it. This access to it is, however, as far as my few observations show, in both the child and adult (I, 212–215) reserved for a female partner.

That successful clitoral masturbation can spread to the extent of furnishing vaginal arousal is, I presume, general knowledge; yet it would appear, although I cannot be definite on this point, that an extensive participation of the "spot" requires subsequent vaginal stimulation.

My original observation concerning the "spot" (that is, the fornices and the womb) and its function came from the analysis of a homosexual woman: I was convinced at the time of never having heard of the subject before. Only lately did I recall that when I was a young doctor and devoid of analytic knowledge a man patient had told me of his overtly bisexual girl friend. He quoted her as saying, "There is a place way up that only a woman's finger can reach." This of course meant nothing to me when I heard it; recalling it lately, I said to myself: How strange of her to express the selectivity of her response in terms of inches; and as for her comparison, how absurd. An erection is certainly longer than an outstretched forefinger; it surely reaches the spot, although she does not react to it. What makes for her choice of words? Only my renewed and intense preoccupation with Freud's formula for the delusion, combined with the frequent amnesia removal for the maternal defloration furnished the answer: the original "woman's finger" that alone reached the spot could only have been the mother's in childhood.

Because I learned only recently that the early activation of the vagina had been known to no less an observer than the great Karl Abraham, I close this report with some sense of awe. It is as though Abraham's voice had reached me from the grave. Some weeks ago I read one of his letters in the recently published correspondence with Freud (Abraham & Freud, 1965):

> Your concept of a change of erotogenic zones in the woman at puberty has always proved correct in practice. I have recently wondered whether in early infancy there may be an early vaginal awakening of the female libido, which is destined to be repressed and which is subsequently followed by clitoral primacy as the expression of the phallic phase. A number of observations seem to bear this out. If my assumption is correct, it would have one advantage for us: we would be better able to understand the female Oedipus complex as the result of an early vaginal reaction to the father's penis (possibly in the form of spontaneous contractions) and the change of the erotogenic zone in puberty would then be a resumption of the original position. One could justifiably follow up this idea some time, since it is based on a number of observations. It could be fitted into our present theory which it does not contradict in any way and to which it might make a small addition. If it seems worth your while, I could report some of my observations which gave me the idea. It has not yet been clarified and the relationship to the phallic phase in particular is so far unclear [pp. 375–376].

Freud was interested but evidently incapable of making the pertinent observations: "According to my preconceived ideas on the subject," he answered, "the vaginal share would tend to be expressed anally. The vagina, as we know, is a later acquisition by separation from the cloaca" (p. 377).

Abraham continues in his very next letter, the day after Christmas, 1924:

> The ease with which little girls can be seduced to coitus-like actions, as well as the tendency to vaginal masturbation and, in particular, the introduction of foreign bodies, must all rest on such processes. Two neurotic symptoms have forced me to assume something which we could call an early vaginal-anal stage: frigidity and *vaginismus*. In the light of all my psycho-analytic experience, I cannot believe that frigidity is merely based on the failure of the libido to pass from the clitoris to the vagina. There must be a prohibition which has an immediate and local basis; this is even more valid for *vaginismus*. Why should the vagina react so negatively to the first attempts at coitus unless something positive has preceded this? Similarly, hysterical vomiting is preceded by a positive and pleasurable experience in early infancy [pp. 377 378].

Abraham did not know of either the neurotic's psychotic parent, or the defloration that enables the small child to masturbate or to be masturbated vaginally and whose repression makes the woman vaginally anaesthetic. In the normal woman who has not had to suffer abuse as a child, Freud's view may well hold true. She may actually after puberty own a new dominant erogenic zone, the vagina (I, 199–201). Certainly she can in her very first intercourse with a man and in spite of the pain caused by the breaking of her hymen become orgastic.

(3.) *The Repression of Sexual and Aggressive Abuse*

If one makes the (so frequently artificial) distinction between sexual and aggressive abuse, one has to state that it is much more difficult to remove the amnesia for the latter than for the former. The patient whose mother boasted publicly at the time of the analysis, "I beat it into her," could not in a long analysis be induced to remember a single beating. Another one, whose analysis abounded in the removal of amnesia for all kinds of seductions, remembered herself at an unspecified time in childhood as having been "black and blue" but would not go any further. This is not always so, as shown in the example where the mother's whippings and floggings are remembered in due course; but it is so more often than not.

(4.) *The Overstimulation of the Child by His Psychotic Mother*

I have previously described a mother who inserted her forefinger far into the rectum of her small boy. This is, of course, but another form of sadistic abuse to which the helpless child reacted with unbearable pain. Yet she also sucked his penis while having him suck her breast. Here the child's reaction may not have been one of outright pain but rather of extreme unpleasure due to overstimulation. Such overstimulation is common and allows for an obvious explanation: the adult imposes upon the immature erogeneity of the child; he insists upon end pleasure which his partner, in the beginning at least, is unable to obtain, and it looks at first sight as though unpleasurable overstimulation would be the only possible outcome. Clinical observation, however, teaches a different lesson: overstimulation is but one of three possible results. The second is hypnosis; the psychotic, without meaning to, hypnotizes the child. This, if you wish to consider it so, is the earliest instance of a hypnotic evasion (cf. Chapter Four: On Exceptional States). The third result should be of interest to the child analyst; it may perhaps correct some of his preconceptions with regard to the sexuality of the child in the phallic phase. I can offer but two authentic observations. In one of them the four-year-old boy enjoyed performing fellatio on a man with whom one can only say he had fallen in love—I do not know whether so small a child is commonly credited with so adult an erogeneity. The other observation is that of the child whose mother never did sexual violence to her; instead she not only had the child masturbate her in many different situations, but—"live and let live"—masturbated the little girl many a time in the bathtub with soap suds, and at least once on the rocking chair. The relation lasted from age three to age seven or thereabouts and was greatly enjoyed by the child who never suffered an overstimulation. She was the only one of my women patients whom a memory not only excited but made mildly orgastic during the session and whom I had to suspect of having been capable of a climax during the phallic phase.

Nature, it would appear, does not fit easily into a book: not even if that book is of the caliber of *The Three Contributions*.

THE PREVALENCE OF THE MOTHER OVER THE FATHER IN THE ABUSE OF THE CHILD

I may be accused of favoring the mother over the father as abuser of their offspring; amongst the 30-odd examples illustrative of the sexual and aggressive exploitation of the child, there are but about 10 in which a man is to blame, and of these only four where the man is the father. This has two reasons, one insignificant and the other significant. The first is accidental: in the cases with only one psychotic parent that I was able to study, the mother usually happened to be the psychotic marriage partner. The significant reason lies in the existence of the preoedipal phase. The preoedipal "twosome" between a mother and her child of either sex, precedes, outweighs and, I believe, shapes the subsequent oedipal "threesome" that follows, but does not replace it. Take but one example, the healthy pubescent boy. He may begin by masturbating in a group, paying his due as it were to his homosexuality, but he will then proceed to masturbating alone with disguised fantasies of the mother; or, if you wish, mother-substitutes he does not recognize as such. In this fashion he finds his way to the girl.

I shall present one example instead of many because it spells out so precisely the prevalence of maternal over paternal seduction. It is taken from the long but nevertheless unfinished analysis of a woman.

When the patient's relation to me became suitable for amnesia removal, innumerable pathogenic sexual activities with the mother emerged. Of the father one heard very little. The child feared him although he regaled her every week at the drug store with elaborate sundaes. He was ignorant of the mother's dealings with the child and was himself the image of respectability: stern at home and successful in his profession. That was all I knew except for his appearance in a brief story recognizable as a screen memory by its periodic repetition and the incongruity of action and affect. He had gone with his little girl to a crowded public affair, in the course of which she reached for his hand and found that she had taken the hand of a stranger. This harmless error precipitated an excessive feeling of shame, and the incident was never forgotten.

Only a short time before the enforced discontinuation of the analysis, two scenes were remembered that showed the true character of the man and revealed him as psychotic. In the first, while the patient was still an infant in the crib the father shoved his erected penis through the slats toward her face. She became frightened and cried loudly, bringing the mother into the bedroom. The mother beat the child without her husband's uttering so much as the slightest protest. It appeared to me that it was her evaluation of the father's character that opened the way for the escape from amnesia of the second scene, which had up to then remained under the cover of the screen memory described above. I believe the event occurred when the child was about five years of age. Here the father placed his erection into the little girl's hand, teaching her how to masturbate him while warning her that "it spits." Some of the product got on the girl, who felt soiled and distinctly remembered washing her hand.

My point in relating this is that while a minor symptom of the patient was selectively traceable to this abuse by the father—a symptom which would never have brought her into analysis yet which disappeared upon the amnesia removal—all the rest of her quite elaborate neurotic symptomatology had its origin *in the abuse by the mother.*

I do not believe it is pure accident that in my observation the abuses of the child by the psychotic mother outweigh so frequently those traceable to the father. It is after all the mother who constitutes the first—preoedipal—object. The subsequent oedipal constellation overlays the preoedipal one but does not replace it.

THE INFLUENCE OF THE PARENTAL ABUSE OF THE CHILD UPON THE CHOICE OF A MARRIAGE PARTNER

One consequence of the abuse of the child that becomes manifest only in adulthood but often goes unnoticed is the frequent compulsion to marry, in the parent's image, a psychotic. Whether or not the individual so compelled is himself a psychotic or only a neurotic is immaterial; and the sex of the partner upon whom the parent from childhood is transferred is as irrelevant as it is in the analytic transference.

A lovely young woman revives her vicious psychotic mother in the shape of a fiendishly psychotic husband. Another woman patient is tortured by her psychotic husband with excessive demands for a perversion and says spontaneously toward the end of her analysis, "I have married my father." Freud's wise technical rule requiring abstention from vital decisions during analysis of course forestalls in most instance such a marriage at the time of the treatment. But it is usually concluded not during but previous to the treatment. It has produced children, bondage, sometimes even *folie à deux*. I must make the sad confession that I personally only twice succeeded in eventually initiating a divorce by a man patient from a psychotic wife representing his psychotic father, and a woman patient from her psychotic husband. If there is any one single factor restricting analysis in giving a patient the happiness it could, it is his marriage.

SOME RESIDUAL QUESTIONS AND OBSERVATIONS

There remain a few residual questions, some answerable, some not. The paucity of the answers is at least partly due to the fact that I have essentially only my own observations to draw from.

When does the child's exploitation cease? With the majority of my patients, soon after they were seven years old. Yet there is the mother who went on using her daughter's finger for masturbation when the latter was 14, and the other who practiced fellatio on her son in his puberty. She, as well as still another one, seduced her adolescent son a few times to full-fledged incest.

The later experiences are sometimes covered by a special resistance. A patient mentioned in several of the preceding examples, who had recalled from amnesia an unusually rich and enjoyable sexual life with her mother, declared that all this had only been possible because her older siblings were in school. When she herself entered school it was discontinued. Her declaration gradually took on the "dogmatic ring" I had come to recognize as a declaration of something less than the truth. I pointed it out and told her that it convinced me of her self-deception about the discontinuation. This caused the scene to shift to a different locale, where for several more years the same intimacies were continued.

These psychotic women seem to need the child. They exploit it so frequently and routinely for a number of years that one cannot but ask oneself how they get along without it. What is their sexual life after the discontinuation? This, of course, leads to the further question: if the patient has siblings, were they also abused? And this in turn makes one ponder the final problem: where are the siblings kept? Why are they never witnesses to the abuse?

The last question is the one that has puzzled me most. A mother's masturbation of her seven-year-old daughter, for instance, took place in the girl's bedroom through which a younger brother had to pass in order to get to his. Where was he at the time of the exploitation? When I pressed the question, the patient finally saw him stand in the doorway with a leer on his face. I cannot exclude this as a memory, but it did not convince me. Otherwise no sibling has ever appeared in the memory of exploitations, although the woman patient who told me directly that she masturbated her children gave me the impression that both were present. The question has often bewildered me, but I must leave answering it to others.

How do the mothers manage sexually after they no longer abuse the child? It is obvious why the analysis cannot furnish a general answer: the child is now excluded and cannot later remember what he never knew in the first place.

It is only in one single case that circumstances, which I do not feel free to report, informed me of almost everything mentioned above. My patient's older siblings were sexually exploited as he had been, and when he was no longer available, the woman ingratiated herself with various relatives, baby-sitting and "taking care" of their children. In other words, she simply went on doing what she had done. Except for this woman's exploitation of siblings, I believe—for reasons that are not pertinent here—that her conduct would not represent the common behavior of the seducing and torturing mothers. I must therefore leave the question unanswered.

CHAPTER FOUR

ON EXCEPTIONAL STATES

The literature on "exceptional states" is filled with confusion. There is a simple way of replacing confusion with order: all one has to do is to identify those exceptional states which although known by various names are basically identical, separate them from the states that differ from each other and from the basically identical ones, and acknowledge, however briefly, the existence of at least some of the exceptional states that are nameless. In so doing, one gains a starting point for the study of the exceptional states because one finds oneself constrained to distinguish three groups.

Group I: *Basically identical (hypnotic) states:*
hypnosis
the hypnagogic state
the hypnopompic state ("aftermath" of certain dreamers.)
"sleepwalking" ("somnambulism")
hysterical twilight ("hypnoid") states

Group II: *States differing from each other as well as from those of group I:*
sleep
derealization
depersonalization
fantasy and delusion

Group III: *Some exceptional states without name:*
the regressive state of creation
the regressive state into which the patient has to enter when associating freely
the same state for the analyst listening with free-floating attention
and, I am sure, many others

The possibilities for discussion of the states listed above are at the time of this writing different for the different groups. There is much to be said about the first group, little about the second, and almost nothing of the third.

I. BASICALLY IDENTICAL (HYPNOTIC) STATES

The question that comes to mind with regard to this first group is: if the five states comprising it are all essentially hypnotic, why different names? The answer: the different names are not indicative of a different nature between these states but merely of their occurrence in a different context; in other words, *of the state preceding and following the particular hypnotic condition. Hypnosis proper* usually replaces complete wakefulness which prevails again after its termination. One may therefore call wakefulness the context in which hypnosis proper occurs and add that it is in most instances possible to sharpen the introspective faculties of an individual to the extent of his being able to distinguish between the two. Yet in other instances the context is unhomogeneous.

When an individual who is awake and consciously trying to go to sleep passes through a hypnotic state, that exceptional state (to be followed by sleep) is called *hypnagogic*. The sleep he passes into is simply sleep; that is, the regressive condition that we undergo every night. This must be stated merely to preclude the misconception of a "hypnotic sleep," which does not exist. The hypnotic *state* preceding sleep is often difficult to observe because it lacks conspicuous symptoms and may be of extremely short duration. If such occurs, it is apt to engender in the observer the deceptive impression that his subject has not been hypnotic at all, but has simply fallen asleep. (The question, what *is* hypnosis? is, I believe, a physiologic one, as Freud has stated for the case of sleep, and therefore one that psychology cannot answer.)

If a hypnotic state is passed through in the opposite direction, that is, from sleep to wakefulness, instead of from wakefulness to sleep, it is called *hypnopompic*. The sleeper before being fully aroused awakens into a hypnotic state which he subsequently exchanges for being fully awake.

The *somnambulistic state* also lies between sleep and arousal, but can be followed by either one of the two. It has been popularly called "sleep-walking," which of course is a misnomer: no one can walk while asleep, but almost everyone is able to walk in hypnosis. One can say that the somnambulist is an individual who, having been asleep, has awakened into a hypnotic state distinguished from the hypnopompic condition by a prevalence of motor- and also speech-motor actions, such as those a hypnotist can suggest to his subject.

The last of the five exceptional states grouped as essentially identical in nature is the opposite of the above. If an individual is already awake but becomes subject to the exceptional state described as typical for the somnambulist, it is termed a hysterical twilight (or hypnoid) state. In other words, both somnambulism and the hysterical twilight (hypnoid) states are hypnotic and characterized by conspicuous motor action. It is only the context in which they occur that distinguishes them one from the other: the hysterical twilight state is preceded by wakefulness, somnambulism by sleep.

It should be noted that four of these five states always occur spontaneously without anyone suspecting that they are being entered. In other words, they are all *autohypnotic*.

A. HYPNOSIS

Since the results of an investigation depend on the method employed, it must be emphasized at the outset of any discussion of hypnosis that the analyst's and the hypnotist's methods are antithetic: the latter suggests to his subject that he *become hypnotic;* the former that he *does not,* but that he remain awake, associate, and remember. The literature on hypnosis has heretofore been written by hypnotists. I attempt, I believe, the first psychological elucidation, however incomplete, based on an analyst's observations made exclusively in the analytic situation and following the strictest analytic procedure. That alone entitles me to entreat the reader to forget for the moment what he has read on the subject (worthwhile as much of it is) and to follow me while I attempt a fresh start. I must extend my plea for a momentary putting aside of the literature on Freud's treatment of the subject as well. That will be discussed in later pages. As to my own former article on a type of resistance I had observed in and out of the analytic session and termed the "hypnotic evasion," it is so full of errors that I can only hope it will be consigned to oblivion. As a hypnotic exceptional state of psychoanalytic importance, both clinically and theoretically, its corrected treatment will be included in several of the following sections.

1. *The Difference Between the Hypnosis of the Child and That of the Adult*

It has never been stated clearly and definitely, although it has been implied, that in the adult *all* hypnosis is autohypnosis; and it has never to my knowledge been either stated or implied that all child hypnosis is not.

The earliest author to imply the first part of this assertion was Ferenczi, who as early as 1909 came to the conclusion

> that in hypnotism and suggestion the chief work is performed not by the hypnotist and suggestor, but by the person himself, who till now has been looked upon merely as the "object" of the administering procedure. The existence of auto-suggestion and auto-hypnosis on the one hand, and the limits of producible phenomena residing in the individuality of the "medium" on the other hand, are striking proofs of what a subordinate part in the causality chain of these phenomena is really played by the intru-

sion of the experimentalist. . . . [pp. 58–59]. The unconscious mental forces of the "medium" appear as the real active agent, whereas the hypnotist, previously pictured as all-powerful, has to content himself with the part of an object used by the unconscious of the apparently unresisting "medium" according to the latter's individual and temporary disposition [p. 60]. *There is no such thing as a "hypnotising," a "giving of ideas" in the sense of psychical incorporating of something quite foreign from without, but only procedures that are able to set going unconscious, pre-existing, auto-suggestive mechanisms* (pp. 84–85).

I omit here, lest I be repetitious, similar intimations by later authors and instead call attention to both the frequency of the phenomenon generally known as "highway hypnosis," and to the frequency of the hypnotic evasion mentioned above, both inside and outside the analytic session (II, 6–7; and below). No one suggests to the driver that he become hypnotic at the wheel; and the analyst, as was mentioned above, does not hypnotize his patient. On the contrary, he wants him to stay awake. If you add to this the different hypnotic states enumerated above under the heading of Group I, it becomes evident, without any help from the statistician, that the incidents where a hypnotist for whatever reason appears to induce his subject to become hypnotic, are, if compared to those of incontestable autohypnosis, relatively so rare that they may be ignored. (This, however, does not mean that I actually intend to ignore them in the course of the present discussion.)

With regard to the child, the conditions are reversed: I have not heard of a single incidence of autohypnosis in an infant. The small child cannot, in contrast to the adult, hypnotize himself; he needs a hypnotist in order to become hypnotic. This hypnotist is an unwitting one; he does not want to hypnotise the child, and one gains the impression that he is almost always unaware that he does. All he wants is to exploit the child, sexually or aggressively or both. *It is the overstimulation inflicted by him on his victim* in the course of the exploitation *that sooner or later makes the latter hypnotic.* Having learned that much, I was at first afraid that whatever occurred while my patient had been hypnotic as a child might not be recoverable; but I soon learned that my concern was groundless; amnesia removal is no more difficult for an event experienced under hypnosis than for one experienced while fully awake.

2. *The Relation of the Autohypnosis of the Adult to That Inflicted Upon the Child. The Hypnotic Evasion*

Since the child develops into the adult, one cannot but ask oneself, is the autohypnosis of the adult related to the hypnosis inflicted upon the child? And, if it is, what is the nature of the relation? Answering the first of these questions is easy; it requires no more than an unqualified "yes." The two are indeed related. Replying to the second question is difficult, not because the relation is unknown but because of its complicated nature. The facilitation of the description of the relation between adult autohypnosis and childhood hypnosis is best served by a clinical observation.

Example #1: A woman patient regularly "fell asleep" on the subway both on her way to and from the session. When complying with the abstinence rule invoked against this acting-out, she instead experienced two orgasms during a single ride. Her report upon this experience in the present was as broken up as though it had concerned a repressed experience from the past: it was given in three installments at three different times in her treatment. At first there was only herself and the subway, which caused me to comment upon "motion pleasure" and vestibular stimulation. When she next referred to the experience, sexual fantasies about women sitting opposite her with slightly spread legs entered the picture. Only much later came a third addendum: her orgasms were accompanied by the thoughts, "Mother rub me!" and "Mother lick me!" These were obviously fantasies about her mother and herself as a child; *and as subsequent amnesia removal demonstrated beyond any doubt, fantasies representing reminiscences of actual experiences in childhood (at age four),* when the patient from the ages of three until about seven had been the sexual partner of her psychotic mother. In the course of their activities she had been *hypnotic.*

Assisted by this "didactic" observation, one may venture to formulate as follows the relation of childhood hypnosis to the autohypnosis of the adult: *the adult is able to re-experience the hypnosis inflicted upon him in childhood through* (in this case) *a sexual overstimulation, now autohypnotically for evading both memory and repetition of the experience.* (Or, in terms of the clinical observation: autohypnosis in the subway assisted the patient in keeping in repression the memory of the overstimulation as a child, and evaded the sexual stimulation by the women passengers. In other words, it insured her against repetition.) I attached therefore the term hypnotic evasion to the phenomenon when I originally observed and published it (1953).

What enables the patient to enter this exceptional state—his hypnotic faculty—will be discussed in the section on the theory of hypnosis (see Section 6 below); his motive for doing so may be discussed now. I imagine a thoughtful but insufficiently experienced reader asking the following question: If these traumatic childhood experiences are repressed, why must their repetition be evaded? The answer: a repetition may endanger the repression. The repression must therefore be re-enforced through a number of resistances, of which the hypnotic evasion is one.[1] If you wish to compare the re-enforcement of the repression through the hypnotic evasion with that through another defense, found by Freud long ago, think, for example, of the phobic abstention. The nature of these two defenses is totally different, yet their effect upon the repressed is the same in that they both assist the repression by forestalling a repetition.

Example #1 (continued): Conversely, what is not repeatable need not be evaded hypnotically; frequently it need not even be repressed. The very patient mentioned above furnished an impressive illustration. She entered her analysis vaginally insensitive and told several times of a sexual childhood experience that had always remained conscious. When she was about five years of age, a maid while dressing her played a game with her: she allowed the little girl's underdrawers

---

[1] The hypnotic evasion as experienced by the analyst as a resistance is discussed in Chapter Five below.

to slide onto the floor repeatedly, which stimulated the most delightful sensation in the child. This is puzzling at first because neither vulva nor clitoris could be touched by such a technique. Only much later when her defloration by the psychotic mother had been recalled did it become clear that in consequence of it the "spot" (I, 212) had become a functioning erogenic zone and the object of the "delightful" stimulation. It remained active even in adolescence when the patient and her girl sexual partner inserted forefingers into each other's vagina. But with her turning to men the region became unresponsive, and she was vaginally frigid. Therefore she could not repeat the experience and hence did not have to subject it to either repression or hypnotic evasion.

I wonder whether or not the reader has noticed that part of the above exposition implies an addendum to the technique of amnesia removal: *whenever repression is re-enforced by hypnosis, one must, before attempting to lift the repression, undo its hypnotic wrapping.* This technical device, however, is valid only for the later stages of a successful analysis; in the beginning, one should, at the proper time and by means of introspection, induce the patient to distinguish full wakefulness from hypnosis. The latter is not, as I earlier erroneously stated, a symptomless state. As far as the patient is concerned, *even the slightest hypnosis feels somehow different from full wakefulness.*

Sometimes the analyst hears pathognomonic complaints restricted to the patient's life outside the session. It is axiomatic that a patient who succumbs to hypnosis in whatever form on the outside will produce hypnotic evasions in analysis. This means the analyst is forewarned.

These complaints are of three different kinds. One of them concerns members of the first group of hypnotic conditions assembled at the beginning of the present section: somnambulism, prolonged hypnopompic states (= aftermaths of a dream: Chapter Two), diurnal attacks of sleep. The second and third kinds correspond to the two main methods employed by the hypnotist with his subject. It is astonishing that lay patients who have never been hypnotized and are ignorant of the hypnotic technique will nevertheless use at least fragments of them for becoming hypnotic. One of these techniques is the concentration on a shiny object. Schilder (Schilder & Kauders, 1956), for instance, stands behind the subject and has him gaze upon a key. Freud has by sheer intuition and without giving an explanation interpreted this as equivalent to the command: "Occupy yourself now exclusively with my person." I believe I can furnish the explanation, stemming, of course, from amnesia removal. It lies not in the present but in the past and that is, in the childhood hypnosis upon which, the adult autohypnosis is founded. Here is a clinical illustration.

The "shiny" object: Example #2: A woman patient complains that she never knows where to "rest" her eyes inside as well as outside of the session. Inside she tries to look steadily at some object in front of the couch; outside on the street she reads the license plates of passing cars. The couch in my office is near a big window; it affords a view of the sky which in winter at the time of her session at five in the afternoon is dark. This helps her settle her problem: she fixes her gaze upon the evening star, in other words, upon a "shiny" object. My notes do not inform me of the relation in time between this settlement and the amnesia removal for an episode in very early childhood. Her severely psychotic mother had the patient, at the age of three or even earlier, masturbate her on the toilet. She recalled the woman exhibiting and orgastically "jumping from one buttock to the other" (her words) while the child became subject to a stupor in which she sat on the floor and had finally to be dragged away in that position.

Having learned to recognize her adult autohypnotic states, she had no difficulty identifying the feeling engendered by them with the infant's "stupor."

This is the first of a number of instances to be described that leave no doubt of the fact that one of the original "shiny objects" in childhood is the moistening and eventually ejaculating maternal vulva.

The other hypnotic technique is the old French method, consisting of monotonous suggestions of sleepiness and motor-inhibitions, accompanied by "passes," that is, a soft stroking of the subject from the shoulders on down.

Example #3: A woman patient reported that her seamstress while fitting her ("passes") was in the habit of talking to her in a "soft monotonous voice," with the result that she, the patient, became "drowsy." I have described the infantile model of this hypnotic reaction in the first volume of this series (p. 223) as follows:

> At the ages of three and four to perhaps five, i.e., after the [psychotic] mother had given birth to the younger sibling and became pregnant with the youngest, a nocturnal ritual was established. The child used to wake up wanting to urinate, and called for the mother. They met in the bathroom. Each took her place: the child, on the toilet, the mother, next to her on the edge of the bathtub. (The patient is sure of the ages, because she remembers how at first her legs stuck out straight and later hung down toward the floor.) The child was unable to urinate, and the mother talked softly to her. "Just relax, darling, it will be all right," etc., while stroking her legs, sliding over her genitals, and her back down to the buttocks. It was semi-dark, only the hall light, covered with a towel, shone dimly. Under the influence of the voice and these "passes," which the child enjoyed, she slid gradually into a condition that the patient now spontaneously calls "hypnotic." The ritual ended with a urinary release, and subsequent to it, urination by the mother . . .

The memory is, of course, incomplete. I have never observed that the psychotic parent gives the child sexual pleasure for the child's own sake; it is always the parent who exploits the child to gain sexual pleasure himself; in most cases a climactic one. This mother in particular was bestial and later gratified herself sexually by flogging the child without mercy. Yet I could not overcome the resistance against expanding the memory to its proper dimension. (This in spite of the fact that the mother kept up the habit of sliding her hand "affectionately" a long way up the inside of her daughter's leg in adolescence and even into adulthood. She did this stealthily and adroitly, even with company present.) I had, instead, to be satisfied with the report of the episode (described in the previous chapter) in which the patient told of being alone in the house with her mother, watching television, and observing the 70-year-old woman in the act of masturbation.

With regard to this patient's hypnotic evasions during the session, it was sheer ignorance on my part that delayed their recognition. Had I learned what I should and could have learned from Schilder's (1956) description in his textbook on hypnosis, I would have known of the "evasions" because of a pathognomonic symptom. The authors report there upon startle reactions, hysteriform myclonus in some hypnoses or in the early stages of hypnotic states. My patient was not infrequently seized by a violent brief contraction of her whole body, an exaggerated shudder, as it were. We were both aware that she did this in reaction, not to the content of what I was saying, but to my voice; but there the matter stood and was left standing for years.

An Abuse of the Analytic Situation: The example contains two lessons: one that will be discussed immediately and one that will be articulated with the assistance of other examples in the next section. In order to grasp the first, it will be convenient to compare the patient's mother transference upon the seamstress and upon the analyst, both of which made her hypnotic. The seamstress repeats the "passes," originally performed by the mother and, for reasons of her own, the mother's sleepily soothing voice. The analyst, however, does nothing of the kind; he speaks in a natural voice, and the patient is never so much as touched.

By what means does he invite the mother transference, which, like all transference is a resistance that in this particular instance takes the form of hypnotic evasions? There is one easy answer: no matter how correctly the analyst acts, trying to analyze in a "state of abstinence" (Freud), *he cannot forestall either the patient's conscious or unconscious fantasies about him or the patient's delusory expectations; if the analyst has not so far repeated the mother's behavior, he will.* This is obvious. If I state it, I do so only in order to make a point: the above explanation is correct but it does not go far enough. The analyst actually does "do" something to the patient, that invites the transference upon him of the damaging mother: *he offers the patient the opportunity to abuse the analytic situation for a repetition of the morbid passivity originally called for in the child by the mother in the course of her exploitations.* This is unavoidable; it would be as senseless to blame the analysis for it as it would be to deny the usefulness of the judicial system because it is not foolproof against abuse. In the case of analysis, all depends on the analyst's recognition of the abuse. He will then demonstrate it to the patient, inducing him to become aware of it introspectively and to exchange this passivity for. genuine free association, the performance 'of which is, against appearances, an "activity." (Only "pseudoassociations"—chitchat that tell the analyst nothing—are "passive." (Cf. Chapter Five, Section One, below.) Without full awareness of this state of affairs there is little chance of abolishing the hypnotic evasion.

Autohypnosis Outside the Session: As for autohypnosis on the outside, one will sometimes be able to recognize which of the techniques the patient has employed for becoming hypnotic and at other times not. One must, of course, never expect him to use the term hypnotic in his reports. "Fatigue," a general "lassitude," "inability to keep awake," or simply "falling asleep" is about all one has a right to expect in the beginning. Although he misnames them, it appears to be easier for the patient to recognize his hypnotic evasions on the outside than in the analytic situations, because they are shallower in the presence of an analyst who is working correctly. *If the patient falls asleep in the hour, the analyst must interpret this to himself as a sign that his technique is faulty.* (It has happened to me only twice, when I was a beginner: the first time I was still working under supervision, the second time was shortly after my premature graduation. It never occurred thereafter, although for more than fifteen years I was still ignorant of the hypnotic evasion.)

A woman patient could hardly make it to her session because "her legs would not carry her"; at other times she complained of cramps in various parts of her legs on her way to the analytic hours.

A somnambulist often induced autohypnotic states which he called "dozing" in response to the newscaster's voice on the radio.

Another man used to awake during the night, "experiencing" the feeling of being beaten, and distinctly "feeling the strokes." It was impossible to remove the amnesia for his childhood hypnosis, although he knew of having been beaten excessively by his father and subjected to witnessing exhibitions by his mother (both parents psychotic); he recalled what he termed his first hypnosis only as an adult: he sat on a bench near the Charles River and became drowsy from listening to the rhythmic lapping of the waves against the river bank.

In one instance, the hypnotic evasion during the session caused the patient to perceive the analyst as being "far away" and uncorporeal ("just a voice").

This, of course, is not purely hypnotic evasion; but a combination of the latter with another exceptional state: derealization.

As has been said before, it is these different autohypnotic experiences on the outside that alert the analyst to watch for his patient's hypnotic evasions during the session.

3. *Hypnosis and the Suppression of Urethral-Erotic Discharge*

Obtaining data is one thing, evaluating them is another. It should be stated that the child in the example mentioned earlier was hypnotic during a period of urinary retention, and that the hypnosis terminated with a urinary release. This release is actually urethral-erotic: for several years prior to her analysis the same patient masturbated without reaching an orgasm but instead each time had to urinate—a sequence that never appeared to her as anything but coincidental.

Before attempting to study the phenomenon in the adult, one may again point to a difference between the investigative situation of the analyst and that of the hypnotist: in the case of the latter this situation is circumscribed by the inception of his suggestion and the termination of the hypnotic condition. His observation begins, in other words, when he gives his first hypnotic suggestion and it ends with the subject's "arousal." If the latter avails himself of the "rest room" later, such is his private privilege and no subject for study. Analysis knows, of course, no such, or for that matter, any other limitation.

Example #2 continued: The patient who solved the problem "where to rest her eyes" by fixing her gaze on the evening star was a completely frigid woman who at one time in her analysis employed her hypnotic evasions in the service of a strong negative therapeutic reaction by having them extend not only over the sessions but also over most of her life. She heard my voice as a "completely monotonous drone" that made her hypnotic; when her lover called her at home she became so drowsy and otherwise so unresponsive that he asked her, "Do you want me to go on?" to which she was barely able to answer with, "Yes, I like it." The previous afternoon she had been too sleepy to work.

If a negative therapeutic reaction is as pronounced as was this one, the analyst must admit to himself that far from helping his patient he is about to make him sicker than he was when he came. He must therefore find a way of being active and break, as it were, the deadlock. Since this patient was one who in the beginning had to be allowed to use the toilet for urination during the hour, I tentatively mentioned my "hunch" (for that was all it was at the time) concerning the connection between hypnosis and the suppression of urination. She responded at first by reporting that she liked using the lover's flaccid penis to stimulate herself and had discovered that the responsive part was not the clitoris, which she knew it should be, but the area around the urethra. There she had felt "something" which she could not describe but which was more than the mere sensation of the mechanical pressure. This is, without doubt, equivalent to the admission that her urethra had actually remained an erogenic zone, and it permits the conclusion that much of her urination actually represented a urethral-erotic discharge. Subsequently she became aware *that her hypnosis during the session and the necessity to urinate immediately after it belonged together.* She left this session with the thought: "How good—today I will for once not have to rush out and urinate!" Nevertheless, in the next session she had to confess that once downstairs she felt compelled to repeat her old behavior.

I described one instance of the same patient's having been hypnotized by her mother through sexual overexcitation at a very early age (Example #2 above); and another, without making a point of the hypnosis, at a later age (between three and four) (II, 360). I repeat my description in part:

> . . . repeated seductions . . . while . . . the child is sitting on the toilet and the mother opposite her on the edge of the bathtub. The mother masturbates poking one forefinger playfully at the genital of the child, who responds with scissor-like movements of the legs. The mother's genital is not really seen: in the "phallic" child's opinion her hand hides a penis. The mother is mildly incontinent, in response to which the child dribbles until she is finally pushed off the toilet by the climactic mother taking her place. The end is excretory for both; the child, during a transient loss of consciousness, makes a stream on the floor . . .

The child's terminal urination, however, took a long time to come out of amnesia. She recalled at first a puddle on the floor, that "worried" her because someone must have made it, and its location excluded the mother. It took my becoming convinced that it was hers and a measure of "working through" before she could actually remember making it, standing up and wetting her pants. Details later remembered were the mother's urinating in a noisy stream with her skirt pulled up, while by talking amusingly she made sure that the child did not leave.

Most striking is the identity of so many details in this episode with those in the episode that concluded the foregoing section. The child's "transient loss of consciousness" was hypnosis in response to overstimulation by the mother's climax, and the hypnosis was again dependent upon urinary retention; it even lasted through the urethral-erotic discharge itself. The original "shiny object" here is the mother's vulva in a state of climactic urination. The relation of childhood hypnosis to the autohypnosis of the adult is that formulated and explained above.

Example #4: A patient recalls the following originally repressed childhood scene. When about four years old she is summoned by the mother from her own room into the bedroom with the familiar call: "X., what are you doing?" She knows from previous experiences what to expect. She enters the bedroom, looking over a wooden footboard at her mother who is masturbating. She perceives a sexual stimulation that she cannot master and feels herself becoming hypnotic. At the same time she is disappointed that the mother "pays no attention" to her. (These women sometimes need the child only in the beginning; the lack of "attention" indicates that the mother is more or less preorgastic.) In the hypnosis an urge for urination arises, is fought, and finally given way to, although it is painful. The hypnosis cannot be shaken off until the girl is eventually able to recathect, on a walk, the beautiful elements of the environment—trees, flowers, and sun. *Much hypnosis in child and adult is based upon suppression of or,* in terms of instinctual discharge, *unsuccessful* (in the present case, painful) *urination.*

Example #5: The next case is not without humorous aspects. It shows the so-called negative hallucination, that is, the not seeing of something that is there by a person in (auto) hypnosis sustained by suppressed urination. A woman patient began her analysis after having lain down on the couch by exhibitionistically equating the analytic situation with that of a gynecological examination. After that she spent hour after hour in hypnosis. The only incident that we both found of note was her need to urinate before and after the hour, near the office. She invariably chose a toilet in Grand Central Station. When I made the obvious interpretation and referred to the alternative possibility—many large hotels in the vicinity—she investigated one of them and reported that it lacked a toilet! She consequently had no choice but to stay with the genital of the mother from childhood (Grand Central Station).

She was without any insight into the absurdity of her report. If I add that the patient has been described in Example #2, and the reader takes the trouble to look back, he will understand why the repetition compulsion enforced the negative hallucination. The hypnotic woman did not see the signs of restrooms in the lobbies of the hotels because the use of these places instead of one called Grand Central would not have represented a repetition. In other words, what looks like a delusion is actually but the result of a hypnotic negative hallucination.

A comparison of the last two examples shows that the first of the two patients makes only moderate and occasional use of the hypnotic evasion and, again in contrast to the second, gives no indication of any urinary retention. I can only ask myself, without being able to answer, whether the first of these differences has to do with a much less frequent exploitation, mostly restricted to *exhibition*. As to the second difference, I was perhaps not active enough to be sure of the facts; for not every patient can be counted upon to acquaint one spontaneously via free association with the urinary suppression requisite to his hypnosis.

Example #6: An overtly homosexual woman patient tried every form of denial even upon being questioned. She has a hypnotic experience during a meeting. Any urination afterwards? Yes, but that means nothing. She had to go to her session and always uses the bathroom before starting. She comes home in the evening and later finds herself waking up fully dressed, sitting in a chair—once at midnight and then again in the small hours of the morning. She urinated each time but that again has no meaning because she had intended to get undressed for bed, and everyone urinates at such a time. Only once she ran out of denials: during the day the Negro maid had been cleaning the floor on all fours and the sight of her caused the patient to feel herself "going off" into hypnosis. At that point she perceived a need, and while the maid was in the kitchen, relieved herself in the bathroom.

Example #7: An adult unmarried patient awakens during a restless night into a hypnotic state in which she is sure of my presence in her bedroom. I am next to her bed, although not visible, and evidently smoking, because there is an unusually strong smell of tobacco about me. At the same time she has a cramp in one foot. Finally she wakes up without the cramp, goes to the toilet, urinates, and is free of her hypnosis.

This example may appear redundant; I must therefore briefly account for its inclusion. In the first place it shows that the hypnosis creates both a delusion (my presence) and a hallucination (the tobacco smoke). This accords with the fact that the hypnotist can suggest both. I remember that forty years ago Hansen the hypnotist put his subject, stripped to the waist, into a refrigerated room and suggested to him: we are in the Sahara Desert (delusion) and very hot (hallucination) because the sun is burning down on us and there is no shade. The suggested situation prevailed over the real one to the extent that the subject instead of getting goose pimples perspired.

In the second place the example revives a question I have asked myself off and on for many years. In Section C of the sixth chapter of *The Interpretation of Dreams* Freud (1900) inconclusively ponders whether sleep, besides dreaming, may engender another phenomenon to be called "fantasies during sleep." Could this be a misnomer? And could the fantasies be, as they are in the above example, "fantasies during *autohypnotic* states" interpolated between states of sleep?

In conclusion, the findings that much hypnosis is dependent upon the suppression of urethral-erotic discharge is theoretically hardly a *novum*. It could, on the basis of Freud's discoveries, have been foretold. If hypnosis draws upon the mobilization and simultaneous aim inhibition and aim deflection of libido, and if the libido is phallic, as it is in so many individuals either by having been arrested in this phase or in consequence of a regression, *it would be only natural to find the phallic climax suppressed.* That climax, however, is, as Freud has discovered, *urethral-erotic.* The paradigmatic woman patient (Example # 1), who abstained from hypnosis in the subway and became orgastic instead, enunciated immediately the wish for purely clitoridean (phallic) gratification from her mother, stemming from the repressed past. Nevertheless, she had to urinate coming to and returning from the sessions, which were filled with hypnotic evasions in consequence of a transference upon the analyst of the mother.

Technically, however, the finding is a significant one. It assists in the abolishment of the hypnotic evasion because it allows the analyst to attack the latter on, as it were, two different

fronts. More important still is the fact that when one fails to
understand certain actions or omissions in the patient's past
behavior but is informed that they were followed by an excretory endeavor, one will hardly go wrong in at first assuming and
eventually ascertaining that the behavior in question was the
consequence of a hypnotic state.

Example #8: In illustration I shall expand upon a previously mentioned example. The mother, one of those women who needs the child
as onlooker only in the beginning (Example #5), having taken a bath,
lay down on her bed in the nude and masturbated in front of the
child. She made sure of the daughter's presence by conversing with
her. Soon she became so involved that she completely disregarded the
child. The little girl, however, remained where she had been standing,
while undergoing the torture of mobilized yet undischargeable excitation. She felt herself growing taller, while the mother's buttocks became larger ("magnification": II, 243–246; and in particular, p. 246,
Ex. #1), and she herself became painfully filled with urine. After the
mother had finished, the child went to the toilet, tried to urinate, but
succeeded only in emitting small quantities while twitching. In the
end the mother entered the bathroom "pleased as punch with herself"
(patient's own words) and said something on the order of, "Now we
must all pull ourselves together."

Because the scene was repeated throughout years and the
patient was able to describe the mother's technique in complete
detail, I asked her, in view of the agony that she underwent
every day, quite naively: "If you suffered so much and your
mother no longer paid you any attention, why did you not simply go away?"

She was unable to answer. Only today I know that she must
have been in hypnosis and thereby glued to the spot. I know
it because of the pathetic attempt to rid herself of the urinary
retention, which still prevailed when she tried to overcome it
on the toilet.

The reason for my failure to recognize the hypnosis in these
childhood experiences was that they had been overlaid, as it
were, by autohypnotic states in the present: the frigid patient

had continued in adulthood to exchange hypnosis for strong excitation. Long before I had understood her use of the hypnotic evasion, she once lay in undress next to her lover, who while stroking her suggested that she reciprocate ("passes"), to which she reacted with fright and the outcry: "Please don't hypnotize me!" Had I recognized her daily hypnosis stretching over several years of childhood and evidently ending only with the beginning of latency, I might have gained a fulcrum for attacking the sexual anaesthesia.

4. *Hypnosis and Suppressed Excretion Other Than That of Urine*

Two examples illustrate that the suppressed excretion need not always be that of urine.

Example #9: A woman patient who broke off her analysis long before the time for its proper conclusion recalled that at 10 years of age she slept with her psychotic mother, woke up, and felt the woman's index finger in her vagina. Her masturbation had been vaginal "as long as she could remember." Material on the occasion of interpreting a menstrual dream compelled the reconstruction that the mother not only deflorated her but on subsequent occasions masturbated her vaginally. She reacted to this reconstruction with what she called an "orgastic dream." The orgasm is vaginal and, as she expresses it, "real." Furthermore, upon arousal she finds the bed shifted from its usual position to one close to the wall, and explains this convincingly as an effect of her strong body movements in the course of masturbation. The arousal is one into an autohypnotic state, which is followed by a second dream whose content is vague: it has to do with her brother talking and eating.

I ask her whether the orgasm left her feeling wet between her legs. She does not know. Why doesn't she? Well, there was certainly much secretion in the vagina; that she could feel. In other words, the suppressed excretion assisting the autohypnosis here was not urinary but vaginal. But suppressed it was.

One may juxtapose to this example that of a man patient, singular in my experience not because of the frequency of his hypnotic evasions or of the difficulty in abolishing them but because every so often during the session he felt on the verge of an ejaculation. Here again the excretion is genital and again its suppression accompanied the hypnotic evasions.

Example #10: A physically healthy patient produced conversion symptoms prior to her analytic session: most painful stomach cramps followed by weakening diarrhoeas. The session contains the report on the mother's habit of giving her enemas as a child. I do not recall whether any of it was ever repressed. The enemas were part of a ritual: the psychotic woman put a pillow into the bathtub for the child to rest on, inserted the hose and began irrigation. From then on the child was allowed to open and close the valve herself, but was admonished to let more and more water in, which produced great pain as did the analysis for a long time in its protracted beginning. The inception of the ritual, that is, the hose insertion and the starting of irrigation, stimulating as they did excretory impulses that the child was forced to suppress, initiated hypnosis: The mother told her a story of which the child heard only the opening sentence: "Once upon a time there was a chicken . . ." because she drifted off into hypnosis which she called "falling asleep."

When 24, the (psychotic) patient fell deeply in love with a psychotic [2] young man who performed coitus *inter femora* with her, abstaining from both immission and ejaculation but furnishing much perineal and anal stimulation to which the young woman reacted, again, with an extremely pleasurable hypnotic state.

Example #11: Another patient was given enemas and suppositories by her mother; she liked the suppositories because their insertion made her pleasantly drowsy or, as she now recognizes, hypnotic. Here surely, defecatory impulses are in play which are not acted upon. I cannot say more because at the time of that analysis I did not know enough to ask the right questions. In her sessions the patient always lay on her left side with markedly drawn up legs and extensive hyp-

---

[2] Lest the reader think me too ready with this diagnosis, I must divagate from the topic dealt with in the text, and report on the fact that the patient, who had for decades lost all trace of the man, met him again unexpectedly and by mere chance during the time of her analysis. Since this meeting led to a short-lived resumption of their association, I was given the opportunity of ascertaining his deviant behavior from the patient's accounts in her sessions.

notic evasions. I was ignorant of the evasions and remained blind to the obvious postural repetition. I also failed her on the occasion of an acute repetition outside of the session, although by that time I knew of the hypnotic evasion. She was a figure skater who had been awarded several medals for winning a number of competitions, but once had a bad fall owing, as she told it, to a rut in the ice. I pointed out that if a skater with only a modicum of experience told me this story, I might believe it; but that I rejected it coming from her because someone with her proficiency knows how to handle a rut. Had she been hypnotic? It turned out that she had. She even answered my question as to how it is possible to go into hypnosis while engaged in such a deliberate and vigorous locomotion by informing me that there was no problem: with the years the motion becomes automatic and allows for hypnosis as easily as does rest.

This hypnotic attack does not at first glance look like a repetition of the hypnosis from childhood. Had I known then that it either must be or at least is likely to be such a repetition, I would have taken a second, an analytic look at it, and in so doing I would have recognized the repetition in disguise. It consisted in the combination of two different kinds of unconscious indirect representation: the projection of an element of the pleasure-physiological body ego upon the environment (II, 246–254) and its symbolization (Chapter One, above). The "rut" is a "dead end" and, as such, representative of the patient's rectum, that the mother stimulated by inserting suppositories. This made the child hypnotic. By means of the fall, which without causing injuries was still quite painful, the patient gave herself one of the unremembered beatings of which the mother at the time of the daughter's analysis openly boasted. Had I interpreted that much, I might have caught hold of some repressed memory, the imminence of whose emergence the hypnosis had to evade.

I shall take the liberty of closing this small section by emending a previous example, even though the emendation fails to fit the title of this section because no demonstrable excretory retention was involved. It nevertheless contrasts profitably with the last example, where I did not function properly, inasmuch as here I did.

It is the example (see Chapter Three, Section II, F) where the memory of the maid in the nude simultaneously masturbating and defecating completed their activities during their association. This amnesia removal was actually more complicated than I have presented it above, where I abbreviated for simplification. For it required the abolishment of a bit of hypnotic evasion, which, had I mentioned it at the time, the reader could not possibly have understood. The analysis was well advanced and the patient thoroughly familiar with her employment of this particular form of resistance. Something made me ask her in the hour in question whether she felt to any degree hypnotic. "No," she answered, "just that very small area in my head; otherwise I am all right." I knew then intuitively that the head in this instance was a symbol ("arse" = head), and translated it for her (cf. Chapter One, II, B). This is what brought her strange experience out of amnesia, immediately and as a whole. It was only later that I recognized the "small area" as the maid's anus. It is, as everyone knows, quite frequent that repressed experiences or fragments of them appear, as did this one, at first in identification with the object involved.

Finally, there appear to be two different reasons for the hypnosis basing itself upon excretory retentions other than that of urine. One, illustrated in the first example of this section is the well known unconscious regressive interpretation of an excretum as urine; in the case under consideration above, that of vaginal discharge. The patient retains it, one could say, in order not to "wet the bed." The other reason, equally well known, is the regression of the libido to beyond the phallic phase; in the second and third examples the libido is anal-sadistic in the child through being arrested in the adult through regression.

5. *What Does the Hypnotic Evasion Evade?*

I hope that the foregoing examples and their discussion have shown that the autohypnotic spells observed by the analyst in-

side and outside the session deserve to be called hypnotic evasions. Their evasion is twofold: they evade memories of traumatic childhood experiences; and, since repressed memories
often give rise to an urge for re-enactment, at the same time
they evade, through a self-induced hypnotic state, the arousal
accompanying that urge. One could say that in this respect the
hypnosis behaves like a conversion symptom, which always
takes the place of an affect.

Example #12: In order to throw the foregoing into relief, I shall
report on the amnesia removal for such an experience in the terminal
phase of the analysis of the woman patient, mentioned in Example
#2, who spent the beginning of her treatment "hour after hour in
hypnosis." The amnesia removal occurred long after she had relinquished all hypnotic evasion. The scene recalled took place at the age
of seven in a cabin on the lake, the floor of which was made of boards
that were not joined, and whose furniture consisted of a bench and a
bucket for rinsing the sand off one's feet. In the episode that came out
of amnesia the mother, who had taken off her bathing suit, was
watched from the rear by the child while she squatted, possibly masturbating but certainly urinating into the bucket. This memory aroused
the patient to such an extent that she experienced a spontaneous climax and a forceful urge to squat and urinate on the office floor (transference).

For a full appreciation of the contrast between these consequences of the amnesia removal and the previous hypnotic
evasions, it must be added that the patient at the time of the
removal had long since lost the impulse to urinate before and
after her session. It is of course perfectly true that the abstention
from acting upon the revived infantile urge also entailed a retention; but the latter was no different from that of a normal
person who feels a need under circumstances that demand a
delay; it was unaccompanied by even a trace of hypnosis.

There is, however, one point in which the examples recorded
so far are misleading: *it is not always the mobilization of libido,
infantile or adult, that is being prevented by the hypnotic evasions, but every so often the mobilization of aggression.* It will

hardly astonish the reader that one of the two basic groups of instincts employs the same resistance against being brought to the fore as does the other. Unfortunately, in spite of having seen this very clearly in patients, neither my notes nor my memory furnish me with a single example. I must, therefore, against my preference, restrict myself to the statement.

It is very different with the third use of the hypnotic evasion. What is evaded here *is the aggression directed by someone else* against the subject of the evasion. This I had not expected to find. I am lucky to be in possession of detailed notes on the sessions in which I became first aware of it, because they furnish the last of the three examples to be presented hereinafter.

It has been discussed previously that the aggression against the victim, originally the child, can be either fused with libido or practically defused. In the former case it will usually occur in the course of a sexual abuse, in the latter case not. The former applies to the first two of my examples, the latter to the third.

Example #13 stems from the analysis of the patient whose hypnosis through sexual overstimulation as a child was reported in Example #4. This time, however, it is recalled that the mother lies on the child, aged between two and three, masturbating against the little daughter's pubic bone whereby the child's head is buried in the woman's belly. The bare region of the child is painfully scraped by the mother's hairy one, and the child is nearly suffocated in the process. The little one struggles in vain and eventually becomes hypnotic. After the mother is through, the daughter simply lies there. She is pushed off the bed by the mother into a standing position, still hypnotic.

Her unfinished analysis did not yield any amnesia removal for the termination of this hypnosis. I have never in all instances of this kind, e.g., the one recalled in the next example, been able to avoid the distinct impression that the manifest suffering of the victim heightened the sexual pleasure gained by the sadistic aggressor.

Example #14: The next example has also been reported earlier (Chapter 3, III, A). It is now to be considered from the viewpoint of the hypnotic evasion of fused aggression repeated through the adult's hypnotic evasions in the analytic situation. The patient had entered analysis with an abysmal compulsive depression. We know from Freud that all compulsion is based upon a regression to the anal-sadistic phase. Throughout the several years of the first part of her disjunct analysis I was as yet ignorant of the hypnotic evasion and became aware only in retrospect of her having exhibited a great number of these evasions. It is therefore perhaps not accidental that the buoyancy of the repressed, meeting with a somewhat lessened resistance in consequence of the analytic work, became channeled into an interpretable dream. The dream has already been transcribed and interpreted (Chapter One, Section II, B, 7). It made possible the piece-meal removal of the amnesia for the sodomitic rape in adolescence. This aggressive assault had not, as far as one could ascertain, made the victim hypnotic but had forced her, as was also reported, into another exceptional state: *derealization.* When the amnesia removal eventually encompassed the infantile model of the assault, that is, the mother's gratification through flogging the child, the hypnotic evasion of this aggression was unwittingly touched upon by both analyst and patient without, however, being recognized for what it was. The patient remembered that the abuse continued into relatively late years of childhood and that it began with the mother's command, "Come here!" given in a peculiar low-pitched voice. I have reported that when the patient, who had been a physically healthy child, was asked why she did not run away from the impending torture, she answered that the voice put her under a spell, like the proverbial paralyzed "rabbit in front of a snake." Even this pregnant description failed to make me realize that the impending aggression had made her hypnotic, glueing her to the spot.

Example #15: The patient in whose analysis I discovered the *hypnotic evasion of aggression directed against the subject* was a male with one of the worst psychotic mothers I have ever heard of. One could not avoid the impression that by right he should never have been able to appear alive in the office, only dead in the newspaper in consequence of a fatal maltreatment. In the first of the few sessions concerned, of which I have detailed notes, he was unable to shake off his hypnosis. I knew at the time only that the hypnotic evasion can be brought to bear against sexual and aggressive strivings, and neither of these possibilities seemed to fit. His retaliatory aggressive impulses had been dealt with. What little material I obtained in this hour, I am not free to offer here. The preceding hours, however, had been filled with a crescendo of maternal abuse. From age two or three to five or six, when his entering school interfered protectively, he was almost constantly cuffed by his mother whose shod foot kicked him practically everywhere and whose knee hit him forcefully in the groin.

This is the kind of aggression whose discharge is suspect of yielding a nonsexual pleasure. I therefore asked myself in this hypnotic-resistance hour, and I asked it aloud: "Can someone else's aggression directed against an object also hypnotize that object?" We were both immediately struck by our response, which was spontaneously an affirmative one. I must also add that the patient was unable to this hour to remember the mother's *face;* he recalled only the parts—her knee and her shoe—that so cruelly hit him. For the face he substituted a certain Japanese mask with a fierce expression and tusk-like teeth. (This is, in the first place, the "faceless woman" that in dreams is the mother; but she is overdetermined by the "phallic mother" who is always the "bad" mother.)

In the next hour, in spite of being hypnotic off and on to the degree of being unconscious, he recalls the long waits as a child for the impending blow to be struck and his fearful observation during the wait of the changes in the mother's facial expression and posture.

Only in the third hour, in the course of further amnesia removal, is the childhood hypnosis remembered. He is hit by the mother with a shoe and an ever-present cat-o'-nine-tails. He takes refuge in a closet with the mother's long clothes in it, which impedes her hitting him. The shoe has caused a huge haematoma above his forehead; he "suffers a concussion" (my correction: he becomes hypnotic), finally comes to, and sneaks away. Here I can only say, with reference to this resistance-interpretation of "concussion" for "hypnosis" that almost everyone prefers a symptom to be "organic" instead of psychogenic.

In another hour (unfortunately my notes fail to give a date), he recalls the mother pretending to faint and watching out of the corner of one eye the terror that her "death" arouses in the two- to three-year-old child.

At the time of these reports he says he is getting a virus attack and inviting a secondary infection by ignoring his temperature, roaming his cold apartment at night, and not going on sick leave or even curtailing his work. He considers his fever a submission to the mother's curse "You should burn!" I have to show him that he is doing his best to invite pneumonia, and, upon his telling me that he feels cold, I put a small electric heater I often use for myself in front of the couch.

He is greatly astonished that anyone would show that much "affection" for him.

His reaction suggests that the hypnotic impediment of the analysis in the hours under consideration were symptoms of a transference of the mother upon me, although I had not known it. They were, in other words, but another example of the "transference as a resistance."

The *Shakespearean illustration* of the subject's autohypnosis evading aggression directed against the subject by someone else was brought to my attention by a colleague. I discussed with him at great length the phenomenon which I was the first to discover, and he called my attention to the fact that Desdemona, mortally offended by Othello, answered Aemilia's question, "How do you, Madam? how do you, my good Lady?" with: "Faith, halfe a sleepe" (IV, 2). That much is true. But so much more is true!

Here I must enter into a brief discourse on at least one formal aspect of Shakespearean language. As was all English music of his time, Shakespeare's language is frequently polyphonic. This would appear to be a contradiction in terms, for one can say only one thing at a time and not oppose several voices to each other as counterpoint implies, and as, for example, a keyboard instrument allows one to do. I shall therefore, in order to resolve the contradiction, quote a few initial bars of a very unusual sarabande (Suite V from a cello suite in C Minor, Cello Solos) by Bach, which, although a two-part piece of polyphony, is written in a deceptively homophonic fashion—in other words, so that one person could sing it:

Actually the eighth notes represent one voice and the quarter notes (as well as the eighth note octave G—G") another, as can be seen by the direction of their stems. If you say loosely that the second "voice" is interspersed in between the first, you have characterized Shakespeare's polyphonic method. The easiest way to recognize this is for the reader to scan the following text slowly. He will find two kinds of utterances interspersed in Desdemona's words: one kind is clear; the other can only be understood if analyzed. These are the two "voices"; they are derivative of *conscious* and *unconscious* thought respectively, and they oppose *adult* to *infantile* experience. Othello, crazed by the paranoia that Iago has succeeded in inducing in him, has called his lovely chaste young wife a prostitute and offered to pay for her services—a mortal blow that sends her into hypnosis. The next passage is sensible only if it is recognized as duplicating my patient's experience. We identify someone by his face; yet my patient did not remember his mother's face. In Desdemona's case:

AEMILIA.   Good Madam,
              What's the matter with my Lord?
DESDEMONA.   With who?
AEM.   Why, with my Lord, Madam.
DESD.   Who is thy Lord?

Othello is, as was my patient's mother, no longer remembered by the hypnotic Desdemona. Yet Shakespeare would not be Shakespeare did not his next two obscure passages supply the suppressed excretion requisite to the hypnotic state and an allusion to childhood in which adult hypnosis is rooted.

AEM. He that is yours, sweet Lady.
DES. I cannot weepe: nor answeres have I none
     But what should go by water . . .

The shedding, that is, the excretion, of tears is suppressed and the word "water" serves as the "enharmonic" element in the modulation from adult sexual to infantile sexual "incontinence." This is not my idea, it is Shakespeare's, who has Desdemona say:

> . . . those that do teach yong Babes
> Do it with gentel meanes, and easie tasks.
> He might have chid me so; for, in good faith
> I am a child to chiding [IV, 2].

Gentle training and loving persuasion to become continent should be administered to the child. And Desdemona has actually the soul of a child; much of her subsequent talk is purely imitative. The small infant, the "child to chiding," does not know that faithlessness actually exists. A bit later (IV, 3) she asks Aemilia about it:

DESDEMONA.
> Do'st thou in conscience thinke—tell me, Aemilia—
> That there be women do abuse their husbands
> In such grave kinde?

In other words, every single feature of the clinical picture of the hypnotic evasion, in this particular case, the hypnotic evasion of aggression directed against the individual, that was laboriously observed and drily set forth in the preceding pages is present as a mere matter of course in Shakespeare's supreme dramatic rendition of the subject.

6. Contributions to a Future Theory of Hypnosis

It is impossible at the present time to put forward a comprehensive theory of hypnosis. One can only assemble some building-stones that a future worker, aided by additional observations, may fit into their proper place in the edifice of an inclusive theory of that exceptional state. Freud (1921), in "Group Psychology and the Analysis of the Ego," had several observations to make regarding hypnosis. These observations contain at least one major error and one fateful omission. In the first place, he declared unequivocally that "hypnosis . . . is identical with it [group formation] . . . distinguished from [it] by [the] limitation of number" (p. 115). He also states: ". . . no one can doubt that the hypnotist has stepped into the place of the ego ideal" (p. 114). And again, "By the measures . . . that he takes, then, the hypnotist awakens in the subject a portion of his archaic heritage which had also made him compliant towards his parents" (p. 127). (It must be remembered that at this time Freud had not yet adopted the term superego, but still referred to this agency as the ego ideal.) Actually the hypnotic relation does not resemble the group and the hypnotist does not, as does the leader of an organized group, occupy the place of the superego of his subjects. Hitler, to use a recent example, in fact did make his followers, to quote Freud, into "criminals without remorse." Yet the hypnotist cannot do so. On the contrary his influence on the subject is restricted by the power of the superego over the ego; he can only work within the confines set by this power. In cases where he seduces sexually or incites to criminal actions, he could have done so without the use of hypnosis: gaining sexual pleasure is often superego-syntonic. Alas, in many individuals so is crime, if the criminal impulse remains unopposed because too little superego, if any, was formed to oppose it.

Everyone knows that the hypnotist's power is restricted by that of the superego, and we know that Freud knew it because he said so himself: "It is noticeable that, even when there is complete suggestive compliance in other respects, the moral conscience of the person hypnotized may show resistance" (p. 116). What motivated him nevertheless to suppose that the hypnotist replaces the superego, I for one am unable to explain.

Anyone who wishes to save Freud's formulation through modifying it would also have to apply the modified theory to the hypnosis of the child. This hypnosis, however, elaborately exemplified as it is in the preceding pages, was unknown to Freud. He has criticized Jung for the "methodological error to seize upon a phylogenetic explanation before the ontogenetic possibilities have been exhausted" and for disregarding "the importance of infantile prehistory while at the same time freely acknowledging the importance of ancestral prehistory" (1918,

p. 97). With respect to his remarks on hypnosis this criticism unfortunately applies to Freud himself. I do not have to prove that; the reader of *Group Psychology* can easily verify it himself.

In the hypnosis of the child, the unwitting hypnotist does not have to replace superego, since it has not yet been established; *he, the parent*—and this is the modification—*represents the "pre-stage of the superego"* before its internalization. Hence the child complies with the demands of the hypnotist whether they induce unpleasure or pleasure. At first too weak to fight, he later still lacks the institution whose demands he could oppose to the hypnotist's; he has therefore no alternative but to yield.

The adult, however, has such a "critical institution," which his hypnotist cannot replace. If the hypnotic procedure is verbal, one needs merely to listen to the hypnotic commands in order to be aware of this: they employ ego language, never the language of the superego. "You feel how your eyelids are getting heavy," "You cannot lift your arms," etc. Never: "Thou shalt . . ." Even in deep hypnosis such as Hansen's (mentioned above), where the subject gets goose pimples in an overheated room or perspires in a refrigerator, the astonishing vegetative results were obtainable only because the superego had no reason to object to a trip to the Arctic or to the Sahara.

I cannot, of course, state that the basis for the hypnosis or autohypnosis of the adult is, in every case, the hypnosis of the child. An analysis, yielding amnesia removal, is the only method for becoming acquainted with the childhood of the adult and thus becoming certain. Yet in the vast majority of hypnotic adults, their childhood is not explored. I can state the above only with regard to my patients. However, I can with good reason suspect it for others, on the grounds of the hypnotist's methods. It is indisputable that these simulate parental behavior, from "passes" and soothing voice, to peremptory command. Ferenczi (1909), speaking of "Father-and-Mother" hypnosis, must have had the same impression.

With regard to the "shiny object," Schilder's key, I have to report some further observations. In most instances the original "shiny object" is the moistening and ejaculating, sometimes climactically urinating maternal vulva. Where the mother does not exhibit, or masturbates so as to cover her genitals with her hand, the original shining object are her eyes, a displacement symbol for the vulva, at that.

Example #16: In a male patient, who had more than once seen his mother masturbate, I had occasion to become acquainted with subsequent transformations of the original "shiny object." At the age of five or even earlier an amateur hypnotist offered to hypnotize him, and he accepted the offer. The hypnotist stroked the boy's penis, produced sexual feelings and light hypnosis, keeping up a flow of suggestive conversation. After a while he exhibited and masturbated in front of the child. The strange element in the patient's memory is that the scene took place in a dark narrow room bordered by four doors, one of which allowed some light to enter below it, which fell on the hypnotist's penis and made it look "shiny." At the age of eight the mother became "procuress" and took the boy to another man, seeing to it that they were left alone. The situation was such that the man had a plausible reason for telling the boy to undress. Having pulled the shades down, he gave the boy "a long, leering stare" which transfixed the child (eyes!), who felt compelled to return the stare. Subsequently the man took his penis out, putting a lubricant on it that made it "shiny." The boy, looking at it, became hypnotic; the seducer seated him on his lap, performing sodomy on him, while reassuring him in an authoritative but monotonous voice. The patient, although not psychotic, enjoyed the performance as a child; while it emerged from amnesia, he had transient rectal soreness and even bleedings in between the sessions.

Another male patient, who had relinquished most of his hypnotic evasions and had recalled innumerable sexual exploitations by his mother, some of them accompanied by climactic urination, reported upon a small relapse. Driving into a tunnel on his way home from the hour of the day before, he experienced a little pull toward hypnosis but was able to get the better of it. Knowing that these tunnels have a band of light on either side, I wondered whether that did not serve as the "shiny object." The patient confirmed this: in order not to succumb to hypnosis he had to avert his glance from the light.

Another building-stone toward a future theory of hypnosis is the concept of *partial hypnosis*. The term is mine; the description of the phenomenon is to be found in the textbook of Schilder and Kauders (1956) but applied only to the specific case of "negative hallucination" (= the nonperception of existing objects). I personally have heard it spelled out only once by a patient. Schilder and Kauders, discussing negative hallucinations, wrote,

> . . . the person who has negative hallucinations nevertheless manifests awareness of the reality which appears not to exist for him. He averts his eyes from the negatively hallucinated objects and is able to find his way around very complicated localities, although he apparently does not perceive them. His responses to hypnotic suggestions frequently convey an impression of weakness and superficiality. . . . In other words, all the regressions mentioned above are only partial regressions, whereas a considerable portion of the personality maintains its normal relations with the outside world [pp. 96–97].

That the concept of partial hallucination is not confined to negative hallucination is explicitly borne out by my patient.

Example #17: She awoke into an autohypnotic state, felt my presence behind her bed, and perceived a strong smell of tobacco. Asked to write down her experience, she records: ". . . part of me knew very well that you weren't there but at the same time the olfactory hallucination of the fragrance of you smelling of tobacco was very real. I didn't quite know whether I wanted to look behind me and verify that you weren't there or not, and I wished that either I would go back to sleep and enjoy my (previous) dream some more, or else really wake up and get rid of the hallucination."

What she actually did was to fall asleep again and have another dream.

The concept of partial hypnosis, in analogy to Freud's concept of "Partial Sleep" (1900), demands in fact a much broader application. Freud's brief description is applicable verbatim if one exchanges the "wish to sleep" for whatever motive it is that makes for autohypnosis. "As is shown by such familiar examples as the sleep of a nursing mother or wet nurse, the fulfillment of the wish to sleep," Freud writes, "is quite compatible with maintaining a certain expenditure of attention *in some particular direction*" (p. 577). I quote Freud's formulation because I could not equal it by one of my own. However, in view of its brevity, I should perhaps elaborate on it. I have italicized "in *some particular direction*" because these words are as crucial in describing partial sleep as they are in depicting partial hypnosis. The nurse or mother may sleep very soundly, but *not all* of her is asleep; "in the direction" of the child under her care, she is awake; and the slightest stirring or whimpering of that child is perceived and induces arousal.

"Part of me knew very well that you weren't there," wrote my patient. That part was, in other words, *fully awake and in contact with reality;* or to phrase it differently, *not all of her was hypnotic.*

No other patient has ever been explicit about partial hypnosis, and for two reasons. For one, it may simply not exist. Just as not all sleep is partial sleep, certainly not all hypnosis is partial hypnosis. On her day off, for instance, the nurse has no motive for maintaining attention with regard to the child; she can let all of herself go to sleep. The same is true of certain instances of hypnosis; in others where partial hypnosis does actually exist, the patient is not aware of it and therefore merely implies it either *by certain associations* or *by their omission.*

The first is well illustrated by the patient as a child in example #7 above. Before I knew of the partial hypnosis, I was unable to reconcile her associations one with another. Some were without doubt hypnotic; she was "glued" to the spot, grew illusorily taller, and her body became "filled with urine." But others made at the very same time; contained accurate observations, such as that of the somewhat unusual but detailed and confirmable masturbation technique of her mother. The knowledge of partial hypnosis eventually solved the contradiction: the observations were made by that part of her that had not been hypnotic.

For the second instance, the implication of partial hypnosis through associative omission, the woman patient (Example #1) who regularly fell "asleep" on the subway is a telling example. At one time she was disturbed because she could not recall whether or not the train had stopped at a certain station; but as far as my office or her home was concerned she never once over-shot her destination. Both patients illustrate the maintenance of attention "in a definite direction": the child was eager to learn all of the mother's activities and experiences; to the pa-tient, it was a matter of complete indifference whether or not the train stopped at an intermediate station, but it was highly important to reach both my office and her home without de-tours. Both underwent *partial hypnosis,* however deep, because it permitted what of them remained wakeful to maintain atten-tion "in the particular direction" of the part of the object world that was of interest to them.

With regard to the metapsychology—in particular, the topog-raphy—of hypnosis I can only make a few disparate and prefa-tory remarks.

(1) That the child can be hypnotized prior to having devel-oped a superego is in accordance with the fact that the super-ego in the adult, although confining the effects of hypnosis, takes no part in their precipitation.

(2) I see no other way but to regard the ego as the seat of the hypnotic process. Since the latter begins with a (conscious or unconscious) sexual stimulation, I must, with respect to the two demi-institutions of the ego, assume that the *partial subject*[3] initiates the hypnosis; and since the sexual reaction is inhibited, I am led to believe that it brings that other demi-institution, the introject,[4] into play. Inhibition, however, does not per se pre-cipitate a hypnotic state. One must therefore posit, besides in-hibition, a *qualitatively different and at present completely un-known influence of the introject upon the partial subject that results in the hypnotic state.*

[3] The *partial subject:* subject of instinctual strivings; and proximal to the id (". . . that part of the ego close to and serving the id"). Cf. *Glossary* and II, Chapter Two: *A New Differentiating Grade in the Ego.* Also Section A, II, *Depersonalization,* below.

[4] The *introject:* the remainder of the ego, proximal to the superego (see Glossary).

(3) Evidence for the reaction of the *partial subject* is the unmistakably sexual expression in the subject's eye and his bodily sexual motions described by Schilder. Evidence for the participation of the *introject,* other than inhibition, is the fact mentioned by Schilder and others that subjects are easier to hypnotize when a group of them are first made spectators to the hypnosis of others. *For the introject is the representative of the group in the ego,* in the present instance, the "group of hypnotized subjects."

(4) If the *hypnotist* is introjected, he could only be introjected into the ego—more exactly, into the introject of the ego. I for one am unable to decide whether it is better to speak of his being introjected *into* the introject or of the introject being *projected* upon him. I am not even sure that this alternative is any more than semantic.

(5) While the opposition of introject and partial subject and their interaction requisite to hypnosis testifies to what I have termed a *"transverse"* split in the ego, *partial* hypnosis would, in addition to the "transverse" split, presuppose a *"longitudinal"* one (cf. II, 117–118).

B. HYPNAGOGIC AND HYPNOPOMPIC STATES.

The identity of these two states, their "topography," and the reason for the psychiatrists' employing two different names for the same state were explained in Chapter Two, Section IV, above. It remains to discuss their hypnotic nature.

Example #18: My notes concern the material from a single analytic session.
Patient's Report on a Nocturnal Masturbation:

> I woke up and had very strong sexual feelings. I pressed and rubbed my genitals very hard but was disappointed and somewhat surprised because it didn't do any good. I felt as if I wanted to be rubbed inside. I squeezed my legs together and moved them up and down which gave me a rubbing feeling inside. I felt

very excited, both emotionally and sexually—more so than I had ever been before. I squeezed my legs very tight because I felt I couldn't stand the feeling.

Comment: This is a step toward getting well: the patient, who had entered analysis wholly frigid, feels more "both emotionally and sexually" than ever before. A certain observation permitted us to conclude with absolute certainty that this was the first night she had not gritted her teeth, undoing the results of an orthodontic treatment for pyorrhea. The report makes it clear what she gritted instead; yet the role of a climax was still occupied by a squeezing, whose anal-erotic origin I have illustrated before (I, Chapter 5, Section II). It was only later that the analysis restored a complete responsiveness of the vagina.

Resumption of Patient's Report on a Hypnagogic Hallucination:

Then I had a fantasy that I saw a dog—a big black one with his head right in front of my face. Then the dog's head turned into a big black penis. It was erected and kept staying right in front of my face. I couldn't get rid of it no matter how I turned my head. I could smell it. [She compares this odor with that of her hand, ascertains the difference, and thinks:] I am not so dirty as I thought. I don't have to worry about being dirty any more.

Comment: The vaginal opening is, in other words, no longer an anus. The rest of the hallucination contains historic material. (For the symbolism of the dog see Chapter One, Section II above.)

Conclusion of the Patient's Report: "I felt as if I wanted a cigarette. I got up and went to the bathroom and urinated. Then I decided a cigarette wouldn't taste good and went back to bed."

Comment: The autohypnotic hypnagogic state was possible because of the retention of both ejaculation and urination.

I shall juxtapose to this report one from the analysis of another patient, who became subject to the same state without demonstrable retention.

Example #19: Here I am forced to express myself only in generalities and to pay for the maintenance of the patient's anonymity by perhaps not being convincing. A woman patient who for many years could allow herself only "partial sleep" until certain members of her household had come home, hears the last of them returning and slamming the apartment's entrance door. She then reports having heard the woman living on the floor above her at first walking around and then moaning pleasurably in masturbatory orgastic release.

Comment: In the first place, I cannot tell whether the patient's state is hypnopompic or hypnagogic; in other words, whether the slamming of the door to her apartment had led to arousal. At the time, homosexual fantasies about the woman upstairs occupied much space in her associations. The woman, a friend of the patient, was unmarried, lived alone, but was "looking for a man." I can assure the reader that I have examined the details of the situation very closely, arriving at this result: It is, in view of the relatively early hour of the patient's auditory experience, quite possible that the woman upstairs was still up and actually walking around; and it is only natural that someone in her situation will at times resort to masturbation. I have, of course, no way of deciding whether or not this was one of those times. Nevertheless, in view of my patient's many reports, I absolutely refuse to believe that the neighbor would ever allow herself to moan loudly enough to be heard in the downstairs apartment, at least unless she knew definitely that for some reason or other the apartment was empty. That, I am sure, was my patient's hallucination.

Both these examples, taken as they are from purely neurotic patients, pose a very delicate question: how far is one justified in reserving the ability to hallucinate for the psychotic? Lacking a comprehensive answer, I must restrict myself to a few disparate remarks, which contain statements, not explanations.

Protracted hallucinations in a state of wakefulness are reserved for the psychotic. He alone, for example, has an "imaginary companion."

A well-known experience that I myself have had once or twice and that was also reported to me by a neurotic patient, illustrates what I mean by "protracted" hallucination: Once, when the doors from my office to the foyer and from there to a hallway to the kitchen were open, I heard the maid in a lively conversation with no one. When I came in she stopped. My patient, who lived in a duplex apartment, came home, and heard her maid talking to what she took for a visitor. She went upstairs and only the maid was there. If I have not raised the question of hallucination in the purely neurotic in the discussion of hypnosis proper but raise it only now while dealing with hypnogogic and hypnopompic states, I do so in accordance with my experience. Frequent as the hypnotic evasion is, I have never found it to precipitate hallucination. The only patient who once produced a transient hallucination on the couch was a psychotic man. However, in those autohypnotic states that we call hypnagogic or hypnopompic, hallucinations on the part of a nonpsychotic individual are not infrequent. In my other notes, which I refrain from reproducing because they would only duplicate the example initiating the present section, the accompanying excretory retention of either urine or stool or menstrual blood is never missing.

Example #20: There is one example, however, that I shall include because it is unique in my experience. It shows what extremely circuitous byways the "buoyancy" of the repressed unconscious must employ in order to surface; and it contains for good measure certain elements that appear to defy interpretation. It concerns the psychotic patient whose widowed mother masturbated, using the patient's finger. For long periods of time they slept in the same bed, lying close together both on the same side, which they called "making spoons." Here the mother put her hands on the daughter's breast and genitals with the result that the daughter went to sleep in a cloud of hypnagogic bliss. In reporting this, the patient emphasizes that the mother never moved her hand; and at the same time she expresses a doubt, corroding the previous amnesia removal for the mother's masturbations: there had also not been any motion then, but merely digital pressure.

While this is debated, the patient abruptly remembers something in the middle of the session that she had intended to tell me at the beginning, asserting, however, that it has nothing whatever to do with the matter under discussion. (Every analyst knows this means the two are most intimately connected.) She committed a parapraxis directly before her session, which was to begin at 5:00 p.m. She had left a certain bank in the neighborhood of my office at five minutes before her hour and was certain (which is realistic) to have two to three minutes' leeway in order to be on time. Entering the apartment house hall, however, she looked at her watch and saw that it was already five. She did not understand, watched the hand for a moment and saw it did not move. She imagined the watch must have stopped. But holding it to her ear, she heard it ticking. Then she suddenly became aware of the fact that she had looked at the small hand instead of the big one. When she now took a second look at the watch everything was all right, and she was actually on time.

I asked her which of the mother's hands was put on her genitals, and she answers without hesitation: the right one. I now show her that if the hands of the watch were those of a person whom she faced as she did the watch, this person, in order to imitate the constellation of a few minutes before five, would have to use his left hand as the relatively immobile hour hand of the watch and his right one as the large minute hand that moves.

This amounts to a circuitous confirmation of the fact that the mother did move her finger when masturbating her daughter. The latter was not, either then or at the time of the analytic session under consideration, capable of an orgastic response to a woman, to a man, or to masturbation. Her ejaculation was therefore suppressed, and the suppression, as theory wills it, produced a hypnagogic state, precursor of sleep.

That state, however, did not in this instance give rise to hallucinations. They or their equivalents appear only in the rest of her story. Naturally she had become addicted to the procedure described above, and when sleeping alone was sleepless. She therefore invented what she called a "trick" in order to go to sleep: she imagined herself as "a dandelion," or she pictured that "it was raining and she was the rain" or that "the universe was flowing through her."

Having obtained no associations to these "imaginations" of a psychotic patient, I am strictly speaking under no obligation to understand them. However, this does not lessen my curiosity and I say to myself, the last picture is directly and the one before it indirectly that of a "flow." Could that be considered what Freud has termed the "unconscious indirect representation through opposites" and therefore mean the nonoccurrence instead of the occurrence of the flow—in other words the above-mentioned suppression of her ejaculation? When the patient entered analysis, her clitoris could not erect; in order to keep in repression the erections provoked by her mother, she had to suppress her present erections. As to the imagined dandelion, it could naturally, as could any flower, symbolize the female genital, in this instance her own. But it is distinguished from many others by a high, leafless stem. Could the latter depict the erection in response to the mother's manipulation?

These tentative interpretations are convincing to me, the more so, the more details of the analysis I bring to mind. That does not, however, entitle me to expect them to convince the reader.

I conclude this section on hypnagogic hallucinations by reporting one discussion with an experienced colleague, in order to show that the problem of hallucination in the psychotic versus the nonpsychotic is at present not settled. We were discussing a late childhood memory of my own which had never gone into repression. I was a schoolboy of perhaps 10 to 13 years when Uncle X.—actually no uncle but an old friend of the family—told us of what he considered a strange experience. He, a bachelor, was sitting one night alone either in his drawing room or his bedroom, reading the paper. Suddenly he saw the hand of his late brother extended to him, over the edge of the paper, and heard the brother's voice saying, "Good evening, Karl." Startled, he looked up from the newspaper and naturally saw no one.

My colleague, who of course knew nothing else of the man, maintained on the strength of this one experience that Uncle X. was psychotic. I had known Uncle X. from the time of my birth until his death soon after we had celebrated his seventieth birthday. At that time I must have been in late adolescence. I have tried to recall everything I had seen or heard of him; some of it normal, some a bit peculiar, but I find nothing that points to a psychosis. And I cannot see why an elderly man who is alone at night, reading the paper, could not drowse, become hypnagogic, and have a hallucination. If the reader answers me: after all, you were a boy, and you may not have witnessed or been told of your uncle's possibly other pathognomonic behavior, I grant him his point. But I must ask him in turn: what about the woman patient's hypnagogic hallucination introducing this section? There I am certain, on the basis of an extended analysis including a consultation some 10 years later, that she was not psychotic.

Example #21: The same is true of another woman patient who long ago had many years of analysis intermittently. There was surely nothing psychotic in her make-up; yet I shall quote two brief excerpts from notes I made at the time of her treatment. She reported then: ". . . as I was going to sleep, I had a clear visual picture of a cockroach larger than lifesize rushing gaily down a gangplank from a boat to a dock smaller than lifesize. I was not scared. In fact I was fond of the cockroach and happy about him. I felt it was not really an insect at all, but I did not realize it was you . . ." At another time she "felt afraid of falling asleep," and after some rumination about a life problem, she became aware of a picture that had been in the back of her mind for several minutes. "It was me slicing pieces off someone's buttocks with a butcher knife. I'm not sure I wasn't both the person doing the slicing and being sliced. The slicing was being done very calmly, and I had no emotion about it one way or the other. I was neither frightened nor horrified. Incidentally there was no association of pain for the victim. The picture lasted a moment. Sometime, not too long after, it was followed by another picture—the face of a woman with a bandage across the lower half of her face. The bandage directly over her mouth was stained with blood. I looked directly into her eyes and they were wild. I could see the whites of her eyes as I looked. That terrified me. It was horrible . . ."

It is noteworthy that hardly anyone seems to mistake a hypnagogic or hypnopompic hallucination for a dream. Personally, I can not agree that the bizarre content of a hypnagogic hallucination renders it pathognomonic for the psychosis. Only after writing this Section have I noticed that this was also the opinion of Freud. The descriptions of hypnotic (hypnagogic, hypnopompic, and somnambulistic) hallucination would, it appears, elucidate his brief statement (1936) about the existence of occasional hallucination of the healthy (p. 244). He even repeats this statement when he says (1937b) that "true hallucinations occasionally occurred in patients who were certainly not psychotic" . . . (p. 267).

I append finally a remark on an observation that I have made repeatedly but have not understood at all. It appears that there is one exception to reserving hallucination in full wakefulness for the psychotic: *olfactory hallucination.* Several times I have been told by purely neurotic patients, particularly upon entering the office, that they had noticed a certain odor in the foyer, usually of certain foods they thought were being prepared in the kitchen. Actually, at the time of their sessions the kitchen was always empty and the stove cold. It is of course possible that these patients were already hypnotic and I did not know it. In that case, however, the statement made above that the hypnotic evasion never precipitates hallucinations would be invalid.

In summary, both the hypnagogic and hypnopompic states maintain themselves as does, it would appear, all autohypnosis, through the retention of excretion. In addition they frequently precipitate hallucination (hardly ever mistaken for a dream) where, with the possible exception of the instance just cited, the hypnotic evasion does not. They thus furnish examples of this phenomenon occurring in the *non*psychotic.

C. SOMNAMBULISM AND THE HYSTERICAL TWILIGHT STATE

Here again the same state has, as was explained in the beginning of this section, two different names only because of the context in which it occurs. If the individual is *asleep* and awakens into an autohypnotic state, distinguished from the hypnagogic and hypnopompic states by elaborate motor and locomotor reactions, he is called a "somnambulist." If, however, the individual is already *awake* and becomes subject to this exceptional state, the latter is called a "hysterical twilight" or a "hypnoid" state. I have had experience with the first and practically none with the second.

To the student of psychoanalysis it must be said that even a genius great enough to create a new science cannot upon occasion avoid an error. He, the student, will read Freud's "Metapsychological Supplement to the Theory of the Dream" (1917), find the author speculating about the different ways in which the unconscious dream wish might find discharge, and encounter the following passage: "[In sleep] direct motor discharge should be excluded . . . But we do meet with exceptional instances in which this happens, in the form of somnambulism. We do not know what conditions make this possible, or why it does not happen more often (p. 227)." If this were true, terms such as "sleepwalking" (or even "sleep acting") would not be the misnomers they are. No one can walk or act in his sleep, but anyone is able to walk or act in hypnosis. Somnambulism, in contrast to Freud's description, is based upon the exchange of sleep for an *autohypnotic* condition. The sleeper, in other words, wakes up into an autohypnotic state, incorrectly called "somnambulism."

> *Example #22:* The report of a patient about a sequence of four different states. The first is a fantasy, possibly at least in part hypnagogic; the second a dream; the third a somnambulistic experience, followed by sleep.

> (1) The night following an hour with you when we talked about Miss X. and my wish that she come to you (I wrote "me" spontaneously) as my giving you a child, I had a *fantasy before going to sleep* of falling in love with a man that *was* a man and marrying him. The main point was the wedding, which you and your wife attended. After the ceremony you came up to me in the vestibule of the church and kissed me. I was so happy and loved you very much. Your wife was there and smiled and was

pleased, and I could shake hands with her and welcome her warmly and happily. The new husband was there too but more by implication than any vital real presence. When you went out the door, the sun went with you.

(2) *I went to sleep and dreamt* that a woman was crouching beside my bed—on the side next to the wall as between your couch and the radiator. She had a knife and I knew she was going to kill me.

(3) I jumped out of bed on the side away from her and stood in the middle of the room staring at the bed trying desperately to see her and what she was doing. Then I realized that I was standing in the line of light coming through the window (I don't know whether this was true, since light comes only from other apartments across the court), and that the woman could throw the knife and kill me. I was a clear target. I moved backward toward the door, still keeping my eyes on the bed. When I reached the door of the room I turned around and went quickly into the bathroom, *turned on the light, and urinated, though I had no urge to do so* . . . I looked at my watch and saw I had only been asleep about 45 minutes.

(4) *I went back to bed* and after a moment went to sleep again.

Comment: Strictly pertinent to the subject is only the comment that the report contains a sequence of fantasy, dream, and somnambulistic state, and that the latter—as does all autohypnosis—depends upon excretory (here urinary) retention.

I have throughout this chapter refrained from unnecessary interpretation. It is the teacher in me that in this case succumbs to the temptation of making at least a few interpretive remarks. I apologize to the experienced because it is my hope that my book may also be read by students.

The initial parapraxis in the daydream speaks, as do all parapraxia, the truth: before she can give me the child, I must naturally give it to her. The rest of the daydream is built exactly as is the dream of Little Karl in his coffin (Freud, 1900, p. 152). There the dreamer does not wish that the child may die, but that the burial may occasion a condolence visit from the man she loves. Here the wish is not to be married to someone but to be kissed by the analyst, for which the wedding is merely an occasion. Yet the deeper, the oedipal meaning of the transference fantasy cannot for long be veiled by the smiling approval of the analyst's wife: the hallucinations here are replete with the fear of the mother's mortal revenge. That the 45 minutes at the end stands for $4 + 5 = 9$, an allusion to pregnancy, not even the student of today need be told.

Example #23: This particular report by a patient on her somnambulistic activities and hallucinations is distinguished by the fact that it occurred in the presence of someone else whose observation is recalled by the patient. The sequence here is (1) sleep, (2) somnambulistic state (called "dream incident" by the patient in her report), and (3) sleep.

> A. [roommate] had left. I was of course very upset and feeling very deserted. That evening I went to B.'s home [girl friend] and spent the weekend with her. All evening I felt good, was in fact in better spirits than usual. I really had a good time. That evening I began to menstruate. B. went to bed an hour or so before I did. I wasn't sleepy, so I sat up and read. When I did go to bed, [1] I fell asleep quickly. [2] This dream incident occurred about an hour later. I remember jumping out of bed in an attempt to rescue B. I thought bags of cement were coming through the ceiling directly above her. They were going to fall on her if I did not warn her in time. I half woke when B. jumped out of bed asking me what was wrong. I tried to tell her apparently. I didn't really know what I was saying. I sat down on the edge of my bed and B. sat down beside me, put her arm around me and said, "Honey, are you sure you're awake?" I was a little indignant and said of course I was. I'd had to warn her and I could explain it. I started to explain and suddenly I was so terribly confused that I couldn't say anything. I don't think I've ever known such a complete feeling of confusion. Finally I said I guessed I wasn't awake after all. B. got up and went to the bathroom. When she came back, *I decided to go to urinate.* I was still dazed. When I came back, B. said, "If anything else starts to fall on me, let it fall. Don't try to rescue me." Still only half there I replied that I couldn't let bags of cement fall on her. She surprised me by say-

ing that was the first she'd heard about bags of cement. I went
right back [3] to sleep. The next morning B. told me what I had
said and done. I had given a startled yell, several of them in a
row in fact. Then I had jumped out of bed and walked to her
bed. She had asked what was wrong. I had told her, "the cradles
are falling from the ceiling." She tried to tell me it was all right,
but I had insisted: "But they are falling." Then I began to get
confused and sat down on my bed. B. asked me what I meant,
and I said, "That woman that was here brought them." When B.
asked, "What woman?" I said, "That's right, you'd gone to bed.
She came after you went to bed." B. sat down beside me, put her
arm about me and asked me if I was sure I was awake. The rest
of the incident was as I recalled it. I had not mentioned the bags
of cement until the end. The next day—Sunday—I was in bed
nearly all day with *the most severe menstrual cramps* I have had
since before the analysis. Aspirin gave little or no relief. Yet de-
spite the pain, I continued to feel happy. I enjoyed B. more than
I ever had, and the day was actually a pleasant one.

Comment: The excretory retention is twofold: the urinary
retention is self-evident, but the urinary release does not, in this
case, terminate the somnambulistic state, called by the patient,
a lay person, "dream-incident" because of the concomitant retention of menstrual blood. The "good" mother may have been
transferred upon the girl friend, and the "bad" mother appears
only during the somnambulistic state—perhaps not as an hallucination but in terms of a delusion—as "that woman" . . . who
"brought" "the cradles" (preoedipal "baby wish"). The disparity between "cradles" and "bags of cement" is that between
child and *Lumpf,* comprehensively explained by Freud in the
case history of Little Hans (1909). Freud has also taught us that
"rescue" symbolizes giving birth.

I think one is entitled to state that the somnambulistic state
in this case follows an unremembered dream in which the censor fails in suppressing the affect. It is the sexual affect concomitant to a preoedipal latent thought that is converted into the
anxiety (the patient's repeated "yelling") and leads so frequently under these conditions to arousal. The arousal, howev-

er, is not into wakefulness but into a autohypnotic, somnambulistic state followed again by sleep.

Analytic Comment: I must begin with a somnambulistic experience of still another patient:

> One of the two other occasions when I experienced the autohyp-
> notic feelings was a few weeks ago. The alarm awakened me in
> the morning. I got up to shut it off, returned, sat on the edge of
> the bed, lighted a cigarette, flicked out the match, and it
> dropped from my hand, and I had the sense I had almost fallen
> asleep sitting up. I really didn't know for a moment whether it
> was the burnt-out match or the lighted cigarette that I had
> dropped, and I didn't much care. This had followed a night in
> which I had gotten to bed late, was very tired, and kept waking
> up during the night, once waking up with an awful cramp in my
> foot. (I don't think that that was the night—I can't remember
> now whether or not it was.)

Comment (quoted from my notes, made at the time of the
occurrence); "In this transcript the problem of urinary continence vs. incontinence, i.e., urinary retention, finds merely its
symbolic expression through fire. The patient is uncertain about
and indifferent to what she had dropped on the floor: the cold
match or the burning cigarette. This, however, is the result of
(re-) repression." The original report on the incident made during the session contained the additional information that this
was a night during which she slept restlessly, got up several
times and *urinated,* and did so again after waking up from the
autohypnotic or, if you wish, hypnopompic state. Here again
the retention of excretion is a prerequisite for autohypnosis.

There remains the discussion of the "hysterical twilight (or
hypnoid) state" with which I have had, as was noted above, little or no experience. I shall therefore confine myself to one single remark. From what I have read, it appears to me to be
identical with another exceptional state with which I have had
no experience: the evidently autohypnotic state requisite to the
execution of a "posthypnotic command."

Schilder and Kauders (1956) have seen some subjects passing

into a "dreamlike" state at the occasion. The propensity of a subject who has been hypnotized before subsequently to go into autohypnosis is enormous. I learned that long ago from an older colleague (who so distinguished himself that Freud had one of his famous signet rings made up for him): Ernst Simmel. During Simmel's service as an army psychiatrist in World War I, he had many psychically damaged soldiers "abreact" their recent trauma by employing cathartic hypnosis (cf. Breuer & Freud's *Studies on Hysteria*, 1895). He told me he did this in barracks which he furnished with a sign reading "Sleep Barracks." After a while the soldiers went into them ahead of their treatment time and lay down. When he arrived he found them all "fast asleep," i.e., in deep hypnosis.

It is the similarity between the descriptions of the two states that causes me to suspect that in spite of their different contexts (in the "hypnoid" state, wakefulness; in the state during the execution of a posthypnotic command, also wakefulness, but *preceded by hypnosis*) they both represent the same autohypnotic condition.

II STATES DIFFERING FROM EACH OTHER AS WELL AS FROM THOSE OF GROUP I

A. THE ALIENATIONS: DEPERSONALIZATION AND DEREALIZATION

The deepest insight into these states—insight so deep that it can only be that of a genius—was Freud's. It is contained in a letter written in his old age to Romain Rolland: "A Disturbance of Memory on the Acropolis" (1936).[5] Before quoting from it I

---

[5] A benevolent reader of my manuscript was dissatisfied with my introduction because it does not elucidate the connection between the Acropolis and the alienations. I am writing for analysts, students, graduates, and their teachers; I have therefore presumed that they are familiar with Freud's paper and thereby with the connection. Since there is not, however, any harm in yielding to my critic, I shall briefly remark that Freud, visiting the Acropolis in 1904, experienced such a strange feeling that he could only assume it to be a "derealization" or its equivalent *(Entfremdungsgefühl)*. In his own words, standing before the Acropolis, he "had (or might have had) a momentary

would like to make a semantic correction: Freud uses the term *Entfremdung* (or *Entfremdungsgefühl* = literally the sense of feeling against) both generically and specifically; generically for the two states we term "derealization" and "depersonalization"—states which Freud said are "intimately connected"; specifically for the states ("derealization") he terms "alienations proper" *(eigentlichen Entfremdungen)*. I will therefore replace his terminology with that used at present because it fits more closely the result of clinical observation.

Freud opposes the alienations to "other phenomena, which may be regarded as their positive counterparts—what are known as *'fausse reconnaissance,' 'déjà vu,' 'déjà raconté'* etc., illusions in which we seek to accept something as belonging to our ego, just as in the derealizations [alienations] we are anxious to keep something out of us (p. 245).

He subsequently describes two general characteristics of the phenomena of alienation. The first is that they all serve the

---

feeling: *'What I see here is not real'* (p. 244)." His belated analysis of this experience, strikingly incomplete though it be, precipitates the fundamental remarks quoted hereinafter on the theory of the "alienations" *(Entfremdungen)*. The paper containing them is the only one in which he has dealt systematically with this subject. As to the incompleteness of the interpretation, it is shared with other of Freud's autobiographical communications: for example, the staircase dream (1900) and "The Subtleties of a Parapraxis" (1935). They are all written so as to give the impression that their author had never read Freud. Neither sexuality (infantile or adult) nor aggression enter his interpretations; yet he never terms them incomplete.

Writing this, I remember a comparable experience of my own. The episode may at first sound fatuous, but because it entered associations in my analysis with Hanns Sachs and underwent thorough interpretation, it is pertinent.

When I was traveling for the first time as an adult on a certain line out of Berlin, my train stopped at a town where the station sign read "Magdeburg." I recalled having said to myself: "There, that is really as the Atlas indicates. Magdeburg actually exists." This affirmative thought must have countered, as it did in Freud's case, a doubt of which I had been unaware—either of the existence of Magdeburg, or of my ability ever to ascertain its existence. (It is noteworthy that occasional visits during my youth from one we called "the aunt from Magdeburg"—a friend of my mother's—did not allay my unconscious doubt.)

Sachs merely said at this point: "Well, *Magde-burg.*" And I, then already a student of analysis, understood him. *Magde* is an obsolete German word for "maiden" or "woman servant"; and of course, *Burg* means "castle," a symbol I had learned. This was the entering wedge for the recall of a traumatic scoptophilic experience in childhood, the neurotic effects of which I was fortunate to exchange for sublimated ones indispensable to my work.

purposes of defence; they aim at keeping something away from the ego, at disavowing it. Now, new elements, which may give occasion for defensive measures, approach the ego from two directions—from the real external world and from the internal world of thoughts and impulses that emerge in the ego. It is possible that this alternative coincides with the choice between derealizations proper [alienations] and depersonalizations. He mentions, finally, the last general characteristic of the alienations: their dependence upon the past, upon the ego's store of memories and upon earlier distressing experiences, which have since perhaps fallen victim to repression (pp. 245–246).

My own experience compels me to make a second correction before going on to add certain details to the framework Freud has established. The correction may or may not be semantic. He avers that the "alienations [*Entfremdungen*, which in this case he even qualified as being spoken of as "sensations"— *Empfindungen*], although very frequent in certain psychic diseases, are not unknown among normal people (p. 244)." I have found this true of derealization but not of depersonalization, which as far as I know is restricted to the psychotic. I hasten to set forth two reasons why this may not be at all a correction of Freud, but on the contrary, a corroboration. If he really means "derealization" by his term "alienation," all contradiction between us is solved. Moreover, my experience with the two states is lopsided: I have observed a fair number of derealizations and experienced two of them myself, while I have had occasion to observe only a few instances of depersonalization and to study analytically only one. Therefore, if depersonalization can occur also in the *nonpsychotic*, I may simply not have seen such a case. Logic alone, however, compels me to this forbearance; actually I do not believe it.

1. *Depersonalization*

I have given the theory of this form of alienation in the second volume of this series (pp. 77–85); in fact it comprised the first step toward a metapsychological innovation, inasmuch as it actuated me to abstract from a number of observations the hypothesis of the two *demi-institutions* and the terms *introject* and *partial subject*. I have explained the complaint of the patient who suffers from depersonalization ("I do not feel myself") by stating that the "I" in the sentence is representative of the introject, the "myself" of the partial subject, and that both instead of "dividing" the ego are "splitting" it, whereby the introject tries to eliminate the partial subject.

Applied to a variety of phenomena now to be understood as arising from what I termed "split" in the ego (morbid self-observation, inhibition, lapses in reality testing, and a defective synthetic function in general, as well as the case of depersonalization), the development of the hypothesis as well as a discussion of its relevance to the "Special Theory of the Neuroses" comprised over a hundred pages. For the present reader I can only recapitulate here briefly.

Borrowing Freud's (1933) term "a differentiating grade in the ego," I applied it to the ego in the narrow sense of the word. And because the two parts I was to differentiate are not on a par with Freud's three "institutions," I proposed calling them *demi-institutions*. They complement each other, forming a transverse line of "cleavage" (as against Freud's concept of a longitudinal one, e.g., in the "multiple personality") in the normal psyche, which in pathology can become a "split."

It should be explicitly stated that the depersonalized individual *knows* that he is himself because the exteroceptive perception of his body or his clothes is not impeded, and because he retains certain memories (name, address, ancestry, family, etc.) that testify to his identity. But he does not *feel* himself on account of a proprioceptive awareness of this split. The awareness engenders a certain form of "unpleasure," to which on another occasion (discussing compulsive action and its suppression) Freud has most fittingly applied the term *Unbehagen* (1930), as in *Das Unbehagen in der Kultur.* (The book title was translated *Civilization and its Discontents;* discontents, however, in German in not *Unbehagen* but *Unzufriedenheit;* and I know of no correct translation for *Unbehagen.* Pondering the problem further with the help of Webster's *Dictionary of Syno-nyms* [1942] I find that "distress" represents the closest approxi-mation.)

In the "ego split," the demi-institutions are functioning in opposition; the "introject" *(I)*, which I defined as that part of the ego close to and serving the *superego*, "observes, disowns, and has eliminated in feeling the other" *(myself)*. This latter part, the "partial subject," I defined as subject to *instinctual* strivings, close to and serving the *id*. In the defusion of instincts leading to a topographical redistribution such as would occur in the ego split, the better part of the aggression is *bound* by the introject, which is opposing itself to the partial subject and has succeeded in eliminating it. "If institutions split up and oppose each other, as for instance, ego and superego in the feeling of guilt, they engender tensions," I wrote in my original discus-sion, "and these tensions cause their owner to suffer. I believe that this is valid for *demi*-institutions as well. However, the suffering is, qualitatively, of a different kind."

Depersonalization, as was said above, is but one of a variety of phenomena caused by the topographical redistribution (cathec-tic rearrangement) in the ego split, and at that, an infrequent one. The suffering is, however, intense, and "in behavior, coun-tenance, [and] tone of voice [the person] suffers in the manner described for the compulsive" (II, 80).[6] One must recall here what Freud has said for the case of the alienations in general, that they "all serve the purposes of defence."

In the case told me by the late Dr. Jekels (II, 78), as well as that to be presented below as example, the defense is against the feeling of guilt. Topographically and dynamically speaking, these patients evaded a split *between* superego and ego through a split *inside the ego* between introject and partial subject; what they actually accomplish through this substitution is the ex-change of one form of suffering for another. The economic gain is in these patients the continuation of certain forms of sexual

---

[6] ". . . a torturing discomfort *(quaelendes Unbehagen)*, a sort of anxiety . . ." (loc. cit.).

gratification that would otherwise have been interdicted by their superego. Dr. Jekels' patient was able to indulge herself by maintaining an extramarital affair without feeling guilty.

The example to follow is perhaps not one of a completed but of an imminent depersonalization. I ascribed this difference at the time to my diagnosis, which declared the patient a neurotic and her obviously psychotic traits as the result of an identification with her psychotic mother. It was only later in the second installment of her interrupted analysis that I saw my error and was forced to change my diagnosis: the patient was actually psychotic.[7] What makes her case so instructive is the fact that she was an *analyzable* psychotic. And, although she would in subsequent consultations and messages at Christmas time give me more credit for her unalloyed happiness than perhaps I deserved, I have no doubt that the analysis helped her substantially.

I shall not attempt to reproduce the circuitous ways taken by the analysis in uncovering the experience of the (imminent) depersonalization, some of which is contained in Volume I, pp. 254–256, but proceed as systematically as I can.

> *Example #24: The (imminent) depersonalization:* I described this patient in a previous volume and will repeat my description here: The girl had in puberty found amongst the mother's belongings and appropriated a crucifix with a glass peephole in the middle, through which one could see Virgin and Child. Once, while looking through it she had experienced the fright of her life: an agonal feeling, difficult to describe, of an imminent, almost mortal, danger of losing part of herself, which she would be unable to retrieve [a depersonalization *in statu nascendi*] [I, p. 256].

---

[7] I do not mean to excuse myself for my misdiagnosis. But the problem is actually not always an easy one. I would, for instance, reserve climactic urination for the psychotic; but I have found it in an analytic patient who was purely neurotic. Prior to her analysis and in the beginning of it, she engaged in clitoris masturbation on the toilet and found an orgastic pleasure in "letting everything go at once." This was indeed a mere identification with her psychotic mother, who had insisted on her witnessing the performance many a time when she was a child. Analysis restored deep vaginal sensitivity and abolished all masturbation.

Interpretation: It was in the last fragment of her analysis that one particular session at the time of her menstruation brought the complete historical elucidation of the (dreaded) depersonalization.

The patient had some dysmenorrhea (sore and swollen breasts, mild abdominal cramps), but felt fine, as she always did, during her period. She had an excess of energy, was at peace with the world and her fellow men, in particular those with whom at other times she was apt to have trouble. Her original description of this menstrual freedom was that during her period she became like a particular woman friend whom she admired: hospitable, affectionate, and serene. This was a partial therapeutic result; in puberty she had been loath to even "breathe the same air with that woman" (her mother), i.e., to have the latter enter the womb at the time of her first menstruations (cf. I, Chapter Six).

In the session under consideration the question of why her improvement was confined to her menstruations was reexamined. She had an idea: she is, menstrually, a woman, and extramenstrually a child. She associates the "crucifix experience" to this idea, and it becomes now suddenly clear to her that the part of herself which she had irretrievably lost while she looked through the peephole, is the child. Because she had the experience when she was 10 years old, it could only be herself as a small child that would be lost. This is traced back to two different occasions in childhood at which her mother disowned her, once temporarily and once for good.

(1) A fairly normal family life—normal at least as far as the child was concerned—suddenly became interrupted when the father deserted his probably promiscuous wife and his children for two weeks. The psychotic mother went completely to pieces and put the three year-old child from one day to the next into a charitable institution. The latter was located below street level, and the patient remembers clinging desperately to the departing mother, who walked up a short flight of stairs to the entrance, and the mother's brutally kicking her downstairs with her foot. The child responded with complete incon-

tinence to the maltreatment. After the father's return, she was taken back but reverted to urinary incontinence and the bottle.

It became evident that the division of the ego into the introject and partial subject requisite to the establishment of continence (II, 124) and based upon (secondary) identification with the (later) mother (parent) remains for a while dependent upon the child's object relation to the mother which supplies the identification with the necessary libido. If the relation is canceled abruptly the division is lost. The traumatic cancellation prepared the patient for the later expectation that her *introject* ("I") would behave as had the mother from which it stemmed, and *expel the partial subject* ("myself") as the mother had expelled the child.

(2) However, another jolt sustained by the ego at the age of about nine, assisted in further preparing the child for the experience a year later. At the time of its occurrence the introject had already become representative not only of the mother but also of the group.

The perverse breast sucking to which the psychotic mother seduced her daughter has been briefly described (I, 112). The practice of this and other incestuous perversions upon which the child had become dependent, lasted from age seven to nine and again came to an abrupt and traumatic end. One afternoon, when the Irish neighbors—mothers and children—were gathered on the stoops of their houses and in the street, chatting and playing, the patient could not contain herself and bragged in front of everybody about her activities with her mother. She remembers the horror in the neighbors' faces and recalls how she was ostracized by the group.

Someone must have notified the authorities, because soon afterward a woman (truant) officer came to the house, gave the mother a severe dressing-down and seems to have threatened her with the courts. The mother became frantic and turned against the child, whom she beat, berated in the vilest terms, and punished by making her do incessant domestic chores.

What occurred subsequently is in part easy and in part not so easy to understand. The mother left the neighborhood, and it so happened that the new district had a good school. The neglected tenement child, covered with vermin, was cleaned up, had her hair cut, and was properly clad. This is understandable, but it was only a beginning.

We were taught in medical school that the study of the physically ill compelled one to assume the "self-healing tendencies" in nature; I am not so sure that one can get along without this assumption when one studies the mind.

The new neighborhood had, of course, a church. My patient who throughout her childhood had heard from both parents only violent expletives directed against religion joined this church at the age of 10 all on her own. There she replaced both mother and the group: the mother symbolically through the church and objectwise through a benevolent lady of the upper middle class working in the church, who befriended her and became her model. She enjoyed the new group and partook in its activities, unruffled by her mother's derision. With such assistance, she suppressed practically all sexuality, rediscovering it later masturbatorily, only at the—apparently often typical—age of 18. She had by that time lost all interest in the church, it having served its purpose; and, while possessed of good moral standards, had become atheistic. During this period of her life she was normal, worked her way through college, and married a potent young man to whom she was perfectly free to respond. It was only in her mid-twenties when the mother died in an institution that her severe adult neurosis broke out.

I have given this excerpt from a case history only in order to supplement the topographical with the historical analysis of the attack of depersonalization. One could call the attack a "return of the repressed in [the product of] the repression" (Freud). It occurred at precisely the time when the church had begun its work. While the church made it possible for the child to re-place her mother, however, it also aroused her interest in the archaic Christian mother, the Virgin. Looking through the hole in the crucifix which belonged to the mother—an ex-Catholic, hating and vilifying everybody in the Catholic neighborhood where she lived—mobilized two traumatic experiences, one from the period of toilet training and one from the disturbed latency period, which had only recently been repressed. Mary holding Christ on her lap alludes for one thing to Mary's breast-feeding her child: the original weaning trauma, undoubtedly also mobilized at the time, was not uncovered in the otherwise successful analysis of the patient. For another thing, however, it alluded to the years of sexually sucking the mother's breast, which aroused the child greatly and made the mother, probably with the assistance of masturbation, orgastic.

However, neither allusion made any of the repressed experiences conscious; nor did it initiate any feeling of guilt. It threatened the girl instead with an imminent *depersonalization;* because the line of cleavage, which in the attack became that of the split, lay not between ego and superego, *but inside the ego itself.*

Only later in the course of her manifest disturbance did the superego express itself in a strong need for punishment: she divorced her husband without any apparent reason (analysis found the reason which she was finally able to voice: "because I had it too good"); she "took up" with a prominent but psychotic man (whom I happened to know) and had him exploit her; mismarried finally a psychotic (whom I saw in consultation), and had to settle sexually for a form of clitoris masturbation that was again determined by a return of the repressed. She stimulated herself in front of a mirror to the point of a climax while taking out her left breast and attempting to suck it. (I do not have to point out the symbolism of left = morally wrong.) Nor do I have to state that, for anatomical reasons, she did not succeed in the *sucking* except in a number of dreams; but that she nevertheless became orgastic because she succeeded in *seeing* the breast, whereby the eye took over the function of the mouth (cf. *The Unit of Mouth and Eye,* I, 55–60).

Here again the depersonalization had for many years spared the patient the feeling of guilt, in this case over the incestuous sexual activities with her mother that had only recently been discontinued.

2. Derealization

There are, descriptively speaking, two kinds of derealizations; in one the whole environment is derealized, in the other only a particular element of it. Nevertheless, the theory is the same for both; and I think that the second can be employed to explain the first.

Neither derealization nor depersonalization affects judgment; the depersonalized individual *knows*, in the typical case, that he is himself, but he does not *feel* it. By the same token the individual in a state of derealization *knows* that the environment is real, but he does not *feel* it. (I am certain of that; even if it should contradict a certain somewhat vague formulation of Freud [1936], set forth in the paper mentioned in the beginning of the present section.) The environment appears unreal; it has lost a "significance," as one patient expressed it, that is difficult to describe; and wherever I have observed the state it had also lost much of its depth dimension.

I have groped for a way of characterizing the "significance" mentioned here; but I found that the opposite of the "lost" significance is demonstrable only through the heightened significance with which the painter, for example, endows his objects. Take at random Cézanne's *"Still Life"* (painted c. 1877, now in a private collection in Paris but reproduced in the authoritative *History of Impressionism* by John Rewald, New York, 1946, p. 320). On the left side of the painting is a stemmed bowl with five apples, while a sixth lies on the table in front of the bowl's foot. Both the bowl and the apples appear rounder, more substantial and, if I may use the words, more strikingly extant for having passed through the artist's eye, than a real bowl and six real apples would if an ordinary person such as myself had arranged them in the same fashion. This is, as was said above, an illustration through opposites: to the same degree to which Cézanne *heightens* the "significance" of the objects, the individual in a state of derealization *divests* them of it. (For the explanation of the relative loss of depth dimension see the conclusion of Example #26 to follow.)

Example #25: A nonpsychotic patient, who was forced much against his will to leave his native country, described in his analysis a typical episode of derealization prior to his departure. He goes for a walk in a park near the home he had lived in ever since he was born. While walking, he traverses a small bridge over a stream. The bridge has a figure on it commemorating the year it was constructed, which took place when the patient was five years old; but he can dimly remember how the region had looked before, i.e., without the bridge. From the bridge he gazes on a wide clump of trees in full leaf and is surprised to see them appear unreal and flattened out.

I believe his experience can be explained if one adds that he took the walk in the park as a convalescent. He had suffered from an extremely painful fistula recti that had disturbed and prolonged his recuperation from a hemorrhoidectomy, at the occasion of which a rectal polyp had been discovered and removed. I am not certain whether or not he could have had the experience without the agony caused by the fistula recti (Freud has stated that pain can precipitate mental representations of an organ that is otherwise not or no longer so represented). As it is, the derealization shows merely his inability to consummate what I have termed, oversimplifying it, the "symbolic equation" (cf. Chapter One, Section I) with regard to the clump of trees. The "word-bridge" (Freud) linking the hemorrhoids to the clump of trees is "growth." The condition of "no more growth in and on him" became projected onto the "growth" of the clump of trees, which for a brief span of time were "not really there." (To repeat: he *knew* of their being there, but he did not *feel* it; had he not known of their existence, he would have to have been either psychotic or in a hypnotic state engendering a negative hallucination.

I have found this formula applicable to every instance of derealization I have succeeded in understanding.

Example #26: To the above experience I juxtapose a derealization which concerned not a single element of the external world but the environment as a whole and lasted for three or four days. It followed the excessive and utterly painful overstimulation by a psychopath of the girl's rectum.

In order to understand why, in this morbid instance, the whole environment became unreal, one has only to recall the normal changes in the representation in the pleasure-physiologic body ego of the genital in the course of its normal function. The aroused genital enters the pleasure-physiologic body ego; during coitus it becomes more and more prominent. During orgasm its most pleasurable proprioceptive perception replaces the exteroceptive perception of the whole environment, and after full gratification it almost disappears from the pleasure-physiologic body ego.

What occurred in the case of the patient could be called a pathologic caricature of the process: overstimulation and pain caused the proprioceptive perception of the pleasure-physiologic organ to replace the exteroceptive perception of the whole environment as well; but it left the pleasure-physiologic element so exhausted in the end, so completely divested of all cathexis, that its representation in the pleasure-physiologic body ego disappeared completely. Instead it was projected upon the whole environment it had previously replaced so painfully. It is thus that the derealization concerned the whole object world and was accompanied by extreme unpleasure (II, 246–247, 251).

This example is also well suited to explain the "flattening out" of the object world (or of an element in it) through derealization. The phenomenon *represents, in projection, the inability to cathect an element of the pleasure-physiologic body ego sufficiently so as to endow it with turgor.*

Example #27: The following example is a more or less literal transcript of notes made after a single analytic session with a male patient. The man was unusually self-perceptive, being aware both of his states of autohypnosis and the derealizations that often accompanied them.

Notes: The patient declares he is and has been before coming to the session, in hypnotic evasion. On the way to the hour he sees a youngish, well-dressed Negress with a very erect carriage (cf. Little Hans, Freud, 1909), who has a flaring skirt which from the rear appears as a sort of "bustle." He has an impulse to pat her on the "behind." His autohypnotic state at the time was, as was noted above, accompanied by a derealization. That morning, drinking coffee with his wife, the state was less pronounced; but when he left her and approached the subway entrance it was again full-fledged.

I interpret: the subway entrance stands for the maternal *anus* leading to the *bowels of the mother earth.* He then remembers an unusually copious defecation of the day before during which some prostatic fluid escaped. This last is obviously an example of a regressively erogenic process with inhibition of any sexual affect. His own interpretation that he must have gotten "something" there from his wife with whom he had had intercourse at the end of her menstruation (in other words, in identification with her) followed the model of his mother having said of her colitis that "if they [rationalized as her doctors, but actually the paranoiac 'they'] say I have venereal disease, I would kill myself." This was evidently her self-punitive reaction to the incestuous act with her son, now my patient.

He asks: May I move? Based on a comment in a previous hour about his rigid position on the couch, I say, Yes, of course. He moves to his left side, becomes sexually aroused to the point of wanting to masturbate, and suffers dizziness—all in complete identification with his mother when he was aged 14 to 15½. I ask about the depth dimension in the objects in his states of derealization during the day. He affirms their incompleteness in that regard, including the Negress with the bustle.

Comment: If one consults that textbook of analytic psychology that is Freud's *The Interpretation of Dreams,* and one's own experience with dreams, with regard to the apparent influence of symbolization upon the censor's ability to suppress affect, one can distinguish descriptively two different cases. In symbolization (Chapter One, Section II) the symbolized element of the pleasure-physiologic body ego is symbolized by a part of the object *world,* and therefore gives the appearance in this substitution of a *de*sexualization. The process of dream formation with its attendant symbolization is itself, as Freud (1933) put it, ". . . subject to the condition of the censorship, which is exercised by the residue of the repression still in operation" (p. 19), displacement being the first consequence of its influence, inhibition of affect, the second. This mechanism is, of course, not peculiar to dreams. In the same lecture, Freud said that the resistance to dream interpretation, hallmark of the dream censorship, "is nothing other than the resistance due to repression by which the two agencies [the Ucs. and the Cs.] are separated" (p. 15). In other words, if the manifest dream or its related psychological formations (such as the exceptional state of derealization under discussion) represents the solution of the conflict, it is, in effect, a compromise. Therefore it will not come as a surprise to know that the success of the censor varies.

In the first of the two cases to be distinguished, it acquieces in the deception of the apparent desexualization inherent in symbolization: affect can therefore be suppressed. In the other case, the forces with which the censor contends in the unconscious are evidently too strong. It is as though it is impelled to "see through" the deception of the symbolization, to quasi-translate it, and in so doing release affect.

To illustrate this latter case first, I will use the brief dream of another male patient. He sees his widowed landlady advancing upon him while cradling an old-fashioned telephone in her arms. With every step she takes he becomes more and more anxious and wakes up filled with terror. Here the symbolic allusion to masturbation through the telephone did not delude the censor at all: it allowed affect to develop, converting, however, the sexual affect into anxiety affect, which results in the dreamer's eventual arousal from a "nightmare."

The first case, that in which inhibition of affect by the censor is successful, is illustrated by the experience of the patient under consideration, not as a dream, but in an exceptional state. Here the mother is symbolized as a "racially foreign" person, the Negress; and her typical, protruding buttocks are displaced upon her clothes (= nudity: Freud) where they appear as a bustle. The mother's anus and her bowel are likewise desexualized through their symbolization: "subway entrance," and "subway." Affect is suppressed.

It is only the analyst's interpretation that divests all these elements of their symbolic disguise and enables the patient to react with sexual arousement. A review of his report makes it evident that in view of the latent incestuous thoughts behind the manifest content of his experience he should have had an erection at the time, which without knowing it he had suppressed. The ensuing *absence* of erective turgor was therefore projected upon the environment, which consequently was *felt as unreal* ("nonextant") and *flattened out* in consequence of his state of derealization.

Example #28: This example may at first sight appear to contradict my explanation of the relative lack of depth dimension in derealization. As a matter of fact it merely refines it. The example is further noteworthy because it confines the derealization to a dream.

> *Associations:* I had at first thought I wanted intercourse but as soon as I kissed my wife I knew I had no desire for her. I touched her breasts—she started violently. She was shaking. She said she wanted sex but was afraid I didn't want it. I felt she "needed" intercourse and started to enter her. *I had only tactile feelings in my penis—no sexual sensations.* I had an adequate erection, however. *I had a fantasy about my penis being in a cloacal opening.* [The patient had previously been acquainted with the fantasy of the cloaca.] My wife had an orgasm, and a while later I ejaculated. There was little change of feeling with this, although I was aware of ejaculation. Later that night I dreamt:
>
> [*Dream*]: The locale of the dream was artificial—resembling a stage setting. The colors were theatrically garish—yellow, orange, and black. There seemed to me a kind of yellow backdrop in the distance. I was at once viewing the scene (as at the theatre) and a participant in it. There was a jet black bridge, organically shaped somehow—like the silhouette of a person

bending over, rear-end facing the observer. On the bridge was a train; from within the train I looked down at the scene far below. Someone said, "It's Peiping," and I saw what appeared to be a group of china houses and figurines.

Then I was inside a hollow tree whose walls seemed to be freshly painted white—everything seemed very clean. I was being besieged, but didn't know by whom. A huge dog—resembling a mountain lion—came into the room. He looked potentially dangerous, yet benevolent. I began searching for a means to get him out, leading him into a number of crevices. Finally I found a door and the animal entered a passage. I closed the door with the feeling that the dog was trapped in the passage.

The patient's associations to the dream: [*Color:*] A glass pitcher I bought for my mother on her 25th anniversary—a rather ugly china thing in the shape of a parrot or a pelican. It was bright orange, yellow, and black. A poster by Toulouse-Lautrec showing a woman (?) in black tights with an orange and yellow background.

[*Yellow backdrop:*] yellow vaginal discharge—[trichinomal] diarrhea.

[*Black bridge:*] Like a woman in black drawers bending over— black pubic hair and hair around the anus. My mother showing me a pimple near her anus [An actual childhood experience].

[*Peiping:*] Peking—peeking.

[*China houses and figurines:*] a colored illustration from a fairy tale about a land made of china showing a man standing on his head, legs apart and waving in the air. This man was a clown, always getting cracked and being mended. Orange, yellow, and black were among the colors in the illustration.

[*Dog mountain lion:*] Balzac's *A Passion in the Desert* wherein the love of a man and a lioness is described [follows an association to an element in the dream, alluding to the name of the dreamer]. Rousseau's painting of a lion and a black woman (man). (Colors here too.) Intercourse from the rear as in animals.

[*Dog trapped in the passage:*] Penis trapped dogs stuck together after intercourse.

Analytic Comment: The patient had experienced frequent derealizations in puberty after masturbation. In the present instance, the derealization is confined to his dream: the locale lacks the third dimension; it resembles, therefore, a setting on the stage.

The first association is to a day residue; but it alludes to the mother, as does the fantasy of the cloaca. The association to the "black bridge" and "Peiping" concern actual scoptophilic childhood experiences with his psychotic mother. The last two associations of coitus *a tergo* between animals or a fictitious man with an animal are evasive. I am sorry to say I did not date these notes but I imagine they were written before amnesia removal had informed us that the patient had in puberty twice been seduced to this performance by his widowed mother while sharing her bed.

This brings one back to the beginning of the associations: he has transferred the mother upon his wife, fantasies an emission into the cloaca—unconsciously the maternal anus—and, although he can produce turgor (erection-ejaculation) and perceive it proprioceptively, the organ does not enter the pleasure-physiologic body ego. Its failure to become pleasure-physiologic —a defense against the commission of incest—in projection upon the hallucinated environment may have caused the derealization in his dream.

One can of course speculate about an overdetermination of the lack of depth dimension, in the light of Abraham's classic paper on scoptophilia (1913). Abraham, who had the finest "analytic ear," noticed that patients with photophobia or hypochondriacal fear for their eyes, never spoke of them in the plural but always as "the" eye. He knew that the eye was a bisexual symbol and cogently explained that " 'The' eye is a substitute for an organ which exists only in the singular" (p. 182), and that displacement upward is responsible. If one were justified in considering the suppression of the genital turgor or, as the case may be, the elimination of the genital from the pleasure-physiologic body ego as castration punishment for incest, one could imagine a displacement of it, as in the Oedipus myth, upon the eye. The latter would then become blind, as did Oedipus. This would leave *only the other eye*, which without its partner cannot reflect depth dimension. A trend of thought such as this is harmless as long as one remains aware that it is no more than pure speculation.

Needless to state that the failure of men and women to experience pleasure when ejaculating is an enigma so far not resolved. I have no idea, and I have never read that anyone else has one, of the mechanism that deprives the proprioception of the sexual act of its pleasure. Nevertheless, I must enlarge upon the explanation of the lack of depth dimension, set forth above, to the extent of including, besides the absence of turgor, the case of those individuals who can produce and perceive it but fail in its pleasure-physiologic proprioception.

I seize the opportunity to contrast the clinical pictures drawn above with a variant of derealization that cannot truly be called one but certainly resembles it. It is an exceptional state accompanied by a hypnotic evasion of a young college girl who was undoubtedly schizophrenic.

Example #29: The patient had recently been exposed to a series of traumatic experiences, the first of which was a nightmare, reactive to her mother's absence and her sleeping alone in the apartment with her father. In between the several parts of the dream (which need not be transcribed here), a somnambulistic episode actually landed her in the father's bed. The second trauma was a protracted "heavy petting" in front of her on the part of her brother and his fiancée. After the brother had left, the two girls were alone and her future sister-in-law openly masturbated in front of the patient through her pyjamas in order to rid herself of the accumulated excitation. While so doing she addressed the patient; but her words were soon forgotten, and the patient tried to maintain that the girl merely scratched herself because of an itch. The third trauma was a gratuitous talk with her married aunt, enlightening her about "coitus infantum," the quality of a sexual feeling, the experience of orgasm, etc. This had occurred about a week before the session under consideration, as had the nightmare; it is not clear whether the conversation followed or preceded the dream. All the traumata share the theme of incest; the last two allude specifically to brother-sister incest which actually belonged to the history of the patient. The scene between brother and fiancée preceded the session by three days, and the onset of the patient's menstruation by one. She felt the onset, but was at first afraid to look; upon coming home she did look and saw blood. This made her fear a return of the nightmare which, however, proved groundless; she slept well and remembered no dream.

Toward the end of the session she described the exceptional state:

> Things are not the same. Everything looks a little morbid. Everything has an emotional meaning to it. The houses, the water tank, the window. [This refers to my window and her favorite view out of it.] It is like a warm current from the rush of the blood down my vagina. It is raining. [One can actually see rain thru the window.] It feels like secretion, secreting blood. [She asks me if one can say that about blood.] Everything is different. That is why it feels as though I were partly unconscious [the hypnotic evasion]. Everything is changed. The whole scenery, not only the outside. [She means not only what is outside the window but the total environment.] For instance the lamp [at the foot of the couch] was always a lamp. Now it is still a lamp, but it looks just a little bit funny. . . . like in the pictures of painters [she gropes for their group name] who paint everything with a mood to it.

It is obvious that the traumatic experiences precipitated a strong arousal, which, because of the (preconscious) incestuous fantasies that both provoked and maintained it, had to be completely suppressed. It appeared instead during her session, although, in consequence of its projection, in an altered form attached to elements of the object world, and in an "exceptional state." What makes her report so significant is for one thing her direct description of the projection by equating the rain with her menstrual flow; and for another her characterizing the object world as "morbid," which in view of the context reported above, can only mean "incestuous." Since the states of alienation serve as defense against the recall of past (repressed) traumata, the patient employs what would appear to be a variant of a derealization: the usual quality "unreal" becomes "mood" in projection, and her own physiologic condition, the onset of which had made her fear a return of her nightmare (cf. I, 216–222), finds its counterpart in part of the environment.

In concluding, when I look critically over my notes I become aware of a lack of more clinical observations of the kind introducing this section, where the derealization does not apply to the whole object world but selectively to one element in it. I find merely a brief notation referring to the case of a sexually anaesthetic male patient whose derealization concerned "more often certain persons on the street; in one instance of an unconscious cloacal fantasy, isolatedly, a trash can." At the time I made no notes in comment. And now memory serves me ill. For a person such as he, passersby on the street (= intercourse—Freud) could well necessitate the defense states of alienation offer. I do not recall the details for his derealization of a "trash can," although overtly its appearance in a cloacal fantasy—a (phallic) container for cast-off (not owned) material—is reasonable enough.

That is really all I have to offer, because the two occasions on which I have personally experienced a brief derealization are, as far as I can see, fairly uninstructive. The instances occurred years apart, and at the time of both of them I was leading a normal sexual life. I shall nevertheless briefly report them.

I was a young man, spending a brief vacation on an island in the Atlantic whose southern shore was separated from the mainland by an expanse of tidewater. I visited that shore only once at low ebb on a heavily overcast day. The sky close above the mudflats was a sight new to me and felt oppressive. It was there that I experienced a general derealization which ended promptly with my return from that shore.

Much later I went for a walk with a friend, and we entered a narrow street flanked by small, identical houses. I do not recall whether or not the street was a "dead end." There again I experienced a derealization, terminating as soon as we left that street.

On both occasions the derealization concerned the whole environment, and at the time of neither of them was I in analysis. I do not therefore have any comment upon them besides pointing to their difference from the derealizations I observed in my patients. When the whole environment is concerned, the patient carries his derealization with him wherever he goes. In the two instances I experienced myself, that was not so: the state was dependent upon one specific environment, and I could shed the derealization promptly upon leaving.

B. FANTASY AND DELUSION: THE INFLUENCE OF EROGENEITY
   UPON THOUGHT

In considering the influence of erogeneity upon thought, it appears to me to be much more far-reaching than is generally acknowledged and as shown by the few clinical examples in my possession. I offer them, as I have said elsewhere under similar circumstances, more as a stimulus to future workers than because they are definitive in themselves.

With regard to that purest and strictest form of thought, mathematical thought, I am of course not competent to judge. I can only say that the more disciplined thought is, the more *independent* it certainly is from the influence of erogenic stimulation. Absence of discipline where it should be present is exemplified by that arch-Freudian, Shakespeare, in the classic berating of the Tribunes by the patrician, Menenius Agrippa in *Coriolanus.*

Holding office as magistrates and therefore supposed to exhibit disciplined juridical thought, they are not only slow-witted but their thought is actually not much more than a product of anal-erotic (sadomasochistic) stimulation. Menenius's tirade against them is a small masterpiece of epitomization:

> MENENIUS: ". . . You weare out a good wholesome Forenoone, in hearing a cause betweene an Orendge [orange] wife, and a Forset-[Faucet-] seller, and then rejourne the Controversie of three-pence to a second day of Audience. When you are hearing a matter betweene party and party, *if you chaunce to bee pinch'd with the Collicke, you make faces like Mummers, set up the bloodie Flagge against all Patience, and, in roaring for a*

Chamber-pot, dismisse the Controversie bleeding, the more intangled by your hearing: All the peace you make in their Cause, is calling both the parties knaves . . . [Italics mine.] (II, i).

The first, nonitalicized, part of the speech depicts bureaucracy as it still is and probably will be forever: a whole forenoon wasted on a petty dispute, and not even then resolved but adjourned for another hearing. The second, the italicized part, shows the influence of (regressive) erogeneity upon thought and refers to what can only be termed an exceptional state, not only by describing the protagonist's changed appearance as having "faces like mummers" (i.e., "masqueraders, making . . . moves with the mouth, making visages and foolish faces" [Foster, 1908]), but alluding to the projection described in derealization through the ingenius ambiguity "and . . . dismiss the controversic bleeding," a poetic "equivocation" as to which is bleeding, the magistrate or the dispute he was to settle.

1. *Fantasy*

The example to follow afforded me an unusual opportunity to study the influence of sexual excitation in one unmarried female caused by the stimulation of *different* erogenic zones upon *different* fantasies accompanying her masturbation. That such a detailed example is from a woman patient is not surprising, the sexual apparatus of a woman being peculiarly suited for breaking down into phases and concomitant observation of stages of excitation. It impressed me sufficiently at the time to make detailed notes after her session.

The patient was psychotic, but one who had made a good adjustment to reality, holding down a responsible administrative post. The record is given more or less as made at the time.

Example #30: The patient had lately made some progress: less compulsive, she had, for example, discontinued making a "work list" for her Sundays. In a Monday session she reported how she had enjoyed her newly gained freedom: did some telephoning, ate when she pleased, etc. In between the calls, a *New Yorker* story titled "Incest" caught her attention and she "got lost in it." Later she had a drink and was answering the first letter from her recently departed woman friend and sexual partner—a letter containing an invitation. While doing so, she interrupted herself, lay down, and enjoyed an extensive masturbation which, while reporting it, she called the "best ever."

The erogenic occurrence can reasonably and naturally be divided into the following four phases:

(a) Beginning of masturbation (clitoris).
(b) Insertion of finger into vagina and vaginal stimulation.
(c) Preorgastic phase.
(d) Orgasm with spontaneous emphasis on the "spot."

Each of these phases was accompanied by a more or less abortive conscious or preconscious fantasy, each of a different kind. What had been preconscious or already repressed I could reconstruct in two instances and thus obtain confirmation. I shall hereinafter render the patient's thought under the heading of each phase and append my comment.

(a) *Beginning of masturbation* (clitoris): Thought about X. (woman partner) lying in bed with her in the morning, with more or less mutual circular clitoris stimulation. X. was capable of an inhibited orgasm with subsequent crying; my patient was not.

Lately X.'s abysmal selfishness and complete disregard for patient or anyone else—in repetition of a totally conscienceless psychotic mother—came into focus in the analysis and was pointed out. This fact might add to the obvious explanation (repetition) of why X. had to be discarded in the fantasy after Phase 1.

(b) *Insertion of finger into the vagina and vaginal stimulation:* She thought of Mr. Y. (a married man). He is her banker, and there was lately a good deal of circumstantial correspondence with him, not without an anti-Semitic touch. She once signed her first name alone, and he answered in the same way. The whole relation resembles her fatuous and abortive "love affairs," which are no affairs at all. He had lately written that if he were to invest he had to know all she owned for the sake of diversification, etc; but she was reluctant to inform him completely. The fantasy itself was vague and evidently poor in content. She just "thought of him."

Interpretation: As I listened to these associations, several features blended into a whole. Dominant of course, was the symbolism of money through feces. The unusually compulsive patient's original preoccupation with her constipation, dating from childhood, agreed with this; and the Jew to the anti-Semite is "dirty." There was, finally, a certain "labyrinthian" (= intestinal—Freud) character to the whole correspondence between her and the banker. All this taken together led me to interpret: "There must have been some anal sensations while inserting the finger into the vagina." She confirmed this by remembering the thought accompanying the insertion, "It is awfully close to the anus."

(c) *Preorgastic phase:* Patient thought about Z., the man she really loves, and how (for reasons that need not here be detailed) she will never have him. She can only "have him in another world."

Interpretation: I recall to myself that she had previously told me that Z. looks exactly like a certain person who had seduced her in childhood and whom, the analysis could establish beyond any doubt, stood in the past, as Z. does in the present, for her father. The "other world," besides fitting the preorgastic state, to my ear alludes to her mother, who had been a clitorally sensitive but vaginally insensitive "Christian Scientist" and had entertained incestuous relations (clitoris masturbation) with the patient when the latter was both a child and adult.

These results of previous amnesia removal support the obvious interpretation: she is transported into "another world" through the preorgastic excitation. I took this occasion to explain to her in popular terms what the psychiatrist calls the "psychic impotence" and the concomitant "inability to love"

on the part of the unhappy Z. He had to put in the place normally occupied by a "love object," his (inanimate) "house" in
which he took inordinate pride (he lives alone—he was always
going to show his house to the patient but never did).

(d) *Orgasm with spontaneous emphasis on "the spot." Interpretation:* The patient described this masturbation as the first complete one
and emphasized spontaneously the location of the orgastic feeling. It
is easily recognizable as the "spot," comprising the fornices and the
womb (I, 212). She reported that while orgastic she thought of the
analyst but that this fantasy had no further content.

Here again two elements blended in my mind. For one thing,
the symbolism of the "house" in the preceding paragraph represents the *Mutterleib,* which is identical with the "spot" (I,
251–252). For another, the fact that the patient, seeing no fresh
flowers recently in the office foyer, concluded that my wife had
left me and had, implicitly, recommended herself for the job.
(This had been interpreted at the time.) I was consequently led
to the interpretation that she could not merely have thought of
the analyst but must have had the fantasy of living with him in
a house.

This interpretation had a most astonishing effect, for it
prompted the patient to undo a recent repression: Yes, she had
that fantasy at the time; she had even called herself "unfaithful" to Z. because in the fantasy he was dead, which made it
possible for the analyst and herself to live in *his* house.

Needless to add that my report is without purpose if it
merely describes another series of masturbation fantasies, of
which every analyst hears so many, or relays some interpretations which any analyst with a modicum of experience would
make. I have included it for one reason only: the *selectivity*
recognizable in it, with respect to the hold of erogeneity over
thinking. Here, excitation of *every single part of the sexual apparatus exercises separately a particular influence upon thought.*
In other words, as the patient's erogeneity moved from peri-
phery to center, so moved her fantasies, step by step, toward

the center of her present emotional involvement, the relation with the transference object.

Example #31: This example is the obverse of the preceding one: in it, erogeneity was arrested because of the specific turn of thought it would have given rise to, had it been allowed to develop.

The female patient became aroused, on the eve of the session, lay down on her stomach, and began to masturbate, finding the vulva well moistened. Nevertheless she could do no more than begin, because far from reaching a climax her activity "petered out" and she went to sleep. In reporting her fantasy she had to overcome a great resistance: she had imagined being licked by a dog.

Before the session began, the door to the foyer was open, and I had not as yet entered the foyer, but the patient experienced a (psychotic) hallucination: she thought she saw me standing in the foyer and watching her. Later, while associating to the masturbation fantasy, much about dogs was remembered and reremembered. It turned out that the patient, a rather prim spinster, at two different ages—in the phallic phase and "later"—had dogs perform cunnilingus on her. In her early twenties she felt strongly aroused upon seeing the erection of a large dog belonging to friends. At this point in her associations she became sexually excited and had the fantasy of the analyst's taking the place of the dog.

Thus, both the recent hallucination and the discontinuation of her masturbation the evening before became understandable. At the place in the foyer where she "saw" me, actually stood a low walnut "bachelor's chest" whose height was that of a big dog. *My watching her,* already lying down on the couch, *instead of her watching the dog's erection,* is a reversal caused, one may safely assume, by the indestructible, unconscious fantasy of the female having a penis that can be watched. Her masturbation of the previous evening had to be discontinued because had it been allowed to go on, erogeneity (as her present associations clearly showed), in the course of increasing arousal, would have compelled the thought of the analyst's replacing the dog in the performance of cunnilingus. This fantasy represented, it would later be revealed, a transference upon the analyst of the mother, who had actually abused the patient in like fashion as a child. Now, due to repression, neither the fantasy nor its origin were allowed to become conscious. Because a strong erogeneic excitation would have influenced thought to take a turn in the direction of the fantasy, the stimulation had to be discontinued.

Nevertheless, one thing did appear from repression that hour: As the dog symbolizes the anal-sadistic partial subject (cf. Chapter One, Section II, above), it will therefore be no surprise to the reader that at the end of the above session the patient reported *for the first time* that her mother, evidently possessed by the fantasy of the cloaca, called "the whole region," as my patient put it, one's "toilet." She often admonished her child: "Wash your toilet," "Take your hand away from your toilet," etc. My patient considered this aberrational term idiomatic and was greatly astonished that I had never heard it before. On questioning, however, she could not remember hearing it from anyone but her mother.

2. *Delusion*

Living in the country limits my access to libraries; yet memory tells me that at least part of what will be described in this subsection as long ago been published by van Ophuijsen, Stärcke, and others in the old *Jahrbuch* and *International Zeitschrift für Psychoanalysis.* Mine may be merely an enlargement and—though systematic—an incomplete one at that.

Concentrating, if my memory serves me, upon the delusion of the psychotic afflicted with paranoia persecutoria, they made what amounts to the statement that the delusory patient feels in his rectum the penis of the man persecuting him. We can enlarge upon this observation today because we know that the delusion is not confined to the psychotic. This has been more recently stressed by Arlow (1949), who also states that fantasies of persecution are observable in nonpsychotics. I recall long ago having tried to impress this upon students, telling them that the compulsive neurotic is full of delusions which may never be found unless one has learned to expect them.

Abraham (1913) testifies to the fact that in the analysis of a young philosopher he found himself confronted with "the identification of the birth and the act of defaecation, and thus to an equation of the products of the brain (thoughts) and those of the bowels" (p. 211). No wonder, therefore, that his patient insisted on forming "a visual image of how thoughts arose in the brain and how they 'come out' of it" (ibid). I am doing an injustice to Abraham's paper, which in range and profundity equals certain papers by Freud, by restricting myself to quoting no more than this passage. It is pertinent to the subject because it establishes a connection between the erogeneity of the rectum and thought.

To complete the theoretical foundation for the clinical observations to follow, I must mention Freud's last formulation about the delusion (1937b, p. 267) insuperable in its basic simplicity and in the conviction which it imparts to the reader. Studying it, you feel that another great riddle is solved. The apparent complication of Freud's formula is merely stylistic; I shall therefore accommodate the reader by undoing it and paraphrase rather than quote: On the face of it the content of the delusion is untrue. That, however, is valid only for the present; in the past it was true and that *past truthfulness contributes to the maintenance of the unshakeable conviction of the delusory individual in the correctness of his delusion.* But the text of the delusion has in the process of its "translation" from the past to the present suffered distortions which become understandable when one is able to ascribe them in part to the "buoyancy" of the repressed unconscious and in part to the resistances against the latter's becoming conscious at all.

This much is general knowledge; there would be no point in illustrating it with clinical observations. My examples are meant to support one small further step: *rectal* stimulation, present or reverberative of one in the recent past, *either felt or suppressed, may give rise to a delusion in the neurotic and precipitate an attack of it or alter its form in the psychotic.*

Example #32: The patient (Example #16 in the hypnosis section), whose seduction to passive sodomy was sponsored by his mother but of course executed by a man, and was described as occurring in a hypnotic state induced by the eight-year-old boy's fixing his gaze first on the eyes, subsequently on the lubricated and therefore "shiny" penis of his seducer. I do not feel that I owe this unknown criminal the complete anonymity afforded him in my previous report, and I shall therefore add that he was a physician, because only this detail explains *the delusion in the transference* that possessed the patient when, by now a young man, he entered his analytic treatment.

He began by expressing his conviction that the analyst was a confirmed homosexual who had "a whole stableful of young men" under the guise of having them as his patients, and who were ready to "do his bidding." This was both fear and wish: if the analyst bore the responsibility, the present prospect of the act would be as attractive as had been its execution in the past.

Everyone knows, of course, that eight is too advanced an age for the foundation of a later delusion; but the word "stable," allusive to horses and thus symbolic of the incest object, *did not fail* in time to "recall" the earliest (around age two) digital penetrations of the rectum by the (phallic) psychotic mother. At the same time the plurality of the compound noun "stableful" testifies to the fact that the mother did not exploit him alone, but also his siblings and probably other children.

I do not know whether this example is convincing, because it requires so much qualification. For one thing none of the data given above were conscious at the time; they became so only step by step in the course of arduous analytic work. For another thing the example involves not only transference but projection—making the analyst instead of himself subject of rectal excitation; and it was the projection that prevented the patient from feeling the erogenic stimulation precipitating his delusion. I shall therefore follow it with a simpler one from a later phase of the analysis of the same patient.

Example #32 (continued): The following is simply a transcript of my notes on a session, slightly revised and extended.

It is the second hour after my 10-day vacation subsequent to a virus infection. Patient is in the grip of a strong desire for passive sodomy and consequently has been impotent with a woman. He is disappointed because he had expected that the previous hour which had merely shown how many things were still not understood—a fact which I had remarked on—would have had therapeutic effect. Very positive transference feeling, however, due to my return.

Negative transference is split off in the following episode: He enters the apartment house hall, finds an older man standing there while he (the patient) announces himself on the interphone. The man ("Is he a doctor?") gives him an admiring glance which he considers an expression of envy about his youth and good looks. Upon entering the elevator the man gestures for him to go first, which makes my patient furious because he feels he is being treated like a woman. (Actually the man was getting out at the fourth floor, and my office was on the sixth, which is the rational explanation.)

I assume that the relation to me is essentially a nonsexual affection because the erogeneity is suppressed. The man who actually shows him that he is "a woman" is, however, myself and not the stranger. The reason for my assumption is that I observe, and tell him so at the end of the hour, that my vacation facilitated his completely re-repressing the two early memories concerning anal and rectal stimulation by the mother. With utter surprise he confirms this.

He compares me favorably with an ignorant colleague of mine, himself adding that this comparison is silly. The reason: the colleague, as I learned only later, coerces his patients and I do not. It is again the anal and *rectal excitation,* this time not projected and therefore unperceived, *that renders the thought paranoid* with reference to the man in the hall.

Example #33: A dramatic illustration of the precipitation of a paranoiac attack in a psychotic through the reverberations of a recent rectal stimulation. The patient had eventually relinquished her paranoiac behavior, and we had established a workable relation. Suddenly she relapsed. The relapse occurred during the course of an apparently undistinguished analytic session in response to a merely descriptive remark demonstrating her morbid bondage to a certain woman: I will not listen to her, will not give her a chance to tell me what she is dying to tell; I interrupt all the time. Presenting her quickly and elaborately with the reality, explaining the nature and purpose of "working through" had no effect whatsoever. She unendingly repeated her delusory accusations. If, having finished a comment, I was silent and waited for associations, she only identified with me by being silent herself. I obtained no more than her delusory rationalization: what is the use of talking, I will only "interrupt" her and not let her speak. The situation appeared hopeless; I felt driven into a corner from which there was no escape. Finally, perhaps counteridentifying with her as she had been before the attack, I said what came to *my* mind: "Now you are in the situation of the child who will not defecate for her mother. She can be made to sit there, but she cannot be made to perform." She: "That is exactly what happened to me this morning." Followed the description of an urge for a bowel movement and a very painful constipation which gave way only after considerable time. I interpret that she evidently now repeats with herself her performance as a child with her mother ("ego split").

It is difficult to describe the effect of this interpretation. So precipitate was it that the whole paranoia appeared shrugged off like a garment. She instantly became reasonable and could be worked with. It was as though what had gone on before had never happened and did not therefore leave so much as a trace.

My trite remark about mother and child was merely expressive of my despair; it was certainly not meant to be an interpretation. Yet it worked as one *because it made conscious*, and therefore deprived of effect, *the aftermath of the rectal overstimulation that*, unknown to me, *had precipitated the paranoid attack*.

Example #34: An illustration of the influence of rectal stimulation upon the form of paranoiac [delusory] thought. I have seen this only once and failed to record it; I must therefore report it from memory. It happened long ago, but my recall of the episode is in all the essentials quite vivid.

A psychotic male patient was ruminating about a conspiracy between his wife and her lover to kill him. It was true that a man friend of the patient was having an affair with his wife; I do not recall their even trying to keep it from him. They might poison him, continued the rumination. In view of the circumstances, this seemed absurd; I was firmly convinced that it had no basis in fact. Suddenly he complained of discomfort in his rectum—I believe a somewhat painful cramp (conversion), but I am not certain of the wording of his complaint. Promptly thereafter the form of his paranoiac thought appeared altered.

To be exact, it had changed in two respects: what had been verbal thought now became visual thought, and what had been a merely general rumination now became a specific fact, furnished with all necessary detail. Clinically it is not easy to describe the combined effect of these two changes. He did not hallucinate, but he saw before his mind's eye, after the fashion in which a normal individual might perhaps recall an impressive scene from a play or a moving picture, exactly how it would happen. He would be invited to have coffee with the pair in a certain room of his own house; his wife would at a specific point of the proceedings surreptitiously put a specific poison into his cup while they were talking about a topic of the day, which he named. It might be of note that his associations were not, either before or after the change, accompanied by an appropriate affect.

The episode reported here illustrates Freud's fundamental distinction (1923a) between *verbal thinking* where thought uses "verbal [auditory] residues" and *visual thinking* where "optical mnemic residues" are employed (pp. 20–21). It differs from Freud's description of visual thinking in only one single point: it does not lack but *includes* "the relations between the various elements of this concrete subject-matter, which is what specially characterizes thoughts," it is not, in other words, limited to making "conscious . . . only the concrete subject-matter of the thought" (p. 21). In the case of delusory thought this apparent difference is obliterated. Textually it appears because the formulation was made by Freud in 1923, long before he was ready to admit delusion in dreams as he did at the end of his long life[8] when (1940) they also are not restricted to the concrete material of thought but express as well the "relations . . . which . . . specially characterize thoughts."

---

[8] "A dream then is a psychosis with all the absurdities, delusions and illusions of a psychosis . . ." (1940, p. 172).

III. SOME EXCEPTIONAL STATES WITHOUT NAME

There exist an indefinite number of other exceptional states. However, they are not only nameless but, what is worse, entirely ununderstood. I shall mention three, of which the analyst is familiar with two.

In order to associate freely and in order to listen with free-floating attention one has to enter a state that may not be regressive but is surely exceptional. Introspection tells the analyst that he is in a condition unlike the ordinary one maintained during the rest of the day. And as for the patient—I recall from my own last analysis how, for example, on the way to a session I would occasionally be preoccupied with something that I was certain would come up in my associations. Yet it did not. Something in the "exceptional state" of free association shut off matter that in my usual state of mind would have reappeared, as it did, indeed, after the hour. Introspection convinced me that its omission was not, however, due to resistance.

It might be instructive to oppose to these states that of extreme concentration, which I believed for a while to be one of them until I recognized my mistake. *Concentration* is not one of these nameless exceptional states and allows, therefore, a degree of theoretical understanding. It is one of "economy": in order to concentrate, that is, to overcathect one activity—for example, my present expository writing—I have to borrow quantities of cathexis by decathecting the better part of the object world. Hence, when I end my extreme concentration I have the somewhat strange experience of an "emerging" of the environment consequent to its recathexis.

Another exceptional state evidently is that of *creation*. The most succinct description of it that I have read stems from a painter. Without giving his source, Kris (1952) quotes Picasso as having said: *"Le dessin c'est une espèce d'hypnotisme; on regarde le modèle tellement qu'il s'assoit sur le papier."* ("Drawing ['design'] is a kind of hypnosis; one so looks at the model that it seats itself on the paper.") *"Kind of hypnosis"* I would read as meaning "an exceptional, somewhat regressive state." The rest is self-explanatory.

Many years later in an interview (Gauthier, 1968), Picasso enlarges upon his "exceptional state": ". . . For me, creation first starts with contemplation, and I need long, idle hours of meditation. It is then that I work most. I look at flies, at flowers, at leaves and trees around me. I let my mind drift at ease, just like a boat in the current. Sooner or later, it is caught by something. It gets precise. It takes shape. You see, if I were interrupted then, weeks of work might be wasted. When future schemes are coming to me, are offered to me through the generosity of mother nature—for all comes from there, and there is no abstraction—my next painting motive is decided." Unfortunately no one, not even a Picasso, can go beyond a description.

He concludes: "Observation is the most vital part of my life, but not any sort of observation. I have trained myself to let nothing pass by: 'One never pays enough attention,' Cézanne used to say, and I have made his word mine. . . ."

PART II

NOTES ON TECHNIQUE

NOTES ON TECHNIQUE

The three sections to follow are disparate. I have been writing for analysts only, and my purpose is not didactic: all three monographs of the *Psychoanalytic Series* are devoted to original findings. Since, however, as I have said before, in a natural science results are dependent upon method, one must account for method before stating results. In Volume I that obligation was discharged simply; I was, with one exception, following the psychoanalytic method laid down by Freud. The exception: a refusal to accept Freud's favoring of fantasy over memory and it corollary—the denial of the ambulatory psychosis in one's patients' past. I also went to some pains to let my reader know that in the period in which psychoanalysis now finds itself entering upon, as from time to time happens to all natural sciences, that is, a period of research on special problems, I was well aware of the methodological difficulties to be encountered.

Results of our research are of necessity discrepant. One cannot "pursue" a subject, bend material to one's interest, let alone experiment with it. One has to take what each patient presents and subordinate one's own interests to his needs. Chance alone dictates what grist comes to the mill.

In this section I attempt to clarify some points I felt merited it. On the Analytic Relation discusses the transference as a *resistance* of the patient, certain resistances of the analyst, as well as what I have called a necessity for *any* analytic work: the gradual revival or establishment of two "infantile" traits. The second section deals with particulars about amnesia removal, that being the road one must travel. No one with any experience can say it is a "royal" one. As I have confessed earlier, it was a long time after graduation before I could obtain it for the patient's earliest years. The title of the last section, Notes on The Diagnosis And Treatment of The Ambulatory Psychotic, is self-explanatory.

349

CHAPTER FIVE

ON THE ANALYTIC RELATION

For a beginning it may suffice to state that the analyst has to earn the patient's respect and affection. The latter may in certain individuals of either sex at times become carnal and therefore in the long run unworkable. It is the responsibility of the analyst, not the patient, to see to it that the analysis is conducted in what Freud has called a state of abstinence. The analysis and eventually the abolishment of a sexual attachment to the analyst is but a part of this abstinence. If he fails, as he will with certain psychotics, he will be unable to help his patient.

The goal is to establish a *workable* analytic relation. The illustration to be given below exemplifies, of course, other points also. But it is, I think, a particularly telling one for the employment of the "analytic eye" and the "analytic ear" to clarify a situation to the patient and then be free to invoke the abstinence rule. The abrupt change in the course of the analysis came about as a direct consequence of the change in the analytic relation.

Example #1: One of my patients in the beginning of her analysis settled for an exaggeratedly conventional relation to me which would have precluded the consummation of any phase of an analysis, let alone her associating freely enough to eventually effect the removal of an amnesia. To be specific: the door to my office gave onto a small gallery, from which two steps led down to the main part of the room with the couch in it. She had the habit of making a veritable stage entrance, greeting me with an affected tinge to her voice as though the analysis were a social occasion. Apprehending this and recognizing that it was her way of defensively keeping her distance are, I suppose, a matter of the "analytic eye" and the "analytic ear." If one avoids the mistake of thinking that what appears obvious is also close to the patient's consciousness, one finds, after having waited patiently, a suitable time for demonstrating and interpreting such behavior convincingly and without offending the patient. This particular one understood promptly. That, she admitted, was no way of behaving toward someone she called a "friend," someone devoted to helping her in abolishing her complaints.

Whereupon memories suddenly began to appear. The first of these had never really been repressed. It told of her strong sexual excitement while standing in the bathtub and watching her mother preparing soapsuds for the purpose of treating the child to a course of most enjoyable genital stimulation. The next memory is an instructive example of amnesia removal in two respects. It had for one thing actually been repressed and in typical fashion escaped only gradually and in fragments. For another thing, one of the fragments precipitated, before all of them could be remembered and put together, a hypnotic evasion.

Here is the story: The mother beckoned to her in the morning after the father had left for his office; this excited the child. Gradually it became a beckoning to join her in the bathroom.

When I quoted her words to the patient in the course of a subsequent hour, she agreed to having spoken of the mother's beckoning and of her own excitement, but *denied* that the beckoning had anything to do with the bathroom. This, she assured me, was an invention of mine. Fortunately I was by then possessed of two data: (1) if a person evades into hypnosis on the outside he will do so, sooner or later, in the session; and (2) *if a patient is oblivious of an association representing a fragment in a coherent series of events*, he has been in hypnotic evasion when he produced the association. The patient discussed here had been, previous to her analysis unknowingly and during it knowingly, hypnotic in certain typical situations. One of these had become the subway ride to and from the analyst's office (see Chapter Four, Example #1). I therefore opposed the abstinence rule to her resistance, and she agreed to remain awake at all costs on her way home. The result: she became orgastic twice during one single ride. I would learn in time, as I reported earlier, that this was the effect of three different but synergistic causes: "motion pleasure" (*Bewegungslust* [Freud]), genital vestibular stimulation through the vibration of the car, and a (at that time still unconscious) sexual fantasy about some female passenger opposite her who must, however, be sitting with slightly spread legs.

Thus the resistance to recall was overcome and the path for further fragments coming out of amnesia freed. The child had joined the mother in the bathroom, masturbated her on the toilet until the mother achieved a climax followed by urination. (The patient had been *enuretic* throughout the better part of her childhood and as an adult had appropriated masturbatory climactic urination.)

No such memory could have come out of amnesia had either the patient's relation to the analyst remained as described above, or had the subway hypnosis been allowed to continue.

ON THE ROLE OF THE TRANSFERENCE IN PSYCHOANALYTIC TREATMENT

"*. . . thorough analysis of the transference situation is of special importance. What then remains of the transference may, indeed should, have the character of a cordial human relationship.*"

(FREUD: LETTER OF 10/22/27 TO DR. PFISTER)

THE TRANSFERENCE: A RESISTANCE

It was, of course, long ago that Freud discovered that the parents, the earliest objects of the child's sexual and aggressive drives, are in the course of his treatment transferred upon the analyst. He drew two main conclusions from his discovery, one theoretical and the other technical. The first amounts to the opinion that the analyst works with the patient's compliance, "deeply rooted in the unconscious parent complex"; the second that he should leave the transference uninterpreted so long as it is not about to become a resistance.

His discovery needs no exemplification; any beginner can easily satisfy himself through the simplest clinical observations that the transference exists. It is different with Freud's conclusions. For they stand or fall—although he never knew it—with his great denial, quoted and commented on above (Chapter Three). If the *"horrible perverse details"* (Freud's own words) reported *are but fantasies,* there is room in the neurotic's past for good parents whom the child loved and to whom he was grateful. Their transference upon the analyst could in the main only facilitate his difficult work.

If, however, the "horrible perverse" details are *memories* of the child's sufferings at the hands of a "horrible perverse" (psychotic) parent, *the transference of the latter upon the analyst cannot but be the greatest obstacle to the work,* regardless of whether or not he is cognizant of its presence. And, as I have stated earlier, most of one's patients suffering from a severe neurosis have been the victims of such parents. As to its form, the transference may be direct or indirect, that is, defensive. It is thus, for example, that a sexual mother-transference of a psychotic woman may make the patient either nymphomaniac or paranoiac. Two examples, the first a simple one; the second extremely complicated and requiring a good deal of knowledge and assiduity for its study:

Example #2: A neurotic patient had entered analysis on account of an abysmal compulsive depression. For a long, long time her analysis remained unsatisfactory, until finally an apparently accidental event wrought a change. I shall probably not raise my stock with the reader by confessing candidly that I could not throughout her treatment understand why this should have changed her relation to me. The change became intelligible to me only while writing the present chapter.

The patient had feared meeting a certain man, with whom she had made a luncheon appointment in a restaurant always crowded at noon. (I have forgotten what compelled her to make the appointment;

actually it turned out to be not with the man she was afraid of, but with an older benevolent friend who had, however, the same name.) She expected violence from the man. While we talked about this I made the trite remark, "Why don't you get there early and seat yourself where you can watch the door so that you can see him first?" All my previous analytic endeavor to help her had made practically no impression, but it was this remark, which any casual acquaintance could have made, that touched her deeply. She responded with strong emotion, "You *are* on my side, aren't you? You are *for* me." And the analysis took on a new complexion.

I pondered and I continued pondering the reason for the crucial effect of my trivial unanalytic remark and found no answer. The reader, however, may need no more information than that this is the patient (see Chaper Three) who in adolescence was delivered to a psychopathic rapist by her depraved psychotic mother. With my advice I protected her from the allegedly violent man. The two situations actually have little in common, but nevertheless bore sufficient resemblance for the patient to bring out the contrast between her mother's attitude to her and mine. Theoretically, the drastic change in the patient's relation to me caused by my rather trite suggestion allows for only one conclusion: the analysis did not go because the patient's relation to me had been encumbered by an unconscious mother transference of which we had both remained totally unaware. This small episode finally enabled me to live the mother down. The example illustrates, by the way, what has been stated above: *the transference in such cases is harmful to the analytic work*, irrespective of whether or not the analyst knows of its presence.

Example #3: An episode in the analysis of the psychotic patient under consideration in the next example has previously been described (I, 92–96) under the heading, A Typical Re-enactment of the "Weaning Trauma" in the Transference. Both parents were psychotic and were simultaneously transferred upon the analyst, who was consequently for years unable to do any productive work. The father, a literate, apodictic, and irascible man, came from a region whose inhabitants are proverbially proud of their ancestry; one of his forebearers had actually been nationally known. He evidently did not exploit the child sexually in the usual fashion, except for having her sleep close to the parents' bed until she was 10 years old. When he learned of his seven-year-old daughter's sexual exploitation by his wife, he heaped scorn upon the child, and threw her out of the house for the better part of the day. The patient expressed her father transference directly: "You do not listen to me; you interrupt me; you do not let me talk; you even speak like my father; you even use the same words. I know you have only contempt for my profession." This puts the analyst into a situation that is not only unpleasant but might prove futile because he cannot win; if he says something, he "interrupts" the patient; if he says nothing, he either "pays no attention" and "does not listen" to her or "refuses to answer" a question. She repays him in kind—a severe test of his powers of perseverance.

I may appear illogical if I state that such a father transference although really precluding analysis, seems, however, the lesser evil if compared to the transference of the mother. What I became through his transference upon me was not a sexual object but the object of a paranoia. The patient was overtly bisexual. She had at different times entertained relations with two men and two women. Both men were psychotic a fact to which she proved blind; but when one of them became dangerous in the beginning of her treatment, she was willing to take my word for it and to heed my advice by terminating the relation. It took me longer than it probably should have to recognize and to understand the paranoia. In view of her past overtly homosexual experiences, I could not understand why I failed in my efforts to make conscious her preconscious sexual fantasying about women, so prominent in her daily life. I argued to myself: her experiences were certainly conscious and belonged to the recent past. She has told me about them in detail. They could not but have informed her about her proclivity in this respect. Her past activities and her present fantasies are essentially of the same nature. Why then can she not own the latter? I considered the argument cogent until I discovered its flaw: her difficulty lay not in owning the *drives, but in not owning their object, the mother.* Having found that out, I had gained a fulcrum for dealing with the paranoia. The result was twofold: I obtained amnesia removal for some of the mother's sexual exploitations, and the paranoia changed complexion until it became demonstrable and distinct.

These early memories were screened by the recall of later hearing (but not seeing) the mother producing a noisy stream and thinking that this was "obscene." At age seven cunnilingus by the mother; at 14 the mother masturbating, using the daughter's hand and crying out, "You will never leave me, will you!" From then on the daughter shared the mother's bed until the first woman friend eventually took the place of the mother.

In the transference now, greatest obstinacy, violent accusations, and desperation: "Someone else, maybe a woman" would do better by her than I. When she "enters" (sic!) the room—i.e., my office—"something happens" to her, causing agitation and rage.

Nevertheless, I was able to work through all this and to bring the analysis to the point where essential changes relieved the patient of most of her suffering; two years after termination she wrote me a warmly grateful letter. I mention these favorable results only to show that they were obtained not with the help but *in spite of the transference.* If the reader refers to Examples #5 and #6 in the next chapter (Amnesia Removal), he will recognize without difficulty that they could be expanded so as to illustrate the same tenet.

Here Example #3 in the hypnosis sections of Chapter Four can, I think, bear being referred to, since in this instance the mother transference (resistance) took the form of hypnotic evasions. The example reports the patient's fittings at her dressmaker's that make her "drowsy." In her analytic sessions she would not infrequently go into a form of autohypnosis that, went for a long time unrecognized by me as such: an exaggerated shudder of her whole body *(hysteriform myoclonus:* Schilder & Kauders, 1926). This was in response not to what I was saying but merely to the sound of my voice. Both mother transferences, that upon the seamstress and that upon the analyst, made the patient hypnotic.

The seamstress repeats the "passes" originally performed by the mother and, for reasons of her own, the mother's sleepily soothing voice. The analyst, however, does nothing of the kind; he speaks in a natural voice, and the patient is never so much as touched. By what means does he invite the mother transference, which is in all such cases a resistance that in this particular instance takes the form of hypnotic evasion? As I wrote above there is one easy answer. No matter how correctly the analyst acts, because he tries to analyze in a "state of abstinence" (Freud) he cannot forestall either the patient's conscious or unconscious fantasies about him, or the patient's delusory expectations. If the analyst has not so far repeated the mother's behavior, he will. This is obvious. If I state it I do so only in order to make a point: the above explanation is correct, but it does not go far enough. The analyst actually "does" something to the patient that invites the transference upon him of the damaging mother: he offers the patient the opportunity *to abuse the analytic situation for a repetition of the morbid passivity* originally called for in the child by the mother in the course of her exploitations. This is unavoidable; it would be as senseless to blame the analysis for it as it would be to deny the usefulness of the judicial system because it, too, is not foolproof against abuse. In the case of analysis, *all depends on the analyst's recognition of the abuse.*

In such cases when sound prevails over speech, the analysis of essential fragments of the transference are precluded through hypnotic acting out. It is then one's task to demonstrate this to the patient, inducing him to become aware of it introspectively, and to exchange this passivity for genuine free association. This last, against all appearance is an "activity." Only "pseudo-associations"—a term I have coined and mentioned earlier (Chapter Four, Hypnosis, Section 2)—that tell the analyst nothing are "passive." This type of utterance is as meaningless as genuine associations are meaningful; they resemble the latter only superficially. Actually they are no more than chitchat, whose content can be compared to the disjunct, uninformed "small talk" made on certain social occasions. They are symptomatic of a resistance, which is sometimes unmistakably recognizable as a sadistic attitude to the analyst who, a captive audience, is forced to listen to nonsense while being deprived of the opportunity of doing any work. He can counter this form of resistance only with its persistent and comprehensive interpretation. A full awareness of what is transpiring in these cases must be summoned up if the hypnotic evasions are to be abolished.

All in all, having come to know even the limited number of parents described earlier, and having learned of their hate of the child, their victimization of him, and their manifold transgressions and malefactions, it becomes impossible to consider their transference upon the analyst as the *carrier* of the analytic treatment. On the contrary, such can be nothing but an obstacle to the treatment which the analyst has to try to remove. It was explained above why this brings one into contradiction with Freud.

RESISTANCES OF THE ANALYST

In the first chapter of Volume II of this series I discussed certain resistances of the analyst to the analysis he is conducting. One, the denial of the ambulatory psychosis in the patient's past, was discussed at the beginning of Chapter Three, above. Two others are of equal pertinence here.

COUNTERTRANSFERENCE AND COUNTERIDENTIFICATION AS A RESISTANCE

If the patient can employ acting out as a form of resistance, so also at times can the analyst. One form results in either a countertransference[1] or a counteridentification.

When the analyst (counter) transfers upon the patient, he revives his own conflicts. The patient, forced to react to a situation which instead of being *in*trinsic is *ex*trinsic to his past, is in

---

[1] Frequently misunderstood as *the relation* to the patient. It is not. It is a *disturbance* in that relation.

this case in an "accident" not a treatment. Ideally therefore, countertransference should not occur. But it does. The technique for abolishing it becomes evident if the definition is kept in mind. Transference of the patient, when it has become or is about to become a resistance, must be analyzed. So too must countertransference. If the analyst becomes aware of a countertransference phenomenon before the patient has done so, all or most of the necessary self-analysis will be performed outside of the analytic hour. If, however, a symptom has been produced of which the patient is naturally aware, although of course without recognizing it as such, then part of the self-analysis may have to be communicated to the patient.

If the phenomena are more than mild and infrequent (e.g., an occasional parapraxis or a transient unreceptiveness toward certain material, particularly with regard to the patient's transference), the analyst should go back into analysis himself. At this point I should perhaps proffer the consolation given in an earlier communication with regard to our coping as analysts with what Freud has termed the "rock-bottom of all psychological stratification," namely the castration complex. The consolation: from the continuing analysis of our countertransferences we are afforded a singular opportunity for its maximal resolution.

Mild as well as severe countertransference symptoms of course play a prominent role in training analyses where the ability for self-analysis necessary to remove countertransference must be gained.°

Counteridentification has not been treated by Freud. As I

° Editorial note: In Freud's early paper dealing with the countertransference (1910a), he remarks with an acerbity not often encountered that if the analyst isn't successful in his self-analysis of his difficulties with the patient, he "may at once give up any idea of being able to treat patients by analysis" (p. 145). Decades later, almost at the end of his long life, he is, as an editor elsewhere has said, "cautiously appreciative" of both the psychic dangers encountered in practicing analysis and the difficulties in surmounting them. In "Analysis Terminable and Interminable" (1937a), he pauses in his discussion of the demand in the practicing analyst for a comparatively high degree of psychic normality and correct adjustment "to assure the analyst that he has our sincere sympathy in the very exacting demands he has to fulfill. . . . It almost looks," he continues, "as if analysis were the third of those 'impossible' professions in which one can be quite sure beforehand of achieving unsatisfying results. The other two, which have been known much longer, are education and government" (p. 248).

wrote, the analyst's faulty involvement with his patient is that found in *folie à deux*. The identification is mutual: a response of the analyst to the patient's identifying with him, and repetitive in both patient and analyst of an early "constituent" identification; that is, of a structural element in the patient's ego. Regressive as it is, it interferes with the *non*regressive identification, which as "empathy" represents a particular phase of the analyst's work.

THE HYPNOTIC EVASION AS A RESISTANCE OF THE ANALYST

Yet another resistance of the analyst bears discussion at this point. Paralleling what his patient may be doing, but in reverse, the analyst not infrequently evades both the libidinal and aggressive demands of his patient in the countertransference (or his own libidinal or aggressive strivings toward the patient). In so doing he mentally absents himself without being aware of it. He fails to lay hold actively on his analysand's associations, may or may not feel himself becoming hypnotic, and often ends up with having been asleep.

Where the hypnotic evasion exists, it is the task of the training analysis to obtain introspection for it and in the end to abolish it, for it is obvious that whether patient or analyst becomes hypnotic, the analysis suffers essential damage. If this has not been accomplished in his training period, the analyst may use the criteria given in Chapter Four for becoming conscious of his own evasions.

I have heard, since first writing of this resistance, that a substantial number of analysts admit in conversation with colleagues that they "fall asleep" during sessions. They erroneously explain this by saying that their patient "bores" them and are completely unaware of the reason, which on the face of it is quite simple. They themselves "evade," through lapsing into a hypnotic state followed by actual sleep, the material they are unprepared to receive. This, of course, vitiates the patient's communication and "punctures" the analytic procedure to an extent few analyses can withstand.

Personally I have succumbed to this subjective form of resistance in only one analytic treatment. Decades ago, I became drowsy and fell asleep in the analysis of a patient who did not bore me at all. Ignorant of the hypnotic evasion at the time, I remember racking my brain for the reason. Was it because this particular session always followed my luncheon when the digestive process might have deflected a flow of blood from the brain? Could the patient's excessively anal-erotic language (I, 290–293) have such an effect? None of my tentative answers produced any conviction; and I was lucky in nevertheless bringing the analysis to what I then considered its conclusion, i.e., a reasonable and, as I later learned, lasting therapeutic effect. Only many years later when I became aware of the hypnotic evasion was I able to solve my problem in retrospect without effort. A bit of self-analysis even permitted me to identify the individual from the fifth or sixth year of my life of whom the patient had become the representative through a countertransference. At the same time I recognized the particular childhood situation, which I evaded hypnotically, that was duplicated under the influence of the repetition compulsion by the analytic situation.

TWO "INFANTILE TRAITS" OF THE PATIENT, ESSENTIAL TO ANALYTIC TREATMENT

If the transference, however instructive, is not the carrier of the treatment but a resistance to it, one asks what does finally underly a workable analytic relation? Earlier in this section I attempted to show an example of a relation that was not workable and how it was repaired. But pressed to give a definitive answer, I can again only present some clinical observations. The first of them is so obvious that I hesitate to set it down. And if I introduce it with some examples from daily life which impress the reader at first as pointless and unconnected, I must ask his forbearance until I can by abstracting from them relate them to each other.

(a) When as a student I visited an older fraternity brother and his wife on a Sunday morning in the suburbs, they asked me to stay for lunch in the garden and we lingered over the meal. Finally, their little daughter planted herself in front of me, looked me straight in the eye and said resolutely, "Don't you *ever* go away?"

(b) I wish I could juxtapose verbatim the words of the patient who snared me once by asking, "What do you think my mother did after having masturbated on the rocking chair?" I promptly fell into the trap: "Well, I guess she got up, put her dress down, and went about her business." From memory I can only paraphrase the patient's response, which amounted to telling me in no uncertain terms and without a trace of politeness that I was an unmitigated ass. Her amnesia for what had actually happened had meanwhile, without my knowing it, been removed. The mother, instead of doing what I had "innocently" surmised, had actually put the child on the chair and masturbated her. The patient vividly recalled their delight.

(c) A woman analyst, who with her husband shared the opinion that it was unwise to expose themselves to their children, told me how one of them, a girl in the phallic phase, complained in tones of dramatic despair appropriate to a Medea, "But I have not even *seen* Daddy's penis!"

(d) As a young analyst I had luncheon with the wife of one of Freud's oldest friends—a woman I remember with great affection. Her other guest was a beautiful and vivacious young actress who told us what she said to her little daughter whom she found playing with herself: "I know how good that feels—I do it myself; just don't do it too often!"

My juxtaposing examples from daily life with an analytic one, by the way, is for didactic purposes only and not meant in any way to controvert two stringent rules laid down by Freud, the first: no matter how strong the drives experienced by the patient in the session, the abstinence rule restricts their gratification to verbalization; and the second: the analyst is forbidden to adduce anything from his personal life.

These examples upon which I may have wasted ink, are to illustrate the first of two observable "infantile traits" of a patient in the analytic relation. One is tempted to qualify by saying "successful analytic relation," for without them it is really impossible to analyze. The first: the uninhibited child will say what is on his mind and do what he feels like doing without concealing it. The patient in the regressive condition engendered by free association has, by agreement, become that child again, the child unfettered by convention.

The second infantile trait is that of the analyst becoming an object of admiration. It, too, like the verbal freedom just cited, is indispensable. Its importance in the analytic relation warrants a few illustrations.

(a) Example #4. One patient, an accomplished amateur pianist, practiced a piece from a very well-known collection and remarked that the absence of sharps or flats in the signature characterized the piece as being written in C. I retorted that my memory told me that the collection had only one piece in C, one that did not fit her description. She still did not understand, and finally her "affective stupidity" forced me to make the elementary, but to her "profound," remark that the piece must be in A minor, the relative key whose signature is the same as C. On another occasion she told me about her French course in college, attributing some of the most famous and ubiquitously known sayings to the wrong authors. My ability to correct her elicited absurd praise for the breadth of my education.

(b) A colleague in analysis had read some of my later original books without offering comment. When the time for "admiration" came, he read an earlier, unoriginal piece and was full of praise for the style, the forcefulness, and the clarity of opinion.

(c) Another unusually intelligent patient finally responded to an interpretation by exclaiming, "But that is sheer genius!" "Yes," I replied, "it is. However the genius is borrowed from Freud."

(d) I recall, by way of contrast, the analysis of a patient, no less intelligent than the last, which had to remain incomplete. She was unable to supply this "infantile component" of the relation, or I was unable to induce her to supply it. In the end I was not satisfied with the results.[2]

I am sure of the validity of my observations, but I am not certain how to abstract from them. It would appear that the patient suitable for analysis is someone in need of a "corrected" parent and willing to take a "second chance." It seems fruitless to speculate about whether or not this is a phylogenetic characteristic or what else endows the individual with it. It is obvious that the need for a "corrected" parent is basically infantile. Two different sets of observations support this contention.

For one thing, the *sequence* of amnesia removal for traumatic events in childhood and the patient's comment upon them is not infrequently determined by this need. Frequently therefore, those *events are remembered first which appear to exonerate the parent*, so that he appears as a good one, while the events contradicting this version are held back by remaining in amnesia for a long time.

(e) A father's treating his little girl to delicious concoctions in the drug store had not even been repressed; yet it took a long time until the patient relinquished amnesia for his putting his erection through the slats of her crib, frightening her so that she cried, whereupon the mother came in and whipped her for crying, while the father stood by without demurring.

---

[2] A critical reader of the manuscript at this point suggested that this last example needed amplification. In attempting to follow his suggestion, I found myself hindered by two factors. In the first place it is always possible to describe something that exists; yet it is often nearly impossible to describe something that is lacking. In the second place I would have to refer to the intricate life situation of the patient and in so doing violate her anonymity. I must therefore limit myself to stating that she was able to acknowledge improvement only in an impersonal almost indirect way by saying, for instance: "I could not have done that only a few months ago, and I do it now without so much as a tremor." She also remarked, upon meeting an acquaintance on his way to my office for reanalysis, "Well, I am glad to see that X. is coming to you. What he had with Y. was a laugh." But she was utterly rigid and opinionated in matters I cannot particularize; it never occurred to her that my opinion might occasionally be the more mature one and that it might at least rate serious consideration. Her relation to me lacked warmth; the basically infantile element of admiration or even of attachment was missing.

(f) Another patient recalled from repression how she awakened the mother, wanting to be taken to the toilet, to which the woman always agreed, stroking the child, calling her "Darling" and masturbating her in the process. Only much later was the amnesia removed for the cruel floggings of the daughter for the benefit of the mother's perverse and overtly sexual gratification.

For another thing, there are my own dreams. They often present my parents, particularly my mother as the young woman of 26 to about 31 that she was during the first five years of my life. And the young woman is not only loved but loving—the latter, according to what my analyses showed me, and what Freud, who knew her well, told me, a falsification: it is the "corrected" mother of whom I dream.

The transference in analysis of the original "uncorrected" parent represents a resistance to be overcome. If that is possible, the analysis may still cause occasionally unpleasant transient symptoms, and the amnesia removal for the severe abuse by the original parent may still at times be quite painful. But on the whole the analysis is *satisfying*, besides being *satisfactory,* because the *corrected parent is found.* I recall a woman patient of great intellect and strong emotion who epitomized this while taking leave. She thanked me for what had been achieved and added, "It was wonderful!"

That, I think, is all I can say directly about the workable analytic relation. The subject will, I hope, be implicit in most of the clinical illustrations to be recorded in the next chapter.

CHAPTER SIX

TOWARD THE TECHNIQUE OF AMNESIA REMOVAL

Strictly considered—and why should this question not be considered with all possible strictness?—analytic work deserves to be recognized as genuine psycho-analysis only when it has succeeded in removing the amnesia which conceals from the adult his knowledge of his childhood from its beginning (that is, from about the second to the fifth year).

Freud, "A Child is Being Beaten"

My reason for attempting this section at all is because of its importance in coming to grips with the etiology of the severe neurosis. If all three parts of my thesis spelled out at the beginning of Chapter Three[1] are to be confirmed, the analyst has to possess himself of the technique of amnesia removal. Yet this technique cannot be given its own definition. It is ultimately identical with the whole of the analytic technique; there is nothing in the analytic technique that does not contribute its share to amnesia removal.[2] The basic necessity, the establishing of a "workable" analytic relation through the maintainance of a "state of abstinence" was discussed at the beginning of the preceding chapter. One may venture to isolate two more re-

---

[1] The thesis: that the patient with a severe neurosis (1) has at least one psychotic parent; (2) has been exploited sexually by him or her in the most bizarre ways; and (3) has suffered the (largely defused) aggression of this parent.

[2] A dialogue with a colleague brings this into focus because it puts it in personal terms. I told of a third colleague who had said after the first volume of this series had appeared that he was not as proficient at amnesia removal as I. I added: "That is a compliment—friendly but undeserved. There is no special technique for such removal; I don't do anything to achieve it." Whereupon my colleague contradicted me, commenting on all manner of things that he knew I did do: I listened absorbedly, with free-floating attention; I interpreted; I translated symbols; I asked questions; I reconstructed, etc. It only illustrates my habitual lack of quick-wittedness that I failed to counter him on the spot with: You mean I *analyze*. Yes, that is very true.

quirements laid down in Freud's technical writings which have a particular significance for the removal of amnesia and which bear closer examination. The two to follow are free-floating attention and the distinction of memory from fantasy. Following their discussion I will attempt to clarify certain particulars in the technique under consideration, which I hope may prove of assistance.

FREE-FLOATING ATTENTION

Freud's (1912) admonition to the analyst is to reciprocate the free association to be engendered in the patient, with free-floating attention on his part. "The rule for the doctor may be expressed: 'He should withhold all conscious influences from his capacity to attend, and give himself over completely to his "unconscious memory." ' Or, to put it purely in terms of technique: 'He should simply listen, and not bother about whether he is keeping anything in mind' " (p. 112). "The technique . . . consists simply in not directing one's notice to anything in particular and in maintaining the same 'evenly-suspended attention' in the face of all that one hears" (pp. 111–112). One could add that sufficient practice in free-floating attention equips the analyst with the "analytic ear," that quintessential attribute for analyzing, eluding description.

Example #1: A single example may stand for many. From the "Studies on Hysteria" and other of Freud's early writings one certainly gains the impression that if there is a puberty trauma repeating infantile ones, one is apt to obtain first the former and subsequently the latter. There is no doubt that this happens, but in the case to be quoted the sequence was in reverse.

Ample childhood traumata had emerged from amnesia, and they seemed to explain the complaints of the patient so fully that I was totally unprepared for the existence of *a trauma in puberty* and for the necessity of removing it from amnesia. However, a certain former girl friend occasionally began to appear in associations which told about breast play. I thought nothing of it. Now to the "analytic ear":

from a certain time on, the insistence on the limitation of the relation to breast play, although clad in the same now familiar words, began gradually to assume an *increasingly dogmatic ring*. At last I verbalized this to the patient explaining that a dogma is to be taken on faith and in analysis *amounts to the request to omit investigation*. The response was a convincing description of a homosexual scene between patient and friend which subsequently broadened into an intense and elaborate relation of considerable duration, finding its abrupt end only because, for reasons that never became quite clear, both girls switched their sexual interest to boys.

In the above example the memory of the initial scene emerged as did Venus (in the legend) from the sea: in its entirety. All detail was remembered at once: the minutiae of the action, the intricacies of the locale, and the circumstances that threw the two protagonists together alone. This is by no means frequent, nor is it always immediately clear whether one hears a fantasy or a fact.

THE DISTINCTION OF MEMORY FROM FANTASY

It is here that a third request from Freud bearing upon amnesia removal cannot be emphasized enough, although in the lines I refer to he deals rather with the patient's reaction to a construction.[3] Adapted to the present discussion, it would be to neglect the question "fantasy" or "memory" altogether, and, he suggests, emulate instead the character in a play by the Austrian writer Nestroy—a domestic who for all queries and objections has only one answer: "It will all become clear in the course of future developments" (p. 265). In our case, if the analysis proceeds as it should, most such fragments will reveal their nature spontaneously as a fantasy or a piece of a larger memory; and if fantasy they may either remain fantasy or become real and take their proper place in a memory about which there can be no

---

[3] Freud avers (1937b, p. 266), by the way, that a reconstruction alone sometimes has the same therapeutic effect as does an amnesia removal. I take this opportunity to state, without comment, that this has never happened in my practice.

doubt. The same is true for the constructions to which the material prompts us and which we communicate to the patient in the hope of further elaboration or confirmation. And here I will repeat a technical note given earlier (II, 339 fn.) about dream reports. In asking patients to write down dreams after they had been reported, I follow Freud strictly. However, I have found that asking certain patients to include associations occasionally in their dream report is of advantage, and I have never observed that it has interfered with their subsequent associations.

Confirmation of Memories Subsequent to Their Removal From Amnesia: The Importance of Detail

It is possible to exemplify characteristics which emerge either at once or gradually in the patient's associations and that stamp them with the mark of truth. The first is *the detail*.

Example #2: In the example given at the beginning of Chapter Five, for instance, the preparation of soapsuds by the mother is never repressed. Even those inclined to regard being masturbated by the mother as a fantasy sprung from a wish, must question whether the anticipatory excitement upon seeing her making soap suds could be invented.

Of the masturbation on the toilet, the further course of the analysis brought out these details: every so often the mother masturbated herself; but for one thing the child had to be present, and for another the woman never failed to seat herself in such a fashion that everything was exposed to the onlooking child. If you juxtapose that to the compulsive fantasying about complexion and odor of the genitals of any woman who relaxed opposite her in the subway, which also became conscious much later in the analysis, do you find room for doubt? Still more gradually emerged. In the morning the mother wore a house coat for the occasion; however, instances were remembered when she was dressed and the bathroom was lit up by rays of sunlight through the window. We mentally examined the layout of the apartment and recognized that this could only have been caused by the sinking sun; in other words; in the late afternoon. Here no beckoning was recalled;

mother and child simply entered the bathroom together before the father came home. We could not escape the conclusion that this woman frequently had to masturbate, or be masturbated twice daily. Can that by any stretch of the imagination be fantasy?

Example #3: In this example, the recall is of two adolescent girls drying themselves from a swim. They stood in an unused bedroom with the bed stripped down to the mattress. The patient was under-developed and scrawny with very small breasts, for which the large-breasted, fully developed friend had a nasty name. The friend kissed the patient and masturbated her standing up, then lay down on the bed and spread her legs apart. The patient accepted the invitation, and in analysis not only recalled vividly how the big girl became ecstatic and threw herself about, but remembered the words that she spoke to her afterward: "Oh . . ., that was really wonderful!" I inserted an ellipsis for what was actually a nickname. Each of the two called the other by such a name; both names were somewhat outlandish and in a foreign tongue; one spoken by neither girl. I must naturally refrain from giving them, as I must also omit several further telling details. But I think I can take the liberty of quoting a brief speech from a later time when the relation no longer existed.

Once the patient exposed herself briefly to the friend in the process of dressing and the friend exclaimed, "What a homey smell!" Can you credit anyone but a great writer with the originality requisite for *inventing* these words if they had not actually been spoken?

Confirmation of Memories Prior to Their Removal From Amnesia

Bizarre Behavior Pattern: In the preceding examples an alleged initial amnesia removal is followed by more and more removal, revealing details on the strength of which one becomes certain that the removal is a veritable one; in other words, that the recall is not one of fantasies but of facts. Here, confirmation follows (and confirms) the removal.

There are, however, two other typical instances where confirmation *precedes* the removal. One of these is the repetition of a bizarre behavior pattern. Such behavior remains incomprehensible for a very long time until one day the amnesia removal, not infrequently for a single occurrence, explains it.

Example #4: In the first volume of this series I have described how ". . . an engaging and frank young girl, crisp and immaculate in appearance, begins her analysis with the description of taking a bath. Lying down in the tub, she urinates copiously into the bathwater and then soaps and dries herself without benefit of a shower . . ." She "could urinate all day long," and does so at intervals just long enough to avoid attracting attention (I, 146).

This last is undoubtedly an illustration of psychotic incontinence mastered sufficiently for the patient to remain "ambulatory." What, however, was behind the strange performance in the bath? I did not know the answer and obtained it only after several years of work.

At the age of four the patient's psychotic mother bathed together with her, putting her at the drain end of the tub and dousing her sneeringly with a partly submerged stream of urine. In adulthood the patient simply had to do the same thing for herself. To be quite explicit, the patient's perverse indulgence was forced upon her by the repetition compulsion. In the course of it she became subject to a double identification: with her mother (who, for example, thought nothing of donning, after a bath, the same dress overdue for the cleaner that she had just taken off, frequently without wearing anything underneath), and at the same time with herself as a child.

Nevertheless, the condensation operative in her original association must not be allowed to obscure the question: what is the transference meaning of the association? Why does she tell it to me in the very beginning? I eventually learned the answer: the same repetition compulsion forced her to invite similar deprecation from me. When at the end of the first year I remarked that she had a perfectly normal intelligence, she lashed out angrily at me, "How do you know?" and refused to accept my reply, that if I talked with someone five times a week for almost an hour, I could not fail to receive some impression in that regard. (Actually I was wrong. Her intelligence, as time went on, proved very far above average. She had concealed this and had kept herself in a menial job. She now has her doctorate and does research in a recondite, highly respected field.)

Example #5: The precedence of its confirmation before the removal of an amnesia through the bizarre behavior, mentioned above, is so important a technical point that I feel justified on presenting two more examples. It is not bizarre that a neurotic woman who had not exchanged the dominance of the clitoris for that of the vagina will masturbate on occasion. Yet the patient to be reported upon, when alone in her apartment, not only felt a strong masturbatory urge but had to gratify it in a particular fashion that, I believe, deserves to be called bizarre. It was necessary that she remain fully dressed in her outer clothing, take off her underdrawers and then slouch in a chair, exposing only the lower half of her body.

I am quoting her when I say that she felt "the contrast of being on top a lady and at the bottom a slut" as representing the height of "obscenity" and inducing the strongest arousal. This remained unintelligible until spontaneously in the course of analysis a single previously repressed event was recalled. I shall report on it not as it came out of amnesia—in bits and pieces which had to be put together—but as the whole episode occurred.

The psychotic mother, fully dressed, entered the dining room with her child on the maid's day out, threw herself into a rocking chair facing the kitchen, one leg over the chair arm, and began vigorous masturbation. She wore, as was her custom, no underdrawers. This particular woman was verbal in situations where most women prove more or less mute. She asked the child standing in front of her these two questions: "Do you see it?" and "Do you like it?" After that she surrendered herself to a loud orgastic vocalization. Sight and odor so excited the child that when the chair was finally vacated she went to it and tried to smell all she could. This was not the only memory establishing beyond doubt that, unlike other women of her class, the mother did not keep herself clean.

Repetition compulsion and mother identification in the patient's bizarre behavior need not be pointed out. Upon the amnesia removal, it ceased without trace.

If I append a third example of this kind I do so not in order to be repetitious but to warn others lest they may make my mistake. It was sheer indolence that caused me to recognize a patient's behavior as bizarre only *after* she had recalled the events her behavior repeated. I am convinced that the analysis would have benefited from my recognition of it earlier, that is, long before the amnesia removal occurred. Naturally the behavior was, I might say in extenuation, more subtle than in the preceding examples.

Another item: One may state without exaggerating that almost every patient has his own way of getting onto the couch. This may or may not be significant, but it certainly should be observed. The woman patient under consideration here proceeded in a manner that I have never seen before or since; it should therefore have attracted my attention sooner. If it had, I would have recognized it for what it was: a pantomimic communication in the transference, stemming, of course, from the past.

Example #6: Here is what she did. She sat down on the couch, pivoted, swinging first one then the other leg onto the couch, both with raised knees and slightly spread for a moment. Whereupon rump and head were put down, the legs straightened and sometimes put together, often accompanied by a slight tug on the skirt. This went on for several years before an amnesia removal explained it and compelled me to a belated and therapeutically futile recognition of it as bizarre. What came out of amnesia was certainly more than bizarre. One day when the child, aged seven, came home from school, the psychotic mother called her upstairs in order to "show her something." Being one of those children who never relinquish the hope for affection, she thought that she would be surprised by a gift. Instead she was made to lie down on the bed, spread her legs, and expose herself. Whereupon the woman began to alternate between rubbing the genitals of the child increasingly harshly until it hurt, and gently rubbing her own. Eventually she lay down next to the daughter and masturbated to the point of a climax. This became for a long time a standard procedure; the child upon returning from school was expected to spontaneously assume the position described above and to suffer pain and humiliation.

In analysis she termed it "the trained dog experience." I have heard another patient recall similar experiences who would not, however, believe her memory when it emerged, just as the reader who has not learned to abstain from the use of empathy with the psychotic will disbelieve my report. The analysis is a daily scheduled event, as is school, and whenever the transference demands it, the couch is regarded as bed; yet I could not convince the patient that her particular way of getting onto it only repeated the repressed scene under consideration, while inviting me to abuse and to hurt her again as had the mother in the past.

The Periodically Repeated, Apparently "Meaningless" Association

The second typical instance where confirmation precedes removal: In some analyses one is told something over and over that appears either meaningless or seems to make no sense at all. Associations of this kind are never accompanied by so much as a trace of affect. When one asks oneself why it continues to come up in the patient's associations, one learns eventually that it represents a fragment of a repressed experience fraught with meaning. The association had become meaningless through an excessive use of the mechanism of isolation. Technically one does nothing, that is, one leaves the association alone.

Example #8: In one analysis, the mother's underdrawers were mentioned again and again, whereof I could, of course, make nothing. Assurance that the mother wore no underdrawers alternated with the certainty that at times she did wear open ones. It was explained that she used to "stuff rags into them." Having learned all about the peculiar way in which this woman dressed—a description that here may be omitted—I was never able to form a judgment as to whether or not this was true. In addition, it was only after she died that the disposable menstrual napkin was introduced. I continued not to react to any of these associations, with the result one day a complete and detailed memory escaped amnesia which the patient, spontaneously and *without doubting,* herself called the story of "her first sexual seduction" by the mother. The patient was then three years old—an age originally singled out by Freud, prior to his denial, as crucial. The woman clad in the open drawers mentioned, sat down on the bed, lifted her skirt, and exposed herself to the child, telling her that she would show her something and admonishing her not to fear what she saw but to smell and to "taste" it. The child liked what she did, went on doing it, and the mother's orgastic spasm was clearly recalled. The association meaningless in isolation, could not have been more meaningful in its context.

Example #8: In another analysis, an association came up periodically for years. The mother took a bath and let the bathwater out while she remained in the tub. In this case the patient herself wondered why the mother should have done that, since it would have made her uncomfortably cold. I agreed but made no further comment. Again the amnesia for an event eventually removed itself, equipping the "senseless" and affectless association with sense and with affect by furnishing an elaborate context.

The mother did take a bath, and the daughter, aged seven, entered the bathroom—it never became clear on whose initiative—and began masturbating the mother, starting with stimulating her nipples and proceeding downwards. When she arrived at the clitoris the mother regularly opened the drain in the interest of less encumbered exhibition and more effective digital excitation. The experienced child interspersed her performance with occasional anal stimulation, eliciting from the mother a more voluptuous shudder. Sometimes, nearing a climax, the mother exclaimed eagerly "More! "More!" but when actually orgastic she invariably pushed the child's hand away and used her own to apply terminal clitoral stimulation while inserting the forefinger into the vagina. Thus she covered her genital and the daughter, scoptophilically frustrated, could only watch the anus emitting flatus, which, besides exciting her, induced the experience of beauty (cf. II, Section III). She compared what she saw to the unfolding of a flower

The mechanism that had originally deprived the association of meaning is in this case a triple one: a combination of isolation, cathexis-withdrawal and displacement onto detail *(Verschiebung aufs Kleinste—Freud).* Those inclined to ponder a fine theoretical point may ask themselves: Does the term cathexis *withdrawal* fit the occasion? Or should one rather speak of the *transformation* of affect into the nameless dynamic factor enforcing the repetition of the association?

I hope that the reader has not overlooked the fact that these last examples, although not chosen for that aspect, are nevertheless filled with specific detail.

Amnesia Removal Consequent to a Dream

Amnesia removal occasionally occurs consequent to a dream. The relation between dream and removal varies. The analyst may, for instance, as he did in the example to follow, stimulate the removal by interpreting a certain dream.

Example #9. The dreamer was someone who had previous to his treatment resorted to a substantial number of dietary regimes which promised to abolish his complaints. He came to analysis on the recommendation of an acquaintance whose judgment he did not trust. He was firmly convinced that analysis could only be another ineffectual fad.

His bizarre behavior was sexual: he praised the performance of fellatio on him by girls as more exciting than anything else, yet after each episode he went into a severely depressive decline. Before entering analysis he discontinued the practice, hoping that this would enable him to conceal it. When that did not work, he gave the name of his partner as Margaret and admitted only under duress of the analytic rule that her real name was Marguerite (cf. Chapter One, II on the symbolism of "French.")

After a year, or a year and a half—it all occurred long ago—he recounted a dream in which he sat in the front row of a number of benches where a band was playing. The main character in the dream was a man, standing opposite him, I believe, who wore a yellow straw hat.

I interpreted the first part of the dream metaphorically (not knowing then that the analyst should ordinarily refrain from so doing) as: he is finally "facing the music"; and the second symbolically, following Freud's interpretation of the "straw hat" as "penis." The straw hat was yellow, and I do not recall what besides youthful insouciance gave me the courage to say: It must therefore be the penis of a Chinese.

This interpretation induced the patient to recall a repressed memory as full of affect as the dream was empty of it: A Chinese laundryman had more than once seduced the four-year-old boy to perform fellatio on him. This resulted in a deeply felt love affair on the child's part. When it ended because of the objection of the laundryman's partner and the threat of police intervention, the boy was booted out of the place and told never to come back. He was heartbroken and felt desperately alone; he found no relief in confession or punishment, but the confession compulsion exhausted itself in a parapraxis to which no one paid any attention. There was a Chinese laundry at each of the two corners of the block, and it was the laundrymen's habit to draw a pictograph on a scrap of paper subsequently torn in half. They retained one, affixing it to the batch of laundry, and let the customer have the other. When the washed laundry was reclaimed, it was identified by fitting the two halves together. One day the boy led the father to the wrong laundry and the two halves did not fit; he expected to be punished severely for his error, but the father merely smiled, went to the other place where the halves fitted, and was given his laundry.

My patient was now completely bewildered by what had come forth, like the genie from the bottle in the old tale. How could a "fake" procedure, a "fad," as he had at times termed psychoanalysis, extract all these memories from a dream? He now doubted the memories and did as one of Freud's patients had done. He took a train to the town of his birth, found the block where he had lived at the time, saw at one corner a Chinese laundry and at the other an empty lot. He inquired and was informed that the lot was empty because the *other* Chinese laundry had burned down.

This was too much for him; he feigned improvement and ran out of analysis. It took him five years and a special circumstance to come back. He was then helped substantially, although his disturbance was a psychotic one. As such it precluded amnesia removal for the original early trauma of which the one here recounted must, of course, have been a repetition. The existence of two psychotic parents, vague memories of excessive paternal beatings, and weird maternal exhibitions at the occasion of toilet functions were all that could be obtained.

A Brief "Harmless Dream" and its Relation to the Recall of a Traumatic Event

Example #10. In the next example the analysis, begun a long time before the dream occurred, had been relatively unproductive. One heard about an unsympathetic mother forcing the patient, as a child, to give her toys to her younger (schizophrenic) sister who broke them. When the patient was a young woman the mother taunted her before family and friends with being too ugly to marry. In puberty there were intimacies with an itinerant preacher, protegé of the mother, the exact nature of which remained unknown, but which had been sufficiently impermissible for the man to push the child away from him when he heard someone approach.

Eventually the extremely short dream: "Someone is driving his car into the driveway next to my [the patient's] house." Here the action appeared so immaterial, so devoid of a motive for dreaming that one had to suspect a "Harmless Dream" of Freud's description: the absence of any trace of an affect, appropriate as it was to the manifest content, attested further to the complete success of the dream work.

Interpretation: I must omit specifying how the dream contained an immediately recognizable picturization of the seducer's name. Could I do so, I would remove any doubt that he was the man driving the car. In addition, the dream employs the car, a bisexual symbol, in this case representative of the male genital. But why the choice of a bisexual symbol for the seducer's organ? The question can only be answered when one has spent a lifetime becoming acquainted with the extreme sophistication of the unconscious. The original trauma in childhood, re-enacted by the repressed traumatic experience in adolescence provoking the dream, has been recounted earlier (Chapter Three). There, the original seducer was indeed a female, the mother. The dreamer's "house" is a genital symbolization of the woman, the dreamer, and the driveway (dead-end) symbolizes her rectum (cf.

Chapter One, II). The dream, in other words, represents the insertion of his penis by the seducer into the patient's rectum.

This was the starting point for a long stretch of painful analytic work that eventually brought the following sequence of events out of amnesia.

When the patient was 16 or 17 years of age the preacher, accompanied by a bad reputation, had come back to town, and the father, prominent in the community and well informed, had forbidden his daughter to see him. The mother, when asked the reason for this prohibition, pretended complete ignorance and arranged for clandestine visits behind her husband's back. On the occasion of one of these, the young girl and the preacher stopped at the house of a man, who the preacher incited to mercilessly flog his little son. This evidently excited both the man and the girl to such an extent that they returned to the car where the girl, who was having her period, allowed the man rectal insertion. The psychopath followed this up with frictions so violent and excessive that his victim suffered indescribable pain, followed by a state of complete derealization lasting three or four days.

Because the complete amnesia for all these events was the result of their having "followed into repression" the period covering the traumatic childhood, conversely the amnesia removal opened the way for gradually obtaining a good deal of the necessary memories from the first five years of life.

One could call these early traumatic memories confirmations of the later one because it repeated them in some essential details. But there were others: a picture of the seducer and a letter from him to the patient, as well as subsequent newspaper reports saying that he had been jailed for impregnating one of his own adolescent daughters. The symbolic meaning of the driveway as "dead end" in the dream was confirmed through a repeated experience of the patient in adolescence: when using the library in her home town she felt often an unaccountable urge to move her bowels. Inquiry showed that this occurred only when she sat reading in an elongated corner of the building without a door, in other words, again a "dead end." (For the projection of pleasure-physiologic elements of the body ego into environment see II, 246–254.)

THE IMPORTANCE OF MEMORY QUALITY

The most instructive lesson to be derived from the preceding example can only be read between the lines because I refrained from being explicit about it. My reason: it is important enough to be allotted a separate section. None of the confirmation for the reality of the scene that emerged from amnesia was really needed because the patient was spontaneously convinced that every detail of it had been real. Her conviction met with my own. I had no reason to doubt it in the first place, and the progress of the analysis made me certain.

Is It a Memory?

Actually all the examples adduced so far (with the possible exception of Example #9) are deceptive in this respect: regardless of whether the amnesia removal was at once for the whole event or only for fragments of it that had to be put together, events or fragments *were always memories for the patient.* In other words—they were something that he recalled or, as one can express it, something that had "memory quality" for him. However, *half the time that is not the case in analysis.* The patient says something concerning his past, and if asked, "Is it a *memory?*" he is not sure. He said what he said because it came to mind; he knows of no other reason. It is here that Freud's admonition to trust that the further course of the analysis will eventually furnish the answer applies. If the answer is positive, that is, if the association actually did describe a fragment of the whole of a past event, it expressed a memory with the memory quality lacking.

The Establishment of Probability for a Memory

With regard to amnesia removal, the acquisition of memory quality for a memory is of extreme importance, *because without it the removal remains therapeutically ineffective.* The analyst cannot, of course, experience memory quality for a memory of the patient; it is the patient, not he, who participated in the event. What he can and must do is establish the probability by applying to the alleged event his knowledge of character, anatomy, and locale, his learning and his experience with other patients.

Example #11: Here is a simple illustration (cf. II, 69). The memory was a fragment, although I had no way of knowing that when it was first remembered. At the age of seven the patient helped her mother with the dishes, broke a stack of them by dropping them on the floor, to which the mother reacted sweetly by saying, "That is all right, darling; it can happen to anyone." This had memory quality for the patient, but it was impossible for me to believe it because I knew the mother as a vicious psychotic, who, even at the time of the daughter's analysis, boasted of beatings administered to the child, which the patient could never remember. In the further course of the treatment, another detail was added: When the child dropped the dishes the father was in the next room. I knew him as one to whom no one in the world was dearer than his daughter, and I was convinced that if he were made to witness punishment of his child he would have turned violently against his wife. Thus the story made perfect sense, and *the memory was a true one,* justifying the presence of memory quality in the patient. The woman had simply feigned affection within earshot of her husband in order to trick him; in his absence she could now beat the child more than ever.

The Feeling of Continuity of Self

Up to this point the discussion has been fairly simple, it will now become complicated because the description of certain disturbances of memory quality cannot be avoided and I fear it may bewilder the reader. A bland, never repressed memory of my own may serve to illustrate, through contrast, what I mean by a certain disturbance in memory quality when the feeling to be described is lacking.

When I was 13 years old my father presented me with a watch that he had been given by his father at the same age. As part of the birthday celebration the whole family attended a circus performance, accompanied by a somewhat younger visiting friend. I recall that the seating order was such that the family separated me from my friend. At one point the unforgettably charming boy, son of highly placed parents in a foreign country, whispered in his neighbor's ear the question, "What time is it?" together with the request that the question be transmitted from person to person. When it finally reached me, I could proudly display my watch.

I take the trouble of telling the little episode not only because it illustrates memory quality, assuring me after 60 years that this actually happened, but in order to emphasize one ingredient of this quality: the "feeling of continuity of the self." The term is neither Freud's nor mine. I have encountered it in epistemological studies and do not know who coined it. As a boy of 13 I was certainly different in almost every respect from the septuagenarian I am now, but something inside myself mysteriously yet unequivocally tells me that even then, I was I. I can distinguish without any doubt what has happened to me from what happened to the closest of my friends. This holds true for events from any age, irrespective of whether they came out of repression or had never been repressed.

One is then compelled to emend the statement made above about the importance of memory quality to the extent that if the quality appears present *but lacks the feeling of continuity of the self, the amnesia removal will be as ineffective as if memory quality had been absent.*

This is a very important emendation. I remember one analytic treatment in which that continuity long remained broken. The highly intelligent and introspectively gifted patient would assure me over and over, "I know that these things did happen, but it feels as though they had happened to someone else." I recall another analysis where the patient failed to verbalize this, but I came to suspect it—on what grounds I cannot remember. When I described it to her, questioning her about it, she replied at once, "I think all my memories are of that kind."

I have naturally pondered the reason and have come to regard the phenomenon as a consequence of the ego split (cf. II, 92) I had not previously known. Actually, when the *split was repaired* and the ego again a whole, the feeling of continuity of the self was restored, and the memories could eventually be "owned." Nevertheless, this is an irreversible explanation. The patient who suffered a prolonged state of derealization after a rectal penetration was a severe compulsive in whom the ego split was, of course, very pronounced (II, 146). I have recounted how slow and how painful the amnesia removal proved to be for, at first, fragments of the repressed trauma from adolescence and, subsequently, for the original childhood traumata. Whatever fragment emerged, however, was completely owned: the patient always felt that what had happened *had happened to her.*

Memory Quality and Fantasies

A comprehensive presentation of memory quality, however brief, must include still another complication. This quality, which was shown to be often absent in the case of actual *events,* can on occasion be present in the case of *fantasies.* The result: a fantasy is then "remembered" as though it had been an event. If this makes it seem hopeless to ever distinguish fantasy from reality, two examples will readily convince the reader that it is not.

Example #12: One female patient contended for a while that she "remembered" how she, age seven, and her mother lay on their backs, raised and spread their legs, rubbing vulvas together. The component events, playing a similar role for the fantasy as do the day residues for a dream, had come out of amnesia; and it was well understandable that they gave rise to the wish which the fantasy represents as fulfilled. The mother actually daily assumed this position in the nude for a long time, insisting that the child watch her masturbating and reaching a climax. The child had no outlet for her excitation and evidently entertained the fantasy that made her a quasi mirror-image of the mother and thus in the "remembered" contact with her.

It would be of theoretical interest to account for whatever it might have been that gave memory quality to the fantasy, because the wish alone, however strong, is not enough. But the interest would really be only theoretical. Technically, if the analyst does his share in examining probability, he easily recognizes that the alleged remembered act cannot, for reasons of both anatomy and position, be performed, at least not as the patient described it.

Example #13: A male patient "recalled" how, when he was about five years old, both he and his father squatted side by side over a small bench in the garden they actually inhabited in his childhood, defecated simultaneously on the bench, resulting in a stylized product of a certain shape he described in detail. This again is, for a number of rather obvious reasons, in spite of the memory quality not a real occurrence. The analysis had to remain incomplete; I did not obtain the repressed events upon which the fantasy must have been an elaboration, "screening" I suspect, the events.

Whether or not the fact that I remember but two instances where a fantasy arrogated memory quality testifies to the rarity of such arrogation I cannot tell: the analyst studies too few patients to make statistical statements. But the examples do show that the acquisition is harmless; the establishment of the criteria probability by the analyst will not fail to undo the deception and mark the alleged memory as spurious.

The Acquisition of Memory Quality in the Course of a Patient's Associating to a Dream

I have experienced such acquisition more than once; but I lack a record of it in my notes or in my memory sufficiently explicit for presentation. I am therefore greatly indebted to a colleague who acceded to my request to furnish one. I have studied it and found it an excellent piece of analytic work. It does not make for easy reading: its absorption will tax the student. I shall quote from it verbatim and if I follow it with a few remarks, it is not so much to amend my colleague's interpretations, which are exhaustive and to the point, so much as to amplify them because of their extreme brevity.

Example #14: The report: A young woman has been approaching a memory of watching her father masturbate when she was in the crib, age *three*. She had previously remembered that this would happen on *Sunday afternoons,* and had recalled the detail of his putting on a condom before masturbating. This detail had led to the following remarks bearing on the question of memory vs. fantasy:

"I want it to be all my imagination, but the intensity of the image [last week in the analysis she 'couldn't help feeling' that I was masturbating in the chair behind her], the many details . . . the realization that I always felt I knew what condoms were for, that this meant masturbation and not intercourse to me . . . that I always knew where father kept his condoms, what the box and the wrappings looked like, without knowing how I knew, all that makes me feel it is a memory."

Convincing as her reasoning was to both of us, still it was plain that there was some interference with fully remembering and acknowledging that the quality of memory was involved.

The dream brought in another detail which gave the definite quality of memory and resulted in a bit of amnesia removal; the amnesia removal is still in progress.

Dream: "I am with the wife of a physician who says that her husband is too busy. He comes in wearing a surgical costume. Underneath his pants I can see he is wearing jockey shorts. Feel fear and excitement and have to leave!"

She had spent the previous evening at the home of a woman friend; they had been discussing the castration anxiety of the friend's *three*-year-old boy. She had felt excited during the discussion.

Associations: "Now I remember that father who usually wore boxer shorts would wear jockey shorts every *Sunday* because of some sports activity. Doctor in the dream is in three layers—first a physician, you. Second—a surgeon who could cut me up . . . [Her recurrent preoccupation: "What happened to my hymen" has been interpretatively connected with fantasies she has of being "castrated" by father. I feel that there are defloration experiences here to be remembered.] "Underneath the third layer—jockey shorts bulging in between his legs with his penis and testicles in a way that my panties never bulged. Now I see the specific image of those shorts he wore on *Sunday afternoons* [this is now clearly memory].

"I think of a thin girl I saw in profile with bulge in her genital area [presumably *mons veneris*], sometimes I am aware of it myself with tight clothes.

"Now I see my father in profile—bulge in his shorts getting bigger—he is starting to have an erection and so am I as I tell you this; I have a feeling of discomfort of having an erection constricted by pants [striving for identification with father]. Something is happening to his body. He is facing the bureau drawer where he keeps prophylactics, he goes to the drawer and opens it up. . . ."

Here there is a pause and obvious resistance. She goes on to tell me of the migraine headaches her father had on weekends, and of the smell of his vomiting. Then there is more hesitation; she says that she is in hypnosis suddenly (for the first time in the session). I reply that my guess is that the hypnosis is needed to ward off the feelings that would be evoked if she continued to remember.

She goes on. "I am looking at him out of the side of my eyes. He gets out a condom and steps out of his pants. Now I understand why I had both a profile view (of his penis) and a more frontal view. He goes to sit on the bed [across from the crib]; he has an erection, puts on a condom. It drives me wild, surge of excitement and clitoral erection I feel now, it is painful; I feel I am spinning away [rotating symbol]. Then he props up the pillow so he is half sitting up with his knees up and his hands on his penis; he rubs up and down. I can see him, penis is not clear because he has his legs up but I see the increasingly fast rhythmic movements of his hands. I am so excited. I wish my clitoris could burst [need for explosive discharge of overexcitement]. Also I have a vaginal feeling now, sharp and painful. I feel that I can't move, that I am not supposed to see and yet at the same time supposed to see that man on my [sic] bed [a slip]. As if I don't recognize my father. Now I feel as if I *am* on the bed with him, between his legs. I can remember the effort to turn over and crawl up nearer his penis, with the wish to put his penis in my mouth. But it is not clear if I am in my crib or on the bed. I can't face look-ing at his genitals and pubic hair." [She had previously remem-bered his penis as seen through the bars of her crib.]

So the amnesia removal ends at a certain point where doubts and uncertainty again take over. She seems to be deal-ing with a series of experiences from the past.

My Comment:
The report is of the greatest interest in several respects. First of all this patient does more than I have described above. She not only recounts a memory *without memory quality*, because it comes to her mind and she must say it by reason of the analytic rule; but she is critical of her association to the extent of recog-nizing *that it must be a memory;* and she experiences the strug-gle of reason telling her why it must be one with the resistance that tempts her with a futile denial. In the process she discovers more or less by herself what I have called "the importance of the detail." At the same time she apparently understands her analyst when he points to the lack of memory quality in her associations.

After the dream she not only repeats the critical—critical because it is the beginning of the phallic period—age of three, originally discovered by Freud, but in her recountal of the eve-ning previous to the dream she identifies with the anxiety of her friend's three-year-old boy, as neurotic women with a marked fear of castration will frequently do. The significance of the protruding *mons veneris* for these girls, which her analyst evi-dently found out for himself, I learned from the late Dr. Ruth Brunswick.

Memory Quality is Acquired

While associating, the memory is not only enlarged but memory quality for it is acquired. Yet the memory is overwhelming: the repetition compulsion enforces an almost unbearably strong clitoral excitation such as had originally accompanied the event. Subsequently it causes her to experience castration, manifested by the sharp vaginal pain I described previously as accompanying the "castration" of a woman patient (II, 315). She had at first tried to evade the excitement through hypnosis, which, however, the analyst's interpretation made impossible to maintain. Consequently the memory endangers her with ego disintegration which she expresses symbolically by association—the rotating symbol (cf. Chapter One, II). In the end it is only too natural that the excessive clitoral urge demands discharge through masturbation, which she forbids herself in the analyst's presence. ("I feel that I cannot move, that I am not supposed to . . .".)

The instructive end of the report demonstrates the apparent paradox: the share of the resistance not in the continuation but in the removal of the amnesia. While the analytic work has corroded the resistance to the extent of allowing recall, it has not failed to extract its due: the particular memory was selected by the unconscious because it maintains that father and child had not contact. Yet the analysis, insatiable as it is, already begins to mobilize future memories characterised by the closest sexual contact between father and child.

Thus the session ends, as a good session in the course of analysis should, by asking more questions than it has answered and letting the analyst glimpse the kind of results he may expect if his future work is as successful as was the past.

THE OCCASIONAL SEPARATION OF TWO SENSORY SPHERES FROM EACH OTHER IN THE PROCESS OF AMNESIA REMOVAL

On rare occasions—I have seen it only twice—two sensory

spheres, both joint participants in the apperception of a past event, become transiently independent of each other, with the result that the amnesia is removed first for one alone and only later for the other. They are the eye and the ear. One obtains, then, at first a purely visual memory which later becomes also acoustic.

A woman patient, who at the age of 12 feigned masturbating in front of her mother, remembered first the woman's facial expression of rage and her outstretched forefinger, and only subsequently in the process of working through, her furious voice and her threatening verbalization: "Don't you ever let me see that again!"

A male patient, the details of whose incomplete analysis I have forgotten, recalled a maternal exhibition at the age of five, and only weeks later the words spoken by the mother on the occasion. He announced the emergence of the acoustic component of the memory with the words: "I am now wiring this thing for sound."

The transient separation described here represents the kind of observation that is unsatisfactory because one lacks any theoretical understanding.

AN ADDENDUM TO THE TECHNIQUE OF AMNESIA REMOVAL

It will be recalled that in the section on hypnosis (Chapter Four, I, A, 2, concerning the hypnotic evasion) an addendum to the technique of amnesia removal was reported. It is of sufficient importance to remind the reader of it here.

As I stated, after the patient has been induced to distinguish wakefulness from hypnosis, *whenever repression is reinforced by hypnosis, one must, before attempting to lift the repression, undo its hypnotic "wrapping."*

The woman patient who regularly became hypnotic on the subway ride to and from my office (see On the Analytic Rela tion. Chapter Five; and Chapter Four, Example #1) exemplified this procedure. Her autohypnotic state (re-experiencing the

hypnosis brought upon her as a child by the mother's sexual exploitations) allowed her to evade both memory and repetition of
the experience. The abstinence rule invoked against her "acting
out," represented by her self-induced hypnosis, finally allowed
amnesia removal for the activities of child and (psychotic) parent. One caution: the above technical advice is suitable only in
the later stages of a successful analysis. I should repeat here
that amnesia removal for an event experienced under hypnosis
is no more difficult than for one experienced while fully awake.

MISCELLANEOUS NOTES

Here I should perhaps remind the reader of original material
in the *Series* that has a direct bearing on interpretation, and
hence aids amnesia removal. In Volume II a thorough familiarity with the pleasure-physiologic body ego (II, Chapter
Three) is of assistance in a variety of ways. The first chapter of
this volume, On Symbolism, should speak for itself, for there I
attempt as thorough a treatment of the subject as is possible at
this time: in the first section theoretically, and in the next by
considering specific symbols either hitherto undescribed or requiring discussion. Many of these symbolize parts of the pleasure-
physiologic body ego, and a knowledge of them is essential to
correct interpretation and therefore the eventual effecting of
amnesia removal.

The final section, The Significance of Symbolization For Clinical Work, should be consulted in its entirety for reasons that
are self-evident, in particular, Symbolic Prediction for the recall
of traumatic events before the analysis has progressed far
enough to inform one of them through other means; symbolic
assistance in distinguishing memory from fantasy; the assistance
rendered by symbolism in distinguishing a memory as a screen
memory and in reconstructing the memory that it screened.
There is also the "symbolic equation," [4] a means of adaptation to

---

[4] Not to be confused with the "symbol equation," a term by which one could designate the unconscious equation of a symbolized element with a symbol.

the environment: the cathectic equation of an element of the object world with an element of the pleasure-physiologic body ego. There is lastly a three-fold safeguard I noted against the misuse of a (potential) symbol in one's work:

(1) Ascertain that a potentially symbolic element is, in the context before you, actually a symbol (Chapter One, D).

(2) If it is, do not overlook its frequent historic, and its occasional metaphoric overdetermination (Chapter One, M).

(3) Know that the symbolic equation (Chapter One, P) is constant; it does not bear tampering with: the analytic symbol has only one *symbolic* meaning. In other words, its correct translation is always the same. Practically the sole exceptions are the few "bisexual symbols" (q.v.).

IDENTITY OF THE RESULTS OF AMNESIA REMOVAL IN THE NEUROTIC AND THE PSYCHOTIC ANALYSAND

If it is true that psychotic people in general are not fit for analysis, it is also true that a minority of them are or can be made to be analyzable up to a point, a subject which will be dealt with in the following section. The present section allows for only one statement. The results of amnesia removal are exactly the same whether the patient is neurotic or psychotic. Why? Abraham (1907) long ago declared that childhood experiences etiologic for the neurosis are not etiologic for the psychosis where they determine only the form of the disturbance in a particular case.

The first example in Chapter Five, above, was neurotic, whereas Example 8, this chapter, had a psychotic disturbance. (She had also, in earlier years, masturbated her mother on the toilet.) The patient in Example 9 was psychotic, whereas the patient in the next example was purely neurotic. Of the two patients exemplifying the spurious attachment of memory quality to a mere fantasy (Examples 12 and 13), one was neurotic, the other psychotic. I could go on with such comparisons almost *ad infinitum*. On the surface one would think that there should be a difference in what is recalled by patients in the two categories. But on second thought the reader will have to admit that the results could really have been foreseen. The reason: we are again dealing with psychotic *parents*, whether their children be neurotic or psychotic. Thus Abraham's statement can today be expanded without contradicting it. It would then read as follows: the psychotic parent of the *neurotic* patient damages him in only one way, namely, *by exploiting him as a child for his sexual and aggressive needs. The psychotic parent of the psychotic patient damages him in two ways: first, by endowing him genetically with the as yet unknown factor causing the organic psychotic disease; and secondly, by exploiting him as a child.* No wonder, therefore, that the amnesia removal reveals the same events in the childhood of both.

CHAPTER SEVEN

NOTES ON THE DIAGNOSIS AND TREATMENT OF THE AMBULATORY PSYCHOTIC

DIAGNOSTIC CONSIDERATIONS

I append in conclusion some notes that might be of use to the practicing analyst who is confronted by the ambulatory psychotic. What I have to say is based on long experience and the commitment of many errors. The indispensable first step toward a perhaps possible treatment, I have become firmly convinced, is the establishment of the diagnosis. This is sometimes easy, at other times not.

EASILY MADE DIAGNOSES [1]

When your patient, for instance, is a psychiatrist and comes armed with reprints, charts, or the like, of his work: his behavior is practically pathognomonic. If he uses every ashtray in the office, including anything looking remotely like one; if he refuses the chair reserved for the patient, snatching another instead; and if the object of scrutiny turns out to be you when it naturally should be himself, the diagnosis is almost as obvious as when he tells you he has once slit his wrists. I remember one, "shopping" for an analyst who would be good enough for him, telling me about more than half a dozen he had seen before. In so doing he made about each of them a—realistic—critical observation that disqualified them in his eyes before asking me what he called a "personal" question about my own qualifications. Moreover, he revealed himself in the first and only consultation as a liar: for one thing he claimed that his sexual life was "absolutely normal," and for another, after telling me that

---

[1] In the Appendix the reader will find, also in the form of notes, some additional observations on the ambulatory psychotic.

in driving a car he was pursued by the idea of having run over someone, when I asked him, "Do you actually *believe* that?" he promptly evaded by answering, "Why, Doctor, I doubt everything." I decided to avoid seeing him again; not because he was an ambulatory psychotic but because his character would have turned any attempt to help him into a waste of time.

The psychotic psychiatrist is apparently not too rare and, alas, the psychotic analyst also can be met with. I recall a professor of psychiatry, student in analysis, whom I gradually recognized as a psychotic, although our contact was confined to supervisory sessions. When he once asked me for a pencil and then promptly put it into his mouth, I felt constrained to communicate my observations to the Chairman on Students of an Institute. With regard to the diagnosis, the latter agreed with me on the basis of his own classroom impressions; whereupon the student was graduated within the week.

DIFFICULT DIAGNOSES

At other times the differential diagnosis is difficult, occasionally very difficult. Sometimes a trial analysis enables one to make a decision. At this point two "don'ts": do not rely on the Rorschach test, for more often than not it does not yield the differential diagnosis. Those made by the late Dr. Oberholzer did; but, as Dr. Brunswick remarked to me once, not because of the potency of the test but because Dr. Oberholzer was such an exceptionally keen psychiatric observer. She was proven right: all Rorschach reports I have read subsequently contained nothing but "double talk." The second "don't" I learned from Dr. Oberholzer himself. He once exclaimed in a conversation, "What is the meaning of all those diagnoses such as 'paranoid,' 'schizoid personality,' 'borderline case,' or 'latent schizophrenia?' Somebody has a schizophrenia or he *doesn't!*" I have since decided that actually all these diagnoses are nothing but psychiatric defense against the acknowledgment of the ambulatory psychotic. Refrain from making them is therefore the second "don't." It is perfectly true that some psychotic patients may not, for shorter or longer—sometimes very long—periods exhibit gross symptoms; but that does not mean that they are not what they are. This is so important a point and one that has caused so much diagnostic confusion that I should illustrate it.

One evening a husband told his psychotic wife that they should get a divorce. Her answer: "If you had said that to me before 2:30 this afternoon, I would have agreed with you; but now I don't." What she meant was that she could pinpoint the exact hour when an unnameable inner feeling had informed her of the onset of one of her remissions: that is, periods in which she was free of symptoms. (She was saying, in other words, "I am all right as of 2:30 this afternoon. You therefore have no complaint. Hence, why divorce?")

There are so many symptoms, behavior patterns and features that prove pathognomonic, they are too numerous to describe. Many are so subtle as to defy description. Take the "compulsive" *délire de toucher:* coming home, the person suffering this must touch the door knob three times, put his hat three times on the rack, etc. He is *not a compulsive* but a *schizophrenic.* Take the so-called "phobic type." He can eat only in one restaurant in the whole city; from all others he is driven by an explosive "claustrophobic" attack. A schizophrenic again. The neurotic has many odd sexual traits; but when a man puts two condoms over his tongue in order to perform cunnilingus, he makes the diagnosis for you. Again, there is the "instant identification." You happen to scratch your temple—in an initial consultation where the patient sits opposite you—he must scratch his. Afflicted for many years with a chronic sinus condition, I had a box of Kleenex handy and once in a consultation blew my nose. The patient asked whether she might have one, took it, found no use for it, and I can still see it fluttering from her hand.

Sometimes the identification lasts longer: it can even be chronic. It results then in the well-known "as if" personality. I recall such a person who, for example, went to the theater because it was the thing to do, although she was incapable of taking in which she saw, let alone form a judgment about it. She listened instead to what her friends said of the play, or waited until the reviews had appeared and then started quoting from them without naming the source—making it seem that the "quotes" represented her own opinion. She even came twice to see me, "wanting to be analyzed." After the second consultation she decided "to forget the whole thing." The only reason for her appearance was a transient identification with her daughter, who had been my analytic patient.

Some psychotics are able to put their ability to withdraw from the object world into the service of mendacity. By ordinary standards they are then the most convincing of liars. However, neither the "as if" personality nor the psychotic liar are in most instances difficult to detect if they are subjected to a correctly conducted trial analysis. This, in my opinion, should take the place of the Rorschach test; unless it is rendered superfluous —as it is in some cases—by two or three consultations that tell you all that you need to know.

A PARTICULAR PATHOGNOMONIC SYMPTOM

There is, furthermore, occasionally a particular psychotic inability to retain recent events, which deserves perhaps two brief illustrations.

I once saw a young girl who lived with friends, a married couple. She was in an acutely confused state. We had a good contact and I learned that about a week before, while the wife was on a three-day trip, she—so far a virgin—had had an affair with the husband. It appeared necessary to obtain some details and I began with the question of how often they had been together. The surprising answer: "I do not know." I am firmly convinced of her honesty; she had actually—one is tempted to say "repressed"—that detail. However, the years have given me the unaccountable conviction that this is not a repression in the usual sense of the word, but something else for which there is at this time no theoretical explanation. (I have subsequently discovered that although this remark is correct, its origin is cryptomnestic: Freud had expressed himself similarly in his essay "The Unconscious," 1915b).

A psychotic woman reported how on the day before the session she had prepared herself for masturbating by removing her underdrawers. About to retire for the purpose, she told her little girl that she now had to change into other clothes and to her surprise was answered: "But, Mama, you are already naked." Here the child verbalized primary process thought, particularly extreme condensation and allusion. A translation into secondary process thought would have been more elaborate and much longer: "But Mommy [why do you lie to me when I know that as far as the lower half of your body, which you want to use, is concerned] you are already naked [underneath your outer garment]." The patient was utterly at a loss for an explanation as to how the child could have known and presented the event without saying so as a sort of extrasensory puzzle. The solution, which could only lie in her having exhibited to the child, did not occur to her; the exhibition, in other words, was already "repressed."

OTHER PATHOGNOMONIC SYMPTOMS

The foregoing has been easy to convey. Yet there is on the other hand the schizophrenic look in the eye, sometimes characterized by a peculiar glitter, at other times impossible to describe. There is an occasional deep vertical fold in the middle of the forehead, that I mentioned once in analysis to a colleague. He answered: "Yes, I know what you mean; but when I mention it to my analytic friends they do not know what I speak of." In rare instances the psychotic person appears literally bothered by something that he evidently locates in his head because he puts his hand to his head and, as though trying to assuage something there, presses and rubs it. In one case in several consultations I still could not make up my mind until I once showed the patient to the door. There she stood for a moment, and the diagnosis was made. What allowed me to make it? Her posture. Yet I am absolutely unable to portray it.

I recognized it only because I had seen it once before in a young woman I had had committed when she alerted me to the imminence of a break through an attack of depersonalization.

Some men wear what I have called to myself "the psychotic shoe." At a social occasion I once entered into a discussion with a psychiatrist who expounded therapeutic procedures that baffled me because they sounded fantastic. Accidentally my glance slid downward and I saw his shoes: high brown boots, loosely laced, and appearing—in contrast to the rest of his conventional, neat attire—neglected. I promptly felt relieved because I wondered no longer. From then on I could confine myself to answering with a polite assent his delusory statements. Again, I recall a patient who was completely disoriented after the first consultation: he bumped into walls, opened a closet, and could not find the big double door leading into the hall. I should have made the diagnosis right then and there. Another patient, described previously (I, 76–77), while working in his office was compelled constantly to watch for girls using the bathroom. Hearing this for the first time in the beginning of his analysis, I responded with the harmless remark: "Well, if you have a part of your mind on that, you cannot put your whole mind to your work. Don't you think it is logical to suspect that consequently your work will suffer?" His answer went something like: "I have never in my life heard such nonsense as that." In a man of average education who appears neither stupid nor confused this is—resistance or no resistance—symptomatic of a thought disorder. Today I would lay it aside toward at least a tentative differential diagnosis.

Another example: a youthful millionairess comes to a consultation in a dark, rigorously plain dress, the sort that would suit a person in deep mourning; sits with her legs spread, exhibiting stockings with round garters below the knees and, of course, some of her thighs. This way of dressing and sitting is also pagognomonic.

The same young woman in a moment of stress was prompted to a certain kind of "silent crying," which I have also at times heard on the phone. Visually it breaks through a face that is almost devoid of expression. There are tears but no heavy breathing or sobbing; the patient tries to suppress the crying but fails. Speech may but need not be momentarily interrupted —all in all it is easy to recognize, difficult to depict and absolutely pathognomonic.

Many of the symptoms of this category appear as caricatures of normal behavior: for example, the married woman who in the first consultation feels that she has to confess an affair with the referring physician. There are many for whom this would be far from easy and would certainly produce hesitation. But this woman, a lady immaculately groomed and dressed, with impeccable manners, froze quite speechless. There she sat, giving me the impression (for which again I cannot, try as I may, account) of someone sitting on the toilet resigned to his constipation. And there I sat, waiting. Soft, friendly prodding: "Well, what is on your mind?" was of no avail. Finally, after a practically interminable period of silence, a terse confession. If the lover, who I later learned had not confined himself to the exploitation of this one patient, had not been the heel he was he would not, of course, have put the burden of informing me on the poor schizophrenic woman.

Another schizophrenic female, who I should never have tried to analyze, had as do many neurotics great difficulties in following the analytic rule. In many patients this may produce pauses. In one ambulatory psychotic, however, these were so exaggerated as to amount to "mutism." But my intellect did not keep pace with my intuition. Once when she simply would not talk, I was desperate because no matter what I tried, I could not break her silence. Finally I resorted to the entirely unorthodox means of getting out of my chair, walking to the foot of the couch, and looking her in the face. She immediately smiled at me and had no further difficulty in talking. Did I recognize that the visual sphere had in this case the same prominence that it has in the dream? Did this lead me toward the diagnosis? It did not. I remained entirely unenlightened for years.

The greatest difficulty with this category of symptoms frequently lies in deciding whether or not they are the caricatures mentioned above. Certain patients are understandably anxious in the beginning, but I remember one who made me spend weeks in showing him his excessive anxiety and in trying to quiet him down. Is this still within the limits of neurotic behavior? It is indispensable that the neurosis be transformed into a transference neurosis, yet I recall a patient, cruelly beaten by his psychotic father as a small child and as an older boy, who, in an absolutely delusory manner, expected me to arise, approach the couch, and beat him. Is this purely neurotic? I learned subsequently that it is not. On the other hand, I am absolutely certain, on the strength of a long analysis, that the woman, cited above, who was aroused to the point of climax by a certain memory, was neurotic. I recall, moreover, the analysis of a man who once became so strongly excited by the memory of a seduction that before I had time to remonstrate, he precipitately began discharging his excitement in masturbation by performing manual frictions through his trousers to the point, as he told me next day, of a copious ejaculation. Should this have made me doubt my original diagnosis, classifying him as a neurotic? Today I know that it should. How does it compare with the woman who in the first session complained of a hirsute breast and asked: "Want to see it?" Her case, by the way, reminds me of another difficulty. She was actually an analyzable ambulatory psychotic in whom I had recognized certain psychotic symptoms from the beginning. Yet I dismissed them all as merely neurotic *identifications* with a violently psychotic mother.

There is one symptom that in my experience, contrary to Freud's, is always pathognomonic: depersonalization. Freud treats this phenomenon ("I do not feel myself") together with derealization ("The environment is not quite real") as states of "alienation," encountered in both neurotics and psychotics. This, if I can rely on certain experiences of my own, is a mistake: derealization occurs in the neurotic (perhaps even the practically normal individual), while depersonalization occurs only in psychotics, sometimes as the only sign of an imminent break. All in all, it is not always easy to draw the line.

IMPORTANCE OF DIAGNOSIS

Why is it necessary to draw it? Why should the establishment of the diagnosis be, if at all possible, your first and foremost task? For several reasons. For one thing one must not be led astray by the limited range of Freud's early article on "Wild Psycho-analysis" (1910b). Its subject is not even an analysis of the period, let alone a procedure that would be called by that name today. An *analysis*, even a *first consultation*, can damage the ambulatory psychotic. I remember a student who was surprised that a patient "came apart at the seams" in an interview as though she were approaching a break. I told him, as any experienced analyst would have told him, that his patient was the kind of psychotic one must prevent from doing anything smacking of free association. Her defenses had to be strengthened, not weakened, and one should forestall, not promote, an onrush of the unconscious her ego could not withstand. He understood, acted accordingly when he next saw her, and reported that she had promptly "mended" and calmed down. I do not personally remember having damaged any psychotic I should have diagnosed instead of trying to analyze. This is, I believe, due to two factors: my generally cautious approach and the prevalence of those psychotics who protect themselves against free association. They outweigh by far, in my experience, those who lay themselves open to damage.

PROGNOSIS

Prognostically speaking, you observe two kinds of ambulatory psychotics: those you can help to a greater or lesser degree and those for whom you, or anyone, can do nothing. Of the latter you meet two different sorts: those you understand, like the characterologically unfit psychiatrist mentioned above, who would rather lie than admit that this fear of having run over someone was a full-fledged delusion, and those you don't comprehend at all. I remember as an example of the latter species a woman whose transference quickly became nymphomaniac.

One day she finally announced that she was quitting. Her analysis (which I had already converted into a mere psychotherapy) did not help her, she said, and the sessions offered her only extreme frustration. I fully agreed both with her reasoning and her resolve. When I started taking this up with her next day, she was greatly astonished, did not know what I was talking about, and claimed she had never said anything of the sort.

TREATMENT

All in all it is so important to lay hold of the diagnosis as early as possible *because your procedure depends on it.* In the case of the ambulatory psychotic you decide to treat, it will either be a psychotherapy, which, although teaching you very little, may improve the life of your patient considerably—and the improvement may last; or it will in rare instances become, after years of psychotherapeutic preparation, a true analysis.

The psychotherapy has hardly to be learned. Your analytic knowledge, although you do not verbalize it, stands silently by your side as Siegfried in the myth stood invisibly behind Gunther. As to interpretative comments: only the scantiest and most superficial. Openings in the material, that in an analysis might be probed as to whether or not they afford an access to the repressed, remain unused. Confessions about the sexual life of your patient are not subject to scrutiny but, if necessary, to reassurance; and there is naturally no interpretation of dreams. Instead, you acquaint your patient, when that becomes requisite, with his symptoms and advise him without insisting that he take your advice. It is only the positive transference that plays a role comparable to the function it exercises in an analysis; negative transference can hardly be dealt with, and it may take all the skill you possess to keep it to the barest minimum; or, better still, to circumvent it. One word of counsel: use the couch. For an approach close enough to lay hold of the patient's unconscious, certain safeguards are necessary—the fee, no other contact than the analytic one, a circumscribed time, etc.

The couch inherited from standard psychoanalysis is one of them. I have come to consider it as an absolute must for all treatment (except, of course, preliminary consultations). The couch is of the same assistance here as it is in a conventional analysis. Use it with the understanding that if need be the patient may look at you or even temporarily sit up (a defense against masturbation). I would not hesitate to say that a patient actually unable to lie down is beyond help.

Mentioning the couch recalls to me the widespread confusion about smoking in the session. I have found it best to let the patient smoke in preliminary consultations if he wishes, but to interdict it on the couch, explaining if necessary that we need all of the mouth for verbalization.

In the case of the potentially analyzable psychotic patient, the treatment will, as was said above, consist of a psychotherapeutic preparation that you allow eventually to blend into an analytic treatment. But even then you will for a while abstain from touching upon or reacting to certain material; in other words, you will exercise much more caution than with a neurotic whose recovery is not jeopardized by a mistake in timing but merely delayed.

PSYCHOTHERAPEUTIC PREPARATION
FOR ANALYSIS

The psychotherapeutic preparation for an analysis of the ambulatory psychotic has not, to my knowledge, been treated in the literature; it deserves therefore perhaps at least two fragmentary illustrations.

#1. In the case of the woman masochist whom a sadistic homosexual voyeur had trained to report daily upon her masturbation fantasies ("Oh, I must hear more about that!"), and who, when we started, continued torturing herself in the same fashion, I responded by rescinding the analytic rule in the very first session. I told her that I had no interest in the subject and no intention of perpetuating her maltreatment. This produced a

wealth of useful information and led relatively soon to the recall of her injurious sexual and aggressive exploitation in childhood and adolescence by her psychotic father and sister. The
mother remained in the background, but not enough for me to
be unaware that she was also psychotic and probably the greatest culprit of all. Here, naturally, not a word of comment. The
lover was presented as "terribly intelligent"; I, by chance, knew
the man and considered him something of an ass. (I need hardly
mention that at the time I kept this to myself.) I learned from
her that he was also a sadist, which evidently made for her
strong attachment. When he lost interest in her, I took the
unorthodox step of asking her to invite him to see me in an
unpaid consultation. Here I informed him in confidence that if
he left her now it would destroy her and requested that he delay throwing her over for a while. Not too long after that, she
dreamt of him as a mean, punitive schoolteacher and began to
see how he was torturing her, giving me an opportunity to
show her that his alleged intelligence was but the result of her
furnishing him with her own. Even this sketchy report explains
why the time was not far distant when she could support the
termination of their liaison. Upon being jilted, she talked of suicide, but she heeded my rather fatuous admonition that one did
not kill oneself in "analysis" since one is bound by an agreement with the analyst to let oneself be helped and if possible to
get well. (I think she obeyed because of a strong positive
transference and because her threat was actually only symbolical:
that of being thrown back upon masturbation [Freud]. She soon
found a somewhat erratic but charming and benevolent lover.
After about three years I was convinced that she had become
strong enough to sustain analysis. Needless to say, the latter
effected amnesia removal, made it possible to deal painlessly with
the fantasies mentioned above, and abolished the need for masturbation.

I am not free to describe the major beneficent changes she
was gradually able to make in her life, but must confine myself
to reporting that she became and has remained to this day a
happy person.

#2. The other case concerned an adolescent with a wealth of typically schizophrenic symptoms. In presenting some of it I must preface my account with Freud's (1912) words, so full of resignation: "As regards the treatment of [the patient's] relatives I must confess myself utterly at a loss . . ." (p. 120). The parents belonged to a group with which I was neither acquainted nor would wish to be. The patient, a bright, honest, and sympathetic girl, was the proverbial "lily on the dung pile." The father sent their physician to see me in order that he, although no psychiatrist, could check on my diagnosis. I can still see him sneering: "Your diagnosis, Doctor, is, of course, based purely on intuition." "No," I answered patiently, "it is not. If a girl tells you that neither bath nor breakfast awaken her and that she comes to only after arriving at school; or that the buildings surrounding the plaza tilt and are bending over, she leaves hardly anything to your intuition." That removed the man, who had already proved himself worthy of his friends, from my office. I also succeeded in dissuading the father from calling me once a week to ask me cheerfully and in a tone reserved by dramatists for the master's use when he speaks to a lackey: "Well, Doctor, how is my daughter doing?" My staving off interference had but a small effect; it gave us three years of preparation and but one of analysis. The reader will therefore not expect a report on an analytic success.

However, shortly after I had begun treating the patient I had an experience I believe worth recounting at the risk of a divagation. I chanced to meet the colleague who had seen the girl before she came to me: a gentle man, older and more experienced than I, and for whose exemplary character I had the greatest respect. He said, "I hear that So-and-So is now with you. There is nothing psychotic, don't you agree?" I told him the truth, described a few symptoms, and could see how hard it was for him to believe me. Later on I found an occasion to tell the patient that I had met Dr. X., that he had chatted about her, and that it turned out that he knew nothing about such and such of her difficulties. How come? She answered promptly, "Because I never told him."

I am not certain what "moral" this little story contains. For one thing the girl was brighter than Dr. X., and that will never work. I have seen it in others and once experienced it myself when the treatment of a psychotic whose intelligence was superior to mine ended in miserable failure. For another thing it takes more than benevolence for the patient to open up. I have observed over the years in preliminary consultations that *the more I understood and the less I said,* the more I was told by the patient. This includes, of course, symptomatic action. I recall a woman who asked me whether it was all right to have relations during her period and who, after being answered, told me mockingly that she had already done it. Had I evaluated her way of playing with her pocketbook at the time of her hypocritical question, I would not have been fooled. Decades later another woman told of her difficulties when she had temporarily been separated from her husband. While she talked, she briefly drew a small semicircle on the arm of the chair with her left forefinger. This was her only way of "telling" me of her conflict over masturbation which (left = wrong) was not confined to her celibate period. I reject emphatically the fictitious idea of extrasensory perception, but I do believe that we do not know all the subtle means a patient may employ in an attempt to bring something to our attention.

This leads back to the adolescent girl. She came to the first—and to the first session only—in evening clothes, lay down in a posture that without the slightest impropriety betokened her unconscious willingness to have me arrogate the *droit du seigneur.* This contrasted sharply with her attire in subsequent sessions: blouse and skirt, with a broad leather belt which had a small pocket bearing the inscription "Mad Money." Her leather purse, clanking with hardware, has been described elsewhere in this volume. Her symbolic resolve to be continent in her sessions was, however, of little avail: In the beginning, I was compelled, against my usual policy, to let her use the bathroom many a time. Her sexual life consisted of placing herself on rare occasions in the bathtub in such a manner that the stream from

the faucet hit her vulva. Her experience was typically schizophrenic in more ways than one: not an arousal but something
else unknown to both of us compelled her to do it; no excitation, let alone a climax was produced; she found herself in a
highly unpleasant, fearful condition, exceedingly difficult to
describe. She had entered what might be called "another
world" clashing with the world as it is. She was not only con-
sumed by utter shame, but she could not comprehend, although
she knew it, that her family was actually in the next room,
unaware of what was going on. This affords an opportunity to
demonstrate why it is impossible to make general statements
about the psychotic. On the one hand I have heard the same
technique described by a psychotic woman in whom both masturbatory act and effect were perfectly normal: she was aroused
and obtained an orgastic climax. On the other hand I have
gained the impression that certain psychotics commit sexual
(probably also aggressive) acts in a certain "exceptional state"
superimposed upon their psychoses and terminating with their
gratification. I am altogether unable to attempt even a description of this state.

To return to the girl: toward her parents she was when she
entered treatment both uncritical and submissive. She told of
some of her father's crooked and even illegal actions in a tone
of admiration for his cleverness and saw nothing irregular in the
mother's doing "beauty exercises" requiring knee-elbow position in front of her two younger brothers. She merely asked me
about "that little piece of flesh" hanging down between the legs
of the mother in that position. (When I informed her about the
labia minora and their often unequal shape and size, I could
hear the relief in her voice.) She told me repeatedly of a certain
well-known book the mother was reading, unaware that the
ostentatious, schizophrenic woman lacked the education as well
as the power of concentration requisite to absorb its content.
The only critical observation she ever dared make concerned
the internist mentioned above. He had her undress completely
under the pretense of an examination, and then "jokingly"

made an improper comment. Without criticizing the comment, she remarked mildly, "He should not have said that just while I was without clothes."

I refrain, lest I be repetitious, from describing the treatment in detail. I will restrict myself to illustrating, each with one example, the impact of the transference upon the patient, her becoming more closely acquainted with a symptom, and the unorthodoxy of the psychotherapeutic technique employed with her.

In re transference, she became able to have her first petting session with a boy more or less her own age. In talking about it she said with charming naïveté, "But I was unfaithful to him; I thought several times of you." The symptom originally described as hearing a disturbingly loud voice changed to hearing angry quarreling voices, an alteration that would, I believe, if the analysis had been allowed to go on, have proven itself the first step toward amnesia removal for a traumatic event. With regard to technique, she surprised me once by appearing with three oil paintings, her own work, representing young women. One was so well done that it could have taken its place in any gallery devoted to this kind of art. We propped them up on the floor and discussed them for the whole length of the session.

During the psychotherapy the mother was cooperative because it took the girl, who had been a nuisance in clinging anxiously to her, off her hands. After a year of analysis the patient began to become a person in her own right, independent of the tyrannical woman's approval, critical of her mother, and rebelling against her domination. I acceded to the mother's request for a consultation, in the hope of smoothing the daughter's path; but I failed. Furious, arrogant, without a trace of respect, the mother proved inaccessible to reason. At the same time something happened that should be mentioned because it bears upon technique. I have never prescribed a drug for an analytic patient because I consider so doing equivalent to breast feeding and therefore an acting out, apt to render the transference both unworkable and extremely regressive. In the rare instances where medication became necessary I have never met with the slightest objection when I told the patient to ask his doctor for the prescription. Not so in this case: the doctor felt that I had "put something over on him" when he heard that I was responsible for his patient's request. From then on it took only two or three days until the parents interrupted all treatment, forcing abrupt "termination."

An epilogic remark: I had deluded myself into believing that I would be allowed to finish the analysis of the girl. On the strength of the last year's results I had no doubt about the immediate outcome. I was merely afraid that when she became 23 years of age the organic process might worsen precipitately and wipe out what I had been able to achieve. I had observed long ago that this age (more accurately the period between 22 and three-quarters and 23 and one-half years of age is a critical one for individuals of her type. There is at the present no way of arresting this process; I could only hope that my patient might escape such an exacerbation. If she did, I was convinced she would be as well off as the patient previously described.

Perhaps two years after I had been "given the boot," another patient, sane, sober, reliable, who knew the girl, chanced upon her in a public place. She saw a young woman who, she reported, looked so unhappy and literally shrivelled up that she refrained from asking her how she was. She also noticed that a cosmetic operation, wished for by the parents but vetoed by me more than once, had been forced upon her, and she knew that she had been married off to someone who, it turned out, had been more strongly attracted by the father's wealth than by his daughter. My tactful informant restricted herself to only two questions: "How is your husband?" which was answered with, "He's not my type," and "How is the baby?" "Well, she cries all the time." I do not think that this report, brief though it be, requires a comment.

The incompleteness of these all too short "notes," based as they are upon the experience of a single analyst, is understand-

able. The purpose was to increase the student's diagnostic faculty by acquainting him with a number of pathognomonic and
potentially pathognomonic symptoms, to convey an impression
of the technique for the psychotherapy of the unanalyzable
psychotic patient, and of the psychotherapeutic preparation of
the eventually analyzable one.

POSTSCRIPT

I have been granted the satisfaction of seeing the three volumes of my Psychoanalytic Series completed: *Erogeneity and Libido* and *Ego and Body Ego* are printed; the last volume, *Symbol, Dream, and Psychosis,* is ready to join them. All three are one work comprised of original findings made over more than three decades of fascinating experience. They were written on a glass-slabbed desk facing a blank wall, conducive to concentration. Above my desk hangs a reproduction of a Duccio, that many years ago in a shop window attracted my wife; she had it framed for me. Against the well-known golden Byzantine background lies a boat with two fisherman (the traditional Christ to the left), lowering their finely knotted net in order to scoop, as I have tried to scoop, from the deep, listening to those who have sought my help. It has sustained me over the years. Two prior books, quite unoriginal, have been well received. My original writings, however, have had a mixed reception. My keenest critic tells me that this is due, in the last analysis, to one finding: the etiology of the (severe) neurosis in the traumata inflicted upon the child by a psychotic parent. He sees the basis of psychic illness not so much in the castration complex as in the parental psychosis.

It has taken me time to recognize my isolation as another blessing: I had never to please anyone, and have been undisturbed in listening to my own "critical institution."

Freud was another Columbus; no one but he could detect a Continent. But as administrator, as had Columbus, he failed. Even in Abraham's lifetime some to whom he entrusted his work were ill chosen. After Abraham's death, his propensity to choose wrongly went unchecked. This eventually made for a "movement" of which, except for some teaching and supervision, I was never part, and upon which I turned my back as soon as I could retire.

Yet the life of a human is short and the life of truth is long. No one can today be confident that the world as we know it will hold together. Should it hold, truth will out as it has always done. When it does, those of my contributions which advance our science will, amongst analysts, become common knowledge.

411

APPENDIX

OBSERVATIONS ON AMBULATORY PSYCHOTICS

The residual observations jotted down here notebook style would not, were I younger, be printed. I would hold them back in the hope that what is more or less aphoristic could be studied further—perhaps understood, but at any rate be expanded. As it is, I must leave that to others who might become interested in the subjects of the remarks to follow. I have placed them in an appendix because they do not exclusively concern, if at all, the "particular type" of ambulatory psychotic described in Chapter Three, but the ambulatory psychotic at large.

(a) *The overcathexis of word images by the psychotic* was discovered by Freud. I saw it three times and mention it here because it seems to take on such radically different forms. Long ago when it was still mandatory for a widow to spend a year clad in black, the evidently psychotic recently widowed grandmother of a patient bought herself a colorful new dress. Questioned by the objecting family she answered, "Well, he [her late husband] always said to me, 'Why don't you get yourself a new dress?' "

A psychotic writer occasionally used Latin words, such as *et al.* and *inter alias,* or the British "albeit" instead of "although." I knew the man well and had the distinct impression that he was convinced of having said something of substance by merely exchanging foreign or archaic words for ordinary ones.

A psychotic woman patient who was unable to own sexual drives told me at two different times: *"If it is necessary for the analysis to have intercourse with you, I would do it."* When I answered, "No, that is not necessary," the matter each time was dropped. The casualness of her tone is difficult to describe; her voice was less inflected or altered than if she had said, "It is raining a little" or, "The sun is in my eyes." Even the slightest approach to an introspective comment was rejected. She would not associate to it, let alone answer questions such as, "Why do you think this now comes suddenly to your mind?" The italicized sentence in the flattest possible voice was all that one obtained. It was as though the overcathexis of the word images of which it consisted were capable of absorbing all affect.

(b) *Some psychotics have difficulty with time.* Two weeks before a certain public performance, I received a charming note from the performer, asking for an appointment. There was nothing in the note to arouse any diagnostic suspicion. My correspondent was well known and unusually accomplished, as I personally knew from experience because I had once listened to her on the radio. She did appear, but was 20 minutes late, which she mentioned in a tone of desperation. She was anxious and greatly worried about being able to carry off the performance. Although the consultation left no doubt now as to her diagnosis, I decided, against all odds, on a psychotherapeutic attempt to save the performance. Her intelligence, her previous accomplishments, and the fact that performing as she did could, as Freud has discovered, easily have a symbolic meaning, were, as far as I can remember, some of the factors going into my decision. For that second appointment she did not, however, appear, nor did she send word of any kind. My bill went unhonored. What became of her I do not know; shortly, before the performance however, the newspapers carried a notice of its cancellation.

The second example stems from a phase of the analysis of a patient with a psychotic disturbance. It is interesting because the circumstances furnished a practically experimental set-up. The patient, head of a department, was free to come and go, and her office was only a relatively short distance from mine. She therefore walked to her session, which eliminated all variables inherent in public transportation. Yet she was always either a few minutes late or too early. I do not know and she did not know how she did it. It happened independently of her trying to avoid it. She even went so far as to ask for the recorded "correct time" by phone before she left. Nor was I able to lay hold of whatever in her analysis eventually abolished the trouble. At one time it simply disappeared.

(c) *The psychotic sometimes goes by opposites.* He acts, I remember saying occasionally to patients, as though the white walls of my office were black. The example under (a) can be used as an illustration; custom demands dark mourning clothes, consequently a colorful dress is acquired. This again is a matter in which I have been remiss by not making notes; I can therefore only offer a few illustrations from daily life. One of these caused me grief: a close friend had injured a tendon on one foot. The orthopedist, who should have kept the foot out of action, said instead: "You can walk on it all you want." (Needless to say the man had been authoritatively recommended and I became aware of his diagnosis only later.) Wanting some fresh air before a concert, we left the taxi a few blocks away from Carnegie Hall, to walk. I still remember being in ecstasy over a rendition of the Overture to *Don Giovanni* such as I had never heard before and will never hear again, while my companion, by then in torture from the abused foot, was unable to appreciate a note.

The few remaining observations are household ones reported to me by friends to whom I told the symptom. Prefatorily I should explain that during the last few years of our life in New York, one could obtain as household help on a part-time basis only maids with short tenure from a bonded service. They were, it would appear, without exception overtly schizophrenic.

The notes (jotted down at my request): "If maids are told to do anything specific, the chances are that the opposite will be done. 'Please clean the glass table with Windex.' (Table left still soiled.) 'Please ring when you come in.' (Given the key of the apartment since they came daily, they invariably entered without ringing.) A sign on a door between professional section and private part of the apartment, which bore a sign to kindly close, was constantly left open, *other* doors carefully closed.

"They came early when requested to come later, and vice

versa. Requested to do light dusting and not a thorough vac-uuming, they did the latter. If requested to speed up a certain job in order to get along with the rest of the regularly pre-scribed work, they would slow up, etc., etc. One finally had to be dismissed because, although hired for a certain number of hours, and paid by the hour, she could not be made to leave. In no case was their behavior due to ill will."

(d) Some psychotics show a need for *"perpetual stimulation."* The term is not mine but that of a colleague with whom I once discussed the subject. It would appear that such stimulation insures the psychotic against an evidently threatening dissolu-tion of ego. This need could perhaps explain a number of data in analysis as well as observations in daily life. There is not only the frequency of masturbation by the psychotic, discussed above, but the complaint of patients that they were perpetually abused sexually by their psychotic mothers. Every dressing, undressing, bathing, etc., involved the imposition upon the child of some sexual contact. However, the stimulation need not always be a sexual one. An errand boy, for example, suspected of being psychotic, carried in addition to heavy grocery orders a large transistor radio that poisoned the air without let-up. Anyone could multiply such observations from everyday life many times.

Far from suggesting that the demand to abolish silence first came from psychotics, I have nevertheless come to appreciate the words of an older colleague, used by him in a private con-versation, when he thoughtfully spoke of "Our schizophrenic age. . . ."

(e) *There are certain psychotics who live with a "secret fanta-sy" about themselves.* A typist who specializes in copying medi-cal and psychiatric manuscripts sends out bills headed "For professional services" and printed exactly like those of doctors. An intelligent training analysand agreed with me that her mother, who did counseling in social work, was, in her own eyes, a psychiatrist.

This secret fantasy is never actually admitted by the ambula-tory psychotic. The nearest to a "confession" I ever recorded was that of a harmless game played by a family after they had

had their dinner. The mother would say, "Now let's all pretend that we are an old Southern family and remain seated while the colored help are clearing the table and doing the dishes." After a while everyone got up and helped clear the table and wash the dishes.

(f) *In sharp contrast to the secrecy* with which the ambulatory psychotic usually conceals his symptomatology from public, acquaintances, and spouse, *one occasionally encounters the manifestation of a confession-compulsion*. Two patients who, in a psychotherapy told of having sexual dealings with children did so with great ease, although they could have concealed it. I also found the following little note in one of my folders on the ambulatory psychotic.

"The maid had asked to use the phone. Before she could put in her call there was an incoming call. After answering it and waiting a while, I walked out and asked the maid if she had finished with the phone. She said she had gone to use it but that she heard voices. I said: 'Yes, a call came in.'

"*Maid* (who had heard the phone ring announcing the call): 'No, this was *before.*'

"I have not the slightest idea of what prompted this woman, whom I hardly knew, to inform me that she 'heard voices.' "

(g) *Confusion combined with complete lack of insight in an ambulatory psychotic.*

I found, finally, in the same folder a newspaper clipping from the *New York Herald Tribune*, dated June 9, 1963:

Lisburn, Northern Ireland

Miss Margaret Hunter, 65, Britain's most determined woman driver, said yesterday she failed her latest driving test because of the tyranny of officialdom.

Miss Hunter, a retired schoolteacher, has been learning to drive since the end of World War II but has not quite made it because, she said, "My reactions are too fast."

Her latest ordeal came Friday when she flunked 12 of 19 points on a driver's test after turning the wrong way down a one-way street and getting stuck for 10 minutes behind a parked taxi.

"I was perfectly calm," she said afterward. "They just don't want to give me a license, that's all."

Miss Hunter first drove into the headlines in her native Stockport, England, last year when her instructor, Stanley Davenport, jumped from her car in mid-lesson and fled, shouting, "This is suicide!" Undaunted, Miss Hunter drove herself home—and was fined $3 for driving without a license.

Since then her driving escapades have involved:

A demonstration spin with a woman reporter aboard that lasted 100 yards before Miss Hunter hit a truck, wrecked her car and was fined $14 for reckless driving.

Two driving tests in which she was flunked—once before she started because she could get no insurance in her home town; once for making seven false starts, running a red light and parking three feet from the curb.

Driving lessons from which two male instructors resigned precipitately.

She came to this Northern Ireland town to make a fresh start.

No one will ask me: Do you know this woman? Have you examined her? Because I would only answer: I do not have to. There is confusion as complete as the lack or insight for it. There is the "They" (fourth paragraph) that one hears from every paranoiac, and the going by opposites: "My reactions are too fast"—when they are obviously too slow (second paragraph). "One way"—she goes the other (third paragraph); taxi parked— taxi in motion (ibid); red light = stop—she goes; and: park close to the curb—she parks a whole yard away from it.

What puzzled me for a while was the question: Why is the report on this sick old woman so funny? Thinking it over I noticed at first the consummate craftsmanship of the nameless reporter: his neutral stance, his terse style, how every sentence makes a point, and how he manages to compress almost 20 years into a few lines. Only later I recognized the weightier reason, which is of a (psycho) economic nature. The protagonist does not suffer. We do not therefore have to expend any affect on compassion. We are free to react with all available affect to the comic.

GLOSSARY

Anal Reversal: A cathectic displacement from the front (oral-erotic and phallic erogenic zones) to the back (anal-erotic zones) in the interest of the mastery of affect and the preservation of continence. Such displacement (Abraham) is undergone because the superior strength of the anal sphincter allows for a greater dependence upon it. Symbolically the reversal can appear as one of right and left, east and west (Jones), cause and effect (Freud), or time (I, 125–128).

Demi-institutions: The two complementary parts of the ego (in its narrowest sense) I have hypothecated and termed *partial subject* and *introject* (q.v.). Their typography may be likened to a transverse "split" in the ego (as opposed to Freud's longitudinal one). Normally, the two are indistinguishable because of their smooth synergistic working together. In pathology they become recognizable in consequence of a split of the ego into its two constituent parts which oppose each other (as in depersonalization: *I* do not feel *myself*") (II, 77–179).

Distal End of the Vagina: The distal third of the vagina combines with vulva and clitoris to form a pleasure-physiologic organ that can be separately stimulated to the point of an orgastic reaction (II, 272).

Gebärmutter: In the German language the symbol equation between womb and mother finds a direct linguistic expression, inasmuch as the word for womb is *Gebärmutter*, literally "parturition-mother." It is the site of the deposition of the introjected mother (I, 208–209).

Introject: One of the two demi-institutions (q. v.) hypothecated for a transverse division in the ego. It develops out of identifications with the group and is proximal to the superego. When studiable, it is the exponent of aggression more or less completely defused.

"Mother comes in": An indirect representation of the partial subject. "If, in the body ego, the "womb" is the seat of the early mother who became located there by introjection, it is expectable that under certain conditions the mother will appear in projection as a symbolic representation of the 'womb.' This is indeed so, for instance, in menstrual dreams.

"At the onset or at the cessation of a menstrual period the womb enters into, relatively speaking, or disappears from the body ego in consequence of its relative prominence in the body as a result of the glandular cycle. In dreams symbolizing this entry the mother enters the room. . . . I have hardly ever heard that such a dream occurred near the middle of the menses; it is almost always dreamt at the beginning or at the end. Why the recess of the womb in the body ego should also be symbolized by the mother's entry is not clear" (I, 216).

Partial subject: The second of the two demi-institutions (q.v.) I have postulated for the ego. The complementary part of the ego centering around an erogenic zone and subject of a particular set of instinctual strivings (oral-erotic, oral-sadistic, anal-sadistic, etc.). It is therefore that part of the ego close to and serving the id and is essentially the exponent of sexuality and/or aggression.

Pleasure-Physiologic Body Ego: A preconscious psychic formation consists, roughly speaking, of the totality of the mental representation of the erogenic zones. This, however, is subject to the following qualifications: (1) There is a constant libidinal cathexis and decathexis corresponding to a libidinization and delibidinization of elements of the body ego, which thereby become descriptively conscious or unconscious respectively. (Examples: ordinarily the representation of the vagina is descriptively unconscious, i.e., preconscious. But during a gynecological examination it can become conscious as an element of the "body image" (Schilder), or body ego. In a state of sexual excitation it also becomes conscious, but now as *an element of the pleasure-physiologic body ego.* (2) Since the "whole body" (Freud) or any part of it can become an erogenic zone in consequence of its temporary sexualization, *the number of elements of the pleasure-physiologic body ego is indefinite and varies from one moment to another.* (3) *The mental representation of erogenic zones* in the pleasure-physiologic body ego *is inseparable from the representation of their function* (II, 206–285).

Pleasure-Physiologic Body Ego—Its Projectability into the Outside World: For clinical observations which suggest the proposition that parts of the pleasure-physiologic body ego are projected into the outside world effecting an "equation" between ourselves and the environment, see II, 246–254.

Refractory Narcissism: The hypothesis of "refractory narcissism" is a small addendum to Freud's theory of the libido. This theory names the ego as the reservoir of the libido from which the latter is sent out toward objects. In cathecting these objects it transforms itself from narcissistic libido into object libido. If an object is decathected, the libido returns as narcissistic libido into the ego. Certain clinical experiences (II, 304–317) led me to propose "that there is an amount of narcissistic libido, varying from individual to individual, that resists the transformation into object libido but lends itself nevertheless to the cathexis of objects. I suggest the term refractory narcissism for this residual narcissistic libido because it resists the only vicissitude undergone by narcissistic libido: the transformation into object libido" (II, p. 307).

Symbolization and the Pleasure-Physiologic Body Ego: The pleasure-physiologic body ego is dominated by the primary process (displacement, overdetermination, condensation, picturization, allusion). Symbolization is but another phase of the primary process (II, 228–230).

Zone Equation: The subjective and temporary equation of an erogenic zone with one of the object has been previously described for the case of the equation of one's own genital with that of the partner during orgasm (I, 274–279).

REFERENCES

Abraham, H. C. & Freud, E. L., eds. (1965), *The Letters of Sigmund Freud and Karl Abraham*. New York: Basic Books.

Abraham, K. (1907), On the Significance of Sexual Trauma in Childhood for the Symptomotology of Dementia Praecox. In: *Clinical Papers and Essays on Psychoanalysis*, ed. H. Abraham. New York: Basic Books, 1955, pp. 13–20.

_____ (1908), The Psycho-Sexual Difference between Hysteria and Dementia Praecox. In: *Selected Papers*. New York: Basic Books, 1953, pp. 64–79.

_____ (1910), Remarks on the Psycho-Analysis of a Case of Foot and Corset Fetishism. In: *Selected Papers*. New York: Basic Books, 1953, pp. 125–136.

_____ (1913), Restrictions and Transformations of Scoptophilia in Psycho-Neurotics. In: *Selected Papers*. New York: Basic Books, 1953, pp. 169–234.

_____ (1922), The Spider as a Dream Symbol. In: *Selected Papers*. New York: Basic Books, 1953, pp. 326–332.

_____ (1924a), The Influence of Oral Erotism on Character-Formation. In: *Selected Papers*. New York: Basic Books, 1953, pp. 393–406.

_____ (1924b), A Short Study of the Development of the Libido, Viewed in the Light of Mental Disorders. In: *Selected Papers*. New York: Basic Books, 1953, pp. 418–501.

Arlow, J. (1949), Anal Sensations and Feelings of Persecution. *Psychoanal. Quart.*, 18:79–84.

Boccaccio, G. (1940), *Decameron*. New York: Triangle Books.

Breuer, J. & Freud, S. (1895), Studies on Hysteria. *Standard Edition*, 2. London: Hogarth Press, 1955.

Deutsch, H. (1932), *Psychoanalysis of the Neuroses*. London: Hogarth Press and Institute of Psycho-Analysis, 1950.

Feldman, S. (1945), Interpretation of a Typical and Stereotyped Dream Met with Only During Psychoanalysis. *Psychoanal. Quart.*, 14:511–515.

Ferenczi, S. (1909), Introjection and Transference. In: *Sex in Psychoanalysis.* New York: Basic Books, 1950, pp. 35–93.

———— (1930), The Principle of Relaxation and Neocatharsis. *Internat. J. Psycho-Anal.,* 11:428–443.

———— (1931), Child Analysis in the Analysis of Adults. *Internat. J. Psycho-Anal.,* 12:468–482.

———— (1933), Confusion of Tongues between Adults and the Child. *Internat. J. Psycho-Anal.,* 30:225–230 (1949).

Fliess, R. (1953), The Hypnotic Evasion: A Clinical Observation. *Psychoanal. Quart.,* 22:497–511.

———— (1956), *Erogeneity and Libido.* New York: International Universities Press.

———— (1961), *Ego and Body Ego.* New York: International Universities Press, 1972.

Foster, J. (1908), *A Shakespeare Word Book.* New York: Russell & Russell, 1969.

Freud, S. (1887–1902), *The Origins of Psychoanalysis.* New York: Basic Books, 1954.

———— (1896), Further Remarks on the Neuropsychoses of Defence. *Standard Edition,* 3:159–185. London: Hogarth Press, 1962.

———— (1900), The Interpretation of Dreams. *Standard Edition,* 4 & 5. London: Hogarth Press, 1953.

———— (1901), The Psychopathology of Everyday Life. *Standard Edition,* 6. London: Hogarth Press, 1960.

———— (1905), Three Essays on the Theory of Sexuality. *Standard Edition,* 7:125–243. London: Hogarth Press, 1953.

———— (1909a), Analysis of a Phobia in a Five-Year-Old Boy. *Standard Edition,* 10:3–147. London: Hogarth Press, 1955.

———— (1909b), Notes Upon a Case of Obsessional Neurosis. *Standard Edition,* 10:153–249. London: Hogarth Press, 1955.

———— (1910a), The Future Prospects of Psycho-Analytic Therapy. *Standard Edition,* 11:140–151. London: Hogarth Press, 1957.

———— (1910b), 'Wild' Psycho-Analysis. *Standard Edition,* 11:220–227. London: Hogarth Press, 1957.

———— (1911), Psycho-Analytic Notes on an Autobiographical Account of a Case of Paranoia. *Standard Edition,* 12:3–82. London: Hogarth Press, 1958.

———— (1912), Recommendations for Physicians Practising Psycho-Analysis. *Standard Edition,* 12:110–120. London: Hogarth Press, 1958.

———— (1914), On the History of the Psycho-Analytic Movement. *Standard Edition,* 14:3–66. London: Hogarth Press, 1957.

———— (1915a), A Case of Paranoia Running Counter to the Psycho-

Analytic Theory of the Disease. *Standard Edition*, 14:262–272. London: Hogarth Press, 1957.

_____ (1915b), The Unconscious. *Standard Edition*, 14:161–204. London: Hogarth Press, 1957.

_____ (1915–1917), Introductory Lectures on Psycho-Analysis. *Standard Edition*, 15 & 16. London: Hogarth Press, 1963.

_____ (1917), A Metapsychological Supplement to the Theory of Dreams. *Standard Edition*, 14:219–235. London: Hogarth Press, 1957.

_____ (1918), From the History of an Infantile Neurosis. *Standard Edition*, 17:3–122. London: Hogarth Press, 1955.

_____ (1919a), A Child is Being Beaten. *Standard Edition*, 17:177–204. London: Hogarth Press, 1955.

_____ (1919b), The 'Uncanny.' *Standard Edition*, 17:218–252. London: Hogarth Press, 1955.

_____ (1920), Associations of a Four-Year-Old Child. *Standard Edition*, 18:266. London: Hogarth Press, 1955.

_____ (1921), Group Psychology and the Analysis of the Ego. *Standard Edition*, 18:67–143. London: Hogarth Press, 1955.

_____ (1922), Dreams and Telepathy. *Standard Edition*, 18:197–220. London: Hogarth Press, 1955.

_____ (1923a), The Ego and the Id. *Standard Edition*, 19:3–66. London: Hogarth Press, 1961.

_____ (1923b), Remarks on the Theory and Practice of Dream Interpretation. *Standard Edition*, 19:108–121. London: Hogarth Press, 1961.

_____ (1925), An Autobiographical Study. *Standard Edition*, 20:3–74. London: Hogarth Press, 1959.

_____ (1927), Fetishism. *Standard Edition*, 21:149–157. London: Hogarth Press, 1961.

_____ (1930), Civilization and Its Discontents. *Standard Edition*, 21:59–145. London: Hogarth Press, 1961.

_____ (1931), Female Sexuality. *Standard Edition*, 21:223–243. London: Hogarth Press, 1961.

_____ (1932), The Acquisition and Control of Fire. *Standard Edition*, 22:185–193. London: Hogarth Press, 1964.

_____ (1933), New Introductory Lectures on Psycho-Analysis. *Standard Edition*, 22:3–182. London: Hogarth Press, 1964.

_____ (1935), The Subtleties of a Faulty Action. *Standard Edition*, 22:232–235. London: Hogarth Press, 1964.

_____ (1936), A Disturbance of Memory on the Acropolis. *Standard Edition*, 22:239–248. London: Hogarth Press, 1964.

_____ (1937a), Analysis Terminable and Interminable. *Standard Edition*, 23:211–253. London: Hogarth Press, 1964.

————— (1937b), Constructions in Analysis. *Standard Edition*, 23:256–269. London: Hogarth Press, 1964.

————— (1940), An Outline of Psycho-Analysis. *Standard Edition*, 23:141–207. London: Hogarth Press, 1964.

————— & Oppenheim, E. (1911), Dreams in Folklore. *Standard Edition*, 12:177–203. London: Hogarth Press, 1958.

Gauthier, S. (1948), Pablo Picasso. *Look Magazine,* December 10, 1968.

Grotjahn, M. (1942), The Process of Awakening. *Psychoanal. Rev.,* 29:1–19.

Heissig, W. (1964), *A Lost Civilisation.* London: Thames & Hudson.

Jones, E. (1916), The Theory of Symbolism. In: *Papers on Psycho-Analysis.* Baltimore: Williams & Wilkins, 1950, pp. 89–144.

————— (1953), *The Life and Work of Sigmund Freud,* Vol. I. New York: Basic Books.

Kempe, C. H., Silverman, F. N., Steele, B. F., Droegemueller, W., & Silver, H. K. (1962), The Battered Child Syndrome. *J.A.M.A.,* 181:17–24.

Klein, M. (1930), The Importance of Symbol-Formation in the Development of the Ego. *Internat. J. Psycho-Anal.,* 11:24–39.

Kris, E. (1952), *Psychoanalytic Explorations in Art.* New York: International Universities Press.

La Bruyère, J. (1688), *Characters.* New York: Oxford University Press, 1963.

Partridge, E. (1960), *A Dictionary of Slang and Unconventional English.* London: Routledge & Kegan Paul.

Peto, A. (1959), Body Image and Archaic Thinking. *Internat. J. Psycho-Anal.,* 40:223–231.

Rank, O. & Sachs, H. (1913), *The Significance of Psychoanalysis for the Mental Sciences.* New York: Nervous and Mental Diseases Publishing Company, 1916.

Rewald, J. (1962), *History of Impressionism.* New York: Museum of Modern Art, 1969.

Schilder, P. & Kauders, O. (1926), A Textbook of Hypnosis. In: Schilder, P., *The Nature of Hypnosis.* New York: International Universities Press, 1956, pp. 45–184.

Searl, M. N. (1932), A Note of Depersonalization. *Internat. J. Psycho-Anal.,* 13:329–347.

Shakespeare, W., *Collected Works.* London: Nonesuch Press, 1953.

Steffens, L. (1931), *Autobiography.* New York: Harcourt Brace Jovanovitch.

Stekel, W. (1910), Rechts und Links. *Zentralblatt für Psychoanalyse und Psychotherapie,* 1:67–68.

————— (1911), *Sex and Dreams.* Boston: Badger, 1922.

Sterba, E. (1940), Child Analysis. In: *Readings in Psychoanalytic Psychology,* ed. M. Levitt. New York: Appleton-Century-Crofts, pp. 287–310.

Webster's (1942) *Dictionary of Synonyms.* Springfield, Mass.: G. & C. Merriam Co.

———— (1947) *New International Dictionary*, second edition. Springfield, Mass.: G. & C. Merriam Co.

Wentworth, H. & Flexner, S. (1960), *The Dictionary of American Slang*. New York: Crowell.

Young, L. (1964), *Wednesday's Children: A Study of Child Neglect and Abuse.* New York: McGraw-Hill.

INDEX

Abraham, H., 254, 421
Abraham, K., 12, 25, 30, 83, 92, 147,
    151, 224, 234, 236, 254–255,
    328, 339, 391, 392, 411, 418, 421
Abstinence rule, 99, 141–142, 143,
    259, 350–352, 357, 362
Abuse of child, see Aggressive abuse
    of child, Sexual abuse of child
Accident proneness, 57–58
Affect
    and symbolization, 324–326
    in typical dreams, 155, 156, 169,
    180
Aggression
    cannibalistic, 104
    defused, 206, 243–246, 286, 288,
    418
    fused, 14–15, 164, 247–251, 286,
    287
    and symbolization, 13–15
    see also Aggressive abuse of
    child, Libido
Aggressive abuse of child, 62, 112,
    164, 205–261, 317, 355, 371,
    381
    and hypnosis, 266–268
    and hypnotic evasion, 285–291
    see also Sexual abuse of child
Aichhorn, A., 238
Alienation, states of, 311–332
Ambulatory psychosis, 204–261
    diagnostic considerations of, 393–
    401
    prognosis of, 401–402
    symptomatology, 395–400, 412–
    417
    treatment of, 402–410

Amnesia removal, 53–54, 336
    and bizarre behavior patterns,
    370–374
    and confirmation of memories,
    370–380
    and early trauma, 205–206, 213,
    223–224, 231, 267, 270, 284,
    285, 351–358, 364–365
    and symbol translation, 56,
    57–58, 60–61, 63, 88–89, 106,
    110, 112, 115
    technique of, 219–220, 269, 366–
    392
Anal excitation and paranoid delu-
    sions, 338–343
Anal reversal, 418
Anal-sadistic phase,
    regression to, 287
    symbolization in, 23–24
Anti-Semitism, 93–94, 334–335
Arlow, J., 338–421
Arousal dreams, 129–134, 170 171,
    178
Associations
    and memory quality, 384–388
    and repressed memory, 374–375
    see also Free association
Autohypnosis, 47–48, 190, 264–311
    during analytic hour, 272–274
    and childhood hypnosis, 267–274
    and hallucinations, 299–300
    in Shakespeare, 289–291
    see also Hypnotic evasion

Bach, J. S., 288–290
Battered child syndrome, 214–219
Beating fantasy, 247–249

Birth, symbols for, 40, 82, 84, 197, 309
Boccaccio, G., 3–8, 11, 15, 16–17, 18, 19, 33, 38, 42, 121, 421
Breuer, J., 311, 421
Brunswick, R. M., 95, 387, 394

Cannibalistic aggression, 97, 104, 193–194
  symbols of, 13–14
Castration,
  fantasies, 386, 388
  complex, 359
  symbols for, 14–15, 24–25
Cathexis
  displacement of, 418
  of external world in sleep, 123–126
  of object world, see "Symbolic equation"
  of refractorily narcissistic libido, 19, 45–48
  of symbols, 9–10, 11, 31
Cézanne, P., 321, 345
Claustrophobia, see sub Freud
Clemenceau, G., vii
Color symbolism, 89, 109–111
Color symbolism, 89, 109–111
Compulsive talking
  as incontinence equivalent, 236
Condensation
  and pleasure-physiologic process, 128
  symbolic, 37–41
Consciousness, states of, see Exceptional states of consciousness
Constructions, 368–369
Continence
  and dreaming, 159–172, 191–193
  and transverse ego split, 318
Continuity of self
  and memory, 381–383
Counteridentification as resistance, 359–360
Countertransference as resistance, 358–359
Couperin, F., 111

Day residue and spoken word in dreams, 137, 139–146

Death
  symbols for, 12, 173, 182
  wishes, 157–158
Defense
  states of alienation as, 315, 330
  symbolization as, 117–120
  see also Hypnotic evasion, sub specific defenses
Delusion, 15–16, 72, 91
  in dreams, 147, 201–203
  and erogeneity, 338–343
Demi-institutions of ego, 199, 297, 314–315, 318, 418
Depersonalization, 313–320, 418
  and derealization, 313, 400
Derealization, 274, 287, 311, 321–332, 333, 379
  and depersonalization, 313, 400
Desexualization and symbolization, 9–10
Detail, importance of, 369–370, 375, 387
Deutsch, H., 47, 48, 421
Diagnosis of ambulatory psychosis, 393–401
Displacement, 375, 418
  of spoken word in dream, 145–151
  see also Displacement symbol
Displacement symbol, 25, 26, 32–33, 41–43, 80–82, 86–89, 108–109, 294, 328
Dream hallucination, 147
  theory of, 122–135
Dream symbolism and symbolism, 7, 156
Droegemueller, W., 214, 424
Dream(s)
  aftermath of, 189–190
  and amnesia removal, 376–380
  arousal, 131–133
  associations to, 384–388
  ceiling of, 189±190
  and continence, 159–172, 191–193
  delusion in, 147, 201–203
  derealization in, 326–328
  ellipsis in, 191–197

floor of, 190–197
Freud's, 124, 125, 144–145, 160–162, 203
"harmless," 155, 378
punishment, 139, 152, 200, 200n
spoken word in, 135–154
topographical analysis of, 187–199
see also Symbolically typical dreams, Truly typical dreams, Typical dreams

Ego, 83
alterations of in dreaming, 187–199
demi-institutions of, 199, 297, 314–315, 318, 418
and hypnosis, 293, 297, 298
transverse split in, 314–315, 318, 383, 418
Ellipsis in dreams, 191–197
Empathy and psychoanalytic technique, 219–220, 224, 360
Enson, B., 24n, 108n
Erogeneity, influence of on thought, 332–343
Exceptional states of consciousness, 262–345
Excretion
genital, 281–283
retention of and autohypnosis, 299, 301, 305, 307, 308–309, 310
see also Continence, Incontinence, Urethral erotism
Exhibitionism, 278
in ambulatory psychosis, 226–227, 242
Experience versus fantasy, 206 212
see also Memory versus fantasy
"Eye-mouth unit," 73–75, 193, 320

Fantasy
beating, 247–249
of cloaca, 91–93, 326, 328, 331, 338
and erogeneity, 333–338
and experience, 206–212
homosexual, 106

versus memory, 53–55, 205–212, 353–358, 368–388
and neurosis, 212
ready-made, 187, 193, 199
see also sub Masturbation
Father and abuse of child, 257–259
see also Aggressive abuse of child, Sexual abuse of child, sub Symbol
Federn, P., 67
Feldman, S., 74, 177–178, 421
Ferenczi, S., 31, 68, 212–214, 216, 265–266, 293, 422
Flexner, S., 94, 425
Foster, J., 333, 422
Free association, 190n
Free floating attention, 210–212
and amnesia removal, 367–368
Freud, E., 254, 424
Freud, S., vii, viii, 5, 9, 11, 18, 30–35 passim, 45, 61, 63, 67, 69, 70, 75n, 83, 85, 86, 90, 95–104 passim, 114n, 116, 121, 143, 154, 159, 186, 187, 193, 204, 205, 206, 218, 219, 238, 243, 250, 251, 259, 270, 272, 279, 303, 314, 321–324 passim, 349, 350, 357, 358, 363, 365, 375, 378, 380, 382, 387, 397, 400–405 passim, 410, 412, 413, 418, 419, 420, 422, 424
on altered states of consciousness, 311–313, 315
on beating fantasies, 247
cases of, 13, 15–16, 59–60, 71–72, 76, 84, 129, 132–133, 133n, 136, 163, 174, 189, 202, 203, 307, see also Little Hans, Rat man
on claustrophobia, 73
on compulsion, 287
on constructions, 368n
on delusion, 339, 343n
on dreams, 21, 66, 122–127, 129–135, 147, 158, 165–181, 182, 188–189, 192, 194, 196, 200, 201–203, 306, 325, 343n

dreams of, 124, 125, 144–145, 160–162, 203
on ego, 83
on fantasy versus memory, 205, 207–212, 353
on free association, 190n
on free floating attention, 210–212, 367
on hallucination, 305
on hypnosis, 291–293
on masturbation, 40n, 117
on mother's role, 208n
on paranoia, 72
on primal scene, 227, 229
on reality testing, 128
on repression, 49
on sleep, 264, 306
on spoken word in dream, 135–140
on superego, 138–139, 152, 200
on symbols, 5–22, 26–28, 39–43, 47, 49n, 53, 59–60, 64, 66, 68, 74, 77, 81, 82, 106–108, 111, 113, 119, 133, 165, 177, 182, 309, 326, 331, 335, 377
on technique, 359n, 362, 366, 367
on thinking, 343
on threshold symbolism, 197–198
on transference, 352–353
on typical dreams, 155–158, 160–161, 172–174
on the unconscious, 45n, 55
on vaginal sensitivity, 254–255
on wish to sleep, 295–296

Gauthier, S., 345, 424
Gebärmutter, 75, 418
Genital excretion and hypnosis, 281–283, 299, 301, 305
Graves, R., 82
Groddeck, G. W., 80
Grotjahn, M., 39n, 424
Guilt
and exploitation of children, 213–214, 216–217, 219
and states of alienation, 315–316, 320

Hallucination, 15–16, 62, 72, 92, 337
and autohypnotic states, 299–305
in dreams, 202–203
negative, 295
olfactory, 305
see also Dream hallucination
Heissig, W., 245n, 424
Hitschmann, E., 67
Hitler, A., 21n, 292
Hypnagogic state, 190, 263, 298–305
Hypnoid state, 264, 306, 310
Hypnopompic state, 190, 264, 269, 310
Hypnosis, 263–298, 389–390
in children and adults, 265–274
partial, 295–298
theoretical considerations, 291–298
see also Hypnotic evasion
Hypnotic evasion, 10, 39, 50–51, 62, 88, 92, 256, 265, 266, 267–291, 324, 330, 351–352, 386
as resistance of analyst, 268, 360–361
and transference, 352, 356–357
Hysterical twilight state, 310
and somnambulism, 264

Id and partial subject, 297–298, 315, 319
Identification
with mother, 318, 324, 371, 372
and symbolization, 15–16
Incest objects, symbols for, 68–75
Incontinence
in ambulatory psychosis, 233–237
equivalents, 236–237
see also Continence
Infantile traits necessary for analytic treatment, 361–365
Interpretation, 49, 342
of Freud's "staircase" dream, 160–162
of spoken words in dreams, 146–151

of symbols, 3–7, 156
of typical dreams, 157–158, 172, 181
Introject(ion), 146–147, 297–298, 314–315, 318, 418
Intuition, 18
Isolation, 374, 375

Jekels, L., 315–316
Jones, E., 44, 418, 424
Jung, C. G., 292

Kauders, O., 270, 295, 310–311, 356, 424
Kempe, C. H., 214, 424
Kennedy, J. F., 199n
Klein, M., 44, 424
Kris, E., 344, 424

LaBruyère, 29, 424
Levitt, M., 424
Libido
and aggression, 14–15, 285–286
and refractory narcissism, 19, 216
see also Aggression, Sexuality
Little Hans, 11, 21, 31, 68, 72, 76, 309, 324

Manifest content
ellipses in, 191–197
of incontinence dreams, 163
and spoken word in dreams, 145–153
of symbolically typical dreams, 177
in typical dreams, 155–156
Masochism, 52–53, 237
Masturbation
in ambulatory psychosis, 224–225
and boredom, 39n
fantasies of, 52–53, 333–338
female, 58–64, 333–338
symbols for, see sub Symbol
see also Sexual abuse of child
Memory
confirmation of, 369–374
versus fantasy, 53–55, 205–212, 353–358, 368–388
repressed, 205–212

Memory quality, 380–383
and dream associations, 384–388
and fantasies, 383–384
Menstruation, 70–71, 78–80
dream of, 169–170, 419
symbols for, 99–101
Mother, 208n
psychotic, 250–253, 256–259
see also Aggressive abuse of child, Sexual abuse of child, sub Symbol, sub Symbolism of
"Mother comes in," 75, 142, 419
Mouth-eye unit, 73–75, 193, 320

Narcissism, refractory, 19, 216, 227, 420
Negative therapeutic reaction, 275
Neurosis
etiology of, 206, 212, 219
and psychosis, 391–392
Number symbolism, 22, 111–116

Oberholzer, E., 394
Oppenheim, E., 113, 131, 159, 424
Oral sadism and symbolization, 13–14
see also Cannibalistic aggression
Overdetermination, 142, 165–166, 198
of symbols, 22, 33–37, 47, 65, 74, 85

Paranoia, 338, 355–356
and homosexuality, 72
Parapraxis, 186, 302–303, 306, 307, 377
Partial object, 90–93
Partial subject, 132, 297–298, 314–315, 418, 419
anal sadistic, 90, 94, 338
Partridge, E., 94, 424
Penis envy, 41
Perception in ambulatory psychosis, 239–243
Peto, A., 44, 103, 424
Picasso, P., 344–345
Picturization, 20–21, 28, 45, 64, 85
Pleasure-physiologic body ego, 419

and body ego proper, 42
and derealization, 328
and partial object, 46
and primary process, 42, 45, 420
and symbolization, 8–10, 17,
    42–43, 45, 118–120, 420
symbols for, 75–94
see also Pleasure-physiologic
    functions, Pleasure-physiologic
    processes
Pleasure-physiologic functions, 323
    symbols for 94–106
Pleasure-physiologic processes
and dreams, 123–135
and symbolization, 15–17, 123,
    130, 132
Potential symbol, 17–19
Primal scene and ambulatory psy-
    chosis, 227–229
see also Sexual abuse of child
Primary process, 42, 45, 49, 121,
    420
Projection of pleasure-physiologic
    body ego, 16, 33, 323, 326, 420
Promiscuity as incontinence equiva-
    lent, 236–237
Psychoanalysis, psychotherapeutic
    preparation for, 403–409
Psychoanalytic technique, 349–411
    and abstinence rule, 99
    with ambulatory psychotics, 393
    and amnesia removal, 219–220
    and hypnotic evasion, 272–273,
        275
    and spoken word in dream, 150–
        151
    and typical dreams, 157
Psychosis and neurosis, 391–392
see also Ambulatory psychosis
Psychotherapy with ambulatory
    psychotics, 402–403
Punishment dreams, 139, 152, 200,
    200n

Rank, O., 43, 424
Rat man, 139–140
Reality testing, 128–130

Re-enactment
in the analytic situation, 357–358
symbolic, 57–58
see also Repetition compulsion
"Refractory narcissism," 216, 227,
    420
and symbolization, 19
Regression, 284–285
in ambulatory psychosis, 229–237
and dreams, 134
and rotating symbol, 102–104
and symbolization, 21
Repetition compulsion, 164, 277–
    278, 371
and repression, 268
and symbolic re-enactment, 57–
    58
Representation and symbolization,
    19–22, 27–28
see also Picturization
Repressed
buoyancy of, 55, 301, 339
return of, 319, 320
Repression, 49, 338
in the analyst, 220
and hypnosis, 269, 389–390
and neurosis, 212
organic, 90
and repetition of trauma, 268
of sexual and aggressive abuse,
    255–256
and symbolization, 31, 324–325
see also Amnesia removal, Hyp-
    notic evasion
Resistance
analyst's, 204–205, 220, 358–361
in children of ambulatory psy-
    chotics, 221
transference as, 357–358
see also Hypnotic evasion
Rewald, J., 321, 424
Rorschach test, 394, 396
Rotating symbol, 32–33, 101–106,
    386

Sachs, H., 43, 312n
Schilder, P., 270, 272, 293, 295,
    298, 310–311, 356, 419, 424

Scoptophilia, 328
Screen memory, 55–56, 226, 258
Searl, M. N., 44, 424
Secondary elaboration, 143–144
Sensory spheres and amnesia removal, 388–389
Sexual abuse of child, 40, 57–58, 88–89, 92–93, 97, 98, 104, 105–106, 112, 164, 205–261, 286, 294, 301, 318, 337–338, 339–340, 364–365, 372, 373, 375, 377
    and hypnosis, 266–268
    and transference, 355–358
    see also Aggressive abuse of child, Hypnotic evasion
Sexuality
    in ambulatory psychosis, 229–233
    perverse and neurosis, 206
Shakespeare, W., 42–43, 76, 80–81, 84–85, 93, 115–116, 127–128, 200–201n, 219, 289–291, 332–333, 424
Shiny object and hypnotic states, 270, 276, 293–294
Silberer, H., 197
Silver, H. K., 214, 224
Silverman, F. N., 214, 424
Simmel, E., 311
Sleep, 264
    autohypnosis in, 279, 306
    diurnal, 269
    and dreaming, 188–201
    dreamless, 190–200
Somnambulism, 269
    and hysterical twilight state, 264, 305–306
Spoken word in dream, 135–154, 199
"Spot," 251, 253–254, 269, 336
Stärcke, E., 338
Steele, B. F., 214, 424
Steffens, L., 173n, 424
Stekel, W., 12n, 34n, 67, 106, 424
Sterba, E., 90, 424
Superego
    and dreams, 139, 152, 154, 200
    and hypnosis, 292–293, 297

origin of, 138
and transverse ego split, 315–316
    see also Spoken word in dreams
Symbol
    bisexual, 25, 106–109, 328, 378
    cathexes of, 31–33
    equation, 44n, 418
    definition of, 8–9, 10–11
    function of, 31–33, 130
    "individual," 27–28
    metaphorical interpretation of, 34–37
    modified, 37–38
    overdetermination of, 33–37, 85
    potential, 17–19
    and representations, 19–22, 27–28
    rotating, see Rotating symbol
    in typical dreams, 155–156
    see also Color symbolism, Displacement symbol, Dream symbolism, Number symbolism
"Symbol aggregate," 38–41
Symbol for
    "arse," 86–90, 284
    birth, 40, 82, 84, 197, 309
    blood, 38, 67
    castration, 14, 15, 24–25
    cunnilingus, 52, 94
    death, 12, 173, 182
    ego disintegration, 101–106
    erection, 54, 67, 161
    father, 31, 67
    fellatio, 52, 94
    female genital, 22, 28, 33, 38, 39, 42, 59–60, 67, 75–76, 80–82, 111–116
    intercourse, 38, 39, 47, 161, 173
    masturbation, 10, 14, 20, 22, 39, 40, 50, 53, 54, 55–56, 58–64, 95–99, 112, 117, 118, 404
    menstruation, 99–101
    mother, 20, 29, 32, 40, 50, 64, 71–75, 288, 325
    parent, 22, 68–71
    phallus, 13, 25, 28, 42, 43, 67, 328

rectum, 20–21, 46
secret, 165, 177
urination, 35–37, 133n
womb, 76–80, 82–85, 143, 179
symbolic equation, 43–48, 322, 390–391
symbolic modification, 29–31, 71
symbolic prediction, 50–51, 390
symbolic re-enactment, 57–58
"Symbolically typical" dreams, 155–156
of analytic hour, 74–75, 176–179
Symbolism of
dead end, 86–87, 283, 378–380
dog, 90–93
French, 94
head, 87–89
horse, 11, 21, 68–69, 106
knee, 80–82
moon, 82–86
mother, 76–77, 142n, 378
"mother comes in," 75, 142
piano playing, 10, 58–64, 117, 118
racially different person, 11, 69–71, 325
riding in trains, 173
sky, 89–90
telephone, 20, 50, 54–56, 95–99, 118, 141–142
two identical persons, 24, 29, 32, 71–75, 81, 120
week, 99–100
see also Color symbolism, Number symbolism, sub Symbol for
Symbolization 3–121
and aggression, 13–15
in Boccaccio's Decameron, 8, 11, 15–19, 33, 38, 42
clinical significance of, 49–67, 390–391
employment of, 28–33, 117–120
onset of capacity for, 22–26
of pleasure-physiologic part object, 15–17, 420
and regression, 21
and repression, 31, 324–325

Symptomatology· of ambulatory psychoses, 220–243, 395–400, 412–417

Thought, influence on of erogeneity, 332–333
Threshold symbolism, 197–199
Transference, 285
and childhood abuse, 353–358
homosexual, 340–341
and hypnotic evasion, 272–273, 279, 287–289
as resistance, 357–358, 368
Trauma
sexual and aggressive, 212–213
and states of alienation, 313, 329–331
symbolic re-enactment of, 57–58
see also Aggressive abuse of child, Hypnotic evasion, Sexual abuse of child
Truly typical dream(s), 156, 160–175, 179–187
see also Symbolically typical dreams, Typical dreams
Typical dream(s), 155–156, 163, 181
and continence, 159–172
"disinterested strangers" in, 162, 165–170
of examination, 172
Freud on, 155–158
of inhibition, 160–162, 173–175, 179, 181
interpretation of, 156–158
of missed analytic hour, 74–75, 179–187
of missing a train, 172–173, 181–182
of "mother comes in," 75, 142, 182
of nudity, 160–162
of partial undress, 162–175, 184–187
of psychotic patient, 183–187
of wave, 182
see also Symbolically typical dreams, Truly typical dreams

Unconscious, *see sub* Freud
Urethral erotism, 233–235, 316n
  and hypnosis, 274–281

Vagina
  distal end of, 418
  sensitivity of, 254–255
Van Ophuijsen, 338
Verbal indiscretion as incontinence
    equivalent, 237

Webster, 37–38, 315, 425

Wentworth, H., 94, 425
Wish
  to conceal in ambulatory psy-
    chosis, 220–223
  dream-, 123, 125–126, 159, 164
  to sleep, 295–296
Word symbolism, 7–8

Young, L., 215–218, 425

Zone-equation, 24, 420